Pioneers on Maine Rivers

WITH
LISTS TO 1651
COMPILED FROM THE ORIGINAL SOURCES

Wilbur D. Spencer

HERITAGE BOOKS
2015

HERITAGE BOOKS
AN IMPRINT OF HERITAGE BOOKS, INC.

Books, CDs, and more—Worldwide

For our listing of thousands of titles see our website at
www.HeritageBooks.com

A Facsimile Reprint
Published 2015 by
HERITAGE BOOKS, INC.
Publishing Division
5810 Ruatan Street
Berwyn Heights, Md. 20740

Originally published Portland, 1930

— Publisher's Notice —
In reprints such as this, it is often not possible to remove blemishes from the original. We feel the contents of this book warrant its reissue despite these blemishes and hope you will agree and read it with pleasure.

International Standard Book Numbers
Paperbound: 978-1-55613-364-0
Clothbound: 978-0-7884-6260-3

To
*Those Little Groups of Intrepid English
Pioneers,
Who Founded Maine,
Under the Banner of Saint George
and in Accord with the
Tenets
of
The Church of England,
Consistent in Their Conduct,
Liberal with Their Countrymen,
Devoted to Their Ideals
and
Irresistible for Achievement,
This Book
Is
Most Respectfully Dedicated.*

BRISTOL, ENGLAND, EARLY HOME OF MANY MAINE PIONEERS

CONTENTS

	PAGE
Dedication	3
Introduction	9
The Founders	12
Maine Visiting Lists Before 1630	13
English Proprietary Divisions	24
The First Plantations in New England	28
Chief Executives of Maine Under Gorges	29
The Location, Size and Character of the Settlements in Maine	30
Piscataqua River	33
Isles of Shoals	46
Pioneers	55
Laconia Plantations	56
Great Island	71
Dover	73
Exeter	79
Newichawannock (Berwick)	85
Pioneers	103
Eliot	103
Pioneers	111
Kittery	113
Pioneers	118
Agamenticus	121
York River	122
Settlement	125
Division of Land on the West Bank	135
Division of Land on the East Bank	137
Incorporation of Gorgeana	140
Pioneers	142
Cape Neddock River	146
Ogunquit River	147

Wells River	149
Pioneers	150
Maryland River	152
Pioneers	157
"Cape Porpoise"	158
Kennebunk River	159
Batson's River	162
Little River	163
"Winter Harbor"	164
Saco River	165
The Second Occupation	168
Division of Land in Biddeford	181
Division of Land in Saco	183
Massachusetts Supremacy	184
Saco Islands	186
Pioneers	186
Scarborough River	191
Stratton's Islands	191
Nonesuch River	193
Pioneers	197
Spurwink River	198
Richmond Island	198
Cape Elizabeth	200
Pioneers	204
Fore River	209
"The Cabin at Casco"	215
Presumpscot River	216
The Second Occupation of Casco	222
The First Islands Occupied in Casco Bay	231
Pioneers	232
Royal River	234
Cousins Island	237
Pioneers	238
Bunganuck River	239
Pioneers	240

CONTENTS

New Meadows and Pejepscot Rivers 241
"Imperial Kennebec" 256
Sagadahoc River 257
    The Old Empire of Moashan 257
    The First Colony 259
    Sagadahoc, Lygonia or Plough Patent 266
    The Parker Family 268
    Pioneers 271
"The Vale of Cushnoc" 272
Kennebec River 273
    The Dawn of Christianity on the Kennebec 280
    Employes 281
Sheepscot River 283
    Pioneers 287
Damariscotta River 289
    Damariscove Island 291
    Pioneers 303
"The White Angel of Bristol" 304
Pemaquid River 307
    John Brown of Pemaquid 324
    Isle of Monhegan 330
    Pioneers 352
"Samoset" 353
Muscongus River 354
    Pioneers 357
Saint George's River 358
"The Lost Province" 363
Penobscot River 364
    Pioneers 388
Machias River 390

Appendices:
    (A) The Old Planters in Massachusetts 392
    (B) The Thirty New England Patents 393
    (C) Ancient Maps of Maine 395
    (D) The Recall of Neal and Associates 395
    (E) The Wannerton Deed 396
    (F) The Anonymous "Relation" 397
    (G) Indian Titles at Sagadahoc 399
    (H) Sullivan's Historical Blunder 399

ILLUSTRATIONS

Bristol, England	4
Pascataqua, 1653	32
Laconia	57
Part of Wood's Map, 1635	66
The River below Newichawannock House	87
Chadbourne Estate, 1764	99
Eliot Lands	107
Point Christian, York River	133
York, 1653	141
Cape Porpoise, 1653	154
Dutch Map, 1631	167
Church Point, Saco River	178
Saco, 1653	185
View of Portland	216
Mackworth's Island	219
Casco, 1653	230
Simancas Map, 1610	257
Plan of Fort Saint George	262
Fort Weston, Augusta	276
Phipps Point	282
Damariscotta River below Newcastle	288
New Harbor	307
Sketch Map of Pemaquid	323
The Cliffs, Monhegan	331
Site of Brown's House, New Harbor	356
Saint George's River	360
Dochet Island, Saint Croix River	365
French Settlements in New France	374

INTRODUCTION

Faint but convincing traces of ancient European occupation of the coast of Maine disclose attempts at permanent as well as transient settlement. French colonists, who sought the island of Saint Croix in 1604, and again in 1611, and the pioneers of Mount Desert Island, in 1613, did not contemplate abandonment within a decade. English projects for colonization can only be understood from careful analysis of the considerations which actuated them.

Of all "adventurers" who were interested in the successful evolution of New England, the name of Sir Ferdinando Gorges should be regarded as preëminent. It is true that he was not absolutely free from mercenary motive, but it is impossible, at this late date, to review his action and examine his personality without a sense of his dignity and sincerity. So large a share had he in all great preliminary movements for Northern Colonization of America, that he took occasion, more than once, to chide himself that results had not been more satisfactory and conclusive.

A striking inference from a critical study of earliest Maine history, as presented by ancient and modern writers upon the subject, is that too much has been taken for granted and that the beginnings of first permanent settlement, in many localities, have been antedated.

A different perspective has been sought by the writer of this story of colonization, which has produced interesting results. The object has been to learn, if possible, how recent rather than how remote were the dates of settlements upon Maine rivers.

The proper position for the study of history is not to be found in the clouds, where all objects appear to attain the same altitude while viewed from above, but it should be taken at the level, so that the true relation of events may be observed in the cross section.

No apology is offered and no quarter is asked for either the substance or arrangement of this treatise. While some of the conclusions may appear to be unsupported by specific records, those particular statements, which a critic might feel disposed to challenge, can be shown to be based upon credible authorities in all cases.

It was found impracticable to note all sources of information, but the extensive reference outline, which covers the important field of available published and unpublished materials, both in this country and abroad, may be given full confidence. Where several reprints of a rare book or manuscript are available for general library reference, the original pages of the more accurate edition have been cited.

Recent publication of ancient documents or letters, heretofore lost or inaccessible, makes possible a sure revision of many important details. For this reason Maine histories, which involve many misleading deductions, are seldom quoted.

Any ancient date in the book may be modernized by adding eleven days and, in case of a hyphenated year, by discarding all numerals between the third and final printed figures.

It is apparent that each primitive plantation was composed of a single household, occupying a common fortified habitation in the wilderness. The casual remark of Ambrose Gibbons, proprietor of Newichawannock House in 1633, "Our number commonly hath bin ten," will apply equally well to all other early locations on the coast of Maine.

Many of the present cities of this State have wandered inland from the original centers of settlement. For comparison they have been arranged in the following list, beginning at the westward.

Piscataqua River: Portsmouth.
Saco River: Biddeford and Saco.
Casco River: South Portland, Portland and Westbrook.
Sagadahoc River: Bath.
Androscoggin River: Auburn and Lewiston.
Kennebec River: Gardiner, Hallowell, Augusta and Waterville.
Penobscot River: Rockland, Belfast, Bangor, Brewer and Old Town.
Union River: Ellsworth.
Saint Croix River: Eastport and Calais.

The term "Eastward," formerly used as an abbreviation for "Eastward Parts," meant Maine to early New Englanders. On account of its indefinite range the word has been found indispensable in this work.

It is the hope of the compiler that this story of Maine faith and perseverance may find a useful niche among the valuable archives of the State and help to inspire future generations with a desire to learn more about its first European visitors.

Great honor is due to Chief Justice Popham, the earls of Arundel and Richmond, to Sir George Calvert and Sir Ferdinando Gorges, as promotors, but the real founders of New England, and especially of Maine, were those indomitable spirits who, now unknown or almost forgotten, donated their humble lives and energies and mingled their dust with our soil as an earnest of their convictions.

What does it matter if for material needs some came thither merely to fish and trade, or if they were outcasts from Europe or the aristocratic colonies of New England! They were bold adventurers and for Maine and America have become pillars in the temple of a new democracy and some of them, possibly, corner stones in the eternal but ever-expanding tabernacle of God.

W. D. S.

THE FOUNDERS

Bold pioneers of bygone days,
   Who left the homes they loved the best
And sailed athwart the trackless maze
   To found an empire in the West.

Tried men and safe were those who steered
   The sea-worn craft among the riffs;
Brave men and true were those who reared
   Rough cabins on the northern cliffs.

Whatever dangers might assail,
   On hopes like theirs the world might wait;
With zeal like theirs no plan could fail,
   In faith like theirs was born a State.

Great motherland of stalwart men,
   Who greet incoming tides and times,
Who seek the mysteries again
   Of modern days and distant climes!

The restless sea roves in their blood,
   The living north wind stirs their breath,
Their souls reflect that motherhood
   That forms a part of them till death.

MAINE VISITING LISTS BEFORE 1630

1498

Sebastian Cabot, Venetian, from Bristol, England, with five ships and 300 men.

1524

John Verrazano, Florentine, with one ship and fifty men.

1556

Durand de Villegagnon, with a small colony established in a small fort at Norumbega on the Penobscot.
Andre Thevet, historian, in the expedition.

1602

Bartholomew Gosnold, sent by Bristol merchants from Falmouth, England, in the *Concord*, with thirty-two men.
John Angell.
Gabriel Archer.
John Brereton.
William Brown.
Bartholomew Gilbert.
Robert Meriton.
Martin Pring, of Bristol.
James Rosier.
Robert Saltern.
William Street, master of the *Concord*.
John Tucker.

1603

Martin Pring, of Bristol, in the *Deliverance* and *Speedwell* with forty-three men, surveyed Saco, Kennebunk, York and Pascataqua rivers.
William Brown.
Robert Saltern.

1604

Pierre du Guast, known otherwise as Sieur de Monts, settled at Saint Croix Island.

Samuel de Champlain, with twelve men, visited Monhegan Island and Sagadahoc River in a boat from Saint Croix.

1605

Sieur de Monts, of Saint Croix, with some gentlemen and twenty sailors, examined the whole coast of Maine and named Monhegan "La Nef," or Ship Island.
Samuel de Champlain, official geographer.
Pierre Angibaut, alias Champdore, pilot.

George Waymouth, in the *Archangel* from Bristol, England, with twenty-nine men, set up crosses at Saint George's Island and at Thomaston; he kidnapped five Indians, Tahanedo, Amoret, Skidwaros, Mannedo and Assacomoit, from the Pemaquid River region.
Thomas Cam.
Owen Griffin.
Thomas King.
James Rosier.
John Stoneham, pilot.

1606

Martin Pring, of Bristol.
Thomas Hanham, who released at Sagadahoc Tahanedo, otherwise known as Nahanada, one of the natives deported by Waymouth.

Jean de Biencourt, of Port Royal.
    Pierre Champdore, pilot.
    Samuel de Champlain, official geographer.
    Daniel Hay.
    Louis Hebert, apothecary.
    Robert Pontgrave.
    Jean du Val.

1607

George Popham, President of Sagadahoc Company, at Sagadahoc from Plymouth, England, with the *Gift of God* and *Mary and John* and 120 men.
Ellis Best.
Lancelot Booker, of Rotherham, York, born 1576.
Gome Carew.
James Davis, in the *Gift of God*.
John Davis.
Robert Davis, in the *Mary and John*.
John Diaman, of Stoke Gabriel, born 1553.
Robert Eliot.
John Fletcher, of Stephney, born 1581.
Raleigh Gilbert, admiral of the *Mary and John*.
John Goyett, of Plymouth.
Thomas Hanham.
Edward Harlow.
John Havercombe, master of the *Gift of God*.
John Hunt.
Edward Popham, nephew of George.
Timothy Savage, of Saint Brigid, London, born 1563.
Richard Seymour, clergyman.
(Other members: Digby, Fosque, Patteson and Turner.)

1608

(All Sagadahoc settlers returned to England.)

1609

(No record of European visitation, but Hakluyt's description of Moashan was derived in part from data secured that year.)

1610

Jean de Biencourt sighted land near Monhegan Island.

Sir George Somers visited the Penobscot region from Virginia, where he had just settled.
Sir Samuel Argal, commander of one of Somers' vessels, ranged the southern coast of Maine.

1611

Jean de Biencourt, late in the year, with sixteen men from Port Royal examined the site of Fort Saint George on the westerly side of Sagadahoc River, which the English had deserted; he found fishing boats left by Virginia fishermen at Monhegan Island, then called Emetenic by the French.
Pierre Biard.
Robert Pontgrave.
(Captain Platrier, of Dieppe, living at Saint Croix Island.)
(Two vessels from Virginia.)

1612

English fishermen quartered at Monhegan Island during the summer.

1613

Sir Samuel Argal, from Virginia, raided Mount Desert Island, where the French had begun settlement early that year.
William Turnell, lieutenant for Argal, took as captives:
Pierre Biard.
Jean de Biencourt.
Isaac Bailleul.
Charles Fleury.
Enemond Masse.
Nicholas de la Motte.
Francis de Quentin.
Gilbert du Thet died in the conflict.

1614

John Smith, from London, with forty-five men and boys in two ships.
Michael Cooper, captain of Smith's flag-ship.
Thomas Hunt, master of Smith's other vessel, called the *Long-Robert*, kidnapped twenty-four Indians and sold some of them in Spain.
Samuel Crampton, and expert whale-fisherman.
(A vessel belonging to Sir Francis Popham.)

Edward Harlow, from the Isle of Wight, with five natives and under instructions from Sir Ferdinando Gorges to investigate a gold mine at Capawick (Martha's Vineyard.)
Nicholas Hobson, captain of the vessel.
John Matthew, a relative of Gorges.
Two relatives of Gorges, named Sturton.

1615

Michael Cooper, for the Virginia Company, with four ships from London and Smith's trained crews of the previous year.
Thomas Dermer, with one of Smith's vessels from Plymouth.

1616

Sir Richard Hawkins, president of the Plymouth Company, with the *Garland* and one other vessel, after wintering at the West Indies, arrived at Monhegan Island, where he found:
Edward Brawnde, master of the *Nachen* from London, with a typical fishing crew of twenty men.
John Bennett, chief mate.
Brian Tocher, second mate.
William Treedel, owner of the ship.
John Edwards, merchant of the ship.
John Hill, boatswain.
John Downs, boatswain's mate.
William Gayne, gunner and pilot.
James Farre, gunner's mate.
John Barrens, Henry Batteshill, Nicholas Collins and Thomas Webber, quartermasters.
John Brimelcome, steward.
Nicholas Head and John Hutton, cooks.
John Hept, Thomas Roberts, Thomas Tobey, John Wiles and Philip Wiles, seamen.
James Edwards, master of the *Trial* from London.
Arthur Hitchens, master of the *Blessing* from Plymouth.
William West, master of the *Judith* from London.
John Winter, master of the *David* from Plymouth.
(Sir Francis Popham's vessel made a prosperous voyage.)

1617

English vessels, delayed too long by unfavorable winds, went directly to Newfoundland instead of visiting New England.

1618

Edward Rocraft, alias Stalling, with about a dozen companions, left at Monhegan Island by a fishing vessel belonging to Gorges.

Richard Vines, with other Englishmen, abandoned at Winter Harbor (Biddeford Pool) by Rocraft, who went south for the winter.

1619

Thomas Dermer, who had resided for two years in Newfoundland, with a few other men, sent to coöperate with Rocraft, landed at Monhegan Island by Gorges' vessel.

John Ward, in the *Sampson* from Virginia, with whom Dermer, bound for Virginia in a small pinnace, shipped his provisions.

1620

Thomas Dermer, returned to Monhegan Island in his pinnace and was fatally wounded by Massachusetts Indians.

1621

William Tucker, master of the *Eleanor*, of Orston, trading and fishing at Monhegan for Abraham Jennings, of Plymouth, and Ambrose Jennings and William Cross, of London, styled Jennings and Company. (Six or seven other vessels fishing and trading at Monhegan.)

1622

Barnstable masters and ships on the Maine Coast:
  Christopher Browning.
  James Cook.
  Mark Cook.
  John Hodge.
  Adam Horden, master of the *John*.

John Lausey.
John Lucks.
Anthony Nichols.
John Penrose.
John Witheridge.
Richard Whilkey, in the *Rebecca*.

Other Englishmen:
Arthur Champernoone, in the *Chudley*.
John Gibbs, mate of the *Sparrow* from London, with a fishing crew under Captain Rogers at Damariscove Island.
Thomas Morton, passenger in the *Charity* bound for Massachusetts, where he was to begin a plantation for Thomas Weston, of London.
Phineas Pratt and five other persons associated with Weston.
John Huddleston, from England, by way of Virginia, in the *Bona Nova*.
Thomas Jones, from London bound for Virginia in the *Discovery*.
John Pory, passenger for England, at Damariscove in the *Discovery*.
William Reynolds, master of the *Charity*, bound for Virginia.
William Vengham, master of a vessel of Jennings and Company.
Edward Winslow, of New Plymouth, at Monhegan for supplies.
(The *Abraham* and *Nightingale*, vessels of Jennings and Company, were on the coast during the summer.)

1623

John Corbin, with a few passengers for Pascataqua and Virginia, in the *Providence* from Plymouth.
David Thompson, at Pascataqua from Plymouth.
William Gibbons at Casco.
Richard Whilkey, from Barnstable in the *Rebecca*.
Thomas Weston, disguised as a blacksmith, arrived at Damariscove.
Employes of Weston at Damariscove in the *Swan:*
Edward Johnson.
Phineas Pratt.

John Sanders.

John Howbeck, at Damariscove from Virginia.

Thomas Squibbs, at Damariscove in the service of Lord Edward Gorges in the *Katherine*.

Joseph Stratton with Squibbs.

Francis West, admiral from England in the *Plantation* at Damariscove.

John Witheridge, at Pemaquid in the *Eagle* from Barnstable, owned by Melchard Bennett.

New Plymouth planters at the Eastward for supplies:
  Myles Standish.
  Edward Winslow.

Robert Gorges, from Wessaguscus, at Pascataqua and Casco in the *Swan*.

Christopher Levett, coasted late in the year with seven or eight men in boats, from Pascataqua to Cape Newagen.

(Five vessels from Plymouth and two from Dartmouth, without licenses, fished upon the coast during the year.)

1624

Prominent Englishmen at Casco:
  Robert Gorges, governor for New England.
  Christopher Levett, builder of the first house.
  Thomas Weston, with 50 men and 17 guns, in the *Swan*.

Fishermen in the *Little James* at Pemaquid Harbor:
  Emanuel Altham, captain, from New Plymouth.
  John Bridges, master.
  Thomas Fell, carpenter.
  Peter Morritt, drowned sailor.
  William Stevens, gunner.
  John Vow, drowned sailor.

John Witheridge, master of the *Eagle* from Barnstable, at Pemaquid.

Traders at Monhegan Island:
  Luke Edan, merchant in the *Return*, from Elizabeth City, Virginia.
  Henry Hewett, factor for William Constable in the *William and John*.
  William Reynolds, master of the *William and John*.

Factors for Jennings and Company at Monhegan:
John Corbin.
Edmund Dockett ("Doggett").
Thomas Piddock.
William Pomfrett.
William Vengham, resident on the premises.
Samuel Maverick, with Robert Gorges at Sagadahoc.
The crew of the *Unity* which arrived, via Canada, at Cape Ann June 25:
Stephen Bolton, of Wapping, England.
James Boyden, who remained in New England.
Gregory Castle, who returned to England.
John Crookdeak, sailor.
William Edwards, chief mate, who remained in New England.
John Harvey, part owner of the vessel.
William Holland, sailor.
Thomas Scott, sailor.
John Wallaston, captain of the *Unity*.
Tobias White, of Radcliffe, England, master of the *Unity*.
Passengers in the *Unity*:
John Anthony.
John Howard.
John Martin, Virginia planter.
Thomas Morton, of Mount Wallaston.
Abraham Pelletier, who removed to Virginia.
Humphrey Rastell, London merchant interested in Mount Wallaston.
Thomas Savage, a servant of Rastell who removed to Virginia.
John Smith, bound for Virginia.
Sackford Wetherell, bound for Virginia.
(The *Charity*, fishing for New Plymouth adventurers at Cape Ann, and the ship of Captain Coke or Cook, visited Portland Harbor on their return to England.)

1625

John Witheridge, of Barnstable, at Pemaquid Harbor.
Fishermen and traders at Damariscove Island:
Jeffrey Cornish, alias Williams, sailor from England.

Thomas Crispe, merchant from Virginia.
Robert Newman, planter from Virginia.
The crew of the *Swan* at Damariscove:
  Arthur Avelling, servant of Robert Newman, from Virginia.
  Edmund Barker, seaman.
  William Foster, who died in Virginia December 10, 1626.
  John Giles, servant of Nicholas Row, of Virginia.
  Nicholas Hodges, seaman.
  Christopher Knolling, seaman.
  Edmund Nevell, of Virginia, master of the *Swan*.
  Nicholas Row, seaman.
  John Saker, of Virginia.
  Thomas Weston, London merchant and owner of the *Swan*.
Edward Winslow, with colonists from New Plymouth, trading with the Indians on Kennebec River.

1626

Mariners at Casco:
  John Cousins, seaman.
  Peter Garland, master of a vessel.
Traders on Kennebec River, from Massachusetts:
  Walter Bagnall.
  Edward Gibbons.
  Thomas Morton.
  John Peverly.
John Oldham, in the *Happy Entrance*, from Canada.

1627

Weymouth masters at Casco:
  Arthur Guyer.
  William Lash.
  Henry Russell.
  Joseph Russell.
Other seamen in Casco Bay:
  Ambrose Bouden, mariner, of Holberton, in the *Consent*.
  John Mills, seaman.
  James Randall, master of the *Providence* from Plymouth.
  John Taylor, of Jalme, fisherman with the *Consent*.

Bennet Wills, boat-master with the *Consent*.
John Winter, in the *Consent*, from Plymouth.
Nathaniel Waters, master of the *Return* from Millbrook.
Traders on the Kennebec River:
  Walter Bagnall.
  Edward Gibbons.
  Thomas Morton.
  John Peverly.
Traders at Monhegan Island:
  William Bradford.
  Abraham Shurt.
  David Thompson.
  Edward Winslow.

1628

Traders resident on Richmond Island:
  Walter Bagnall, from Wessaguscus.
  John Peverly, his companion.
Traders living with the Indians at Castine:
  Edward Ashley, from Bristol.
  John Deacon, his servant.

1629

Those who took a "vew" of the Maine Coast:
  Richard Bonython.
  Thomas Lewis.
  Walter Neal.
  John Oldham.
  George Vaughan.
  Richard Vines.
Isaac Allerton at "The Eastward."
Edward Winslow, with others from New Plymouth, at Cushnoc.

ENGLISH PROPRIETARY DIVISIONS

April 10, 1606, James I, of England, granted to the London and Plymouth Companies all of North America situated between the thirty-fourth and forty-fifth parallels of latitude.

November 3, 1620, James I allotted to the Council of Plymouth, in severalty, all of that part of North America comprised between the fortieth and forty-eighth parallels.

WESTERN DIVISION.

July 24, 1622, Ludovic Stewart, Earl of Richmond as well as Duke of Lennox, was granted a tract of land which extended for fifteen miles eastward from the middle of Saco River and for thirty miles inland. An island, since known as Richmond Island, was included in this concession. On the same date, Sir George Calvert was given a tract of equal proportions situated on the western bank of Sagadahoc River, together with the island of "Setquin" (Seguin).

August 10, 1622, the entire district between Pascataqua and Sagadahoc rivers was assigned to Sir Ferdinando Gorges and Captain John Mason.

June 27, 1623, the twenty surviving members of the Council of Plymouth, including Calvert, Gorges, Mason and Stewart, renounced all former rights to individual concessions in New England and had their allotments on the Atlantic seaboard between the Hudson and Saint Croix rivers determined by lot in the presence of the king. Even after this agreement no lines of division between the patentees were ever defined, and seven years later the council began to confer lesser patents of a private character describing the following locations:

Pascataqua, to Gorges, Mason and their associates.

Agamenticus (west side), to Ferdinando, son of Sir Ferdinando Gorges; (east side) to Ferdinando, son of John and grandson of Sir Ferdinando Gorges, and his associates.

Cape Porpoise, to John Stratton.
Winter Harbor, to Oldham and Vines.
Saco, to Bonython and Lewis.
Black Point, to Thomas Cammock.
Richmond Island, to Walter Bagnall.
Cape Elizabeth, to Trelawney and Goodyear.
Casco, to Christopher Levett.
Brunswick, to Purchase and Way.
Pejepscot, to Richard Bradshaw.
Cushnoc, to Plymouth Colony.
Lygonia, to John Crispe and Company.

February 3, 1633-4, the members of the Council of Plymouth, who with the approbation of the king were preparing to surrender their charter of New England, consented to an entirely new apportionment.*

April 22, 1635, the western division, known as the "Province of Mayne," was confirmed by Charles I to Sir Ferdinando Gorges in severalty. The king also, as a special reason for this royal favor, explained that Gorges had suffered "ye losse of manny of his good friends & servants in making this first discovery of those Coasts, & taking ye first seizure thereof as of right belonging to us." The district was named "New Somerset County."†

CENTRAL DIVISION.

July 24, 1622, a district extending "as the coast lyeth" twelve miles eastward from the southernmost point of "Pethippscott" (Pejepscot), with the islands of "Menehiggan," was granted to Thomas Howard, Earl of Arundel and Surrey.‡

February 19, 1622-3, all rights in the mainland of this division were withdrawn and Arrowsic and Raskegon islands were included in a plan to create a municipality, to be known as "State County," and to provide the site for a city to be named by the king.

February 29, 1631-2, Pemaquid lying on the eastern border, between Damariscotta and Muscongus Rivers, was allotted to Robert Aldworth and Gyles Elbridge, merchants of Bristol who lived within five miles of the estates of Gorges.

* Me. Doc. Hist., 7-121.
† Am. Ant. Col., 1867-119.
‡ Me. Doc. Hist., 7-61.

April 22, 1635, the Council of Plymouth by virtue of its agreement of the previous year induced Charles I to confirm 60,000 acres situated on the eastern side of the Sagadahoc River to Lord Edward Gorges, Marquis James Hamilton, Thomas Howard, Earl of Arundel and Surrey, James Hay, Earl of Carlisle, Captain John Mason and Esme Stewart, Duke of Lennox and Earl of Richmond. This land was never apportioned. In 1665, a royal commission reported that in the case of the Marquis of Hamilton it was unable to "find the 10,000 acres at the head of Sagadahoc in the east, it having two streams but the head unknown," nor could there be discovered "any land Lord Gorges had there, of which the 10,000 acres were to be set out."§

EASTERN DIVISION.

September 10, 1621, James I, of England, with the consent of Gorges, who was then the most influential member of the Council of Plymouth, conferred upon William Alexander, Earl of Stirling, an immense district which included all of the present territory of Maine situated east of Pemaquid and Kennebec rivers. This division was to have been designated "Canada County," but no settlement was made within it by the grantee.

July 19, 1629, after their principal strongholds had been reduced, the French colonists in Canada ceded all of their territory to the English.

March 13, 1629-30, Muscongus, which was comprised in the district known as "Canada County," was granted by the Council of Plymouth to John Beauchamp, of London, and Thomas Leverett, of Boston, Lincolnshire, England, who formed a trading partnership with Plymouth Colony and others and established a post on the Penobscot River at Castine.

March 29, 1632, by the treaty of Saint-Germain-en-Laye, Charles I restored to the former French settlers all of the Canadian territory which had been ceded to the English three years before, but this concession did not include the mainland of Eastern Maine, as at that time it had never been occupied by either Flemings or French.

§ Sainsbury's Col. Pap., 2-334.

April 22, 1635, the Council of Plymouth apportioned to Sir William Alexander all Maine territory to the eastward of the Muscongus and Kennebec as far as Saint Croix River, but August 1, of that year, the French evicted the English tenants of the post at Castine, then known as Machabitticus, and sent them home to New Plymouth; the invaders claimed to be acting within rights derived from the treaty of Saint-Germain-en-Laye. November 1, 1638, the Council made Sagadahoc River the western boundary of the grant to Alexander, intending to enlarge his proportion by the union of Canada and State counties, but the plan failed because it never received royal sanction.

THE FIRST PLANTATIONS IN NEW ENGLAND

1607-8   Phippsburg by Popham Colony.
1620   *New Plymouth by Plymouth Colony.
1622-6   Damariscove by employes of Sir Ferdinando Gorges.
1622-3   Weymouth (Wessaguscus) by Thomas Weston's Colony.
1622-8   Braintree (Passonagessit) by Thomas Morton.
1623   *Hull (Natascot) by John and Thomas Gray from Weymouth.
1623-6   Monhegan by Plymouth merchants.
1623   *Rye (Pascataqua) by David Thompson and Plymouth merchants.
1623-4   Sanders' Point by Weston's Colony from Weymouth.
1623   *Weymouth, again, by Robert Gorges' Colony.
1624   *Boston Harbor by Blackstone, Maverick and Thompson. (Boston by Blackstone; Mystic by the others.)
1624-6   Cape Ann by Dorchester merchants and Plymouth Colony.
1624-8   Casco by Christopher Levett.
1626   *Salem by Dorchester colonists from Cape Ann.
1626-8   Saco by John Cousins, John Mills and Thomas Purchase.
1628   *Dover Point by Edward and William Hilton from New Plymouth.
1628-31   Richmond Island by Walter Bagnall from Braintree.
1628   *Pemaquid by Abraham Shurt for Bristol merchants.
1628   *Pejepscot by Thomas Purchase and associates.
1628-35   Penobscot (Machabitticus) by Edward Ashley for Bristol merchants; taken by New Plymouth, in 1631, and by the French, in 1635.

* Permanently settled; all others were abandoned at the end of the period indicated; most of the eastern settlements were deserted during the later Indian wars.

CHIEF EXECUTIVES OF MAINE UNDER GORGES

1. Robert Gorges, Weymouth, Massachusetts, Governor of New England, 1623-1624.
2. Walter Neal, Rye, New Hampshire, Governor, 1630-1633.
3. Richard Vines, Saco, Maine, Steward General, 1634-1636.
4. William Gorges, York, Maine, Deputy Governor, 1636-1637.
5. Sir Ferdinando Gorges, Governor of New England, 1637-1639.
6. Thomas Gorges, York, Maine, Deputy Governor, 1640-1643.
7. Richard Vines, Saco, Maine, Deputy Governor, 1643-1646.
8. Henry Jocelyn, Scarborough, Maine, Deputy Governor, 1646-1649.
9. Edward Godfrey, York, Maine, Governor, 1649-1652, when the province was absorbed by Massachusetts Bay Colony.

THE LOCATION, SIZE AND CHARACTER OF THE SETTLEMENTS IN MAINE IN 1630

BASED UPON STATEMENTS OF VISITORS TO NEW ENGLAND SHORES.

Samuel Maverick, in a description of New England in 1626, said: "Wee could not make in all three Hundred men in the whole Countrey, those scattered a hundred and ffiftie Miles assunder," and added, "about those times also there were not within the now Great Government of the Massachusetts above three Shallops and a few Cannoes."*

He described the dwellings as of little value, since all of the buildings from New York to Nova Scotia, with exception of three or four at New Plymouth and his own at Winnisimet, were not worth two hundred pounds.

According to representations, made by Edward Winslow and Isaac Allerton and reaffirmed in the Plymouth charter of January 13, 1629-30, Plymouth Colony had less than three hundred inhabitants at that date. On the other hand, Massachusetts Bay Colony, upon the arrival of Thomas Dudley upon May 30, 1630, contained but two hundred and twenty, of whom one hundred and eighty were sent the year before.

These figures prove that in 1630 the entire population of the Commonwealth was only 500 persons.†

According to Captain John Smith, Massachusetts was "the paradise of all those parts." Thomas Morton, also, in his New English Canaan published in 1637, asserted that "The Massachusetts, being the middell part" (of New England) "is a very beautifull Land," and that "the rest of the Planters are disperst among the Coasts between 41. and 44. Degrees of Latitude, and as yet have" (made) "very little way into the inland."

* 2 Mass. Hist. Proc., 1-247.
† Appendix A.

The anonymous writer, assumed to be Walter Neal, writing of the country in 1635, said: *"The English in their severall patents are planted along the sea coast and have their habitations nere adjoyning to Rivers navigable ffor shippinge, or Barkes, the charge and difficultie of transportinge provision by land, ffor want of horses causes the Inland parts to bee yett unpeopled."*‡

July 14, 1638, John Jocelyn voyaged from Boston to the home of his brother Henry, who had just left the service of Ann, widow of Captain John Mason, at Pascataqua, and settled upon his grant at Scarborough. This writer then remarked: *"The Countrey all along as I sailed, being no other than a meer Wilderness, here and there by the Seaside a few scattered plantations, with a few houses."*§

A reproduction of the map of 1653, which was found in the British Museum, disclosed only sixty-five English dwellings in the *Province of Mayne*.

May 17, 1665, Samuel Maverick supplemented his earlier description of the country with the following special reference to Maine: "In this province there are but few Townes, and those much scattered * * * *They are rather farmes than townes."**

As late as 1677, according to the historian Hubbard, "The uncertain and fallible Reports of such as have only sailed by the Country, or viewed some of the Rivers and Havens, but never passed through the Heart of the Continent" described Maine as "a barren and rocky Country * * * of little worth, unless it were for the Borders thereof upon the Sea-coast and some * * * desirable Land upon the Banks of some Rivers." In the opinion of the author the whole district was "scarce worth half those Mens Lives that have been lost these two last Years, in hope to save it" from Indian depredation.

Upon the same authority, litigation over Maine real estate had been "enough to have maintained a greater Number of Lawers, than ever were the Inhabitants."†

‡ N. E. Hist. Gen. Reg., 40-72.
§ 3 Mass. Hist. Col., 3-226.
* Me. Doc. in Eng. Arch., 67.
† Hubbard's Wars, 2-2, 8.

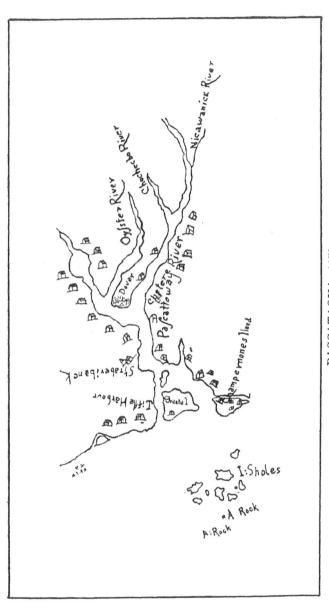

PASCATAQUA, 1653

PISCATAQUA RIVER

In 1548, the British Government enacted its first legislation for the encouragement of the fishing industry on the Banks of Newfoundland, and many years later the opposition of Sir Ferdinando Gorges and Sir John Bowser to the exercise of the right of free fishery in New England was severely criticised in Parliament.

Under the date of May 2, 1621, the following passage occurred in the official record of proceedings: "And theis men which are the northern plantation of New England, have not one man there, in theis 70 years * * * theis New England men will neither plant themselfes, nor suffer others." Apparently, it was the almost unanimous opinion of statesmen of that period that all of the colonization which then had been effected had been promoted through private initiative, or at least, like that of New Plymouth, without the united coöperation of the royal proprietors.*

At that juncture Gorges realized the necessity for immediate action in order to save the Northern Charter. Assignments of territory in New England were projected and plans for permanent occupation were begun.

March 9, 1621-2, Captain John Mason secured a grant of land at Cape Ann from the Council of Plymouth, and Ambrose Gibbons, of Plymouth, was designated to take possession of the premises.

Subsequently, it was claimed by Mason's heirs "That in the year 1622 the said John Mason did send over several Servants and passengers to be tennants with store of cattle, provisions and necessaries unto his lands at Cape Ann and did build sundry houses and set up the trade of ffishery upon that Coast and employed for his Steward there Ambrose Gibbons Gentleman."

There is no definite proof that the patentee did anything that year to perfect his title to the concession at Cape Ann, although the grant had been made and Plum Island had acquired already

---

* Brit. Proc., 1-37.

the significant name of Mason's Isle. If possession was taken at that time, it may have been effected by Gibbons in conjunction with other projects. He may have been associated with Thomas Morton, or Phineas Pratt, who in May, 1622, arrived at the Eastward with a small party of colonists in the *Sparrow*.

That ship had been dispatched from London by Thomas Weston and John Beauchamp, merchants of the English city, with orders to fish and trade at Damariscove Island during the summer.

The colonists had been instructed to locate their plantation in the vicinity of Plymouth Colony, because Weston as an original subscriber to that venture anticipated substantial assistance from that quarter.

After delay in securing a satisfactory pilot at Damariscove and Monhegan the expedition proceeded westward in an open boat. Landings were made at the Isles of Shoals and Cape Ann and both localities must have presented advantages, but the site selected for the plantation was at Wessaguscus (Weymouth, Massachusetts). If Gibbons were one of the party, he may have taken possession at Cape Ann at that time.

Morton was personally acquainted with Mason and styled him "that Heroick and very good Common wealths man * * * a true foster Father and lover of vertue."

Although English court records indicate that the former was involved in litigation at home during the period of his first visit to this country, there is nothing in the files which disproves his absence from London after April, 1622.*

At any rate, he declared that "In the Moneth of June, Anno Salutis 1622, it was my chaunce to arrive in the parts of New England with 30. Servants, and provision of all sorts fit for a plantation: and whiles our howses were building, I did indeavour to take a survey of the Country."†

From this statement it is plain that Morton sailed from London with Weston's colonists, amounting to about sixty members, in the latter part of April and arrived at New Plymouth about the last of June; that, about the first of August, he removed to Passonagessit (Braintree), where he lived alone. It may be inferred that his "servants" were some of the "servants and ten-

* Mass. Hist. Proc., 58-169.
† N. E. Canaan, 59.

nants" of Mason who were quartered at Weymouth with those of Weston.

Many of the settlers had soon "forsaken the town, and made their rendezvous where they got their victuals." They were described as "scatered up & downe in ye woods, & by ye water sids, wher they could find ground nuts & clames, hear 6 and ther ten."*

In the "Depth of Winter" Morton, as the solitary pioneer at Passonagessit, left his dwelling and "reposed at Wessaguscus" in order that he might "have the benefit of company." He referred to residents at Wessaguscus as "my neighboures" and to their buildings as "our howses." While he was sojourning abroad the Indians extracted some corn from his house at Passonagessit, across the river, and complaint was made by him to Chicataubut. That sagamore delegated "a Salvage, that had lived 12 moneths in England," to make restitution for the loss. The native chosen was Squanto, also known as Tisquantum, who had lived in London three years before with Thomas Dermer. He was the last known representative of the Patuxit tribe, which had been located at New Plymouth, and his death occurred suddenly in December, 1622. Its date was corroborated by Winslow. Hence, the incident happened in the late fall before the death of Squanto and soon after the advent of Morton at Braintree.†

August 10, 1622, Gorges and Mason had secured from the Council of Plymouth a grant of all of the territory situated between Merrimac and Sagadahoc rivers. The concession comprised all of Coastal New Hampshire as well as Western Maine. It was secured largely through the influence of Gorges himself. It was to be operated in severalty and regulated by a proprietary form of government.

About two months later, specifically upon October 16, David Thompson, a Scotch apothecary of Plymouth, England, obtained from the same council a grant of 6000 acres of land, to be located within the confines of New England. It was unassigned to any particular district, but after a selection had been made the premises were required to be surveyed and registered with the council. Seventeen days later the grantee had procured a license to transport ten men and provisions thither.‡

* Mass. Hist. Co., 8-266; Bradford, 2-93.
† N. E. Canaan, 46, 124; Mass. Hist. Col., 8-250.
‡ Appendix B.

In the spring of 1623 he arrived at the mouth of Piscataqua River, the name of which was properly spelled Pascataqua—the form generally adopted in this text.

He seems to have possessed advance information concerning that locality. In a map of 1612 Champlain gave Pascataqua Harbor the name of "baeu port." Two years later Smith alluded to it as Passataquack. Dutch maps of 1616 and 1621, drawn by Hendricksen and Jacobs respectively, designated the mouth of the river with the legend "schoon haven."

He selected Odiorne's Point in Rye, New Hampshire, as the site for a fortified house and began construction forthwith. His situation was called Little Harbor, to distinguish it from Great Harbor, which lies on the north, or Maine, side of Great Island.†

Samuel Maverick, who came to New England with Robert Gorges later in the year and was associated at Pascataqua and Winnisimet (Chelsea), with Thompson, married the latter's widow and acquired part of his estate. While in error about the date of the patent of Pascataqua, which was executed before his advent in the country, Maverick asserted that Thompson, financed by Abraham Colmer, Leonard Pomery and Nicholas Sherwill, merchants of Plymouth, "went over with a Considerable Company of Servants and built a Strong and Large House, enclosed it with a large and high Palizado and mounted Gunns * * * This house and ffort he built on a Point of Land at the very entrance of Pascatoway River * * * and for the bounds of this land he went up the River to a point called Bloudy Point."‡

By their agreement the Plymouth merchants were obligated to furnish seven men to settle upon the plantation. These colonists were to be provided with transportation in the *Jonathan* and *Providence,* ships of Plymouth which were bound for Virginia with other passengers.§

From a subsequent petition in which the son of William Hilton, of Plymouth Colony, maintained that his father and uncle Edward Hilton "were the first Inglish planters" to settle on the Pascataqua River, it has been assumed by Belknap, Hubbard and early writers, that both Hiltons were members of the original Thompson colony.*

† Bradford, 2-107; Mass. Hist. Col., 8-276.
‡ Mass. Hist. Proc., 21-234.
§ N. H. Gen. Rec., 2-2.
* N. E. Hist. Gen. Reg., 36-41.

But this could not have been possible, because the Hiltons did not remove from New Plymouth to Pascataqua until after the arrival of the petitioner in the country in August, 1623. Hence, they could not have been associated with Thompson in the construction of the first English house in New Hampshire. There is no doubt that they were, as claimed by themselves, the first Englishmen to settle upon the inland banks of Pascataqua River and that their operations were begun in Dover, at the point where that stream flows out of Great Bay, but their plantation was not undertaken until several years after that at Little Harbor.

Proof that the station of Thompson at the latter place was the first established in New Hampshire was furnished in the reminiscences of Pratt, one of Weston's colonists.

In February, 1623, when the plantation at Wessaguscus became destitute, John Sanders, its director, sailed in an open boat for Eastern Maine, where he expected to obtain supplies from fishing craft about Monhegan Island.

A month later, and before the return of Sanders, all of the members of his colony who had not succumbed to the exigencies of Indian conflict or starvation—except a few who had withdrawn to New Plymouth from preference—embarked in their small vessel, the *Swan*, for the Eastward, where they hoped to meet Weston himself or find employment on the fishing boats and obtain funds for return passage to England.†

The story told by Pratt, who was sick from exposure when the settlement at Wessaguscus was abandoned and had been left with a few others at New Plymouth, was as follows:

"9 of our men weare ded wth ffamine and on died in the ship before thay Came to the place whear at that Time of yeare ships Came to ffish—it being in March. At this Time ships began to ffish at ye Islands of Sholes and I haveing Recovered a Little of my strength went to my Company near about this Time" (to) "the first plantation att Pascataqua the" (overseer) "thereof was Mr. David Tomson at the time of my arivall att Pascataqua."‡

"Sanders' Point" is one of the oldest names in New Hampshire. It was given to the promontory which lies between Little Harbor and Sagamore Creek and now forms the southerly ap-

† Bradford. 2-94.
‡ 4 Mass. Hist. Col., 4-486.

proach for the bridge to Great Island. It must have marked the second location of the Weston Colony in New England.

At the Isles of Shoals, near this point, the fugitives from Massachusetts had encountered the first fishing vessels of the season and could gain no advantage by going farther east. Here Weston himself, according to accounts of Bradford and Morton, found his disheartened colonists that spring. Disguised as a blacksmith on a fishing sloop, he had just come to Monhegan and transshipped for Massachusetts in a small sailboat, which was wrecked "in ye botome of ye bay between Meremek river and Pascataquack," where he was plundered by the Indians of Agawam (Ipswich). From Pascataqua Weston succeeded in reaching New Plymouth where he refinanced himself. Later, in a retaliatory spirit, his colonists conducted an aggressive campaign against the Indians of Dorchester and Agawam, in which they obtained supplies of corn and captured some of the natives.

Many years afterward Samuel Maverick, who claimed to have seen "the first settellment of those pts" by the English, alluded to the strength of the plantations at Monhegan and Pascataqua and asserted that these eastern colonies were chiefly instrumental in subduing the savages, who were arrogant in their conduct towards the first weak planters of Massachusetts.*

Pratt also intimated that the station at Pascataqua was well protected against the Indians. He related incidents that happened there late in 1623, when a sagamore gave two of his subjects to Levett and Thompson. One of these natives was Wat Tyler, who had been found destitute, upon an island in 1619, by Thomas Dermer, and the other was Jack Straw, who formerly had been carried to England by Sir Walter Raleigh.†

In the fall of 1623 Robert, son of Sir Ferdinando Gorges, who had begun a second colony on the premises abandoned by Weston at Wessaguscus, came to Pascataqua from New Plymouth in the *Swan* which he had just confiscated from Weston under an order issued by the Council of Plymouth May 31, 1622.

At Little Harbor Gorges proceeded to organize the Council of New England, which then consisted of Admiral Francis West, Governor William Bradford from New Plymouth and Christopher Levett.

* N. Y. Hist. Col., 1869, 31, 49; Mass. Hist. Proc., 21-234.
† Winthrop, 1-52.

Levett was engaged in surveying at Pascataqua and remained there about one month. He made it apparent that there could have been no English settler on the inland reaches of the river at that time, since the only available information relative to conditions in the interior was derived from the natives. The statement of this visitor was: "But for the ground I can say nothing, but by the relation of the sagamore or king of that place, who told me there was much good ground up in the river about seven or eight leagues."*

The prior grant of Maine and New Hampshire territory to Gorges and Mason precluded Thompson from acquiring title to the premises which he had occupied at Pascataqua. He was but a trespasser, and Colmer, Pomery and Sherwill with all of their influence could not prevail against the superior rights of the original patentees, who were insistent in preserving their claims.

In fact, five Plymouth and two Dartmouth ships were "arrested" after their return to England in 1623, "because they went to fish in New England" within the patent limits of Gorges and Mason. Two of these may have been the *Jonathan* and *Providence,* in which the Thompson Colony had been transported to Pascataqua. At any rate, the renewal of opposition to free fishery in New England by Gorges on this occasion resulted in further hostile criticism of his patent rights by Parliament.†

Accordingly, the visit of Robert Gorges to Pascataqua cannot be regarded as purely friendly. While there he arrived at an agreement with Thompson to relinquish that location to his father Sir Ferdinando and his partner Captain Mason, whom he represented in New England in the capacity of attorney.

The subsequent petition of Mason's heirs alleged that from the year 1623 the decedent "did settle a considerable Colony at Pascattaway River." The inference must be that some of Mason's men took possession there immediately, and, if so, that some came from Massachusetts where they had settled temporarily.

The first intimation that Thompson intended to remove from Little Harbor is found in a letter, written by Governor Bradford on September 8, 1623, after he had been in conference with Gorges, Thompson and Weston. In that communication it was stated that both Thompson and Weston were anxious to obtain

* Me. Hist. Col., 2-80.
† Brit. Proc., 1-57, 58.

a grant of Cape Ann—a desire which on the part of the former indicated a marked reversal of plans, since he was reported by Winslow, in the preceding July, to be well pleased with his location at Pascataqua.*

Cape Ann, which had been granted previously to Mason, was regranted January 1, 1624, to Plymouth Colony, which was not oversolicitous for the interests of others.

Thompson "removed down into the Massachusetts Bay within a year after" his advent at Pascataqua, where he took possession "of a fruitful island, and a very desirable neck of land, since confirmed to him or his heirs by the Court of the Massachusetts, upon the surrender of all of his other interest in New England, to which yet he could pretend no other title, than a promise, or gift to be conferred on him, in a letter by Sir Ferdinando Gorges."†

The Council of New England was soon dissolved. West immediately withdrew to Virginia, where he became prominent in political affairs; Gorges abandoned his new establishment at Wessaguscus the following spring; and Levett, after completing a fortified post in Casco Bay, returned to England the next summer.

Whether Morton deserted his premises at Braintree with Sanders in February, 1623, or with the remaining survivors in March, was not disclosed, but he was in England the next year and had perfected plans to return to the New World.‡

Before Levett left the country in the summer of 1624 he had entertained some of the other unfortunate members of the Weymouth colony at Casco. They had been unable to secure return passage in the fishing fleet and may have been employed by him through the previous winter. Their vessel, still known as the *Swan*, was engaged in coastwise trade between Damariscove and Virginian ports.

Thompson had a major interest in the first dwelling built at Winnisimet, which, in 1660, Maverick declared to be the most ancient house then standing in Massachusetts. Obviously, it had been located upon the "very desirable neck of land" to which Hubbard had afterwards alluded. It was constructed in 1624, for only twenty years later, in his historical data of New England,

* Ford's Bradford, 1-358.
† Hubbard, 105.
‡ N. H. State Papers, 17-496.

the pioneer governor of Massachusetts asserted that the earliest settlement in Boston Harbor was begun by Englishmen seven years before 1631.*

In 1625, Thompson and Maverick, who had left the plantation at Wessaguscus to form the partnership, fortified the post at Winnisimet with four cannon and other means of defense against the natives, with whom they were engaged in trade. Maverick stated that his home was provided "with a Pallizado and fflankers and gunnes both belowe and above in them which awed the Indians who at that time had a mind to Cutt off the English."

In 1627, during that part of March which formerly was assigned to the previous year, Thompson joined the merchants of New Plymouth and purchased the entire stock of merchandise offered for sale at Damariscove and Monhegan islands.

Many years later Bradford referred to Thompson with an inapt description of residence as one "who lived" instead of one "who *had* lived" at Pascataqua. During the year of his transaction at Monhegan the pioneer of Pascataqua and Winnisimet erected "the forme," meaning *the frame,* of a house upon Thompson's Island in Boston Harbor, but he died before the structure was completed.

He may have been killed or fatally injured by the Indians in their attack upon his house at Winnisimet, which Maverick claimed was assaulted by them soon after it was fortified. The sequel of that incident, so far as the savages were concerned, was reported in the following excerpt: "They once faced it but receiveing a repulse never attempted it more although (as now they confesse) they repented it when about 2 yeares after they saw so many English come over." The attack must have been made in 1628.†

Amias, Thompson's widow, was still living at Winnisimet in June of that year, when she subscribed to the fund for the deportation of Morton from Mount Wallaston (Braintree).‡

Maverick did not subscribe at that time for the reason that he was not in sympathy with the movement, as indicated by him in a subsequent extended criticism of the action. He maintained that the Massachusetts colonists were not wholly guileless and

* Mass. Hist. Proc., 21-236; Winthrop, 1-43.
† Mass. Col. Rec., 2-206.
‡ Bradford, 2-161.

that Morton's description of the people and conditions in New England during the earliest period was true to life.

However, he was but a young man when he arrived in the country, for he was born in 1602 and was but eleven years of age when Amias Cole was married at Plymouth. He had been a member of her family at Winnisimet for several years while Thompson was at its head and subsequently married her. Before his marriage he may not have been rated for himself.

The Maverick family occupied the old house at Winnisimet until 1633, when the grant of Noddle's Island was made. The assertion of Edward Johnson that Maverick was residing upon that island in 1630 may be accounted for as but another instance of mistaken reminiscence.†

June 9, 1628, the English plantations agreed to assume the expense of extraditing Thomas Morton, of Mount Wallaston, Massachusetts, for the offence of selling arms and ammunition to the Indians. In describing the event Bradford employed this language: "Those that joyned in this acction (and after contributed to ye charge of sending him for England) were from Pascataway, Namkeake, Winisimett, Weesagascusett, Natasco, and *other places wher any English were seated.*"

The complete list of settlements which participated was reported to have comprised the following items only:

<table>
<tr><td>Plymouth,</td><td>£2.</td><td>10</td></tr>
<tr><td>Naumkeak (Salem),</td><td>1.</td><td>10</td></tr>
<tr><td>Pascataquack (Rye),</td><td>2.</td><td>10</td></tr>
<tr><td>Mr. Jeffrey and Mr. Burslem (Wessaguscus),</td><td>2.</td><td>00</td></tr>
<tr><td>Natascot (Hull),</td><td>1.</td><td>10</td></tr>
<tr><td>Mrs. Thomson (Winnisimet),</td><td></td><td>15</td></tr>
<tr><td>Mr. Blackston (Boston),</td><td></td><td>12</td></tr>
<tr><td>Edward Hilton (Dover),</td><td>1.</td><td>00</td></tr>
</table>

Evidently there were on that exact date no English plantations in Maine, where the results of Morton's activities would have provoked general criticism and his keen competition would have been most disastrous. Casco must have been deserted by Levett's colony that summer, and Richmond Island was not inhabited by Walter Bagnall and his associate until after the departure of Morton from Mount Wallaston, for Bradford said: "Some of ye worst of ye company were disperst, and some of ye

† Mass. Col. Rec., 1-96; Winthrop, 1-39.

more modest kepte ye house till he should be heard from." Bagnall was one of the Morton colony of seven.*

The accuracy of an ancient list of servants sent by Mason into New Hampshire has been questioned, but its only apparent defect is incompleteness. It was made from the composite memory of many persons. It contains the names of early settlers who had lived in the country before organized government existed and can only be accounted for because they escaped mention in records or were located primarily in Massachusetts.

When Roger Clap arrived in Boston Harbor May 30, 1630, the only settlers he found in Massachusetts were living at Charlestown, which included Winnisimet, Salem and Plymouth. After the advent of Winthrop, two weeks later, plantations were begun at Dorchester, Lynn, Medford, Roxbury and Watertown.

At Agawam (Ipswich) a settlement had been undertaken by some of Mason's and Levett's pioneers. It did not have the full sanction of the prevailing government.

September 7, of that year, before Levett had embarked on his homeward voyage in the *Gift* a secret order was passed in the new council relating to Agawam. It was then decided that a warrant should "presently" be sent "to comand those that are planted there forthwith to come away."†

Not satisfied with the mere annihilation of the infant colony at Ipswich which was situated within Mason's limits, the same authorities resorted to the persuasive means of criminal prosecution to induce all competitors in Indian trade to leave their neighborhood. Those who could not be made to depart by the imposition of severe penalties for minor offences were banished or forcibly deported.

During the first year of the Winthrop administration, according to official records, twelve Massachusetts pioneers were banished summarily by judicial decree. The deputy governor, too, congratulated himself on being rid of many who, because of dislike for the "government," returned in the vessels in which they had just arrived. And he mentioned others who, "hearing of men of their own disposition, which were planted at Pascataway, went from us to them."‡

Some of these who are recognizable as Mason's men were

* Bradford, 2-162.
† Mass. Col. Rec., 1-58.
‡ Young's Mass. Chron., 315.

Ambrose Gibbons, John Peverly, Thomas Moore, Jeremiah and Thomas Walford, the householder found in Charlestown in 1629, and his sons-in-law William Brookin, Alexander Jones and Thomas Peverly.†

Reverting to the charges made by Mason's heirs in later years, one may be almost convinced of the truth of their allegation that Gibbons continued to occupy Agawam, interruptedly perhaps, "untill the year 1630 at which time the Massachusetts Colony violently seized upon that part of the Province stretching their bounds three miles to the Northwards of Merrimack River and turned the servants and tennants of the said John Mason out of their possessions, under pretence of a Charter from his late Majty King Charles in 1628."‡

Before the death of Mason an agreement was made, but never consummated, to the effect that the colony should surrender its title to land east of Merrimac River in exchange for that proprietor's interest in Cape Ann.§

Friends of the colony, both at home and abroad, characterized Gorges as an "enemy." Some accused him of secret plans to usurp the local government through the annulment of all patent rights granted by the Council of Plymouth in New England.

The attitude of the grand patentee towards Massachusetts oppression was described by John Humphrey, one of the chief advisors of the colony. In a letter to Winthrop, dated December 9, 1630, he reported that "from verie high matters" Sir Ferdinando had "come to this, to desire that his people & planters (by vertue of his sons pattent) may live quietly & uninjured by us."**

Among early fugitives from Charlestown justice were Sir Christopher Gardiner, Henry Lynn and John Pickering, who went to Pascataqua for refuge and may have been members of the original Gorges immigration. At least they were in sympathy with the interests of that patron.

In spite of the successful denouement of its attempts to be rid of undesirable citizens by rigorous abuse, the leading political factors in the new government could not be mollified. The

† N. E. Hist. Gen. Reg., 2-39.
‡ N. H. State Papers, 17-534.
§ Me. Doc. in Eng. Arch., 66.
** 4 Mass. Hist. Col., 6-3.

dwelling of Morton at Mount Wallaston was burned before his eyes in the winter of 1630, previous to his second extradition to England. A few months later, although Gardiner himself had been decreed to banishment and successfully evaded his inquisitors, his house was reduced to ashes.*

April 25, 1635, the Council of Plymouth, in which Gorges had been an active agent, surrendered the Grand Patent of New England to Charles First. The chief reason for the action was the insistence upon observance of new forms of religion and laws prescribed by the Massachusetts regime, which had acquired power enough to enforce any edict by "punishing divers that would not approve therof, some by whipping, others by burning their houses over their heads, & some by banishing & the like." The victims were described as "Servants & certain other Undrtakers & Tenants" of the council.†

In 1676, the heirs of Mason incorporated the same charges in their petition for recovery of the decedent's former territorial rights in New England. Testimony was adduced by the Commonwealth to disprove the statements by such "old planters" as then could be found in the country, but only Edward Johnson, of York, could testify to occurrences previous to 1630. He was one of Weston's colonists who had withdrawn to Pascataqua in 1623.‡

Individual settlers can be determined only from subsequent allusions.

Henry Alt deposed, in 1678, when he was seventy-three years of age, that John Smart had mowed a marsh on Great Bay twelve years before Dover became a township. As that municipality was recognized as a town by Massachusetts Bay Colony as early as 1639, the year of reference must have been that of 1627, or an earlier one, and both must have been residents at the time.§

John Ault was listed as one of Mason's men. Smart may have been a member of the colony of Gorges or Weston, who had gone back to England, but had returned and was living at Hingham in 1635.

John Oldham may have been a transient resident at Pascataqua. Although Bradford asserted that his family remained in

* N. E. Canaan, 183.
† Am. Ant. Col., 1867, 125.
‡ N. H. State Papers, 17-521.
§ Essex Inst., 59-282.

Massachusetts, he had sojourned for a while at New Plymouth and Nantasket, but in 1626 he was in Virginia as passenger on board a vessel from "Canada," which then included Northern Maine. In the deportation of Thomas Morton he was an active agent and took charge of the prisoner, from the time he was transferred from one of the uninhabited Isles of Shoals, near the mouth of Pascataqua River, until he was confined in an English jail.

In 1629, Massachusetts authorities were apprehensive lest Oldham might return and settle within their limits where he could create further dissensions. By that time he had secured an interest in the old patent of Robert Gorges and was engaged in obtaining a grant at Saco with Vines. Furthermore, his name appeared as a witness upon the Wheelwright deed of Pascataqua territory and his trading goods were forwarded to that port the following year in the *Warwick*.

THE ISLES OF SHOALS.

This group of nine rocky islands, part of which lie within the state of New Hampshire, was first known to mariners as "Smith's Isles." Those in Maine, situated about six miles south of the entrance to Pascataqua River, are Appledore, Cedar, Duck, Malaga and Smuttynose. In 1614, they were first visited by Captain John Smith, who claimed that they were afterwards designated by his name because they comprised all of the territory that had been assigned to him from the vast domain of New England. He described them as "barren rocks, the most overgrowne with such shrubs and sharpe whins you can hardly passe them; without either grasse or wood but three or foure short shrubby old Cedars."*

Phineas Pratt, one of Weston's unfortunate pioneers, who in 1622 had found no English settler between Monhegan and New Plymouth, said that "ships began to ffish at ye Islands of Sholes" in March, 1623.†

Christopher Levett landed at the islands during the fall of the same year and remarked concerning their character: "Upon these Ilands, I neither could see one good timber tree, nor so much good ground as to make a garden. The place is found to be a good fishing place for 6 Shippes, but more cannot well be there

* Smith's Trav. & Works, 2-947.
† 4 Mass. Hist. Col., 4-486.

for want of convenient stage-roome, as this yeare's experience hath proved."‡

From Levett's statement it appeared that until the time of his advent none of the Isles of Shoals had been occupied for any purpose and all were uncultivated; neither did there appear to be any accommodation for more than half a dozen vessels.

Appledore, the largest island in the group, contains 350 acres and was called "Hog Island" at first, because, like others upon which there were springs of fresh water, it was stocked with pigs. These animals were permitted to run at large over the entire premises and subsist upon fish scrap until their removal at the end of each fishing season. In the early days, other islands along the Maine coast were similarly christened, including two in Casco and one in Muscongus Bay. In fact, swine had been transported to Monhegan Island as the first experiment and were maintained there for the express purpose of utilizing the most worthless by-product of the summer fishing industry.

The settlement of David Thompson at the mouth of Pascataqua River was contemporaneous with the first fishing ventures at the Isles of Shoals and provided a convenient rendezvous for pioneer fishermen in the vicinity. Fishmongers of Barnstable and Plymouth appeared as the earliest adventurers on this part of the coast. Their entire operations, however, were confined to the spring and summer seasons.

Hog Island naturally acquired the distinctive title of "The Isle of Shoals," since it was the first and for many years the only one of the group to be occupied permanently by fishermen. So, at the end of the first half of the Seventeenth Century, at least, it may be regarded as the only inhabited island in this group and main port of entry for Western Maine.

The early population was very small, but after the plantation had become established and its inhabitants felt their dependency upon their limited resources, a large majority began to insist that swine should be excluded to prevent pollution of the indispensable water supply.

Before settlements were attempted upon the mainland generally the larger islands were resorted to by Europeans because they afforded greater advantages for security from the savages and were more accessible to fishing grounds and coasting vessels.

‡ Baxter's Levett, 89.

Later, competition forced new arrivals to occupy the protected headlands along the shore itself, and finally the interior where fortified trading stations, called by the islanders the "houses in the rivers," were located.§

The earlier occupants at Hog Island built dwellings, stages and flakes for the benefit of the summer industry only, but it was not the place for a gentleman, and in 1628, when Thomas Morton was marooned there by Massachusetts authorities until a ship could be secured to deport him for England, he described his own predicament as follows: "They tooke mine Host into their Shallop, hoysed Saile, and carried him to the Northern parts; where they left him upon a Island * * * without gunne, powther, or shot or dogge or so much as a knife to get any thinge to feede upon * * * Home hee could not get to Ma-re-Mount."

"Upon this Island he stayed a moneth at least, and was releeved by Salvages that tooke notice that mine Host was a Sachem of Passonagessit . . ."

"From this place for England sailed mine Host in a Plimmouth shipp (that came into the Land to fish upon the Coast), that landed him safe in England at Plimmouth." The following spring the exile returned to New Plymouth over the same course.*

Early in June, 1630, English colonists bound for Salem passed within two leagues of the Isles of Shoals, but noted only one ship anchored there and "five or six shallops under sail up and down."†

The shallops seen plying about the islands at that time were boats belonging to the larger vessel which was a belated fishing sloop. Levett found that the fishing season then terminated on the Northern Coast about the last of May or the middle of June. Mariners had already frequented that locality for seven years.

This same year Walter Neal and his associates arrived at Pascataqua, where they found shelter in the house at Little Harbor, which had been built by Thompson and his Plymouth colleagues seven years before. In addition to other projects it was the intention of the Laconia Company, as soon as the colony was established in the country, to undertake fishing operations upon a large scale at the Isles of Shoals. Edward Godfrey, selected by

§ Me. Doc. Hist., 3-462.
* N. E. Canaan, 151, 144.
† Winthrop, 1-24.

the adventurers to supervise this part of their proposed industry, had a small quota of men thus engaged in the spring of 1631.
November 3, of that year, the "Isles of Shoals, and ye ffishings thereabouts" were granted by the Council of Plymouth to Laconia Company as appurtenant to Pascataqua territory.‡

March 6, old style, of the following year, Henry Fleet, another factor of the same company, en route from Pascataqua River for Virginia in the *Warwick*, which had been employed in coastal traffic, docked at the Isle of Shoals for provisions. Stocking the vessel at this point by fishing and trading took five days.

About two months later John Gibbs, master of the *Lyon's Whelp* of London, arrived on the premises where he proposed to develop the fishing industry for the company. William Seavey, afterwards a resident upon Hog Island, may have been a member of this crew, since he was subsequently identified as one of Mason's men and testified that he came thither that summer on a "fishing account."§

Late that season Godfrey was instructed to increase the number of fishermen employed by him on the mainland, but the experiment in deep-sea fishing had failed so completely that no more vessels were chartered by the company for that purpose. After the return of Gibbs, complaints of his "ill dealing" throughout the voyage were made to Ambrose Gibbons, of Pascataqua, and though the reason given by the latter for its failure was that "A Londoner is not for fishing," yet the late advent of the vessel upon the fishing grounds was held to be mainly accountable, so that the next year operations at the islands were continued for divers English syndicates by John Corbin, John Raymond and George Luxon, from Plymouth, London and Barnstable respectively. Raymond had been a factor for some of the Laconia merchants, but June 24, when about to depart from the Isle of Shoals, he dispatched his unsold merchandise to Gibbons at Newichawannock for safe-keeping. Luxon had sold provisions at the latter station during the same month. His home was Bideford.

Discouraged by reverses which had been met in their joint management of Laconia plantations, the members of the company met in London December 6, 1633, dissolved their partnership

‡ N. H. State Papers, 17-482.
§ N. H. State Papers, 17-522.

relations and agreed upon a division of all of their properties at Pascataqua except the Isles of Shoals and Newichawannock House.*

The following spring there were seventeen fishing vessels stationed at Richmond Island and the Isles of Shoals. In fact, Winthrop himself recommended the eastern route as the most expeditious for the transmission of English mail to Massachusetts. The forwarders suggested were Edward Hilton and Thomas Wiggin who were both resident at Pascataqua.†

A list of ten of the ships referred to comprised a single fleet, "lying in the River of Thames" and awaiting permission to sail for New England. They proceeded in April with the *Elizabeth* and *Francis*, of Ipswich. The master of the latter ship was John Cutting afterwards identified with the political affairs at the Isle of Shoals.‡

April 22, 1635, the northern half of the island group was assigned by royal conveyance to Gorges and the residue to Mason, who were regarded as the most influential members of the Laconia partnership. Heretofore, these fishing grounds had been a common resort. During that summer George Luxon fished and traded at the "Isle of Shoals, as he had done for many years, and returning to sell his fish at market, was taken in foggy weather, and carried into the bay of Port Royal, and there wrecked upon a small island."§

On the afternoon of August 13, in the same year, the *James* of Bristol anchored in the lee of "Hog Island," but Richard Mather, a clergyman bound for Boston in this vessel, reported that he had found no inhabitants at Monhegan and but few at Richmond Island. The fishing season was then over and he mentioned no one as a resident at the Isle of Shoals, where all of the ship's passengers lodged on board their own vessel during that night.

The opening of 1636 presented a dismal outlook for New England planters. All of the settlements were nearly destitute, and supplies could not be secured to the southward where like conditions prevailed. In the crisis it was manifestly unsafe to depend wholly upon the surplus stores of the fishing ships and in

* N. H. State Papers, 17-487.
† Winthrop, 1-464.
‡ N. E. Hist. Gen. Reg., 8-137.
§ Winthrop, 1-163.

order to obtain adequate stocks from abroad it was necessary to get early communication with England. With this object in view Isaac Allerton was licensed by Massachusetts government to sail as far eastward as the French post at Penobscot "for ye better conveace of our letters."*

The result of this unseasonable voyage was disastrous for the messenger. In the words of the governor: "His bark was cast upon an island, and beat out her keel, and so lay ten days; yet he gate help from Pemaquid, and mended her, and brought her home." He reached Boston before March 30, 1636.†

At the beginning of the next month Allerton and Thomas Mayhew, as agent of Matthew Cradock at Medford, visited the Isle of Shoals to trade with the fishing masters, where they got "but little provisions, and at extreme rates, but six hogsheads of bread, and a few peas." The narrator added, "Some pork they brought, but so lean as I have not seen the like salted. The Indians killed up all their swine."

The trade conditions at the islands were described by Mayhew himself in these words: "Touching my journey to Ile of Sholes to buy 80 hogsheads of provission, when I came I fownd noe such thinge as unto me for trueth was reported; to procure 8 hogsheads of bread I was fayne to lay out one hundred pownds in ruggs & coates unnecessaryly: and for pease I gott but 1 hogshead & $\frac{1}{2}$."‡

Presumably, Mayhew made the voyage from Medford in the bark *Rebecca* which had been named for Cradock's wife and belonged to his plantation. The supplies were needed at Saco, where men were engaged in the clapboard industry, as well as in Massachusetts.

April 12, of the same year, it was regarded as a dispensation of Providence when the *Charity* from Dartmouth arrived in Boston Harbor with supplies from England. Winthrop asserted that "The Lord * * * sent us a ship * * * with provisions, but she put in at Pascataqua, and sold much there."

The cargo of this vessel belonged to Alexander Shapleigh, whose daughter Catherine Hilton, in a plea addressed to the Massachusetts authorities for the release of her younger brother Nicholas Shapleigh, alluded to the incident in 1674 in these

---
* Bradford. 2-221.
† Winthrop. 1-182.
‡ 4 Mass. Hist. Col. 7-31.

words: "About 38 years since, in a time of great scarcity, in this land, our ffather layd out a good estate, for the supply of this Country, & the seteling some part of it, & in A season of there want, supplyed them soe reasonabley with provisions, that it was thanckfully accepted, and acknowledged by the Authority then in being."§

During the month following the arrival of the *Charity,* Thomas Bradbury, agent for Gorges, influenced by Shapleigh's benevolent treatment of the colonists, assigned to him the whole of Kittery Point, except the extremity, and valuable fishing privileges at the Isles of Shoals.

Under the direction of his grandson John Treworthy, Shapleigh maintained "a fishing" at Hog Island for some years. A house for fishermen was erected at Kittery Point by Treworthy, who chartered the *Bachelor* for fishing purposes from the younger John Winthrop as early as 1637 and moored it in a cove near his building on the mainland.

By 1640 ownership of the island fishery had been acquired by James, father of John Treworthy, and the title was recognized officially by the magistrates of Yorkshire Court—of which the owner was a member—in a decree which described Thomas Wannerton as a resident of Strawberry Bank (Portsmouth) and his neighbors on the Isle of Shoals as fishermen that lived "near him upon the Island belonging to Mr. Treworthy."

Two of the tenants to whom reference was made must have been Stephen Crafford and William Seavey who had "Howses on the Ile of Sholes." These fishermen appear to have arrived together in the *Charles,* of Bristol, which belonged to Gyles Elbridge and was licensed to sail from the home port July 21, 1639.

Most of their fellow passengers were bound for western points. The vessel was docked at Pascataqua for weeks. Seavey had been in the country before, but Crafford who brought his family had not been mentioned previously. Later, both owned dwellings on the mainland.

English mariners, although prohibited by early royal edict from trading on the coast, continued to transport surplus commodities for exchange with the fishermen and Indians. In June, 1641, John Winter visited the islands to procure "pitch & som liquer Casks, & som other nessessaries," to complete his new

§ Me. Doc. Hist., 6-38.

bark at Richmond Island. He found the ships were about ready to sail for England.

Crafford was drowned while on a fishing trip during the following spring. Seavey's boat and servant were lost at the same time. The family of the deceased was maintained by Seavey, who as a partner in the houses at Hog Island administered the estate. Other residents on the island at that time were Thomas Trigs and Peter Turbett, who married a daughter of John Sanders, of Hampton. According to Winthrop, only two vessels fished at the islands that year, but Richard Gibson was employed by them as their pastor throughout the season. He returned to England on one of these ships.*

The unused houses owned by the partners on Hog Island may have been leased by Winter, who reported that fishing results had "proved well" for mariners who were "well provided for that place with good fishermen." Later, William Hingston, master of the *Hercules*, of Plymouth, left with Winter the keys of two small houses at the "Isle of Shoals," which had been vacated by his fishing crew at the end of the season.†

During the year 1642 Nicholas Shapleigh, merchant of Kingsweare, acquired all of the Maine estate which had belonged to his father, including the valuable fishing rights at Pascataqua and Hog Island, and in addition to numerous activities undertaken at Kittery and in Massachusetts, personally conducted a fishery at the Isle of Shoals for about a year, at the end of which period he appointed his nephew John Treworthy agent for New England and returned to Devonshire.‡

In 1645, Richard Cummings and Thomas Turpin were resident at Hog Island and the latter was designated constable, but soon removed to Portsmouth. John Seeley, from Kingstanton, England, was also described as a constable the same year. He, too, retired to the mainland subsequently, leaving his brothers George, Richard and William at Hog Island.§

Massachusetts merchants became interested in the fishing industry about the islands, but Treworthy as manager for his uncle refused to proceed in the business because his principal had neglected to send more boats and supplies from England as

---
* Winthrop, 2-21, 66.
† Me. Doc. Hist., 3-336.
‡ Aspinwall, 185.
§ Aspinwall, 350; Mass. Arch., 3-215.

originally agreed. The fishing shallops that remained were drawn up on the beach and beaten apart by the tides.*

However, on his own account, Treworthy made several unprofitable ventures along the coast and finally contracted to provide part of a cargo of fish, valued at £1100, which Major Robert Sedgwick, of Charlestown, and Valentine Hill, of Boston, had agreed to procure for shipment from Cape Ann, Isle of Shoals and Monhegan. Delivery was to be completed by the middle of June, 1647, to Edward Wetheridge for the account of Thomas Tucker, of London, and Ferdinando Body and David Stephens, of Teneriffe, merchants.

In consequence of unusually bad weather the catch failed to meet expectations and reimbursement of the funds advanced to pay wages was demanded from the contractors. In compliance Treworthy gave Sedgwick a mortgage of all the property at the island with two furnished dwellings, a stage and flakes, seven shallops and provisions, as well as a ketch or pinnace at Pascataqua "sometimes belonging unto this place a fishing."†

June 19, 1647, Antiphas Maverick, of Pascataqua, sold to Henry Sherbourn "all my tittell and interest that I have or ever had in Hoge Illand at the Isle of Shoals to have two houses, one stage and the moreing places wch belong unto the stage or cove." From the similarity of descriptions it might be reasonably inferred that they covered the same property in the cases of this grantor and Treworthy.

In October, of the same year, complaint was made against John Reynolds that he had arrived at Hog Island from the mainland with a great stock of goats and hogs, which wasted the fish and polluted the common spring of water on that island, that was "the only relefe & subsistence of all the rest of the Illands." A further demand was made that his wife be removed from the island since her presence was contrary to an unwritten law that would exclude all women. To its credit, the court decided that Reynolds' wife could share his home, but that his live stock was a public menace. The consort of William Wormwood, who had had more or less controversy with her neighbors at Kittery, was ordered to be deported by Richard Cutt and John Cutting.

* Me. Doc. Hist., 6-5.
† York Deeds, 1-3, 9.

At this time there were a few inhabitants on some of the New Hampshire islands, but they were fishermen who probably did not live on the premises during the winter season.

PIONEERS

ANGER, SAMPSON, fisherman at Isles of Shoals, 1640; York, 1640; wife Susanna, 1668; died 1691-4; widow Sarah married Arthur Hughes.

BALL, JOHN, born 1635; fisherman at the Isles of Shoals, 1649; York, 1650; Kittery, 1687-1694; wife Joanna, born 1646; children Elizabeth (Pettigrew) and John.

BATTEN, JOHN, fishing partner of William James and employe of William Brown, of Salem, at the Isles of Shoals, 1647; married Sarah, daughter of John Maine, and removed to Westcustego; children Abraham and John.

BICKFORD, JOHN, fisherman, 1647; Dover, taxed 1648-1661; died at Isles of Shoals, 1662; son John.

CADOGAN, RICHARD, born 1635; fisherman at the Isles of Shoals, 1648; York River, 1648; sold land at York by attorney, 1659; died at Charlestown November 5, 1695.

CRIMP, WILLIAM, fisherman at Isles of Shoals, 1649; deceased 1652.

CULLANE, MATTHEW, came from Ireland; lodged with his cousin Dermot Mahoney, of Boston; had no other relative in America; died at the Isles of Shoals December 25, 1650.

EDWARDS, OADES, formerly of Ipswich, died at the Isles of Shoals, 1651; left widow and brother, John Edwards, who was administrator.

GORRELL, PHILIP, fisherman at Isles of Shoals, 1649-1651.

HORRELL, HUMPHREY, fisherman; Isles of Shoals, 1650; Muscongus, 1653; estate in Beverly; widow Elizabeth; son Humphrey.

HUNKINS, HERCULES, or Archelaus, fisherman, at Hog Island, 1649; died at Star Island, leaving widow, 1659; children Ann, Benton and Mark.

KELLY, JOHN, attorney at the Isles of Shoals for Stephen Oliver, of Exeter, England; contract made jointly with John Treworthy, of Kingsweare, and Thomas Purchase, of Dorchester, February 27, 1647-8; may have been the father of Roger of the Isles of Shoals and of Reginald, of Monhegan.

MAVERICK, ANTIPHAS, son of John and brother of Moses of Marblehead and Samuel of Noddle's Island; removed from Isles of Shoals to Kittery, 1647; Exeter, 1661; died July 2, 1678; children Abigail (Gilman) and Catherine (Paul).

NEWCOMB, ELIAS, fisherman at Isles of Shoals, 1649; bought half of Champernoone's Island, 1650.

PHILLIPS, THOMAS, fisherman at Isles of Shoals, 1642; Damariscove, 1649; Pemaquid, 1652; widow at Hippocras Island, 1671; children Thomas, born 1647, and probably William, of Pemaquid.

SEAVEY, WILLIAM, born 1601; fisherman at the Isles of Shoals, 1632; loaned passage money to Stephen Crafford on board the "Charles" of Bristol, 1639; Portsmouth, 1640; fishing at the Shoals, 1642; living 1676; children Elizabeth (Odiorne), John, Stephen and William.

SEELEY, JOHN, mariner at the Isles of Shoals, 1646; from Kingstanton, England, 1650; house on Doctor's Island in Salmon Falls River; died 1670; children, born in England, George, John, Richard, William, who died March 22, 1679-80, and Joanna (Topping), of London.

TURBETT, PETER, fisherman at the Isles of Shoals, 1641; Cape Porpoise, 1653; died 1669; widow Sarah married Daniel Goodwin; children Elizabeth (Banks), Hannah, John, born 1651, only one to leave issue, Nicholas, Peter and Sarah.

TURPIN, THOMAS, fisherman and constable at the Isles of Shoals, 1647; removed to Portsmouth; drowned October 29, 1649; children Anne (Endell), Elizabeth (Adams) and Jane (Leach).

WAY, THOMAS, fisherman at the Isles of Shoals, 1649; Cape Neddock, 1649-1651; Pemaquid, 1653.

THE LACONIA PLANTATIONS.

On account of the existence of many great lakes within it the territory granted to the Laconia Company by the Council of Plymouth November 17, 1629, was called the Province of Laconia. The description indicated a previous general knowledge of the region about Lake Champlain.

It comprised "All those lands & Countrys lying adjacent or bordering upon the great lake or lakes or rivers commonly called or knowen by ye name of ye river & lake or rivers & lakes of ye Irroquois a nation or nations of salvage people inhabiting up into ye landwards betwixt ye lines of west & North west conceived to passe or lead upwards from ye rivers of Sagadahock & Merrimack in ye Country of New England aforesd Together also wth ye lakes & rivers of ye Irroquois & other nations adjoyning ye midle part of wch lakes is scittuate & lying neerabout ye latitude of fourty four or fourty five degrees reckon'd from ye Equinoctial line Northwards as alsoe all ye lands soyls & grounds wth in tenn miles of any part of ye said lakes or rivers on ye South or East part thereof, & from ye west end or sides of ye sd lakes & rivers soe farre forth to ye west as shall extend halfway into ye next great lake to ye West wards & from thence Northwards unto ye North side of ye maine river wch runeth from ye great & vast Westerne lakes & falleth unto ye river of Canada, including all ye Islands wth in ye precinct or perambulacon described. As alsoe * * * trade & traficque wth ye Solvages."*

Whence the English information was derived is not known, but it may have been secured from the Indians themselves.

The great lake is clearly depicted in ancient maps.†

The principal object of the grantees in obtaining this concession was the right to trade with the Indians who, on account of

* N. H. State Papers, 17-476.
† Nova Belgica et Anglia Nova; Mass. Arch., 11-61; Appendix C.

the abundance of fur bearing animals, were known to frequent localities like that described. Furthermore, the French fur trade upon the Saint Lawrence River was a matter of early knowledge and consideration by English adventurers.

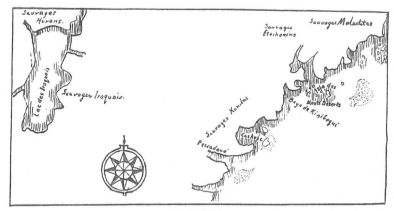

LACONIA

Under the date of April 10, 1630, Winthrop noted in his journal the report that "the bark *Warwick* was taken by the Dunkirkers, for she came single out of the Downs about fourteen days since, intending to come to us to the Wight, but was never heard of since. She was a pretty ship of about eighty tons and ten pieces of ordnance, and was set out by Sir Ferdinando Gorges, Capt. Mason, and others, for discovery of the great lake in New England, so to have intercepted the trade of beaver."‡

As a matter of fact, the *Warwick*, under commission of the Laconia Company, sailed from The Downs March 28, touched at Plymouth April 8, and arrived safely at Pascataqua May 31, one year after the execution of the Wheelwright deed.§

The rumor circulated in Salem that the *Warwick* had been captured by pirates seemed credible, as in those days there was strenuous rivalry to reach New England. It is apparent that the Laconia expedition was under orders to anticipate, if possible, all other departures.

‡ Winthrop, 1-7.
§ N. H. State Papers, 1-62.

The location of Pascataqua River had induced the belief that a feasible pinnace route could be found and maintained into the region of Laconia and the heart of Canada.

Upon arrival the employes of the Laconia Company occupied the house built by David Thompson at Little Harbor in 1623. Obviously, this building was the meeting place selected by John Oldham and the Laconia pioneers, since it was called "Rendezvous" in later years. The structure was rebuilt of stone materials, fortified with cannon and styled the "Great House" and "Mason's Stone House."*

The names of Laconia employes were Thomas Blake, Thomas Cammock, William Cooper, Thomas Crockett, William Dermit (Dennett), Ralph Gee, Ambrose Gibbons, Edward Godfrey, Henry Jocelyn, Stephen Kidder, Roger Knight, Henry Langstaff, Charles and Walter Neal, John Reynolds, the physician, Thomas Spencer and Adrian Tucker.

Hubbard asserted that the colonists spent the summer and fall of their first year in preparation for the coming winter which was delayed but severe. December 14, Neal and three associates visited Massachusetts, where they were poorly entertained. With their return to Pascataqua and the disappearance of the last English sail from the coast, the little band resigned itself to the prospect of its first New England winter in the wilderness, "far from neybers."

March 6, 1630-1, the *Pide Cow*, with men and supplies in charge of Captain Henry Keyes, sailed from Portsmouth, England, for Pascataqua. It was a vessel of only thirty tons capacity and June 25 its arrival at destination was announced in Boston where it was described as a "small English ship come thither with provisions and some Frenchmen to make salt."†

Francis Williams came in this vessel as overseer of the salt works and assigned to the Frenchmen a small rocky point or islet, containing only about one acre at that time and lying opposite Eliot shore, still known as Frank's Fort, where they were engaged for a short time in an attempt to produce salt from sea water. This enterprise was intended to facilitate the curing of fish, but proved unsuccessful. The names of these employes of the Laconia Company were Peterfore, Charles and Labrisse.‡

---
* N. H. State Papers, 17-552; 29-157, 163.
† Winthrop, 1-56.
‡ Winthrop, 1-226; N. H. State Papers, 1-72.

July 7, of this year, Edward Hilton took possession of his patent at Dover and transferred it to Thomas Wiggin, who had arrived, with Isaac Allerton by way of Saco, in the *White Angel* from Bristol. Wiggin was to act as sole agent for some Bristol merchants who had purchased the Hilton plantation. On an ancient map of this year the name of the plantation was designated Bristol.

During the same month Neal arraigned Edward Ashley of Penobscot, who had been arrested for retailing arms and ammunition to the Indians contrary to royal edict. Captain Henry Keyes assisted in the investigation. The offender was transferred to England for further examination.

Realizing his need of greater authority in the administration of justice, Neal petitioned for and obtained a commission from the British government, which gave him jurisdiction as a chief magistrate from "Boston Patent" to Saint Croix River. He was afterwards recognized as governor of Maine territory.§

July 4, 1631, the *Warwick* which then belonged to Henry Gardiner and George Griffith, merchants of London, sailed from The Downs in command of Henry Fleet who had a commission from the Laconia Company to trade for one year. The master of the bark was John Dunton.

In the words of Fleet, this vessel "arrived in the harbor of Pascattouaie, the 9th of September, making some stay upon the coast of New England. From thence on Monday the 19th of September, we sailed directly for Virginia." On his way south Fleet secured some trading goods at Massachusetts, as he had at Pascataqua, for which he was to make payment in Indian corn from Virginia.

A passenger in the *Warwick* was Thomas Wannerton who was then described as a "soldier for discoverie." He began the construction of a house at Strawberry Bank that fall. His location was later called Portsmouth after the port from which he had hailed.

The year when the Wannerton house was built may be fixed by reference to a deposition of Edward Colcord, of Dover, who stated that when he arrived in that part of the country in 1631, there were but three houses upon Pascataqua River.*

§ Me. Doc. in Eng. Arch., 81.
* Hubbard, 219.

He must have alluded to the "Rendezvous" of Neal at Little Harbor, the building occupied by Weston's colonists at Sanders' Point and the post of Edward Hilton at Dover Point, which Colcord came to occupy as an employe of the Bristol Merchants.

Other passengers in the *Warwick* were Shadrach Miller and two "servants" engaged by the colony to cleave clapboards and pipe staves. The names of the servants were not given, but Langstaff may have been one.

October 3, 1631, Walter Bagnall and his companion, who had lived on Richmond Island since the dissolution of Morton's Colony near Wessaguscus, were killed by Indians. The tragedy occurred in the evening and was the result of injudicious sales of liquor and English weapons to the natives. Further, it was claimed that Bagnall had been dishonest in his methods of trading with them and had acquired wealth by reason of exorbitant profits.

Neal voyaged eastward in pursuit of the criminals who were reported to have lived in the vicinity of Presumpscot River, but he failed to apprehend anyone at that time. He did, however, secure from friendly Indians some evidence of the identity of the persons responsible, although he found none of them in the native villages on the coast.

The cases of Ashley and Bagnall illustrate the entire absence of any police protection or coöperation among the scattered Maine plantations. At that time, according to Maverick who was familiar with the true conditions in New England, there were no roads and but few boats, and without such means of transportation strict enforcement of law was impossible.

From the situation then existent it is apparent that all of the small plantations in Maine were powerless to protect themselves against indignities of the savages, to say nothing of their inability to administer discipline in cases like those mentioned, where only a few members of a single tribe were implicated. George Cleave and Richard Tucker were living on the mainland near Richmond Island when Bagnall was murdered.

The hostility of the eastern Indians was again in evidence late in the year. Henry Way, a fur trader of Dorchester, sent his son and three men to the Eastward in a boat, to trade with the natives, but they were all murdered and the boat was destroyed. This event occurred at about the same time as the tragedy at Richmond Island in which Bagnall was killed and may have represented part of a concerted plan to exterminate all of the English planters.

However, it is more likely that conditions, for which former traders were responsible, had not improved materially since the report of Bradford, four years before, that it was then unsafe for coasters to remain long upon the eastern shores after the departure of English fishing crews at the end of each season.

William Wood was an early visitor to New England and was conversant with its affairs. He explained that the hostility in all cases was occasioned by new comers who had sold liquor to the Indians to obtain unfair advantages in trade. He believed that the practice had resulted in "many evill consequents, as disorder, quarrels, wrongs, unconscionable and forcive wresting of Beaver and Wampompeage: and from over-flowing Cups there hath beene a proceeding to revenge, murther and over-flowing of blood. As witnesse Maister Wayes Boate, which they sunke with stones, after they had killed his son, with three more."†

Way, like Richard Collicott, of Dorchester, was licensed by Massachusetts Bay Colony to trade with the natives for furs.

Since controversy had arisen between the employes of the Bristol Merchants and those of Laconia Company over the land on the south side of Great Bay, it became necessary for the latter to secure title to the premises to prevent encroachment.

Accordingly, November 3, 1631, Sir Ferdinando Gorges, Captain John Mason and their associates John Cotton, Henry Gardiner, George Griffith, Edwin Guy, Thomas Wannerton, Thomas and Eleazar Eyre, who then constituted the Laconia Company, obtained a grant of Pascataqua from the Council of Plymouth. Many of these grantees were gentlemen of wealth and influence. Thomas Eyre, secretary of that company, had been clerk of the Canada Company and was custodian of the original of the Grand Patent of New England.‡

The grant recited that the patentees had already expended more than £3000 and "much tyme in the discovering of the Countrie," alluding, probably, to their recent contributions to the "vew" taken by Oldham, Wheelwright, and their associates two years before.

† N. E. Prospect, 68.
‡ Appendix B.

The other considerations expressed were "the advancement of the sd plantacon" by the manufacture of clapboards and pipe staves, making salt pans and salt, transporting vines to promote the wine industry and prospecting for iron ore.

The territory ceded was situated on both sides of the mouth of Pascataqua River. The New Hampshire tract extended westward along the coast for five miles and inland as far as Bloody Point, where it overlapped the Squamscott section of the Hilton patent. The Maine tract was only three miles wide on the seashore, but extended up the river bank for thirty miles, including the present areas of Kittery, Eliot, South Berwick, Berwick and Lebanon, which was called Towwoh by the Indians.

The patent also ceded "All that house and cheife habitacon situate and being at Pascataway al's Pascataquack al's Pascaquacke in New England * * * wherein Capt. Walt: Neale and ye Colony wth him now doth or lately did reside togeather wth the Gardens and Cornegrounds occupied and planted by the sd Colonie, and the Salt workes allready begun * * * for ye use of the Adventurers to Liconia (being in the latitude of 43 degrs or thereabouts."§

In the meantime the *Warwick* had arrived at Virginia. Another quotation from Fleet read as follows: "I was engaged to pay a quantity of Indian corn in New England, the neglect whereof might be prejudicial both to them that should have it, and to me that promised payment."

After stating that the bark had been laden with its cargo, consisting principally of southern corn bought from the natives, Fleet continued: "We set sail from Point Comfort and arrived at Pascattoway, in New England, on Tuesday the 7th of February, where we delivered our corn, the quantity being 700 bushels."

"On Tuesday, the 6th of March, we weighed anchor and sailed to the Isle of Shoals, where we furnished ourselves with provisions of victual. Sunday the 11th of March, we sailed for the Massachusetts Bay, and arrived there on the 19th day. I wanted commodities to trade with the Indians, and here I endeavored to fit myself if I Could. I did obtain some, but it proved of little value."

By reference to Lechford and Winthrop the log of this vessel may be reconstructed.

§ N. H. State Papers, 29-41.

At the Isles of Shoals the crew was engaged in fishing and curing fish and trading with other ships for supplies. At Salem, corn for summer delivery was sold to Roger Conant. At Natascot, where it arrived March 14, the vessel was nearly wrecked, but reached Winnisimet, then known as Massachusetts, five days later. There the bark lay at anchor for some time, in view of Maverick's dwelling, which the owner claimed to have been the "Ancientiest house" in the Bay, and near the farms of Cradock and Winthrop on Mystic River. March 23, Fleet was at Watertown, where he sold southern corn to Robert Feake, to be delivered the last day of July. April 8, accompanied by Maverick's pinnace, the *Warwick* sailed again for Virginia.

Fleet arrived at his destination in May and his narrative concluded with these words, "There I gave the pinnace her lading of Indian corn, and sent her away the 1st of June, with letters from our company to their friends in London, and elsewhere in England, which were safely conveyed from New England."*

There is no indication that the *Warwick* ever returned to Pascataqua. Subsequently, suit for recovery of their property was brought in the Admiralty Court of England by Henry Gardiner and George Griffith, lessees of the vessel and members of the Laconia Company. Their plea alleged undue retention of their bark by John Harvey, while he was governor of Virginia. At any rate the corn engaged that spring by Conant and Feake was never delivered. In 1636, the hull of this early factor in transatlantic and coastwise commerce was dismantled in a Dorchester inlet, afterwards known by the name of "Barque Warwick."

Early in June, 1632, Thomas Willett and Abraham Shurt with others were wrecked at Pascataqua in the shallop of Captain John Wright. Their vessel was laden with goods which had been discharged at Penobscot in transit for Massachusetts consignees. The account of the casualty stated that "One Abraham Shurd of Pemaquid, and one Capt. Wright, and others, coming to Pascataquack, being bound for this bay in a shallop with £200 worth of commodities, one of the seamen, going to light a pipe of tobacco, set fire on a barrel of powder, which tare the boat in pieces. That man was never seen; the rest were all saved, but the goods lost."†

---
* Scharf's Hist. of Maryland, 1-14.
† Winthrop, 1-79.

During their absence on this occasion Willett and Wright, who were in charge at Castine, were informed of the intrusion of the French upon their trading post and the seizure of Dixie Bull's shallop and goods at the Eastward. Another historical item disclosed that "The mr. of ye house, and parte of ye company with him, were come with their vessell to ye westward to fecth a supply of goods which was brought over for them."‡

As already related the murderers of Bagnall and of the employes of Henry Way had escaped punishment since the previous fall. A new offence against the public peace could not be tolerated, and to discourage further overt acts of lawlessness Neal organized all of his available forces and accompanied Shurt's party homeward, where he proposed to administer strict punitive justice.

July 23, according to a letter written by Thomas Cammock, who was then inspecting his prospective grant at Black Point, Neal was still detained beyond Richmond Island, while Vines who had been "coasting" was returning to Saco. Cammock used the expression "urgent occasions" to describe the importance of Neal's mission.§

Either because he had an insufficient force to accomplish his object or because of doubt as to his legal authority to inflict capital punishment upon the criminals, the captain signally failed in his eastern expedition.

Massachusetts magistrates, however, still manifested a sense of moral responsibility for their part in the tragedy. Four years before they had insisted upon the forcible ejection of Bagnall from the colony and he had sought a refuge among the savages in the Maine wilderness. There had been some early criticism of their summary proceedings in his case.

Accordingly, August 7 and more than ten months after the massacre occurred, partly to allay public criticism the court passed an order in these words: "A boate shall be sent forth, sufficiently manned, with comission to deale with the plantacon to the eastward" (Pascataqua River) "& joyne with such of them as shalbe willing thereto, for examinacon of the murder of the said Walter Bagnall, & for apphending of such as shalbe found guilty thereof, & to bring the prisonrs into the Bay."*

‡ Bradford, 2-189.
§ Me. Doc. Hist., 3-18.
* Mass. Col. Rec., 1-92.

William Wood, who returned to England the next year in the same vessel with Neal and must have obtained his information first hand, described the fates of the murderers in the words "as many as were caught, were hanged."†

October 18, 1632, Thomas Cammock and Edward Godfrey, a merchant, brought sixteen hogsheads of Indian corn from Pascataqua to the mill at Watertown to be ground.‡

Some of this grain was raised in Eliot, where it had been planted that spring by William Hilton. Twenty-one years later Hilton recovered damages for the trespass committed in this case, which was tried in the first session of a Maine court under Massachusetts jurisdiction. The decision indicated that Cammock had deprived the plaintiff of his house and crops in Eliot. Such a verdict was inevitable against a tenant of Gorges and Mason.

Hilton was also engaged in raising swine, but he yarded them across the Pascataqua River at Bloody Point, where they could not raid his cornfields. Wood's Map assigned a large point of land in Eliot to Hilton, which may be inferred to imply extensive ownership. It may be assumed that, when Hilton's Point in New Hampshire was sold to the Bristol Merchants in 1631, William Hilton removed to the location across the river, where he was mentioned in Maine records the next year.§

After delivering their cargo of grain from Captain Neal's pinnace to the Watertown mill, Cammock, and probably Godfrey, continued the voyage to Rhode Island upon an exploratory expedition. The purpose of this visit was explained previously when Cammock had written to Trelawney from Richmond Island, under the date of July 23, as follows:

"I doe purpose before winter to goe and see the Narragancett, which is to the Southward of Cape Codd, if our shallop comes from the Eastward time enough; and if I see any good to be done ther, to drive a trade, and you please to Joine in the proceedinge of itt, which shall be very probable or els I will nott stirr in itt, lett me alone for the procuringe off a patent, for itt is my lorde of Warwickes owne devision, and he was willinge I should gon upon itt. But itt is very populus of the Indians, and itt will requier a plantation of good force and strength, which so soone

† N. E. Prospect, 68.
‡ Winthrop, 1-90.
§ York Deeds, 1-60.

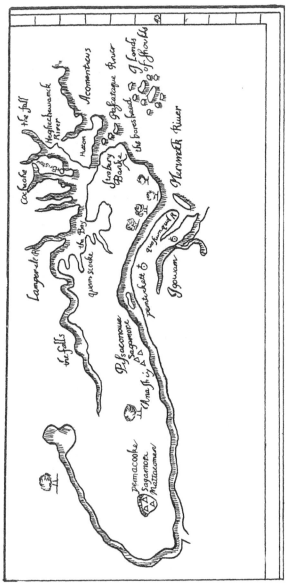

PART OF WOOD'S MAP, 1635

as I have bin ther, I will acquaint you of the state of the cuntrye."*

Cammock was a nephew of the Earl of Warwick and their kinship accounted for the liberties which the former proposed to take in the premises at Narragansett, if the conditions found there proved to be satisfactory to him. The title of Warwick was based upon the old division made in the presence of King James June 29, 1623, when the coast of New England was apportioned by lot to the members of the Council of Plymouth. Their investigation of the country beyond Cape Cod could not have appealed to the Laconia pioneers, since neither subsequently acquired any interest there.

While Cammock and Godfrey were in Massachusetts the magistrates there were informed of a piracy committed at Pemaquid by Dixie Bull and fifteen others. Neal had already gone eastward with two shallops, two pinnaces and forty men—all that could be mustered at Pascataqua plantations. After they had been windbound in Pemaquid Harbor for three weeks the fleet returned to Richmond Island, then deserted by everyone but Andrew and Thomas Alger and John Baddiver, Trelawney's servants. There they found and executed Black Will for complicity in the murder of Bagnall. Wood claimed that the criminals were betrayed by other Indians, but this was the only reported instance in which the death penalty was exacted.

The operations of the Laconia Company at Pascataqua had proved disappointing and expensive to all concerned. In the spring of 1633 Neal again visited the Eastern Country where he gave possession of lands at Scarborough to Cammock in the presence of Abraham Shurt, Richard Smith and John Winter. Four days later he delivered seizin to Abraham Shurt at Pemaquid in the presence of Cammock, William Hook, Robert Knight, George Newman and Christopher Burkett, master of the *White Angel*. This was the last time Neal ever saw the coast of Maine, for he was recalled by the Laconia proprietors in a letter that was then awaiting him at Pascataqua.†

In its instructions to Gibbons the company directed that all the employes be dismissed from its service except those who could support themselves upon the premises. At the same time Neal was authorized to grant land to the agents of the company.

* Me. Doc. Hist., 3-20.
† N. H. State Papers, 1-68.

June 2, he had returned from the Eastern Country to Little Harbor, where he conveyed to Cammock the premises in Eliot, on which William Hilton had planted corn the year before. This occupation by Cammock's predecessor was mentioned in 1641, in the premise to Wannerton's deed of adjoining land, and the tract was bestowed upon the grantee as a reward for "desertful endeavour," in which the principal inducement may have been recognition of the forcible eviction of Hilton himself.‡

During that month Neal bought the first cattle acquired by the plantation. This live stock was brought from the West Indies by Captain John Stone and sold along the coast from Boston to York. The inventory at Pascataqua July 2, 1633, listed ten cows, one bull and two calves.§

Just a week after the inventory was completed Neal deeded the first lot below that of Cammock to Thomas Wannerton and the second to Henry Jocelyn in consideration of company services. At about the same time Sanders' Point, then unoccupied, was assigned to Gibbons.*

July 15, Neal left Pascataqua for Boston, whence he sailed for England August 15, with eight associates, who appear to have been Thomas Cammock, Henry Jocelyn, Henry Langstaff, Shadrach Miller, Thomas Spencer, Adrian Tucker, George Vaughan and Francis Williams.†

Employes left by Neal at Newichawannock House were Gibbons and his wife and child, Thomas Blake, Thomas Crockett, Stephen Kidder and Charles Neal, who had resided there for nearly two years. At Little Harbor Thomas Wannerton remained in charge with William Cooper, William Dermit, Thomas Furrall, Roger Knight and his wife, Ralph Gee and a boy.‡‡

Some of these men were still engaged in their original employments after the departure of Neal. Cooper, Furrall and the boy assisted Gee in caring for the live stock. Others devoted their whole energies to cleaving clapboards. The earliest allusion to a saw pit was at Kittery Point about 1637.§§

The tragic deaths of some of these early colonists have been described. Cooper and the boy went "to an island, upon the Lord's day, to fetch some sack to be drank at the great house,"

‡ York Deeds, 1-3, 1.
§ Winthrop, 1-104; N. Y. Hist. Col., 2-3, 43; N. H. State Papers, 1-80.
* N. H. Prov. Deeds, 4-185.
† Winthrop, 1-106.
‡‡ N. H. State Papers, 1-81.
§§ Mass. Arch., B38-37; N. H. State Papers, 2-530.

but "coming back in a canoe (being both drunk) were driven to sea and never heard of after."

Another casualty occurred to a woodsman "At the same plantation" when "a company having made a fire at a tree, one of them said, 'Here this tree will fall, and here will I lie'; and accordingly it fell upon him and killed him." At that time trees were burned rather than cut down and the process sometimes required several days.*

April 22, 1635, Gorges was invested with a royal title to the Province of Maine and September 17, following, in consideration of the grantee's release of all other territory between Pascataqua and Sagadahoc rivers, confirmed Newichawannock to Mason. The premises described were identical with those allotted by agreement two years earlier.†

The other Pascataqua patentees were ignored; Gorges did not favor full recognition of their claims; consequently, he did not confirm their divisions during his lifetime and, in 1650, they engaged Captain John Littlebury, of Hatfield, England, to prosecute their demands. In Boston this agent, who was operating at his own expense on a commission basis, allied himself with Captain Thomas Lake, in order to secure influence with the stubborn eastern planters. Champernoone and Shapleigh, who were in possession of the coast between Kittery Point and Brave Boat Harbor, were the chief objectors in Maine, refusing to recognize any other title to their lands than that of Gorges, their predecessor.‡

During his first attempt to recover lands at Pascataqua, Littlebury entered and "layed clame unto the Ile of Shoales" and, in his own words, "tooke Quiet posession of the house & Lands in littell harbor where Capt Neale lived with servants we sent him out of old England for the use of the patentees."§

However, nothing of importance was accomplished at that time, and, in 1659, the surviving proprietors of Pascataqua joined with Godfrey, Rigby, and the heirs of Gorges and Mason, in a petition to the British Parliament, asking for restoration of ancient rights by Massachusetts.**

July 4, 1664, Littlebury was again called into action and promised a quarter of all the land he could recover in New Eng-

* Winthrop, 1-120.
† 2 Me. Hist. Col., 8-179.
‡ Aspinwall, 299.
§ Me. Doc. Hist., 4-318.
** New Eng. Vind., 41.

land for the surviving patentees. The claimants then living were Eleazar Eyre, Henry Gardiner and George Griffith.

Three years later the agent disposed of his interest in all Laconia lands to Thomas Lake, John Feake and Nathaniel Fryer. So far as known he had never recovered anything of value to reimburse his clients for their expenditures at Pascataqua. He had become discouraged at the outlook, although he reported that he had taken "posession of house and Land in great harbor with mr ffryers Consent." At that time the only building owned by Fryer at Great Harbor had been derived through mesne conveyances from Champernoone and was called "Champernoone's Lower House." It is a reasonable inference that the building had been occupied originally, before 1633, by Cammock and Godfrey as agents for the Laconia Company.†

The house at Little Harbor had been in possession of Joseph Mason during the sojourn of Littlebury in England. The former had been engaged in litigation to recover for Ann, widow of Captain Mason, lapsed interests in personal and real estate. The results had proved discouraging and Mason decided to abandon the service and return to England with Littlebury. Accordingly, he leased the Great House at Little Harbor to Abraham Corbet and Nicholas Shapleigh upon May 13, 1667, and it was not mentioned subsequently in any official record.‡

The building at Sanders' Point, formerly known as Strawberry Bank House, was assigned by Gibbons to his son-in-law Henry Sherbourn, who in turn conveyed the premises to his son in 1678.

The tract of land called Sanders' Point then contained "about three acres." The Sherbourn homestead, in which it was included, was described as situated "near Little Harbor by the Piscataqua River, bounded east by the said Little Harbor, north with land of Tobias Lear, south with the creek commonly called Sherburne's Creek, and so up the creek till it comes to the place commonly called *the old house.*"§

Apparently, Strawberry Bank House — the second oldest building of English construction in New Hampshire — stood upon the northerly side of the creek and but a short distance from the river.

† York Deeds, 1-77.
‡ Suffolk Deeds, 5-202.
§ Granite Monthly, 46-218.

GREAT ISLAND.
The earliest history of this island is obscure. It is situated in the mouth of Pascataqua River and forms Little Harbor to the south where the first plantation was made by Thompson on the New Hampshire shore; to the north it surrounds two sides of Great Harbor, through which the main channel leads upriver. It was first recognized as a place of defence against the French, Dutch or Indians, and was partially fortified by Walter Neal before 1633. Tradition says that he found two fishing huts there.

Neal lived at Little Harbor in the service of Gorges and Mason but three years in all. One of his workmen, Henry Langstaff, testified later that he had lived with him for two years and that "Capt. Neal did build a fort on Great Island whiles agent for sd Mason."*

The extent of fortification was described by Vines and Jocelyn in a statement, dated August 20, 1633, and regarded by some as spurious. The substance of this document may be relied upon, because all of the collateral facts could have been refuted by settlers who were fully conversant with them at the time they were offered in evidence.

The statement asserted that "There was ffoure Grete Gunes brought to piscatequa Which ware given by a Marcht of London for the Defence of the River" and that Neal and Thomas Wiggin, as governors at Pascataqua, were instructed to choose "the most Convenient place in the Said River to make a ffortefecatyon for the Defence therof, and to Mount those ffoure Gunes given to the place."

The plan of this fort, sent to the proprietors at the time, was alleged to have contained "all the Necks of Land in the North Este Side of the Grete Island that makes the Grete Harbor" and the founders "gave it the Name of ffort Poynt and alloted it so far bake in to the Iland about a bow shoat to a grete high Rocke Where on was Intended in time to Sett the Principall fforte."†

The fact that Neal did construct a fortification on Great Island is confirmed by collateral evidence. Before he left the country an inventory of all personal property belonging to the Laconia Company was completed. The list at Pascataqua, dated

* N. H. State Papers, 2-530.
† N. H. State Papers, 29-54.

July 1, 1633, contained two distinct sets of small ordnance, widely separated by unrelated items, some of which were found at Portsmouth. It was necessary to pass the island to reach the latter point.

In the rear of Fort Point was a tract, called Mosquito Hall, which comprised the northwestern corner of the island. October 1, 1637, this land with the buildings was sold to Francis Mathews, in escrow for John Hurd of Sturgeon Creek, by Jocelyn, Vines and Wannerton, who were acting respectively for Mason, Gorges and the Laconia Company. The premises were acquired by John Walton in 1646 and passed through the ownership of Richard Tucker to George Walton, when they were described as a "neck of land upon Great Island, in Pascataqua River, lying toward the west" and known as Mosquito Hall, "or nigh adjoining to it."‡

Two cannon were removed from Pascataqua to Hartford in 1642 by order of Sir Richard Saltonstall. These appear to have been the guns taken from Fort Point by the Waldrons who were associated with the Shrewsbury Merchants. Saltonstall had been a large patentee in Dover in 1633 and a dealer in heavy ordnance. It is likely that he was the unnamed London donor of the cannon at Pascataqua and had authority to transfer them later to the new southern colony where he had an interest.§

Fort Point was mentioned as a shipping rendezvous in 1650. Unlike Little Harbor, it lay near the middle channel of the river. The name also occurs in Portsmouth records in 1657, and in 1661 when Bryan Pendleton obtained permission from the town to erect a windmill on the point near the beach.*

In 1666, Massachusetts had authorized the establishment of a fortification at Portsmouth. May 19, 1669, the new fort may not have been completed but the Commonwealth decided that "the neck of land upon the east end of the great island at Portsmouth shall be sequestered for the use of the fort there planted, taking in ye *great Rock*, & from thence all the easterly pte of the said island."

The next year Walton, who still possessed Mosquito Hall, complained "of wrong donne by the County Court at Portsmouth for taking away of his land at Fort Poynt, upon the great island in Portsmouth." The tribunal decided that there was "no ground

‡ N. H. Hist. Col., 8-120.
§ Conn. Pub. Rec., 1-70.
* York Ct. Rec., 1-134.

of complainte," because the petitioner had no "legall or true title to ye land in question."†

As late as 1685 Walton deposed that he "remembered ye ffort built by Capt Mason upon the Great Island in the Same place where the ffort now Stands & that it was * * * furnished with Great Guns of which Some were Brass & were Afterwards taken away by Major Waldron and his Brother William."‡

In 1651, Captain John Littlebury took possession of the house at Little Harbor and put Joseph Mason in charge of the premises at that time. The latter lived in the Great House for several years as representative of Ann, widow of Captain Mason. That tenant asserted that the first battery on Great Island had consisted of ten cannon, but when he arrived everything had been "caried away (except one peece of Ordnance)." He also stated that all of the military equipment at the fort as well as several houses on Great Island had been provided at the expense of Gorges, Mason and their associates, alluding to the Laconia Company. Mosquito Hall was one of the buildings.§

May 30, 1693, Great Island and part of the New Hampshire shore, situated between Sagamore Creek and the sea and extending westward as far as Hampton, were invested with the privileges of a town and called "New Castle." The royal charter emanated from William and Mary of England.

In later times Fort William and Mary, which stood upon the site of Neal's original fortification, became the scene of the first overt act of the American Revolution, when the premises were raided on the night of December 24, 1774, by Langdon, Sullivan, Scammon and other local patriots, and all available war material was removed.

At Hotel Wentworth, on the southwest corner of the island and diagonally across from the enclosure of the ancient fort, the Russo-Japanese plenipotentiaries met in 1905, to formulate their national peace proposals.

DOVER (Hilton's Plantation).

In 1654, a commission, consisting of John Allen, Thomas Lake and Nicholas Shapleigh, was chosen to investigate proprietary

† Mass. Col. Rec., 4-2, 569, 635, 654.
‡ N. H. State Papers, 29-134.
§ N. H. Doc. in Eng. Arch., 38, 41.

claims to Wecanacohunt (Dover) and Squamscott (Bloody Point).

Their report stated "That Mr. Edward Hilton was possessed of this land about the year 1628, which is about 26 years ago." At that time Hilton was a living proprietor from whom all others had derived their titles, and no doubt the information upon which the decision was based was furnished by him.

He had come thither from Massachusetts, and June 9, 1628, had contributed to the fund for the deportation of Thomas Morton. May 17, 1629, both he and Thomas Wiggin, from Bristol, England, witnessed the execution of the Wheelwright treaty at Squamscott.

March 12, 1629-30, a patent of Hilton's Point and the opposite shore of Great Bay, now known as Newington, was issued to Hilton and his associates by the Council of Plymouth.*

The western boundary of the former tract, upon which the Hiltons had erected a dwelling, was afterwards fixed at Lamprey River, but the Squamscott tract, which was only three miles in width, extended to the falls at Exeter.

The report also stated, that "Mr. Hilton sold the land to some merchants of Bristol, who had it in possession for about 2 years." The record did not disclose the extent of development nor mention the names of the new English purchasers of the Dover tract. Some of these were John Hocking, John Wright and Thomas Wright, of Bristol, England.

The sale was negotiated by Thomas Wiggin, who had come to Saco in the *Swift* with Thomas Wright's colonists. They were to reside in the "House at Casco," which had been acquired from Christopher Levett the preceding year.

June 25, 1630, Wiggin and Captain John Wright, brother of the Casco proprietor, were present when Richard Vines took possession of his grant on the westerly side of Saco River. It may be assumed that the *Swift* had just arrived on the coast at that date, for Stephen Reekes, master of that vessel, also signed the certificate of seizin.

John Wright established his headquarters at Monhegan Island, the fishing plantation of the Bristol merchants, but he was engaged much of the time in sailing a shallop upon the coast of New England from New Plymouth to Penobscot. In September,

* N. E. Hist. Gen. Reg., 24-264.

of this year, while on his way eastward from the former port, he discharged some passengers at Pullin Point.

Wiggin, who visited Massachusetts during the year 1630, became friendly to Winthrop and his interests. Other settlers at Pascataqua had been inclined to be critical in religious matters and had left Massachusetts Bay Colony because its constituents, unlike themselves, did not adhere to the discipline of the Church of England. Thomas Dudley commented upon the depletion of his colony by the withdrawal of some to Pascataqua, where they were better entertained by the inhabitants, or, in other words, found "men of their own disposition." He mentioned merely Christopher Gardiner, who had gone northward, "hoping to find some English there like to himself."†

Because there was little religious or political sympathy between the colony and Hilton's plantation and on account of mutual jealously with respect to control of the eastern trade with the Indians, the Massachusetts magistrates were fearful lest Wiggin and the Bristol merchants, whom he represented in this country, should acquire, and dictate the affairs of, the Hilton settlement at Dover.

Accordingly, Winthrop forwarded to John Humphrey and Emanuel Downing, London members of his company, letters in which he commended Wiggin as a worthy man, but urged that his plan for the acquisition of Hilton's plantation should be discouraged. December 9, 1630, Humphrey, with this proposition in mind, advised Winthrop that his letter to Downing should be delivered at once, but added: "For Mr. Wiggin & your thoughts concerning him, & those who set him on worke, I thinke you will heare little more."‡

Humphrey was mistaken. June 28, 1631, Hilton and Wiggin were present at East Saco when the premises were assigned to Thomas Lewis. Nine days later both arrived at Dover with the Hilton patent, which had been brought from England to Saco in the *White Angel*. At Dover Point Lewis delivered official possession to Hilton, in the presence of James Downs, William Hilton and Samuel Sharp, and the entire plantation was transferred to Wiggin and named Bristol, in honor of the English origin of its new owners. Although the name appeared on Wood's Map of

† Young's Mass. Chron., 315, 334.
‡ 3 Mass. Hist. Col., 8-321 ; 4 Mass. Hist. Col., 6-3.

Southern New England in 1635, the information must have been secured by him at least two years earlier.

Thereafter, Wiggin professed to be a "neighbour" to Massachusetts and, while in England in the fall of 1632, was induced by Emanuel Downing, as attorney for that colony, to subscribe a statement directed to Sir John Coke, the King's Secretary, in opposition to Dixie Bull, Gardiner, Morton and Ratcliff in their combined efforts to repeal the Massachusetts charter.§

Edward Howes, who prepared Wiggin's statement, was an amanuensis in the office of Downing. November 28, 1632, Howes advised Winthrop that he had just met four English sailors in London, who had recently come "from Capt. Masons and the Bristoll plantation." These men—one of whom might have been Morton himself—described the hostile sentiment which prevailed at the latter plantation. They reported, among other criticisms of the "Bay" government, that one of the "Pascataweyans" had declared in their hearing "that fellowes which keepe hogges all the weeke, preach on the Saboth."

This claim resembled that made by Morton that "there is not any of these, though hee be but a Cow keeper, but is allowed to exercise his gifts in the publik assembly on the Lords day." While some of the antipathy between the settlements was due to religious intolerance and persecution on the part of Massachusetts, some was due to provincialism. Ambrose Gibbons, alluding to an event that happened the same year, advised the Laconia proprietors that "A Londoner is not for fishing; neither is there any amity betwixt the West cuntrimen and them."

December 19, following, the petition for annulment of the Massachusetts charter was heard and Wiggin was an indispensable witness for the colony before the Council of Plymouth. While his first impression upon Boston magistrates had not been favorable, his testimony, more than anything else, influenced the committee to which it had been referred, to subsequently dismiss the proceeding.

March 25, 1633, Howes again wrote Winthrop from London that "There are honest men about to buye out the Bristoll mens plantation in Pascataque, and doe purpose to plant there 500 good people before Michelmas next. C. Wiggin is the chiefe Agent therein." This transfer was effected that summer with Lords

§ 3 Mass. Hist. Col., 8-320, 322.

Say, Brook and their associates, known as the Shrewsbury Merchants, to the satisfaction of the magistrates of Massachusetts, who had encouraged them to purchase "the said lands of the Bristol men, in respect they feared some *ill neighborhood* from them."

Winthrop used an analogous expression a few years later with reference to the Wheelwright adherents at Exeter when he alluded to "their dealing as *against good neighborhood*, religion and common honesty."

In the words of the report, "The lords and gentlemen engaged the said land (so purchased) about 9 years, and placed more inhabitants at Dover, some of which came over at their cost and charges."*

June 22, 1633, Howes, in England, advised Governor Winthrop's son, "I must not forgett to put you in minde of one that is cominge to you, whoe hath deserved exceedingly of your father & the plantation, many wayes; he discovered (under God) our enemies plotts, and helpt to prevent them; he hath also dispossest our enemies of their hope, Pascataqua, and intends to plant him selfe and many gracious men there this sommer * * * You all have cause to blesse God that you have soe good a neighbour as Capt. Wiggen."†

The enemies of Massachusetts Bay Colony to whom Howes alluded were Gorges and Mason and their adherents, who claimed title to Eastern Massachusetts under original patents, and settlements made in accord therewith upon premises near Cape Ann and Boston Harbor, before those of the Dorchester Merchants and London Company. Howes as confidant of Emanuel Downing, who was an attorney for the new colony in London, was fully conversant with its affairs.

Winthrop himself attributed the beginning of the contention with Gorges and Mason to disclosures contained in letters, written by some of his indiscreet colonists and opened at Bristol, England, after the death of Christopher Levett, who had them in his custody when he died at sea in 1630. By this accidental means Gorges and Mason had been apprised of the plans of the new administration to evict their tenants and assume exclusive control.

* N. H. State Papers, 1-147, 157.
† 4 Mass. Hist. Col., 6-485, 489 ; 3 Mass. Hist. Col., 9-257.

From the statement of Howes it appeared that Wiggin, who was friendly to the magistrates of the new colony and jealous of the Laconia Company, must have opened the incoming mail of Gorges and Mason, which came by way of Pascataqua the following spring. In letters to Gardiner and Morton, Winthrop claimed to have discovered a new plot of Gorges to recover, if possible, his contested rights in Massachusetts.

In the latter part of 1632, Bull, Gardiner, Morton and Ratcliff, who had personal reasons to be inimical, had combined to institute proceedings in England to have the Massachusetts charter annulled. Through the influence of its promoters the new colony had won and absorbed the old planters by force of numbers on the premises.

Under the new regime Wiggin, as agent of the proprietors, arrived at the plantation in a vessel which reached Salem October 10, 1633. He was accompanied by about thirty colonists, including William Leverich as pastor and Thomas Brooks, alias Basil Parker, as overseer.

This clergyman did not remain long at Pascataqua. In 1638, possibly after some profound dogmatic controversy or sinister political upheaval among the communicants of the Dover parish, he had been superseded by George Burdett, who came from Salem and like Leverich had been engaged by the Shrewsbury Merchants to minister to the spiritual needs of the struggling hamlet. Suits were brought subsequently to recover from the patentees an unpaid balance of Burdett's salary.

Soon after the advent of the latter John Underhill, banished from Massachusetts, appeared on the scene and a series of political conflicts ensued, in which Underhill gained the ascendency over his rival, and in his honor the name of the town was changed to Dover. However, two years of supremacy sufficed and, in 1640, the new dictator withdrew from Pascataqua, leaving Hansard Knowles and Thomas Larkham, who had become a patentee of Dover Point, to contend for future control. Both were English clergymen of divergent views, and an animated dogmatic controversy followed, in which Larkham was successful. The town was renamed Northam in recognition of the popularity of the latter, but with the return of Knowles to England the new name became obsolete.

Dover did not prove to be a source of profit to the Shrewsbury merchants and June 2, 1641, with their unanimous consent, control was transferred to Massachusetts.

The early occupations at Dover were fur trading, raising maize and cleaving pipe staves and clapboards. While vessels were sent annually to the plantation by some of the proprietors during their period of tenure, these were employed in deep-sea fishing off the coast. The salmon industry, on account of its seasonable character, was never an enterprise of commercial importance there, as claimed by some modern writers.

In 1642, a distribution of unappropriated land, situated on Back River in the rear of their original house lots, was made and the persons entitled represented the earliest settlers of Dover who had remained in the vicinity.

May 22, 1656, the Dover and Squamscott tracts were surveyed and the whole district was allotted to the joint owners on the basis of twenty-five shares. The third division which contained the original site of the Bristol plantation was described in the report and disclosed that the maximum development within it to that time consisted of only three fields, amounting to but sixteen acres of cleared land, with some dwellings upon the premises.‡

EXETER (Squamscott Falls).

A hiatus in the records of his English parish disclosed the fact that its pastor, John Wheelwright, was absent during the years 1628 and 1629. It may be inferred that he came to New England with Endicott in September of the former year, and lived with associates in Massachusetts during the succeeding winter.

Edward Johnson described the dispositions and subsequent movements of these colonists in a clear and convincing way when he said that spring "being come, they addrest themselves to coste it as far as they durst for feare of loosing themselves, or falling into the hands of unknown Indians, being kept in awe by a report of a cruell people, not far off, called the Tarratines."§

The local Indians were friendly with the English but feared the Tarratines. In 1615, Captain John Smith, influenced by the solicitation of the natives of Southern New England, said that he "had concluded to inhabit and defend them against the Tarentines with a better power then the French did them; whose ty-

‡ Mass. Hist. Col., 3-180.
§ Wonder Working Prov., 45.

rannie did inforce them to embrace my offer with no small devotion." William Dixy and Humphrey Woodbury, two settlers who lived at Salem in 1629, said that the Agawam Indians sought protection against this hostile eastern tribe from the English.*

The conditions were favorable for Wheelwright, or any other congenial foreigner, to obtain a right of settlement within the limits of New Hampshire. There were precedents for such action at New Plymouth, Salem and Wessaguscus, where the first colonists had bought land of the Indians.

Early in 1629 an opportunity presented itself for Wheelwright to lay the foundation for his preconceived plan of establishing an English settlement in New England. He associated himself with John Oldham.

There must have been a common bond of interest and sympathy between these men which caused them to unite forces and "coast" towards the country of the hostile Tarratines, as an alternative to settling in Massachusetts, where Oldham previously had been subjected to court discipline and the religious beliefs of both are known to have been unpopular.

Furthermore, Oldham, according to the terms of his Saco grant, had already lived in the country six years and was fully conversant with the entire coast from Maine to Virginia.†

The principal result of Wheelwright's activities at this time appears to have been the execution of a settlement treaty or option with the Indian sagamores of Southern New Hampshire, to which Oldham was a witness.

The validity of this document has been questioned on the ground that the English participants were not present in America when it was dated.‡

In the first place, reference to the document itself will show that it was an executory contract, possessing mutual advantages, that its orthography and phraseology were ancient, that its characters were real persons, that its considerations were reasonable and historically accurate, and that its execution was more significant than mere delivery.

Oldham was the first witness to the transaction. He had been in England for nearly a year. April 17, 1629, it was reported by the London Company that he with some others was "pvyding a

* Thornton's Cape Ann, 81.
† Virginia Col. Rec., 121.
‡ Bell's Wheelwright, 79, 143.

vessell, and is mynded, as soone as hee can despatch, to come for New England, ptending to settle himselfe in Mattachusetts Bay." It was reported further that Oldham claimed the right to trade for beaver with the Indians as an original planter, and that he was not "satisfyed to trade himselfe with his owne stock & meanes" which were known to be small, but had been able to "interest other men" who were "never likely to bee benefitiall to the planting of the country, their owne pticuler pfitts (though to the overthrowe of the genall plantacon) being their chiefe ayme and intent."

The letter from which the preceding extracts were taken suggested that trouble might arise from the same source in New England. The words were these: "Wee feare * * * hee will psist and bee ready to drawe a partie to himselfe there, to the great hinderance of the comon quiett. Wee have therfore thought fitt to give yow notice * * * to settle an agreemt wth the old planters, soe as they may not harken to Mr Oldhams dangerous though vaine ppositions."§

Oldham may have arrived in the country before that letter or have crossed the Atlantic in the next month, which afforded ample time with favorable winds. At any rate, he was in New England in the spring of 1630, when his schedule of trading goods was made up and forwarded to Pascataqua in the *Warwick* by the secretary of the Laconia Company.*

Another witness who signed the Wheelwright deed was Samuel Sharp. There were two men of this name. One was a capitalist who had loaned money to Plymouth Colony in 1626 and had later become associated with the London Company. The other was employed by the company March 3, 1628-9, at a salary of ten pounds a year. He was reported to have been ready to sail by March 25 "at ffurdest" and had sailed from England before the middle of April. The presence of his name with that of Oldham on the deed made at Squamscott indicated their early arrival in the same vessel.†

The "other men" whom Oldham had interested in his New England project were clearly indicated in the events of the next twelve months. They were members of the Laconia and Saco companies, whose objects were common and whose relations were

§ Mass. Col. Rec., 1-389.
* N. H. State Papers, 1-62.
† Mass. Col. Rec., 1-5.

congenial. Both Saco companies must have been organized for some months before the issuance of their patents. This fact is evidenced in the language of both grants in the use of specific grantees and the additions "& Company."

Ambrose Gibbons, who was also a witness at this time, was alleged to have lived in Massachusetts before his advent at Pascataqua in 1630.‡

Richard Vines had visited the coast several years before. Late in 1628 he had accepted from Isaac Allerton, as agent for Plymouth Colony, over thirty pounds for his influence with the president, prominent members and eminent legal advisors, of the Council of Plymouth in the attempt to secure a patent at Cushnoc on the Kennebec River.§

Upon the authority of the Plymouth historian, over five hundred pounds were paid to Vines in all, of which "30 li. given at a clape, and 50 li. spent in a *journey*," were significant items.*

This voyage must have taken place in 1629 and it is reasonable that the payment of fifty pounds to Vines was Allerton's contribution to the fund for the expedition. This assumption is further strengthened by the claim of Bradford that the preliminary description for the Kennebec patent had been so uncertain in its original form that it became necessary to procure another the next year, to perfect the transaction. The very next year Vines and Oldham were made partners in the grant of Saco by the Council of Plymouth, and Allerton afterwards associated himself with both in the coasting trade.

Richard Bonython, another witness, was also interested in the Vines voyage. His partner, Thomas Lewis, had been in New England before his plantation was selected, because no less an authority than the Council of Plymouth recited as a consideration for their grant, dated February 12, 1629-30, "That Thomas Lewis, Gentle: hath already been at the Charge to transport him selfe & others to take a vew of New England in America, aforesd, for the bettering of his experience in advanceing of a plantation."†

John Wheelwright himself, afterwards confused in his recollection of the event, testified that Runacwitts executed some deed

‡ N. H. State Papers, 17-534.
§ 3 Mass. Hist. Col., 1-199.
* Bradford, 2-187.
† York Deeds, 2-111.

to himself and his adherents, and he must have had the conveyance of 1629 in mind, since no other bore the sagamore's name.‡
A collateral allusion to Wheelwright's purchase at Exeter was preserved in the files of the Laconia Company, dated August 13, 1633, and bearing a certificate of deposit at York one week later. One of the two extant copies of the document has been predated. It was subscribed with the names of Walter Neal and Thomas Wiggin as agents for their respective companies and has been presumed to have been forged because at the time of its execution the latter was in England and the former was on the way thither.§

June 12, 1644, the inhabitants of Dover, when in controversy with Portsmouth over the ownership of marshes at Bloody Point, pleaded "that the land in question ought not to be taken from them by the Generall Cort, being theirs by purchase of the Indians & possession * * * wthout any interruption or opposition made against them, excepting onely what was done by Capt Neale, whose pceedings therein were illegall & injurious, as is affirmed by Capt Wiggens."*

Evidently, the document that purported to have been signed by Neal and Wiggin was drawn by the former before he left the country in 1633 and not sanctioned by Wiggin. While it may have been made with fraudulent intent, it contained an array of facts that were recognized, by all parties, as previously existent.

The commissioners on New Hampshire titles in 1679 reported that "Those lands also are all of them in the possession of particular persons that did originally purchase the right of Natives" and that their assigns had "enjoyed them for the space of 50 yeares." The Wheelwright deed is the only extant basis for such a statement.†

Using the vessel which Oldham and his English associates had provided for exploratory purposes on the northern coast, Wheelwright appears to have sailed with them up the Pascataqua River for about "two leagues," where he found the habitations of Edward and William Hilton already established at Dover Point. Undoubtedly, at this season they encountered there Rowles and Runacwitts, the Indian sagamores who cultivated planting grounds

‡ Suffolk Court Files, 15-1372.
§ N. H. State Papers, 1-83.
* Mass. Col. Rec., 2-55.
† N. H. State Papers, 17-531.

a few miles up the Newichawannock branch of the Pascataqua River, at Thompson's Point, in Maine.‡

The deed to Wheelwright recited that a general meeting had been arranged with the natives across Great Bay from Hilton's Point, at Squamscott, a name that five years later was inscribed upon William Wood's map of the locality as "Quamscooke."

The sagamores who signed the treaty probably did so upon shipboard May 17, 1629, and their names were: Passaconway, of Penacook (Concord), Runacwitts, of Pentucket (Haverhill), Wahangnonawit, of Squamscott (Exeter) and Rowles, of Newichawannock (Berwick). The ancient planting grounds were reserved by the grantors.

The grantees besides Wheelwright were Augustine Storer, Thomas Wight, William Wentworth and Thomas Levett, all described as resident in Massachusetts.

Besides those of the witnesses which have been mentioned, the additional names of Edward Hilton, Walter Neal, George Vaughan and Thomas Wiggin appeared on the instrument.

The transaction itself cannot be construed as anything more than a settlement treaty or option for the period of ten years, for consummation of which both parties claimed advantages and in which the hope of protection from "the Tarratens, who yearly doth us damage" seemed an adequate consideration to the Indians, who were aware that from such compacts benefits had accrued already to their neighbors in Massachusetts.

A reduction of New France by the Kirks, consummated July 19, 1629, gave a decided impetus to the prospects for colonization of Maine and New Hampshire. The victorious fleet reached England November 7 and ten days later the Laconia Company secured its grant of territorial jurisdiction over an immense tract located in the interior beyond Pascataqua River. The grants to Oldham and Vines and Lewis and Bonython at Saco, to Plymouth Colony at Cushnoc and to Beauchamp and Leverett at Penobscot, followed in a few months.

None of these concessions conflicted with the settlement compact with Wheelwright and his colleagues and some were in real conformity with it.

Wheelwright and the other grantees subsequently exercised their option at Squamscott (Exeter Falls), where they had taken

‡ York Deeds, 1-3, 6 ; 3-10.

possession of marsh land as early as 1637, which was the year after their return to New England.

The boundary of this settlement on the Dover side was fixed at Lamprey River, known as Pocassock.

A list of those living in Exeter June 5, 1639, disclosed the fact that they were adherents of John Wheelwright who had removed thither from Massachusetts on account of religious oppression.§

NEWICHAWANNOCK (Berwick).

It had been made a condition of the Laconia Grant that within three years from the date of issuance its proprietors should establish "upon ye sd porc'ons of lands or some part thereof one fforte wth a competent guard & tenn ffamillyes at ye least of his Mats subjects resident & being in & upon ye same premises."

The location of Pascataqua River between the Merrimac and Sagadahoc early contributed to the belief that a feasible pinnace route could be found and maintained to the region of Laconia and into the heart of Canada, where the main fortress might be established.

It was known later, however, that the upper course of the Pascataqua did not suit the purposes of the company, because it was bent to the westward through Great Bay, parallel to the seacoast, and at no point reached far inland. Hence, the only trading post ever constructed by the Laconia Company was stationed upon the Newichawannock River, as the northerly branch was known.

The location of Newichawannock House at the head of tidewater in this river, however impracticable it may now appear, was selected with the intention of establishing other posts farther inland to utilize the waterway into the interior. By this route it was proposed to intercept the Indian trade upon the Great Lakes and the Saint Lawrence River.

Heretofore, no one has undertaken to fix the date of construction of the first European dwelling at Newichawannock. It can, however, be determined with reasonable accuracy.

It was not until the summer of 1631 that the wife and daughter of Ambrose Gibbons first arrived at Little Harbor from England, and two years later they were the only female occupants of

§ N. H. State Papers, 1-132.

Newichawannock House. In a letter to the company, dated July 15, 1633, Gibbons asserted with emphasis that for twenty-two months previous he and his men had had but two barrels of beer and two barrels and four bushels of malt. Part of this period they had had no liquor at all. In his complaint he must have intended to comprehend the interval of his occupancy of the post at Newichawannock. This computation fixed the date of entry in September, 1631.

Gibbons claimed that his household had previously been ten, but when Neal left the plantation in 1633, it had been reduced to Charles Neal, Stephen Kidder, Thomas Crockett and Thomas Blake. Who the other three members of the family had been can not now be determined, but all of these men had had insufficient food and clothing for three years.*

The location of Newichawannock House has been a subject of inquiry for many years and it has been assumed to have been in Maine, upon the hypothesis that Newichawannock was identical with Berwick. But this was not true. In the theory of Indian nomenclature the former embraced both sides of the northerly branch of the Pascataqua, because it was applied by the natives to the stream instead of the contiguous region. The name meant "My wigwam place."

Newichawannock River began a quarter of a mile below the mouth of Assabumbadock, or Great Works River, at a large stone in the bed of the stream, called by early settlers Newichawannock Rock, and extended upward to the source in Great East Pond.

The site of the post occupied by Gibbons may now be determined with accuracy from ancient records and traces of occupation. The tract upon which it stood was not mentioned in the description of Pascataqua Patent, which was issued November 3, 1631, to reimburse the Laconia Adventurers for the expense of operations at Pascataqua in their attempts to develop the Laconia District. They had already succeeded in manufacturing clapboards, pipe staves and lumber, cultivated extensive areas for corn and peas and undertaken to make salt for fishing purposes.

The construction of Newichawannock House was begun so late in 1631 that its existence may not have been known to the petitioners for the Pascataqua Patent in England. In fact, that

* N. H. State Papers, 1-81.

concession only comprised a tract which extended westward from the mouth of Pascataqua River for five miles and inland as far as the southerly edge of the earlier grant to Edward Hilton. The other area on the Maine side of the same river was only three miles in width, but embraced the entire easterly bank as far into the interior as the Town of Acton.†

Newichawannock House stood upon the point of land that lies opposite the mouth of the Great Works River, in the Town of Rollinsford, New Hampshire. Proofs of this are to be found in English and colonial records of that state.

THE RIVER BELOW NEWICHAWANNOCK HOUSE

A letter from Laconia Company, dated December 5, 1632, conferred upon Gibbons full supervision at Newichawannock, but he had other plans for his own personal future. He was advised at that time: "You desire to settle yourself upon Sander's point. The adventurers are willing to pleasure you." This point was situated at the present approach to Great Island, between Little Harbor and the City of Portsmouth, and the only building then standing upon it was called "Strawberry Bank House" by the patentees. It could not have been built by the Laconia Company,

† N. H. State Papers. 17-479.

since the testimony of William Seavey proved that the only house constructed by that company, or Captain Mason, on the south side of Pascataqua River, was that at Newichawannock.‡

As the name indicated, this building must have been erected in 1623 by John Sanders and other refugees from Weston's plantation at Wessaguscus. In that year the account of Phineas Pratt, a straggling member who had been detained by sickness at New Plymouth, stated that he rejoined his companions at Pascataqua, and his subsequent reference to David Thompson as overseer of the "first" colony at Little Harbor indicated a second establishment at Sanders' Point. Gibbons may have been a member of Sanders' refugees. The only other dwelling in that vicinity was that built by Thomas Wannerton in 1631.

At any rate, the house at Sanders' Point had been put in the custody of Wannerton by the company's letter of 1632, but as soon as Gibbons was assured that it was to become his, which was early in the following June, he removed the corporate property from the premises to the other two houses, where it was inventoried during the first two days of the next month. The only items then listed elsewhere were some swords and belts, which Wannerton had retained at his residence in Portsmouth, where he occupied the position of military dictator.

During the latter part of June, Gibbons visited "The Bay." At Salem he engaged John Pickering to remodel the vacant building at Strawberry Bank as his future home. From what transpired later it was evident that the contractor resided on the premises for more than a year while he was making the alterations.

December 6, 1633, the members of the Laconia Company met in London and divided all of their territory on the northeast side of Pascataqua River. By mutual agreement, the first three miles from the coast up the river were assigned to Gorges, the next three and three-quarters miles to Henry Gardiner, the next eight miles to George Griffith, Thomas Wannerton and Eleazar Eyre, and the last fifteen and one-quarter miles to Mason. The disproportionate length of the last share was due to its interior location and the necessity for landing facilities below the first fall.

The only houses mentioned in connection with this allotment were those at Pascataqua, Strawberry Bank and Newichawannock, all of which were located in New Hampshire. That none of

‡ N. H. State Papers, 17-522.

them stood in Maine was evident from the fact that they were not excepted in any of the specific tracts assigned. Furthermore, Captain Mason himself, in his first letter to Gibbons, dated May 5, 1634, and signed by Gorges also, announced the recent division in these words: *"Wee wth the consent of the rest of our partners have made a devision of all our Lands Lying on the north-east side of the harbor and River of Pascattaway."* §

A distinct reference in the division places Newichawannock House "next to," or just above, "The Lowermost Falls" in the Newichawannock River. This first obstruction to tidewater, later called "Newichawannock Falls," was situated at the outlet of the Great Works River.

Recently, it was possible to find upon the premises where the fort stood bits of English pottery, hand-wrought nails and other evidences of early occupation by tenants of Newichawannock House. The fact that the spot has been undisturbed by city or village development and that the site has been lost to the public for many years may make the location more apparent today.

Unlike the sites of the Great House at Little Harbor and the Wannerton House at Portsmouth some definite proofs of the ancient post still persist. Since no other dwelling in Rollinsford antedated it, the spot should be marked by the State with an appropriate memorial.*

The main buildings consisted of a large mansion and storehouse, fenced with a strong palisade and fortified with six guns, described in an inventory as two robenets, two murderers and two chambers. Gibbons reported that he had dug a well within the palisade and proposed to enclose it with timber.

His men were engaged "to pale in ground for corne and garden." He advised the company that, while it might expect him to maintain the post with fewer assistants, that was out of the question, since at times he entertained more than one hundred Indians and was situated "far from neybors." At that time his nearest neighbors were living at Dover, then called Bristol, in the westerly angle of the Newichawannock and Pascataqua rivers.

By the end of three years the Laconia proprietors had become discouraged. Their fishing ventures had yielded no profits and the fur trade, although of considerable volume, was conducted at

§ N. H. State Papers, 29-55.
* N. H. State Papers, 1-68; 2-525; 17-487; 29-51, 56; Dover Records, 1-81.

great expense. While some of their factors had been accused of dishonesty and lack of interest, the unsatisfactory results of the fishing industry were explained by Gibbons to have been due to the late arrivals of the fishing ships from London, whereas those hailing from Bristol and Barnstable came early and returned with full cargoes. Furthermore, there was no spirit of coöperation between colonists from London and those from the Western Ports.

Neal, as governor of the colony, was instructed to return to England forthwith and confer with the patentees about the advisability of continuing operations. He was ordered to discharge all employes at Little Harbor and Newichawannock and let them support themselves as best they might. Large tracts of land were given to Gibbons at Sanders' Point, and to Cammock, Wannerton and Jocelyn on the Eliot Shore opposite Bloody Point.

Cammock, who already had a dwelling upon his land in Eliot, and a clergyman by the name of Card removed their furniture to Newichawannock House and left the country for England in company with Neal July 15, 1633.†

Wannerton continued to reside in his house at Strawberry Bank and had supervision of the premises at Little Harbor for the company. Gibbons still retained charge at Newichawannock. Schedules of the property of the company were made at both posts, signed by both agents and delivered to Neal, and with his departure marked the end of corporate operations in this country. Later inventories, similarly endorsed, appear to have been spurious.

By the following spring Captain Mason had acquired the interests of several of the dissatisfied partners, including John Cotton's share in the company, and decided to develop his tract in severalty. To effect his purpose, he executed a contract, dated March 13, 1633-4, with three carpenters named William Chadbourne, John Goddard and James Wall, who had agreed to remain in the country for four years with their families and build houses for themselves and mills for him.‡

Elaborate plans were laid and no expense was spared by Mason to make the project a success. Gorges had made similar arrangements with carpenters and planters to build mills and houses for him upon his son's grant at Agamenticus.

† N. H. State Papers. 1-78.
‡ Mass. Arch., 3-437.

Final preparations for colonization were completed about the first of May and the *Pide Cow* sailed from Portsmouth with the colonists, bearing letters from the proprietors to Gibbons and another, dated May 4, from Thomas Morton to William Jeffrey, of Wessaguscus.

Gibbons was advised by Gorges and Mason, "We have not onelie each of us shipped people present to plant uppon our owne lands, at our owne charges, but have given direction to invite and authoritie to receive such others as may be had to be tenants, to plant and live there, for the more speedie peopling of the countrie."§

Mason's individual message to Gibbons, who then occupied the premises, was: "You must afford my people some house roome in Newitchewanocke house, and the cowes and goates, wch are all mine, and 14 swine, with their increase, some grounds to be uppon, till we have some *place* provided upon my new divided lands."*

From the nature of his request it is evident that at that time there were none of these accommodations upon Mason's separate territory near Great Works and that the word "place," as used in the context, signified both shelter for the mechanics and pasturage for the cattle. In the London contract it had been stipulated that each carpenter should be provided on the plantation with three cows, four pigs and four goats.

In the same letter from Gorges and Mason instructions were given to Gibbons to divide all of the personal property, which belonged to the Laconia Company, in proportion to their shares in the schedule presented to the proprietors by Neal upon his return to England the previous year. Half of all "saide matters," excluding "the cattell and suites of apparell and such other things as belong peculiarly to Capt. Mason," was to be delivered to Henry Jocelyn for the use of the new plantations about to be begun at Agamenticus and Newichawannock.

In due time Gibbons, who probably boarded the incoming vessel at Little Harbor, advised Mason that "The Pide-cow arrived the 8th of Julie; the 13th day she cast ankor some halfe a mile from the falle; the 18th day the shippe unladen; the 19th fell downe the river." The ship was discharged at Pipe Stave Land-

§ N. H. State Papers, 1-88.
* N. H. State Papers, 1-90.

ing, less than a mile from Assabumbadock Falls (Great Works), and later proceeded with the colonists of Gorges to Agamenticus.†

In connection with the advent of the mechanics at Newichawannock, Gibbons assured Mason: "Yor carpenters are with me and I will further them the best I can." The new comers, incorrectly transcribed from a deposition of Francis Small "eight Danes," instead of "eight hands," consisted of William Chadbourne and his sons Humphrey and William, John Goddard, Henry Jocelyn, Thomas Spencer, James Wall and John Wilcocks. The full number is checked by reference to Jocelyn's receipt for household utensils which he had borrowed for their use from the stock of the Laconia Company.

The principal articles acknowledged to have been taken from that company's store July 20, 1634, which was the day following the departure of their vessel, were "one great iron kittle" for which Thomas Spencer was to be held accountable, some Irish blankets, one Kilkenney rug, one pair of sheets, one pintado coverlet, one brass kettle and *seven spoons.*

The items charged to the contractors were not fully specified until August 27, 1639, when Jocelyn, who had then removed to Black Point (Scarborough), endorsed them upon the original receipt with the explanation that they had been borrowed "for Capt. Mason's use, of Ambrose Gibbens" and had been "spent and worne out in his service."‡

Upon arrival Humphrey Chadbourne was only a boy. Jocelyn, who was a son of Sir Thomas, of Kent, had not only agreed in his compact with the proprietor to act as Mason's agent, but to undertake the belated discovery of Laconia.§

Hence, at that late date the interior of the country had not been explored by the English, for even at that advanced post in the wilderness the Laconia factor could only advise Mason: "I prceive you have a great mynd for the lakes and I as great a will to assist you, if I had 2 horses and 3 men wth me, I would with God's helpe soone resolve you of the ciutation of it, but not to live there myself."

Thomas Spencer was referred to many years later in the suit of Allen versus Humphrey Spencer, a grandson, as one who had

† N. H. State Papers, 1-92.
‡ N. H. State Papers, 1-94.
§ N. E. Canaan, 98.

been "Sent over a Servtt into this Country by Capt. John Mason & putt upon his Lands att the Eastwards."
While the appellee's answer did not directly controvert the allegation that Spencer was sent into the country by Mason, it did deny "that old father Spencer Gained his possession wrongfully and * * * that the Appellee or his predecessors ever paid any ffee or acknowledgmt to mr Mason, Sr ffardinando Gorge or the Appellant for the Lands in Controversie."*

It is evident from the import of these records that Spencer came with his father-in-law July 8, 1634, in the *Pide Cow*, and that in 1676 he had not lived in New England forty-six years as represented in the deposition framed for him by Edward Colcord, but that when he died December 15, 1681, he had lived continuously in South Berwick but forty-seven years. He had arrived in the country in 1630 and returned with Neal three years later.†

July 22, following their arrival, the carpenters began at Great Works the construction of the first water power gristmill in New England. It does not appear to have been completed.

Gibbons surrendered possession of the premises at Newichawannock to Jocelyn and removed to Sanders' Point, where his own house had been completed by Pickering. The account of the contractor with the owner, which was concurrent with but distinct from that of the Laconia Company, was settled September 6. In it the latter was debited with three weeks' diet for Thomas Crockett, his employe who had left Newichawannock House soon after the arrival of the carpenters and boarded with Pickering while he was working at Sanders' Point.‡

Jocelyn leased Newichawannock House from the Laconia Company, and it was in relation to the previous activities of that company and the occupation of its premises in Dover by Mason's new employes in 1634 that the New Hampshire commissioners afterwards alleged that "An house was hired in this province but the disbursements laid out were chiefly in the Neighboring Province of Meyn on the other side of the River, and for carrying on an Indian Trade in Laconia, in all wch" (Mason) "was but a partner, however" (his heir) "would appear amongst us as sole proprietor."§

* 2 Me. Hist. Col., 8-185, 187.
† Appendix D.
‡ N. H. State Papers. 1-71, 87.
§ N. H. State Papers. 17-552.

Two of these commissioners, Elias Stileman and Richard Waldron, had lived in the province before the house was hired. The character of its occupancy would not readily escape notice. Where the house had stood was then known to the others by common report.

In connection with what transpired immediately after Jocelyn's advent, the deposition of James Wall, one of the mill mechanics, is illuminating. His statement was sworn to before George Smith, a magistrate of Dover, and was recorded in the following form:

"This Deponent sayeth that aboute the year 1634, he with his partners William Chadbourne and John Goddarde, came over to New England upon the accompt of Captaine John Mason of London, and also for themselves, and were landed at Newichawannock, upon certaine lands there which Mr. Goieslen, Captaine Mason's agente brought them unto, with the ladinge of some goodes, and there they did builde upp at a fall there (called by the Indian name Ashbenbedick) for the use of Captaine Mason & ourselves, one sawe mill and one stampinge mill for corne wch we did keep the space of three or foure years next after; and further this deponent saith, he builte one house upon the same lands, and soe did William Chadbourne an other & gave it to his sonne in law Thomas Spencer who now lives in it; and this deponent also sayth that we had peaceable and quiete posession of that land for the use of Captaine Mason afforesaide, and that the said agent did buye some planted ground of some Indians which they had planted upon the saide land, and that Captaine Mason's agente's servants did breake up & cleare certain lands there and planted corne upon it."*

Jocelyn was recognized by Wall as Mason's agent, and since the principal died in November, 1635, he never had any other agent upon his lands at the Eastward. And so, in all subsequent allusions to such an official, either in Maine or Dover, Jocelyn must be regarded as the person intended.

Of the other servants sent to New England by Mason, some were dispatched to his lands in Massachusetts to the westward and others to Maine, in the later period, because of the political disturbances aroused by Bay magistrates among his constituents. Both Gorges and the patentee of New Hampshire were

* Mass. Arch., 3-444.

avowed enemies of the Winthrop colony, but tried to avoid interference by development of their remoter territories.

It was destined, however, that the Western Colony should eventually overlap the Maine coast by adopting a legal fiction that the upper thread of the Merrimac should define its eastern boundary.

The houses erected by Chadbourne and Wall were the first to be built within the limits of the Berwicks. They were constructed upon Brattle Street, which was the first road or cart path and led from the Lower Landing to the mill at Great Works.

The fields lying on both sides of this street were bought by Jocelyn from the natives. Upon some of this land the maize crop planted by the Indians in 1634 was then growing. The locality is called Old Fields to this day.

The dwelling built by William Chadbourne stood in the northwesterly angle of Brattle Street and the highway which leads from the mouth of the Great Works River to Eliot. Appurtenant to it were ten acres of land donated by Mason in accordance with the terms of the London contract, made with the three carpenters in the spring of 1634.

When Chadbourne left Berwick, about 1638, he gave his dwelling and land to his eldest daughter Patience, who had married Thomas Spencer. The house was the largest in the settlement and was conducted as a public tavern. When Spencer died in 1681 he left his homestead, still fenced as a ten-acre lot, to his eldest son William, who operated the mill at Great Works and built the Spencer Garrison. This was the largest fortified dwelling in the country at the time of the Second Indian War and accommodated one hundred persons. It stood upon the southerly side of Brattle Street opposite the tavern and the site is now occupied by the mansion of the late General Ichabod Goodwin's descendants.

Humphrey, a nephew of William Spencer, succeeded to his estate and, in 1707, became defendant in a leading case of colonial jurisprudence, entitled Allen versus Spencer. The action was brought by assignees of the heirs of Captain Mason to recover possession of the original homestead of Thomas Spencer, situated on the southerly side of the Great Works River, and contiguous tracts granted to him during his lifetime by the Town of Kittery. It was admitted at the trial of the issue that the premises had been in the uninterrupted occupation of the Spencers for more than sixty years. Since the defendant denied and the plaintiff was unable to prove any right by former leasehold, the case was dismissed, but the decision has since been recognized as the American precedent for the doctrine of ownership by adverse possession.

Spencer was one of the first permanent settlers in the Town of South Berwick, and it has been claimed by some that the house built by Chadbourne, in which he spent the greater period of his New England existence, is to-day the most ancient building in the state.

But this contention is unfounded. Catherine Hammond, who was born in Eliot and attended church services at Old Fields, passed the home of Thomas Spencer frequently in her youth, and she testified, in 1704, that this structure had once been located near that in which his grandson Humphrey Spencer was then living.†

More than one hundred years after the Chadbourne house was built, the tract upon which it had stood was described in a Spencer conveyance as the "Old House Field." To-day the parish cemetery at Old Fields encloses a part of the ten acres that were assigned to Chadbourne by Jocelyn, as agent for Mason, transferred to Patience Spencer and sold by a lineal descendant of hers to members of the First Congregational Society of the South Parish of Berwick. The nucleus of the present cemetery was originally the private burial lot of Thomas Spencer and his family.‡

The only other residents at Old Fields, who were rated as the heads of families in a court record of 1640, were Humphrey Chadbourne, Basil Parker, Peter Weare and John White.

The house built by James Wall had been erected on the next ten-acre lot between the Parish Cemetery and the mill at Great Works. When this dwelling became vacant, about 1638, by the removal of Wall to New Hampshire, it was sold by John Wilcocks as agent for Francis Norton, of Charlestown, to Thomas Brooks, otherwise known as Basil Parker, and Peter Weare, an Indian trader. Norton, in turn, was the accredited representative of Captain Mason's widow, and Wilcocks married the niece of the former, subsequently, in England.

† 2 Me. Hist. Col., 8-184.
‡ York Deeds, 19-280.

"Parker's Field" was the easterly boundary of the Spencer homestead and it was adjacent to "White's Marsh" on the south. These are among the oldest local names on the western side of the state.

A part of Parker's land was described later as the "Vineyard," and marked the attempt of Gibbons to produce grapes in commercial quantities, on the banks of the Great Works River, before Mason had obtained title to this land by division with the Laconia Company.

Basil Parker was, at the time of his death in 1651, registrar of deeds for the whole district of Maine. After the decease of his associate, Weare removed to York and their property at Old Fields was absorbed by Richard Leader who had acquired the mill privilege at Great Works from the Town of Kittery. The claim of Mason's heirs to the Wall tenement was compromised afterwards by the Hutchinsons, as assignees of Leader.§

After the decease of Captain Mason in 1635 Henry Jocelyn continued to reside in Newichawannock House. During the summer of the following year Thomas Purchase, of Pejepscot, with some of his employes, visited this post in a long boat which he sold to John Treworthy. Purchase subsequently alleged that this bargain was effected at Newichawannock in a house which was then occupied by tenants or employes of the widow of Captain Mason.

When Jocelyn withdrew to Black Point two years later and associated with Thomas Cammock in that settlement, some of the other employes continued to occupy Newichawannock House. In fact, no other course appears to have been open for them in a country where the titles were constantly in controversy. They were accused afterwards of dissipating what property then remained from the estates of Mason and the Laconia proprietors. Apparently, John Wilcocks, from whom the pond in South Berwick derived its name, and Thomas Canney, of Rollinsford, were two of these.

May 10, 1643, when but nineteen years of age, Humphrey, son of William Chadbourne, bought his first tract of land of Sagamore Rowles. That he was a minor was attested by Savage who alluded to him as "young Humphrey Chadbourne" and reported that he had died before arriving at middle age.

§ York Deeds, 1-30.

The deed was witnessed by Thomas Spencer, in whose household the grantee appeared to have been living, and its description embraced "Half a Mile of Ground which lieth betwixt the Little River & the Great River to begin at the Norther Side of ye old Ground." The reference to the "old ground" alluded to the land which Rowles had previously sold to Jocelyn, in 1634. That tract had extended above the Great Works River and included the northerly slope of the basin, where Gibbons had formerly undertaken to cultivate a vineyard. The name "Vineyard Pasture" was a term used many years later in Chadbourne conveyances.*

The house built by Humphrey Chadbourne, who had learned his trade as a carpenter from his father, was located at the confluence of the rivers, according to an ancient map of the district. Here he operated a sawmill in company with Thomas Spencer.

Passage across the river to Old Fields at this point was made in canoes or over a footbridge fashioned from a single log. The only cart bridge across this river was located at Great Works soon after the settlement of Old Fields. There was no bridge near Chadbourne's house as late as the second Indian massacre in 1690, because the English then escaped to the lower plantations over a log crossing. The Salmon Falls River was fordable at the head of Little John's Falls in front of Newichawannock House.

Chadbourne's wife was Lucy, a sister of John Treworthy, who was sent to Pascataqua in 1636, when but nineteen years old, as supercargo in his grandfather's vessel. She was born in 1632, according to her deposition, taken in 1704 and used in the case of Allen versus Spencer; she was then seventy-two years of age. She testified that she came to New England in 1646. This ancient document was abstracted from the files at Alfred, Maine, or from Suffolk files in Boston, where an appeal was taken. Only a copy of the first line was preserved by Seth Chadbourne who has long been dead. Another deposition gave the same year of birth.†

Humphrey Chadbourne and Lucy Treworthy were both young when their marriage was solemnized, and he died in 1666, leaving a large family of children, all of whom were minors. The widow later married Thomas Wills, and after his decease Elias Stileman. The Chadbourne homestead remained in possession of

---

* York Deeds, 1-6.
† 2 Me. Hist. Col., 8-184.

the lineal descendants of Humphrey for more than two hundred years, and part of it is occupied to-day by Berwick Academy.‡

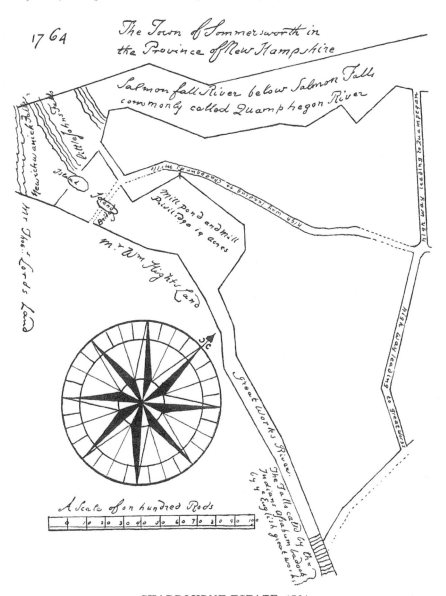

CHADBOURNE ESTATE, 1764

‡ York Prob. Rec., 11-177

Newichawannock House was destroyed by fire. About 1645, according to the recollection of Francis Small, the "house & buildings were burned to the ground, but by what means" he did not know.

In 1654, the line of jurisdiction between Berwick and Dover, as also between Maine and New Hampshire, was established at the middle of the channel of Newichawannock River, and the abandoned site of Newichawannock House was officially determined to be a part of the latter municipality.

Two years later, when one hundred and twenty acres of land opposite the mouth of the Great Works River were allotted by the Town of Dover to Thomas Canney, the tract was described as bounded in part by the original lot seized by the Laconia Company in 1631.

According to an ancient survey of Canney's land, made in 1656, it lay between Saint Alban's Cove and Quampheagan Falls and was bounded "on the soeth est partly by Newichnecke River & *partly ba sartayn parcell of land that was sometime possessed by Capt Massons agent and on the north Est by a highway that goeth from the Southest End of the sayd lott up into the woods to the N. W. end* & on the N. W. by Thomas Hanson his land & on S. W. partly by the common & partly by James Grants land."§

The contiguous tract of James Grant, consisting of twenty acres, particularly defined in a town allotment in 1658, was sold by the grantee to David Hamilton. In his description of these premises Grant, who had previously removed to York, averred that the property was situated "at Nechewanick in Dover."

The upper line of the Canney lot is still defined by the original highway near the river.

The third lot above Canney's, in the same tier, was assigned to John Dame, of Dover, the same year. Henry Clay Dame, a lineal descendant of the pioneer, who died in Rollinsford in 1906, claimed throughout his lifetime that family tradition fixed the location of the first English habitation upon the Garvin farm opposite the mouth of the Great Works River.

The land "sometime possessed by Capt Massons agent" was the ancient field of the Laconia Company, which had been occupied subsequently by Henry Jocelyn as Mason's agent. Apparently Canney, who had also been one of Mason's employes at

§ Dover Records, 1-81.

Newichawannock House, or the municipal officers of Dover at his suggestion, recognized his employer's presumed title to the appurtenant tract.

Hannah, a daughter of Thomas Canney, married Henry Hobbs, of Dover, and her father's lot, granted only five years before, was assigned to her husband as an endowment July 12, 1661. Hobbs had no compunction against trespassing upon the early holdings of the Laconia Company or of Mason's heirs in the tract lying between his land and the river and, because it was adapted to his own uses, claimed it. Hence, it was never granted to anyone by the Town of Dover. In 1687, Samuel Sewall, circuit judge of Massachusetts, alluded to the cove in the lower extremity of that little point, which he then visited, as "Hobs his Hole, Quamphegen." The water there is still forty feet deep at high tide.

Hobbs' Hole had furnished a fair haven for the seagoing vessels of the Laconia Company and Mason and later was utilized as a favorable place to build and launch small sloops. It faced directly down river.

As late as 1691, when Henry Child, David Hamilton and five others were reported to have been slain by Indians in Newichawannock, that district was still understood to comprise both banks of Salmon Falls River; the former decedent lived on Child's Hill at the upper edge of South Berwick village and the latter was a neighbor of Henry Hobbs in Rollinsford.

In 1707, assignees of Mason's New Hampshire rights undertook to eject the successors of Richard Waldron and other residents from lands occupied by them in Dover. The decisions of the inferior court had been adverse to the defendants and their reasons for appeal recited the transient character of occupation by Mason's agents before his death in 1635, and the fact that only one garrison was ever built by the London proprietor or his predecessors.

Proof that the post at Newichawannock in Dover was the only one ever established by Mason or his associates in New England may be adduced from the testimony of William Seavey taken about thirty years before the Waldron suit was finally decided. In his deposition, recorded *in perpetuam memoriam,* Seavey stated that "neither Capt Neale nor Capt Mason nor any by from or under ym did ever set up or exercise any Govermt in this Countrey more than over the family that Capt Neale brought with him. Nor ever built any house or settled any family here except a trading house at Niwichewanacke to trade with the Indians."*

In the language of the appeal it was alleged that "whatever possession or Improvements the said Mason's Agents or successors might have or had in these parts of New England, it really was noe other than the settlement of a Factory and Trade with the Natives; And principally, for a Discovery of a place they called Laconia; and that alsoe in company with several other Merchant Adventurers in England, who for the support and security of their factors and Servants, and Especially from the Salvages, did Erect a Garrison or Fort as they call it, but never Amounted to a possession in Law, soe as any ways to make or confirme a Title to the Land of this Province."†

The language used by Waldron contains a tacit admission that he knew that the fort styled Newichawannock House had been occupied by the tenants of the patentees and that it had been located in Newichawannock at Dover.

May 9, 1709, a highway was laid out, partly along an ancient cart path made by early settlers from Saint Alban's Cove to Quampheagan Falls. This road followed the old way "on the north side of Thomas Cannies lott to the old wadeing place opposite to Chadbourn's mill" until it came "to the mouth of Little John's Creek on the south side of James Stackpole's house."

In 1715, when Captain Ichabod Plaisted made his will, he had negotiated with Samuel, a grandson of Thomas Canney and nephew of Henry Hobbs, for the purchase of the tract formerly occupied by Gibbons for the use of the Laconia Company. April 22, 1722, after Plaisted's decease, Canney confirmed the sale of his interest in the tract to a son of Captain Plaisted, of the same name, describing the premises as three acres situated at a place in Dover called Hobbs' Hole, bounded southerly and easterly by Newichawannock River; westerly by the lot of Henry Hobbs, deceased; and northerly by property belonging to the grantee.

In this connection it is interesting to note that the settlement at Hilton's Point in Dover was situated between two establishments of the Laconia Company: one undertaken at Little Harbor by David Thompson and his Plymouth associates in 1623 and the

* N. H. State Papers, 17-522.
† N. H. State Papers, 2-525.

other at Newichawannock by Ambrose Gibbons, of Plymouth, in 1631.

Pioneers

BROOKS, THOMAS, alias Basil Parker, agent for Shrewsbury merchants at Dover, 1633; Great Works, 1640; registrar of deeds, York County, 1645; died 1651, without issue in this country.

CHADBOURNE, HUMPHREY, planter, arrived at Berwick with his father, 1634; died 1666; widow Lucy (Treworthy) married Thomas Wells and Elias Stileman; children Alice (Donnell, Moulton), Catherine (Weighmouth), Elizabeth (Alcock), Humphrey, born 1656; James, Lucy (Lewis), and William.

CHADBOURNE, WILLIAM, carpenter, arrived at Berwick in the "Pide Cow," July 8, 1634; gave his house at South Berwick to his daughter Patience, wife of Thomas Spencer, and removed to Portsmouth, Rhode Island, 1642; sons Humphrey and William.

CHADBOURNE, WILLIAM, baptized at Winchcombe, 1610; carpenter, arrived at Berwick with his father, 1634; Boston, 1644; Berwick, 1652; wife Mary; daughter Mary (Foss) at Dover, 1666.

GODDARD, JOHN, carpenter, arrived at Berwick from London July 8, 1634, in the "Pide Cow"; Newmarket, 1638; died November 12, 1666; widow Welthen married John Symonds; children Benjamin, Dorcas (Bennick), Elizabeth (Gilman), John and Mary (Thomas).

NASON, RICHARD, planter at Dover, 1645; South Berwick, 1649; wife Sarah, daughter of John Baker; second wife Abigail, widow of.Nicholas Follett; died 1696; children Baker, Benjamin, John, Jonathan, Joseph, Richard and Sarah (Child, Hoyt).

PARKER, BASIL, alias Thomas Brooks.

SPENCER, THOMAS, born 1596; came to Pascataqua with Mason's employes, 1630; returned to England in 1633 and came back in the "Pide Cow," July 8, 1634; died December 15, 1681; widow Patience Chadbourne; children William, Margaret (Goodwin), Susanna (Gattinsby, Joy), Mary (Etherington), Elizabeth (Chick, Turbett), Humphrey, born 1647, and Moses.

WALL, JAMES, carpenter, arrived at Berwick July 8, 1634, in the "Pide Cow" from England; Exeter, 1639; Dover, 1642; died at Hampton October 3, 1659; second wife Mary was widow of Edward Tuck; children Elizabeth, Hannah, Mary and Sarah.

WEARE, PETER, born 1618; Indian trader at Dover, 1638; Berwick, 1640; York, 1642; registrar for York County; killed by Indians January 25, 1691-2; widow Mary, daughter of John Gouch; children Elias, Joseph and Peter.

WILCOCKS, JOHN, agent of Francis Norton of Charlestown, who was attorney for Ann, widow of Captain John Mason at Berwick and Portsmouth, 1638-1640; subsequently married Norton's niece in England.

Eliot.

This locality offered many natural advantages to the prospective settler. It was adapted to cultivation, as well as for fishing and commerce with the Indians.

Near the shore in Pascataqua River there is a small island which, according to an ancient deed, once contained an acre and was known as Watts' Fort. An early map depicted that and Frank's Fort as two small points situated on the Eliot shore about one mile apart.

In 1627, John Watts was sent to Cape Ann as a factor for the Dorchester Merchants. The company was engaged in fishing and trading with the Indians in that vicinity. Watts landed at Cape Ann but Pascataqua was near and must have lured him with prospects of superior trading possibilities. His occupation was merely seasonable, but he appears to have built a fortified trading post upon the little island at Eliot to develop his industry. Only the local name now suggests any historical significance for the islet, once a promontory but now almost annihilated by river tides.

Three years after the departure of Watts for England, the Indians, James and John Sagamore, of Ipswich, complained to Winthrop of the unfair dealings of the Dorchester factor, who was still in England. The tradition was preserved that the native chieftains followed the English trader to his lair, presented an address to King Charles and recovered full reparation for furs which had been taken from them by force or deceit near Agawam.‡

With the possible exception of the trading post at Watts' Fort, probably the first English habitation in Eliot was a building erected at Frank's Fort in the summer of 1631, to provide protection as well as shelter for French employes of the Laconia Company. These men arrived at Pascataqua in June of that year, prepared to begin the salt industry. Francis Williams, from whom the fort took its name, was overseer in charge of the experimental work undertaken by the company at that time.§

The entire project was a failure and the French mechanics did not remain long in the country. The only names mentioned were those of Charles, Labrisse and Petfree who, undoubtedly, were possessed of more than ordinary scientific knowledge, since Petfree was afterwards captain of a French man-of-war in the West Indies.*

Another early settler on the eastern bank of Pascataqua River was William Hilton who appeared there after 1631, when Dover patent had been sold to Bristol merchants by his brother Edward. During the year following that sale he owned a house and planted

‡ Mass. Hist. Proc., 43-493; Winthrop, 1-49.
§ Winthrop, 1-56.
* N. H. State Papers, 1-72; Winthrop, 1-226.

corn in Eliot. In August, 1632, he delivered to George Ludlow a stock of merchandise, left with him by John Hocking, the Indian trader who then represented the Bristol Merchants, but was killed two years later at Kennebec in the service of the Shrewsbury Merchants. The indications are that Ludlow, who obtained the goods at Eliot, was one of Hocking's associates at Dover.†

Soon after, as the result of a controversy over Bloody Point, which Neal claimed to have been included in the grant issued to Laconia Company November 3, 1631, Hilton was ousted from Eliot by agents of that company. The vacant premises were conveyed by Neal, as agent of the proprietors, to Thomas Cammock June 2, 1633, and transferred by the grantee to John Treworthy for the account of his grandfather Alexander Shapleigh, then in England, January 20, 1636-7. After eviction Hilton withdrew to Exeter, but Wood's map of Southern New England, based upon information secured in 1633, assigned the entire Pascataqua shore to him.

The lot south of Cammock's was given to Thomas Wannerton, by Neal July 9, 1633, at the request of Laconia Company. At that time Wannerton was living in the house at Little Harbor, whither he may have removed from his own house at Strawberry Bank and where, at the departure of Neal about a week later, he assumed full control. With the exceptions of "18 swords and 4 swoards at Mr. Warnerton's house" at Portsmouth, all property belonging to the company had been stored in their Newichawannock and Pascataqua buildings, where inventories had been completed July 2, 1633. Sanders' Point had just been conferred upon Ambrose Gibbons by Neal, but the owner remained in charge at Newichawannock until the next summer and permitted John Pickering, who was remodeling the house for him, to occupy the premises during the interim.‡

October 9, 1632, Nicholas Frost had been banished from Massachusetts with orders not to return or a severe penalty would be exacted. With such an alternative he went back to England in some fishing vessel from Pascataqua or the Isles of Shoals.

In June, 1634, he returned to New England with his family, sailing from Plymouth in the *Wulfrana*, which with a few pas-

† York Deeds, 1-60.
‡ N. H. State Papers, 1 80.

sengers may have come on a fishing voyage to the Isles of Shoals. Upon arrival at Pascataqua his family was entertained by Wannerton at Little Harbor for several months and April 17, 1635, during the period of sojourn, one of his daughters was born there. He and his host either had been, or became, congenial friends. It it possible that they may have been associated in England. Philip Swadden, who was then living in Kittery at the mouth of Pascataqua River, testified that about 1635 Wannerton had given Frost some land in Eliot to induce him "to come to bee his Neighbor." Frost was living upon part of this land, which formed a nucleus for his homestead, in 1637, and his child Catherine was born there on Christmas Day of that year. This daughter subsequently married Joseph, son of William Hammond, of Cape Porpoise, resided in Eliot and deposed there when she was sixty-eight years of age.§

Wannerton sold his Laconia grant to Alexander Shapleigh March 1, 1637-8, without reservations. It was then bounded on the south by the tract given to Henry Jocelyn by Laconia Company in 1633 and sold by him to Hansard Knowles, pastor at Dover, five years later, when Jocelyn removed to Black Point where, like Cammock, he had had an earlier concession from the Council of Plymouth.*

The families known to have been resident in Eliot in 1638 were those of Abraham Conley, Nicholas Frost, John Newgrove, Edward Small, James Treworthy and John White. Agamenticus was more populous and had built a meeting-house in 1636. After it was completed William Thompson conducted services there, but in 1639, after a period of probation, he was ordained at Braintree. Then, or later, there was no mention of land occupied by him at Gorgeana, but his pastorate was described in one record as established at "Agamenticus or Pascataqua." Hence, it may be assumed that his domicile had been at Thompson's Point in the latter settlement during 1638, or prior, and that his entire circuit included communicants living in lower Berwick, upper Eliot and coastal York.

There are several distinct allusions to Eliot territory which prove that it was the original Kittery.

§ York Deeds, 3-13; 2 Me. Hist. Col., 8-184.
* Appendix E.

The Cammock tract had been occupied soon after its purchase by James, father of John Treworthy, and John White, an employe, and that locality, which lay opposite Dover Point, derived the name of "Kittery" from members of the Shapleigh family who had emigrated thither from Kittery Point in Devonshire. The name first appears in a deed of land at Eliot, dated January 1, 1638-9.

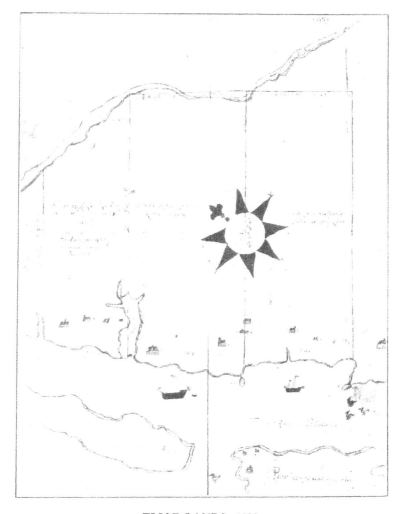

ELIOT LANDS, 1699

Only a few years after settlement John White deposed that his employer, John Treworthy, had been instrumental in inducing John Hurd of Great Island to come "up to Kittery" and build a dwelling at Sturgeon Creek.

Again, the oldest extant map of the Province of Maine, now in the British Museum, bears upon its western margin opposite Dover Point the imprint "Chetere," misspelled by some engraver who was unfamiliar with the English name. Within the area so designated was located, according to county records, the original manor afterwards inherited by Shapleigh heirs at Eliot and styled "Kittery House."

Finally, the ferry tolls from the mouth of Pascataqua River to Dover and Kittery were the same and that to Portsmouth, which was also based upon distance, was six pence less.

Aside from its central situation at Kittery, the reasons for Thompson's choice of the Eliot district are obvious. Clergymen of that period were planters from necessity. The site selected had been cultivated by both Runacwitts and Rowles and for time immemorial and was well adapted to agriculture.

Furthermore, Rowles was friendly to the English and subsequently conveyed to them valuable tracts, including this one which was definitely described by himself as "Tomsons Poynt." Another possible reason for the selection of the Eliot parish was the proximity of planters at Dover, who on account of religious dictation at home sought spiritual counsel abroad.

August 13, 1635, Sir Ferdinando Gorges in England had made an agreement with Francis Williams, who had had supervision over the Laconia Company's salt operations at Frank's Fort, to convey to him the choice of any lands on the Maine shore which had not been granted to others. When Williams arrived at Pascataqua he found that Champernoone had secured title to the premises which he had had in mind. His complaint was that his plans had been disrupted by Thomas Bradbury, of York, who was then resident land agent for Gorges. The agent was charged with accepting a bribe in favor of the successful purchaser, who had the special advantage of being a close relative of the proprietor.

As an alternative he solicited title to a large tract on the upper edge of Eliot, adjoining Thompson's Brook. Later he obtained his deed from Thomas Gorges who had reached Agamenticus in the summer of 1640. At that time Williams was established as governor at Strawberry Bank, and Gibbons, who then lived at Sanders' Point, was acting as his assistant under the original combination compact.†

The Williams tract lay in Eliot adjoining the present South Berwick line. It was described as situated on the "northeast side of the River Pascattaquack over against Tompsons pointe, wch is bounded wth the most northerly brooke or creeke commonly called the blacke creeke, next adjoyneing to Sagamor Runacwitts old planting ground on the north, and from thence alongst the said River to run Downe towards the harbours mouth unto a creeke or cove next adjacent Amiciskeg point so called by the natives on the south, containeing in length upon the said River aboute halfe a mile more or lesse."

This land was located below the river projection, which was subsequently described in a deed from the chief sagamore as "my Poynt of Land Commanly known by the name of Tomsons Poynt, an ould Corne ground which I the sayd Mr Rowls have formerly made uss of." Samuel Treworthy, a subsequent owner, referred to the same premises as "all that my Necke or Tract of Land, scituate above Sturgeon Cricke In the Town shipp of Kittery in Pischataqua River aforesayd fformerly Called Tomsons poynt."‡

This estate was to be held by free and common socage and, like the manor of Sir Ferdinando Gorges at Agamenticus known as Point Christian, exempt from knight's service, but subject to a small annual rental charge.

It was a condition of the original agreement with Gorges that the grantee should settle upon the premises with a family of eleven immigrants and the later deed recited that this warranty had been fulfilled. It is not known who comprised the settler's household besides his wife Helen, but it is obvious that he maintained his own legal residence in Portsmouth though he had built a commodious dwelling below Black Creek which was styled "Thompson's Point House." The title to the premises was confirmed to Williams in 1644 by the justices of Yorkshire Court, including Henry Jocelyn, but like Vines and his associates at the Eastward this planter soon wearied of agriculture and politics at Pascataqua and resolved to emigrate to Barbadoes.

† N. II. Prov. Papers, 1 111.
‡ York Deeds, 1-3, 5 ; 3-10.

December 5, 1645, he sold his farm in Portsmouth to Richard Cummings and Thomas Turpin, of the Isle of Shoals (Appledore), and soon after left New England for good. He could not dispose of his land in Eliot in a similar way on account of the nature of his title.§

But the premises at Thompson's Point did not remain vacant long for two years later they were tenanted by Edward Starbuck and Richard Waldron, both of Dover, who were engaged in furnishing masts to English shipbuilders. The location was described as only three miles from that of Nicholas Frost and his associates "with bounds not possessed by any & remoat from other manes lottes."*

The lease to the Dover men appears to have been given by the Yorkshire Court with the sanction of Williams, but Frost and his neighbors objected strenuously to their proceedings in the province. October 27, 1647, the Inhabitants of Pascataqua began a suit against Starbuck and Waldron by attachment of their masts in Eliot. The gist of the action was defined as "felling timber upon the land which they were tennants unto." Feeling ran high and some of the townsmen even threatened to remove Jocelyn from the bench, presumably on account of his major influence in securing court approval of the deed of the premises given by Gorges to Williams. At any rate, the offending justice had been the first to sign the confirmation. The prosecution was dismissed the next year by agreement.

December 19, 1648, Thompson's Point House was assessed in New Hampshire without specification of ownership. However, the building had been in the possession of Dover residents and was recognized as taxable personal property of that province, although situated in Maine.

Turpin, who had acquired the interest of Cummings in the New Hampshire estate of Williams, was drowned while on a fishing trip October 29, 1649. Soon after, it was reported that his administrator, John Manning who was a resident of Massachusetts, had decided "to Cease upon the Farme at ye Eastward."†

It is difficult to say what disposition would have been made of the Eliot tract and Thompson's Point, which adjoined it on the north, but February 14, during the year of Turpin's decease, the

§ Suffolk Deeds. 1-67.
* 4 Mass. Hist. Col., 7-378.
† York Deeds. 1-62.

organized inhabitants of Pascataqua had assumed complete control of the territory on the Maine side of Pascataqua River and granted lands above and below Black Creek to influential citizens of the new municipality.‡ The confiscation of lands in upper Eliot by the town was not accomplished without some disturbance. Former employes of Turpin at Strawberry Bank farm or on the Eliot tract brought suits against his estate in Maine to recover unpaid wages. Some of these claimants were William Hilton, Abraham Radiver, Sylvester Stover and Nicholas Treworthy, who had lived on Bloody Point or elsewhere about Great Bay. Stover removed to York. The outcome of this litigation was not disclosed by the records.

After Massachusetts had secured control, in 1653, Hilton procured a judgment in York Court against Captain John Mason's widow for acts of trespass committed against him by her agents in 1632. The gist of the action and the basis of recovery were compensations for the disseizin of his land, "which the defendant took from him, and for the vacancy of one year's time, and cutting down his house and for other injuries * * * and for the interest * * * for the term of one and twenty years." His corn had been confiscated by Cammock and conveyed to Watertown in Neal's pinnace, to be milled with what had been raised at Little Harbor. The vessel reached Boston October 18 in charge of Cammock and Godfrey.

Another suit brought by Hilton against Gorges at the same session was subsequently discontinued, and neither of the actions affected the title of Nicholas Shapleigh in the Cammock and Wannerton tracts at Eliot. February 22, 1653-4, all of his land about Kittery House, containing about 500 acres, was confirmed to him by the town.

PIONEERS

BACHILOR, STEPHEN, born 1561, clergyman; Oxford, 1581; arrived in Boston June 5, 1632, in the "Whale"; Lynn, 1632; Ipswich, 1636; Sandwich, 1637; Hampton, 1638; wife Helen died and he married Mary, of Kittery, 1648; died at Hackney, England, 1660; children Deborah (Wing), born 1592, Stephen, born 1594, Henry, Theodate (Hussey) and Ann (Sanborn), born 1601.

BEARD, THOMAS, servant of London Company at Salem, 1629; servant of Treworthy in 1640; died at Dover, 1679; widow Marie; children Elizabeth (Watson), Joseph, Marie, Martha (Bramhall) and Thomas.

‡ York Deeds, 1-5.

BEETLE, ROBERT, assigned land at Eliot by Thomas Gorges, 1641; widow married Stephen Bachilor, 1648, and later Thomas Turner; child Christopher.
BUNKER, JAMES, Kittery, 1646; employed by widow Catherine Shapleigh in 1648 and 1649, when Ellingham hired the Shapleigh mills at Sturgeon Creek; Oyster River, 1651; died 1698; widow Sarah; children James, John and Joseph.
BURDETT, ED, at Eliot with John Treworthy, 1645.
BURSLEY, JOHN, planter who came to Weymouth with Robert Gorges, 1623; Dorchester, 1631; married Joanna Hull, November 28, 1639; Exeter, 1642; Eliot, 1647; died at Dorchester, 1660; children Mary (Crocker), born 1643, Joanna (Dimmock), born 1644, Elizabeth (Goodspeed, Clap), born 1649, and John, born 1652.
CAMMOCK, THOMAS, son of Thomas and Frances, daughter of Robert and sister of Robert Rich, Earl of Warwick, baptized at Maldon, England, February 18, 1592-3; Eliot, 1630-1; 1632-3; planter at Scarborough, 1634-8; died in Jamaica, 1643; widow Margaret married Henry Jocelyn; no issue.
CONLEY, ABRAHAM, planter at Eliot, 1638; Dover, 1657; died 1677; name of widow unmentioned; daughter Judith (Lord).
DAVIS, DANIEL, planter, 1647; submitted to Massachusetts, 1652.
DOWNING, DENNIS, blacksmith, 1650; wife Ann, 1656; wife Patience, 1679; killed by Indians July 4, 1697; sons Joshua, born 1643, and John.
EMERY, ANTHONY, son of John and Agnes, of Romsey, England, arrived at Boston with wife Frances June 3, 1635; Portsmouth, Rhode Island, 1636; Newbury, 1638; Dover, 1640; Eliot, 1648; returned to Portsmouth, 1660-1680; children James, John and Rebecca (Sadler, Eaton).
EVERETT, WILLIAM, at Eliot, 1640; died 1653; widow Margery married Isaac Nash, of Dover; children Martha (Lord), born 1640, and William.
FROST, NICHOLAS, born at Tiverton, England, April 25, 1585; married in January, 1630, Bertha Cadwalla; employe of Holman and Way at Damariscove, 1632; returned from England in the "Wulfrana" in June, 1634; at Little Harbor several months; Eliot, 1635; died July 20, 1663; children (the eldest sons born in Tiverton, Anne at Little Harbor and the rest at Eliot: Charles, July 30, 1631, John, August 7, 1633, Anne, April 17, 1635, Catherine (Leighton, Hammond), December 25, 1637, Elizabeth (Gowen), May 10, 1640, and Nicholas, May 30, 1645.
GREEN, JOHN, at Eliot, 1647; died 1680; widow Julian; children Barbara (Jellison), Elizabeth (Abbott), John and Mary (Searl).
HAYNES, SAMUEL, born 1602; wrecked in the "Angel Gabriel" in Pemaquid Harbor, August 15, 1635; Kittery, 1640; removed to Dover, where he was living in 1684; children Mary (Weeks), Matthias, born 1650, and Samuel, born 1646.
HILTON, WILLIAM, fishmonger of London, 1616; New Plymouth, 1621; Dover Point, 1628; Kittery, 1632; died at York, 1655; widow Frances married Richard White that year; children Anna (Beal), Mary (Wiggin) and William.
JONES, THOMAS, born 1609; servant of Alexander Shapleigh at Eliot, 1640; living, 1679.
KNOWLES, HANSARD, clergyman at Dover, 1638; bought the "Bay Lands" in Eliot of Henry Jocelyn, 1638; removed to Virginia October 7, 1643, after conveying his real estate to Massachusetts.
MARSH, HUGH, born 1619; servant of Stephen Kent; came from Southampton to Newbury, 1638; Eliot, 1646; wife Judith died December 14, 1675; wife Dorcas Blackleach, died November 22, 1683; died December 12, 1693; widow Sarah Haley; children, all born at Newbury, except the eldest, George, 1646, Judith, January 3, 1652-3, Hugh, November 3, 1656, John, June 10, 1658, and James, January 11, 1663-4.

MARTIN, JOHN, servant of John Treworthy before 1645; Dover, 1647; died 1664; widow Sarah; children Abraham, Hannah, Mary, Mehitable and Sarah.

NEWGROVE, JOHN, tenant of Henry Jocelyn on the "Bay Lands," 1636-1641; Dover, 1642; Boston, 1647; wife Mary.

NUTTER, HATEVIL, born 1604; planter at Dover, 1642; Eliot, 1649; Dover, 1652; died 1675; widow Anne; children Abigail (Roberts), Anthony, Elizabeth (Leighton), John and Mary (Wingate).

PAUL, DANIEL, mariner of Ipswich, England; came from London in the "Increase," 1637; Boston, 1640; New Haven, 1643; bought the house of John Symonds at Eliot, 1646; Portsmouth, 1658-1666; wife Elizabeth; children Abigail (Alcock) and Stephen.

PICKERING, JOHN, born 1600; carpenter at Pascataqua, 1633; Portsmouth, 1640; Eliot, 1640; wife Mary; died in Portsmouth January 18, 1668-9; children Abigail, John, Mary, Rebecca, Sarah and Thomas.

PIKE, JOHN, laborer, emigrated from Langford and sailed from Southampton in the "James," 1635; Ipswich, 1635; Kittery, 1640; died at Salisbury May 26, 1654; children Ann, Dorothy (Hendrick), Israel (True), John and Robert, born 1616.

SHEARS, JEREMIAH, planter at Eliot, 1649; wife Elizabeth; removed to Cape Neddock; died 1664; widow Susanna, former wife of Nicholas Green; child Elizabeth (Spencer).

SMALL, EDWARD, Eliot planter, June 25, 1640; secured title to his land from Thomas Gorges, 1643; sold premises to Antiphas Maverick, 1647; Isles of Shoals, 1653; son Francis lived in the country since 1634, when he was fourteen years old.

STARBUCK, EDWARD, born 1604; planter at Kittery, 1640; lived on both banks of the Pascataqua; tenant on Thompson's Brook in Eliot, 1647; removed to Nantucket, 1659, and died February 4, 1690; widow Catherine (Reynolds); children Nathaniel, born 1635, Dorcas (Gayer), Sarah (Story, Austin, Varney), Abigail (Coffin), Esther (Varney) and Jethro, born 1651.

THOMPSON, WILLIAM, born 1599, clergyman; Oxford College, 1620; Kittery, 1637; Braintree, 1639; wives Abigail, who died 1643, and Ann; died December 10, 1666; children Samuel, William, Joseph, born May 1, 1640, Benjamin, born July 14, 1642, and Ann born March 3, 1648.

TREWORTHY, JAMES, merchant, married at Kingsweare, England, Catherine, daughter of Alexander Shapleigh, March 16. 1616-7; Eliot. 1640-2; widow married Edward Hilton; children John, born 1617, Elizabeth (Gilman), Joanna (Amerideth), Samuel, born 1628, and Lucy (Chadbourne, Wells, Stileman), born 1632.

WANNERTON, THOMAS, soldier at Portsmouth, 1631; killed in a military expedition at Castine, 1644; widow Ann married Thomas Williams; children Edward, who died at Scituate October 17, 1715, aged 85, Joanna (Smith) and Thomas.

WHITE, JOHN, born 1604; employe of Alexander Shapleigh at Eliot. 1638; wife Lucy; died after 1680; children Abigail (Allen), John and Mary.

WILLIAMS, FRANCIS, superintendent of the salt industry at Frank's Fort in Eliot, 1631-3; returned from England, 1640; wife Helen and several children; removed to Barbadoes, 1646, from Portsmouth, where he had a farm.

KITTERY.

The first known resident at the mouth of Pascataqua River in Maine was Philip Swadden who had been a servant to Robert

Seeley in Massachusetts until freed by the court August 16, 1631.§

His wigwam stood at Kittery Point upon land confirmed to him by Gorges. In February, 1634, Ambrose Gibbons bought corn from him which may have been raised on the premises the previous year.

In 1636, John Treworthy from Dartmouth, England, arrived in the river in charge of a vessel and merchandise for his grandfather Alexander Shapleigh. He made his port at Kittery Point.*

He obtained permission from Swadden to erect a magazine or storehouse on the outward side of the Point. The building was also occupied as a dwelling, according to the statement of William Reeves, who was employed as a fisherman on Treworthy's bark, called the *Bachelor*.†

May 5, very soon after his arrival, Treworthy who was a minor, negotiated with Thomas Bradbury, of York, as agent for Gorges, to sell to Edward Johnson on behalf of his grandfather 500 acres of land which extended eastward from Swadden's grant to Cutts' Island. The conveyance included all of Kittery Point but the extremity. This exception by Bradbury in the deed to Shapleigh disclosed the fact that the few acres reserved had been alienated to Swadden by Bradbury since his advent at York in July, 1634. The record of such a transaction is not extant.‡

June 28, 1636, John Winter complained to Trelawney that John Billings, Oliver Clark, William Freathy, William Ham, John Lander and John Symonds, who had arrived at Richmond Island the previous year, had left his service at the island and gone "westward by land." The deserters visited Agamenticus and Kittery before their return. Subsequently, Billings, Lander and Symonds became residents of Kittery and Freathy a citizen of York.§§

December 12, 1636, according to a deposition of Edward Johnson, Francis Champernoone, son of Sir Arthur, of Dartington, England, bought Champernoone's Island and five hundred acres more on the mainland at Kittery. To the island he assigned the name of his father's residence and to the tract lying along the shore between Kittery Point, which then belonged to Shap-

§ Mass. Col. Rec., 1-80.
* Me. Doc. Hist., 6-38; N. E. Hist. Gen. Reg., 5-349.
† Me. Doc. Hist., 4-106, 112.
‡ York Deeds, 1-11.
§§ Me. Doc. Hist., 3-93.

leigh, and Brave Boat Harbor he gave the less romantic one of Godmorrock.*

Johnson testified further that he had assisted Champernoone in effecting a bargain with Thomas Bradbury, of Agamenticus, who at that time was acting as Gorges' agent for the disposal of his lands in New England. The consideration was stated to have been "two kowes or heifers."

The first English house at the mouth of Pascataqua River in Maine was begun by Alexander Shapleigh on his land at Kittery Point in 1637 or 1638 and near by, on land leased from Swadden, a brewhouse was erected by John Treworthy for the use of his fishermen, who were employed on the *Bachelor*. Two of these fishermen were William Reeves and Richard Thomas; others may have been John Andrews and Thomas Crockett.†

Before the organization of any proprietary court was effected in Maine, some form of self-government was required to provide mutual protection against raids by pirates and interlopers. Even the early invasion by the French and hostile acts of the natives had severely overtaxed the police powers of Captain Neal.

After his departure from the country the eastern plantations feared that there might be no legal restraints upon crime and formed a voluntary combination for common defence. Proof of the existence of such a compact may be found in the records of New Somerset and in private correspondence of the period.

February 7, 1636-7, Thomas Lewis, the patentee of Saco, was cited before his associates, at the house of Thomas Williams, to answer suits brought in his own court against himself and "to show cause why he will not deliver up the combination belonging to us." Obviously, his plea would have been want of jurisdiction by the new tribunal. The officials who demanded the surrender of the old combination were Thomas Cammock and Henry Jocelyn, early of Pascataqua, Edward Godfrey and William Gorges, of Agamenticus, Richard Bonython and Richard Vines, of Saco, and Thomas Purchase, of Pejepscot. At that date the list represented all of the communities in the district.‡

The next year George Burdett, pastor at Dover, recommended to the Archbishop of Canterbury "That a speedie Course be taken

---
* York Deeds, 3-97.
† Me. Doc. Hist., 4-106; York Ct. Rec., 1-138; Suffolk Deeds, 1-128.
‡ York Ct. Rec., 1-10.

to setle his Maties Govrnt amongest us; there yet being none but Combinacons" on Pascataqua River.§

Two years later George Puddington was accused, by Burdett at York, of disloyalty to the dominant administration when he made the statement: "We hold that the power of our combination is stronger than the power of the King."*

Probably, the very same year that development was begun at Kittery Point, dwellings and fishing equipment were completed by Champernoone on his island.

In the description of New England, published in London in 1638, Captain John Underhill observed, that "The northern plantations, and eastern, as Puscataway, would not be neglected; they are desirable places, and lie in the heart of fishing. Puscataway is a river navigable for a ship of a hundred tons some six leagues up. With boats and pinnaces you may go a great way further. It is the only key of the country for safety. With twelve pieces of ordnance, will keep out all the enemies in the world. The mouth of the river is narrow, lies full upon the southeast sea; so as there is no anchoring without, except you hazard ship and men. It is accomodated with a good soil, abundance of good timber; meadows are not wanting to the place. Pity it is it hath been so long neglected * * * There was grown in Puscataway the last year, and in the Bay, as good English grain as can grow in any part of the world."†

January 10, 1639-40, John Lander, who had acquired the interest of Swadden at Kittery Point, conveyed the westerly end of his lot and half of his house, just finished, to his fishing partner, John Billings.‡

June 25, of that year, all residents of Kittery had been cited to attend the first session of a proprietary court to be holden at Agamenticus and to signify their acquiescence in the administration of local government by Gorges.

The names of those who recognized the summons were recorded in the following order: James Treworthy, Edward Small, Nicholas Frost, John Hurd, Philip Swadden, John Pike, William Everett, Andrew Heifor and Peter Weare.

Those who failed to appear were: Francis Champernoone,

§ N. H. Doc. in Eng. Arch., 32.
* York Ct. Rec., 1-69.
† 3 Mass. Hist. Col., 6-14.
‡ York Deeds, 1-10.

Stephen Crafford, John Lander, William Wormwood, John Andrews, Thomas Withers, John White, John Newgrove, Abraham Conley, Samuel Haynes, Edward Starbuck, John Hall, Thomas Spencer, Humphrey Chadbourne and Thomas Brooks. In the record of this court it appeared that Thomas Wannerton, who then lived at Strawberry Bank, had complained of local fishermen for pilfering timber which had been used in fishing stages at Pascataqua. The owner of the stage destroyed was John Baple, a fishing master of Barnstable, England. The offenders were found to be Stephen Crafford, of Brave Boat Harbor, and William Seavey, of the Isles of Shoals. Crafford was drowned two years later in a fishing voyage off the coast whither he had ventured with a shallop and "servant" belonging to Seavey. His estate included houses at Brave Boat Harbor and at Oyster River in Dover.

Champernoone, who had been living upon his island, purchased, sometime in 1640, a tract of land at Greenland, New Hampshire, where he built a house. Afterwards, the dwelling at Great Harbor was designated "Champernoone's Lower House" to distinguish it from that at Great Bay which stood upon a point near other land of Robert Saltonstall, from whom it had been acquired.§

June 27, 1648, Yorkshire Court conferred upon William Hilton the sole right to maintain an "ordinary" at the mouth of Pascataqua River on Kittery Point, where for six years he had been a tenant in the house, built by Alexander, and leased by Nicholas Shapleigh. By virtue of his license Hilton was required to serve as public ferryman upon the river and the tolls from his tavern were fixed as follows: Great Island, six pence; Strawberry Bank, twelve pence; and Dover and Kittery, eighteen pence.

October 20, 1649, all of Pascataqua Plantation, comprising Champernoone's Island, Kittery Point, Kittery (Eliot) and Newichawannock, were incorporated by the proprietary government as a town by the name of Kittery.

Champernoone spent the winter following the organization of the municipality in Barbadoes where Parker, Vines, Williams and the Robinsons had been stationed for three years. He left the custody of his house at Greenland to Samuel Haynes and Thomas Withers and subsequently sold it to the former. The

§ N. H. Hist. Col., 8-365.

farm and house on the island were leased to John Hurd, who removed soon after to Agamenticus and built a dwelling of his own. November 20, 1652, forty-one residents of Kittery united in the act of submission to Massachusetts authority.*

PIONEERS

AMEREDETH, JOHN, born at Dartmouth, England, 1615; cooper at Kittery, 1647; died January 26, 1690-1; widow Joanna, daughter of James Treworthy; children Joanna (Alcock) and John.
ANDREWS, JOHN, born 1600; planter at Pascataqua, 1636; Kittery Point, 1640; Brave Boat Harbor, 1649; died 1671; widow Joan, born 1621, married Philip Atwell, 1672; children Ann (Billings), Elizabeth (Manwaring), Joanna, John, Robert and Sarah (Mitchell).
BASTON (Boston), THOMAS, planter at Kittery, 1642; York, 1648; Wells, 1651-1678; Ipswich, 1679; children Daniel and Thomas.
CHAMPERNOONE, FRANCIS, son of Arthur of Dartington, England; merchant at Kittery, 1636; Greenland, 1640; married Mary Hoel, widow of Robert Cutt, after 1675; died 1686; buried on Champernoone's Island; widow Mary; no issue.
CRAFFORD, STEPHEN, Brave Boat Harbor, 1640; fisherman, drowned off the Isles of Shoals, 1642; widow Margaret married Thomas Willey, of Dover; daughters Sarah and Susan.
CROCKETT, THOMAS, born 1606-11, laborer at Newichawannock House, 1630-3; Kittery Point, 1640; died 1679; widow Ann married Diggory Jeffrey; children Ann (Roberts), Elihu, Ephraim, Hugh, Joseph, born 1651, Joshua, born 1657, Mary (Barton) and Sarah (Parrott).
CUTT, ROBERT, ship-builder, 1647; died 1674; widow Mary (Hoel) married Francis Champernoone, 1675; children Bridget (Scriven), Elizabeth (Elliot), Mary, Richard, Robert and Sarah.
GODFREY, EDWARD, born at Barnend, England, 1589; merchant, in the service of Laconia Company at Little Harbor, 1632; York, 1633-1654; married widow Ann Messant at York; died in England, 1666; widow survived; son Oliver, by a former wife, in England.
GUNNISON, HUGH, servant of Richard Bellinghan, at Boston, 1635; wife Elizabeth died January 25, 1645-6; married Sarah, widow of Henry Lynn, May 23, 1647; innkeeper at Kittery Point, 1651; died 1660; widow married John Mitchell and Francis Morgan; children, born in Boston, Ann (Lynn), 1636, Sarah, February 14, 1637-8, Elizabeth (Seeley, Cowell), April 25, 1640, Deborah, September 18, 1642, Hester, February 20, 1647-8, Joseph, March 31, 1649, Elihu, February 12, 1649-50, Mary (Rogers).
HALL, JOHN, planter at Dover, 1633; Kittery, 1640; died at Greenland, 1677; widow Elizabeth; children Joseph and Sarah.
HURD, JOHN, planter at Dover, 1633; Great Island, 1637; Kittery, 1640; died 1676; widow Isabel; children James, John and Warwick, who was shot March 24. 1646-7.
HURD, JOHN, tailor at Boston, 1639; Champernoone's Island, 1649; wife Mary; had new house at York, 1650; removed to Dover and died January 17, 1688-9; widow Elizabeth, daughter of Joseph Hull, of York; children, born in various places, Benjamin February 20, 1643-4, William, Mary (Ham), January 26, 1649-50, Abigail (Jones), August 2, 1651, Elizabeth (Nute, Furber), September 15. 1653, Hannah (Nason), November 25, 1655, John. February 24, 1658-9, Joseph, January 4, 1660-1, Samuel, August 4, 1663, Tristram. March 4, 1666-7, Nathaniel, September 20, 1668, Dorcas and Elizabeth.

* Mass. Col. Rec., 4-1. 116.

JAMES, WILLIAM, planter at Salem, 1636; at Kittery with wife Elizabeth, 1647; sold homestead at Spruce Creek, 1651; Kennebec, 1654; Sheepscot, 1665.

JOCELYN, HENRY, born 1606; Pascataqua, 1630-3; arrived at Berwick from England in the "Pide Cow" July 8, 1634; as agent for Captain John Mason; removed to Scarborough, 1638; married Margaret, widow of Thomas Cammock; sold homestead in 1664 and removed to Pemaquid, where he died in 1683, without issue.

JONES, ALEXANDER, born 1615; married a daughter of Thomas Walford; witnessed a deed at Sarah Lynn's house, 1645; sold land at Kittery to William James.

LAWSON, CHRISTOPHER, born 1616; Exeter, 1639; married Elizabeth, sister of William James; cooper at Boston, where he sold his house to Thomas Lake, 1648; wife went back to England, but he removed to Kennebec, where he bought land of Abbagadusset and Kenebis, 1649; sold eastern lands to Lake, 1650, and returned to Pascataqua, where he had acquired 14 shares in Dover patent; children Thomas, born May 4, 1643, and Mary born October 27, 1645.

LUCKHAM, JOHN, planter at Kittery, 1647; died July 8, 1647; no children.

LYNN, HENRY, merchant at Boston, 1630; Pascataqua, 1631; York, 1640; died in Virginia, 1644; widow Sarah (Tilly) married Hugh Gunnison; children born in Boston, Sarah, August 20, 1636, Elizabeth, July 21, 1638, Ephraim, January 16, 1639-40, and Rebecca, February 15, 1641-2.

MENDUM, ROBERT, born 1604; innkeeper at Duxbury, 1639; wife Mary; Kittery, 1647; died a widower, in May, 1682; child Jonathan.

MILES, JOSEPH, born 1619; cooper at Kittery Point, 1640-7; Dover, 1649; Kittery, 1652; married Mary Whelase February 18, 1661; Salem, 1668.

MILLER, JOHN, servant of Alexander Shapleigh, 1636-1640; Sheepscot, 1665.

NEAL, WALTER, governor of Pascataqua, 1630-3; lived at Little Harbor in Rye, New Hampshire; left for England July 15, 1633.

NUTE, JAMES, sent by Mason, 1634-5; Dover, 1640; juror at Kittery, 1646; Dover, 1648-50; wife Sarah; children James, born 1643, Abraham, born 1644.

PALMER, WILLIAM, at New Plymouth in the "Fortune," 1623; Portsmouth, 1640; Kittery Point, 1642; died at Great Island, 1685; widow Abishag; children Edward and Stephen.

POUNING, HENRY, ship-helper at Kittery, 1641; Dover, 1645; Boston, 1649; died 1664; widow Elizabeth; children, born at Boston, Elizabeth (Bridgham), 1649, Mary, 1651, Henry, April 28, 1654, Sarah, August 3, 1659, Daniel, August 27, 1661, and Ann, February 29, 1663.

REEVES, WILLIAM, born 1615; sailor at Salem, 1635; employed by John Treworthy, 1636, at Kittery Point; Boston, 1638; Kittery, 1665.

REYNOLDS, JOHN, fisherman; Kittery, 1640; constable at Isles of Shoals, 1647; married.

SEARL, JOHN, planter, 1647; married November 16, 1661, Catherine, widow of Thomas Warner; later married Mary, daughter of John Green; drowned at sea January 4, 1675-6; child John, born November 19, 1664.

SHAPLEIGH, ALEXANDER, merchant of Kingsweare, England; bought Kittery Point of Gorges, 1636; arrived 1640; dead 1650; children Alexander, born 1606, Catherine (Treworthy, Hilton), born 1608 and Nicholas, born 1610.

SHAPLEIGH, NICHOLAS, born 1610; merchant of Kingsweare, England; son of Alexander; Kittery 1641-7; children born in Bristol, England, Nicholas, 1631, and Jeffrey, 1632, both died in infancy; widow Alice and nephew John succeeded to his estate.

SWADDEN, PHILIP, born 1600; servant of Robert Seeley at Boston, 1631; Kittery Point, 1633; Saint George, 1651; living 1673; no issue.

THOMAS, RICHARD (spelled Rice), born 1614; servant of John Treworthy at Kittery Point, 1636; married Elizabeth, widow of John Billings; living 1652.

TREWORTHY, JOHN, son of James, born 1618; arrived at Kittery as agent for his grandfather Alexander Shapleigh, 1636; married Penelope Spencer at Newbury January 15, 1646-7; governor of Newfoundland, 1651; children born at Newbury James and John, born 1649.

WHITE, PAUL, born 1590; mariner and merchant at Champernoone's Island, 1649; owned half of the island and land at Pemaquid that year; wife Bridget died in Newbury, 1664; wife Ann (Jones), 1665; died July 20, 1679; no issue.

WITHERS, THOMAS, born 1606; planter at Kittery, 1631; died 1685; widow Jane married William Godsoe; children Mary (Rice) and Elizabeth (Shapleigh).

WORMWOOD, WILLIAM, planter at Kittery, 1639; wife Catherine, 1651; children Ann, Jacob, Margaret (Bussey) and William.

AGAMENTICUS

Trimountain of the purple haze
  And filmy cloud-wreaths, dun and gray;
Reminder of those youthful days
  So dim and far away!

Mysterious mountain of the East,
  Bold landmark of the plain and sea,
Enduring symbol of the past
  And of eternity!

Belovèd mount of Aspenquid—
  On which at last he chose to die,
In foliage forever hid
  Betwixt the earth and sky.

Memorial to one who sought
  A higher level for his race;
Where, though his realm survived him not,
  He still retains a place.

Fair mountain of the lights and shades,
  With peaceful grandeur in its heights,
As restful as the star which fades
  At dusk on summer nights!

YORK RIVER

The first distinct reference to the discovery of any part of York was that of John Verrazano in 1524.

He reported that to the northward of Cape Cod he had encountered Indian peoples so "barbarous" that they could not be made to understand simple signs. He said that when he desired to exchange commodities with them his boats would lie under the cliffs, where the natives, as he expressed it, "used to come to the seashore upon certain craggy rocks, and * * * let down with a rope, what it pleased them to give us, crying continually that we should not approach to the land, demanding immediately the exchange, taking nothing but knives, fishhookes, and tools to cut withall, neither did they make any account of our courtesie."

In spite of some opposition a party of twenty-five armed sailors penetrated the wild interior for several miles.

After describing the natives and the locality in brief terms, Verrazano concluded: "We departed from thence, keeping our course north-east along the coast, which we found more pleasant champion and without woods, with high mountains within the land."*

It is evident that the "craggy rocks," where the natives lowered their barter with ropes, were the cliffs at York, now known as "The Nubble." The high mountains mentioned were peaks of Crawford Range, which become visible after passing that point. In this vicinity, too, the change in the general course of a vessel would be a natural one since the coast line trends from the north towards the east into the Gulf of Maine.

It is more than a matter of tradition that "The Nubble" was the habitual resort of Indians during the summer fishing season. There food was not only readily obtainable, but it was abundant. It was, also, an ideal position for observation of the sea and the approach of coastwise vessels. In recent years, the discovery of numerous Indian relics upon the premises is evidence of the particular preference of the natives for that locality.

* Me. Doc. Hist., 1-264.

Seventy-eight years later Bartholomew Gosnold sighted the same shore and Gabriel Archer, chronicler for his voyage, observed that it was about six o'clock, on the morning of May 14, 1602, when they first "descried land that lay north." A promontory to the right, now known as Cape Elizabeth, they named "the north land." Five leagues to the west was another "out point of woody ground" (Cape Porpoise), where the trees stood "very high and straight." The other extreme to the left, now called "The Nubble" and "lying twelve leagues west," they named "Savage Rock," since it was the spot where "the savages first showed themselves."

The narrator added: "From the said rock, came towards us a Biscay shallop with sail and oars, having eight persons in it, whom we supposed at first to be Christians distressed. But approaching us nearer, we perceived them to be savages * * * One that seemed to be their commander wore a waistcoat of black work, a pair of breeches, cloth stockings, shoes, hat and band, one or two more had also a few things made by some Christians; these with a piece of chalk described the coast thereabouts, and could name Placentia of the Newfoundland; they spoke divers Christian words, and seemed to understand much more than we * * * could comprehend."

"Finding ourselves short of our purposed place, we set sail westward, leaving them and their coast. About sixteen leagues south-west from thence" (reckoning from Cape Elizabeth to Portsmouth Harbor) "we perceived in that course two small islands, the one" (Boone Island) "lying eastward from Savage Rock, the other" (Isles of Shoals) "to the southward of it; the coast we left was full of goodly woods, fair plains, with little green round hills above the cliffs appearing unto us, which are indifferently raised, but all rocky."

Brereton's account of the same voyage offered an explanation for the previous contact of the Indians with Europeans. His clear diction proved the writer to have been well educated. The statement was: "It seemed by some words and signs they made, that some Basques or of St. John de Luz, have fished or traded in this place, being in the latitude of 43 degrees." The forty-third meridian passes between the Isles of Shoals and the mouth of Pascataqua River.†

† 3 Mass. Hist. Col., 8-73, 86.

In 1603, Martin Pring, with William Brown who had been one of Gosnold's seamen, returned to New England and explored the coast, including York, Kennebunk and Saco Rivers. In 1614, Captain Smith charted the entire seaboard from Cape Cod to Penobscot River. The Indian name for York River was mentioned for the first time in his statement that "Accominticus and Passataquack are two convenient harbours for small barks." He remarked also that "a good Countrie" was to be found "within their craggie cliffs."

Ten years later Christopher Levett visited Pascataqua on his way eastward and his description, written in 1624, contained this paragraph: "About two leagues further to the East is another great river called Aquamenticus. There I think a good plantation may be settled, for there is a good harbour for ships, good ground, and much already cleared, fit for planting of corne and other fruits, having heretofore ben planted by the Salvages who are all dead. There is good timber, and likely to be good fishing, but as yet there hath beene no tryall made that I can heare of."‡

Levett, Underhill and Winthrop, who were all familiar with the coast, estimated the distance between Agamenticus and the original Pascataqua plantation at Little Harbor at about two leagues, or six miles. Maverick, however, who was a patentee of Agamenticus, specified in an involved description that the shortest distance between the mouths of the two rivers was three miles; he had in mind the more easterly channel of the Pascataqua at Kittery Point, while Little Harbor in Rye, New Hampshire, lay much farther westward.§

The Indian name for York River was spelled variously, but the fact that Winthrop adopted the form "Aquamenticus" proves that he had had access to Levett's earlier report when he began to collect the materials to be used later in a compilation of his history of New England. Agamenticus mountain which he styled "The Three Turks' Heads" was called "The Mount of Sassanou" by Smith. The Indian namesake was a sagamore of prominence in Central Maine during the colonization period.

The natives of York were destroyed by a plague which raged from 1617 to 1619, inclusive. That the river had been a popular

‡ Baxter's Levett, 92.
§ 3 Mass. Hist. Col., 6-14; Winthrop, 2-29; Mass. Hist. Proc., 21-233.

resort of the Indians was apparent from the wide areas of cultivation before the epidemic occurred.

SETTLEMENT.

York was included in the original grant from the Council of Plymouth to Gorges and Mason, in 1622, but the former, by a subsequent agreement with his partner, became sole proprietor.

December 30, or about five months after the issuance of the patent to Gorges and Mason, a similar concession of territory about Boston Harbor was bestowed upon Robert, the eldest son of the Maine proprietor. In 1623, under the patronage of Robert Gorges, colonists settled at Wessaguscus. Five years later their location was claimed by Massachusetts Bay Colony by virtue of the royal patent of 1628.

In 1630, some of Gorges' colonists were still living in Massachusetts, although they looked to his father for their protection. December 9, of that year, Sir Ferdinando Gorges, perturbed by previous acts of usurpation on the part of the colony, had expressed the hope that "his people & planters (by vertue of his sons pattent)" might be permitted to "live quietly & uninjured." William Jeffrey was one of his "old planters" who had expressed great dissatisfaction with the treatment that had been accorded by the new government.*

Colonel Walter Norton and his associates, then living at Charlestown, Massachusetts, were the first persons to solicit grants at York from Gorges. The grand patentee explained his proposed participation in the following language: "I gave him (Norton) my word I would be his intercessor to the Lords for obtaining him a Patent for any place he desired, *not already granted to any other.*"

Edward Godfrey, a near relative of Norton and one of the first governors of Maine, claimed to have been the first settler who had ever built a house at York. In a petition to the General Court of Massachusetts in 1654 he asserted that he had been interested in the settlement of New England for "above thirty-two years," as "an adventurer on that design."

Henry Gardiner, one of the Pascataqua patentees, claimed that Godfrey was a London merchant who had joined with some

---

* 4 Mass. Hist. Col., 6-3.

of Robinson's "Tenants of Amsterdam" in their attempt "to settle a Colony nigh Cape Cod" at New Plymouth.†

Godfrey claimed to have settled at York in 1630, but it is well known that he came to New England in company with Walter Neal in the *Warwick* at that time and that he was employed as a merchant at Pascataqua by the Laconia Company. He had charge of the fishing industry at the Great House in Little Harbor, but insisted that he had built the first house at York, probably a fishermen's hut of temporary character at Brave Boat Harbor or on Stage Island, which were directly accessible to the Isles of Shoals.‡

Hence, it was Godfrey who had induced Norton to secure a location at Agamenticus from the Council of Plymouth through the intercession of Gorges. December 1, 1631, grants were ceded on both sides of that river. With reference to these concessions the grand patentee remarked later: "I was contented my grandson Ferdinando should be nominated together with him and the rest" (Norton and his associates); "to whom was passed a Patent of twelve thousand acres of land upon the east side of the river Agomentico, and twelve thousand of acres more of land on the west side to my son Ferdinando."§

The grantees on the eastern side of the river were Ferdinando, son of John Gorges, of England, Ralph Glover, Thomas Graves and Walter Norton, of Charlestown, John Bursley and William Jeffrey, of Wessaguscus, and Samuel Maverick, of Winnisimet. The charter was revised March 2, 1631-2, when the council struck out the names of other English patentees and inserted that of Dixie Bull, a merchant of London. Some of the partners were brothers, brothers-in-law, or otherwise related by blood or marriage connections.*

At the time of the grant John Gorges, father of the first proprietor on the east side of the river, had acquired title to the premises claimed by his deceased brother Robert in Massachusetts, but his rights had been usurped by the new colony. Bursley, Jeffrey and Maverick, members of Gorges' colony at Wessaguscus in 1623, were concerned as tenants. Obviously, some or all of the other patentees at York had once belonged to Gorges'

† N. E. Vindication, 24.
‡ Me. Hist. Col., 1-390; N. H. State Papers, 1-68.
§ Me. Hist. Col., 2-49.
* Essex Ant., 17-98.

colony at Wessaguscus and the later grant in Maine was provided to furnish a refuge in case of their eviction from precarious tenures in the Commonwealth.

October 18, 1632, Godfrey and Thomas Cammock, described as hailing from Pascataqua, carried sixteen hogsheads of corn to the mill at Watertown in Neal's pinnace. This grain may have been raised from some of that delivered at Pascataqua by Henry Fleet that spring.

In a letter from England, dated December 5, following, the Laconia Company confided the care of the house at Little Harbor, which was then utilized chiefly as a fishing station, to Godfrey, and suggested that he increase the number of fishermen employed there on its account.

These items indicate that Godfrey was living at Pascataqua plantation very late in 1632 and that the Massachusetts colonists did not remove to Agamenticus until the next year.

Referring to Norton and his companions, Gorges continued, "Hereupon he and some of his associates hastened to take possession of their territories, carrying with them their families, and other necessary provisions." Godfrey in subsequent statements clearly indicated that possession was taken permanently in 1633 and that he participated in the event.†

In the settlement of York there was concerted action between the patentees in Massachusetts and citizens of Bristol, England. In fact, York later was called Bristol and made subject to ordinances similar to those of the British municipality of that name. While its electorate was small, the city officials were not wanting. William, son of Mayor Humphrey Hook, of Bristol, asserted that he with several others, en route for York, was landed at La Tour's fort at Cape Sable, and that the French captain gave them the free use of his pinnace to transport them across the dangerous reach of the Bay of Fundy.‡

On their way westward three of these colonists, Hook, Robert Knight and George Newman, met Governor Neal from Pascataqua and were present at the delivery of the premises at Pemaquid to Abraham Shurt on May 27. When they arrived at York a few days later they found the patentees from Massachusetts already in possession.

† Me. Hist. Col., 9-342, 358.
‡ Winthrop, 2-125.

Late in June, Captain John Stone, of Virginia, arrived at York from Saint Christopher's Island in the West Indies with a cargo of young cattle. Some of these had been disposed of at Little Harbor, but the rest were left at York.

In September, after visiting Charlestown and vicinity where Norton had recently resided, Stone sailed for Virginia with Norton as his passenger. When they arrived at the mouth of the Connecticut River a desire to trade with the natives induced them to proceed with their vessel into the interior, where the hostile Indians killed Stone and Norton and the six members of their crew. The massacre was afterwards detected by some Englishmen who had encountered an Indian wearing the scarlet coat of Captain Stone. This event was one of the causes of the Pequot War.§

Godfrey, many years later, referred to Norton in his allusion to his nearest relative who had been killed by the Indians, but he did not name him nor state the circumstances.*

Captain Norton of Agamenticus had been a British soldier of distinction and the story of his death was characteristic of the man. After the Indians had disposed of Captain Stone, "They likewise killed all ye rest, but Captaine Norton defended him selfe a long time against them all in ye cooke-roome, till by accidente the gunpowder tooke fire, which (for readynes) he had sett in an open thing before him, which did so burne, & scald him, & blind his eyes, as he could make no longer resistance, but was slaine also by them, though they much comended his vallour."†

During the massacre the savages had taken possession of five loaded guns belonging to the vessel's crew and had discharged them at the English with fatal results. While the natives did not fully understand the proper methods of charging them, these weapons were accounted a serious menace to the public safety of the whole country while in their hands.‡

Norton's widow Eleanor married William Hook and removed to Salisbury with her husband, but his only daughter Jane became the wife of Henry Simpson of Agamenticus. A court record of 1650 disclosed the death of the latter and her remarriage to

§ Young's Mass. Chron., 363; Winthrop, 1-122.
* N. H. State Papers, 17-506.
† Bradford, 2-203.
‡ 4 Mass. Hist. Col., 7-56.

Nicholas Bond of the same town. Henry Norton, who was living at Agamenticus upon an adjoining lot, then recognized Jane (Norton) Bond as a "cousin." He was, presumably, the son of one of her father's brothers—obviously the child of one of the other patentees of Agamenticus of the same name. The only descendants of Captain, or Colonel, Walter Norton appear to have been derived through his grandson Henry Simpson.

Both patents at Agamenticus, like that at Pemaquid, were granted in consideration of agreements "to transport divers persons into New England, and there to erect and build a Towne." The requisite quota may never have been provided.

As sponsor for the undertakings Gorges himself was interested in the development of the tract on the west side of Agamenticus River. His own statement in relation thereto was the following: "I sent over for my son, my nephew Captain William Gorges, who had been my lieutenant in the fort of Plymouth, with some other craftsmen for the building of houses and erecting of saw-mills * * * by which the foundation of the Plantation was laid. And I was the more hopeful of the happy success thereof, for that I had not far from that place Richard Vines, a gentleman and servant of my own, who was settled there some years before, and had been interested in the discovery and seizure thereof for me."§

The action alluded to by Gorges was taken in 1634. In the spring of that year Captain Mason volunteered the information, to Gibbons at Newichawannock, that not any of their associates would "adventure this yeare to the plantation, besides Sir Ferdinando Gorges and myselfe." Another letter from Gorges and Mason to the same person referred to the adventure at York: "We have not onelie each of us shipped people present to plant uppon our owne lands, at our owne charges, but have given direction to invite and authoritie to receive such others as may be had to be tenants, to plant and live there, for the more speedie peopling of the countrie."*

The pioneers sailed from Portsmouth in the *Pide Cow* during the first week in May and arrived at Agamenticus two months later. Their advent was reported at Boston under the date of July 9, in these words: "Sir Ferdinando Gorges and Capt. Mason

§ Me. Hist. Col., 2-49.
* N. H. State Papers, 1-88.

sent to Pascataquack and Aquamenticus, with two sawmills, to be erected, in each place one."†

Norton and Godfrey were delegated to make an equitable division of the territory on the east side of Pascataqua River, where the Laconia patentees had concluded to operate in severalty.‡

Some of the colonists who disembarked at York at that time were Bartholomew Barnard, Thomas Bradbury, William Freathy, Roger Garde, William Gorges, Edward Johnson and Thomas Jones.

The first sawmill was begun on the west bank of the main river above Rice's Bridge. The tributary on which it was built was later known as Old Mill Creek.§

The mechanics sent by Gorges also erected for William Gorges, agent of the proprietor, a mansion on the opposite shore. This building was called "Sir Ferdinando Gorges' House." Its style, suggesting the long type of English dwelling outlined in the plan of Fort Saint George at Sagadahoc, may be inferred from a description of the first parsonage at York: "Mr. Godfrey * * * keeps a very good howes and if wee will goe thither, a hows with 3 chimnyes hee promiseth." It was liberally estimated that "possibly, through unexperienced or ill management, a thousand pounds" might have been disbursed by Thomas Gorges and Richard Vines "in a house & some land, broake up at Yorke."*

October 31, 1634, Samuel Maverick, then of Winnisimet, bought a "house & land" of George Newman at York. They were situated on the east side near the mouth of the river. For some time he had been subjected to criticism by Massachusetts magistrates on account of his indiscriminate hospitality and may have intended to remove to York, where he still held patent rights. However, the next spring, when finally ordered to leave their jurisdiction, he did not go to Agamenticus, although he did sell his home at Winnisimet to Richard Bellingham February 27, 1634-5.††

April 22, 1635, Gorges by agreement with Mason obtained a grant in severalty of coastal Maine from the Pascataqua to Sagadahoc River, and March 25, following, instituted the first proprietary court at Saco, with Godfrey and Roger Garde partici-

† Winthrop, 1-137.
‡ N. H. State Papers, 1-88.
§ York Deeds, 7-96.
* 5 Mass. Hist. Col., 1-37; Brown's Genesis U. S., 1-190; Mass. Col. Rec., 4-2, 530.
†† York Deeds, 8-209; Suffolk Deeds, 1-15.

pating for York. At this session the properties of William Hook and Thomas Jones were distrained to meet the assessments which had been made against them for the construction of a meeting-house at Agamenticus. This is the first allusion to such a building in Maine. Its location was on the easterly bank of "Meeting-House Creek," southwesterly but not far from that of the present Congregational society at York Village.

The settlement at York advanced but slowly. It was asserted by Gorges that he had sent "by other shipping from Bristol, some cattle, with other servants," but these did not arrive until September, 1636, when their vessel was described as "Another from Bristol * * * with some cattle and passengers * * * at Pascataquack for Sir Ferdinando Gorge his plantation at Aquamenticus."‡

In 1637, Captain John Underhill, who had lived at Pascataqua, described Agamenticus as "a place of good accomodation; it lies five miles from Puscataway river, where Sir Ferdinando Gorge hath a house. It is a place worthy to be inhabited, a soil that bears good corn, all sorts of grain, flax, hemp, the country generally will afford."§

July 23, 1637, Gorges was made governor of New England by royal appointment and he forwarded invitations to influential members of the Massachusetts government to coöperate with him in that capacity. All declined. Agamenticus was destined to continue under an ecclesiastical administration. While William Blackstone, the first English settler of Boston, had promised to accept the position of pastor at York, his agricultural pursuits proved more alluring and William Thompson supplied his place.*

In a petition addressed to the General Court of Massachusetts to confirm his former rights, prior to seeking relief abroad, Godfrey complained that, on account of the oppression of Gorges who had permitted it, he had been cited before the Court of Star Chamber to account to George Cleave of Casco for imaginary wrongs. October 11, 1637, he appeared for himself, Richard Vines and John Winter at a session holden in England and recovered costs for attendance.

While in England Godfrey procured a renewal, dated March 22, 1637-8, of the original Norton patent, in which his own name was substituted for that of Norton in the list of surviving pat-

‡ Winthrop, 1-196.
§ 3 Mass. Hist. Col., 6-14.
* N. E. Hist. Gen. Reg., 14-345.

entees. At that date young Ferdinando Gorges was but eight years of age.†

That same year, in association with Gyles Elbridge and members of the Hook family, of Bristol, he secured from Gorges a concession of 1500 acres at Cape Neddock. William Hook, one of the patentees, owned a dwelling above George Newman's on the east side of Agamenticus River near its mouth; at this date he had cleared land on the upper edge of the plantation and built a farmhouse, where his employes were chiefly engaged with agriculture and stock raising.

Some of his cattle had been brought to York by Captain Stone before the death of Norton and came into the possession of Hook when he married the widow. Some of his other stock may have been purchased from Gorges three years later, but in the spring of 1638 William King, master of the *Exchange* of Bristol, landed ten cows at the farm that had been sent to the pioneer by his father Humphrey Hook, who was owner of the vessel. This ship made the passage from Bristol in ten weeks.‡

While the elder Hook had been interested formerly in Newfoundland fishing and still employed some land fishermen in connection with his New England shipping, his son was not particularly interested in that industry. The son, however, was manager of affairs in this country and in at least one instance succeeded in extricating his ambitious parent from financial disaster.

Some time in 1638 George Burdett, of Dover, was chosen to succeed William Thompson as pastor at York. The new clergyman had a farmhouse and cultivated land, located between Godfrey's Cove and Brave Boat Harbor. He was also interested in stock raising. His housekeeper was Ann Messant, a widow who afterwards married Godfrey.

Burdett may be regarded as a degenerate. At any rate, some of his parishioners were exceedingly perverted. The stories of John Baker and his neighbor Swain, who hung himself because of a bad conscience, have been recounted in the History of New England. These men lived in Burdett's parish.§

April 3, 1639, Gorges obtained a royal charter for the District of Maine and was invested with sole powers of governmental administration as far east as Sagadahoc River. Five

† Am. Ant. Col., 1867-130.
‡ 4 Mass. Hist. Col., 6-94.
§ Winthrop, 2-29.

months later, as proprietor of the realm, he issued a joint commission to Thomas Jocelyn, Richard Vines, Francis Champernoone, Henry Jocelyn, Richard Bonython, William Hook and Edward Godfrey to conduct local government under a special code of laws.

A fair estimate of the loss of political prestige which Gorges had sustained in this country prior to the issuance of his charter may be inferred from his own words to a friend in England: "Had I not obteyned the graunte I lately gott from his Majesty I should not have beene Mr of more than I ocupied wth my servants and those entrusted by me in that parte my house standes in." The date of this letter was January 28, following that of his charter.*

Thomas Jocelyn left Black Point for England before he could qualify as councilor for the District of Maine. Thomas Gorges, a cousin of the royal proprietor, who had been selected as the successor of William Gorges, was appointed to fill the vacancy.

When the new agent arrived "with other necessary servants" in the ship *Desire*, during the early summer of 1640, he secured for his residence the proprietor's house situated on the easterly side of York River at Point Christian. Although this dwelling had been occupied by his predecessor several years, and had been

POINT CHRISTIAN, YORK RIVER

* Me. Doc. in Eng. Arch., II

abandoned but recently, he found no other personal property on the premises "save an old pot, and a pair of cob irons and tongs."†

With the moral support of a larger part of the community Thomas Gorges, as deputy governor, assumed control of civil affairs. Left to his own inclinations at York, Burdett had opposed all attempts at reformation for a long time, but against his protestations the proprietary court was reorganized in the district and effectually curbed his sinister influence. His homestead and estate, which was composed largely of live stock, were transferred to his housekeeper, widow Ann Messant, who disposed of them in her own right long after the deposed clergyman had left the country. Burdett withdrew to Pemaquid in 1641, where he was living in a riotous manner.‡

The names of the heads of families known to have been living in York in 1640 were the following: John Alcock, Sampson Anger, John Baker, Bartholomew Barnard, Ralph Blaisdell, Thomas Bradbury, Arthur Bragdon, George Burdett, Richard Cornish, John and William Davis, William Dixon, Henry Donnell, Thomas Footman, William Freathy, Roger Garde, Edward Godfrey, Thomas Gorges, John Gouch, Philip Hatch, William Hook, Edward Johnson, Thomas Jones, Daniel and Robert Knight, Henry Lynn, George Puddington, George, John, Robert and William Rogers, Henry Simpson, John Smith, John and Nicholas Squire and Rowland Young.

Bradbury and Hook were dissatisfied with the religious and political situations at York, or Bristol as it was also known. They were not strict Royalists. Massachusetts ideals were more in accord with their ideas than the doctrine of the English Church. This made it uncomfortable for themselves and their colleagues who were stanch Episcopalians, if anything. Both withdrew that year to Salisbury. Jones was killed by an explosion on board the *Mary Rose* of Bristol while the vessel was lying in Boston Harbor.

Agamenticus was incorporated as a town by proprietary grant April 10, 1641. There was no highway from Kittery and during the month of incorporation John, son of Nathaniel Ward, the Massachusetts divine, who had been invited to supersede Burdett in York parish, was lost in Pascataqua woods while seeking his parish for the first time.

† Hubbard, 361; 4 Mass. Hist. Col., 7-332.
‡ York Deeds, 4-20; 3-116; 2-34.

The territory comprised in the new town was seven miles long and six wide. The half lying on the westerly side of Agamenticus River was held in trust by Sir Ferdinando Gorges for his minor son of the same name.

DIVISION OF LAND ON THE WEST BANK.

The territory between Brave Boat Harbor and Godfrey's Cove had been assigned to George Burdett, as minister of the parish, before 1639 and was transferred by him with his farmhouse and cattle, then in possession of John Alcock, to widow Ann Messant, to repay funds borrowed from her while she was his housekeeper.

The earliest inhabitant at the mouth of Agamenticus River was William Hilton, an original settler of New Plymouth, who came to York from Kittery Point after 1649, when the county highway was cut through the wilderness from his tavern to Rogers' Cove. His successor at the new location was Richard White who married the widow in 1655. A son William Hilton was an heir to his estate and sons-in-law secured later grants of land in the vicinity. The concession to James Wiggin by the town adjoined the farm of Burdett at Godfrey's Pond and the land of Arthur Beals situated at the mouth of the harbor was styled "Beals' Neck."

Above the Hilton home on the river was a deep indentation in the shore called Rogers' Cove on account of the proximity of the early residence of John Rogers, who had been named by Gorges as a member of his council in 1641. On the upper margin of this "cove of flats" was located a lot of ten acres which had been given Burdett in connection with his farm at Godfrey's Cove. The original concession had been twenty acres but the residue was laid out on Harker's and Stage islands near the cove. Ann Messant succeeded to the ownership of these tracts and Godfrey, who subsequently married her, took control.

The former island contains three acres and lies near the entrance of York Harbor. It was transferred to John Harker in 1647, to settle a controversy over the title to the house of Allen Yeo and company which had been erected there for fishing purposes. The head of the company, a resident of Boston, had died in debt to Godfrey, and John Batten, John Bolt, William James and William Widger were other creditors who attempted to recover wages for services performed on the island. Godfrey's first fishing operations appear to have been conducted on Stage Island where he maintained two houses in 1648. His wife disposed of this island with the premises at Rogers' Cove to Sampson Anger and Henry Donnell, fishermen, before 1659.

Above Rogers' Cove was situated Point Ingleby, which had been appropriated by an early colonist of that name. The grant had contained 100 acres, but had lapsed in 1643, when at his departure from the country Thomas Gorges confirmed the western bank of York River to the City of Gorgeana. The inland edge of this tract was defined as a line extending southerly from Sir Ferdinando Gorges' house at Point Christian to the pond near the dwelling once owned by Burdett at Godfrey's Cove, but then described as "Mr Edw: Godfrey his farme house."§

By reason of this special franchise the municipality later regranted to townsmen all of the territory from Rogers' Cove to Old Mill Creek and the distributees were Johnson Harmon (Rogers' Cove), William Hilton (Point Ingleby), Andrew Everett (Hilton's Cove, 1668), Thomas Donnell (1668), Arthur Bragdon (1669), Job Alcock (1678), Thomas Adams (1678), Henry Sayward (1666), Thomas Beeson, or Boston, and Matthew Young. The depth of some lots was 160 rods or back to Kittery Line.

The section assigned to Beeson was resurveyed to Edward Rishworth in 1687 and included twelve acres which had belonged to Richard (Rice) Howell in 1652. Above this tract was a house which had been built by some of the early carpenters. It stood on a lot adjoining the first mill ever built in York. The premises were conveyed by Bartholomew Barnard to Robert Knight in 1646. Subsequently they passed through the possession of Edward Rishworth and others to Thomas Trafton.*

Gorges' mill, the first in York and contemporaneous with that built by Mason at Great Works in South Berwick, was landed at Old Mill Creek in July, 1634. It was erected near the mouth soon after. A sketch including its site is recorded in York registry and discloses the proximity of Kittery Line at this point and a nearly straight stretch of river above the creek, early known as "Long Reach."†

§ York Deeds, 4-46.
* York Deeds, 3-30.
† York Deeds, 7-96.

YORK RIVER 137

Some of the first employes of the proprietor at Old Mill Creek, or Point Christian on the opposite shore, may be inferred from the list of plaintiffs in suits begun in 1647. Besides Robert Nanney, other claimants for unpaid wages were Bartholomew Barnard, who lived below the mill, and Robert Mills.

Above Eddy Point, which lies in the lower angle of Old Mill Creek and York River, no land was assigned by Vines except a few acres of marsh near the mill and a tract at the head of Long Reach in Scotland Parish. The latter was conveyed to Roger Garde March 25, 1639, and the former to Henry Norton before Vines left the country. These allotments may have been in payment for services rendered.

DIVISION OF LAND ON THE EAST BANK.

June 11, 1641, the eastern bank of York River had been apportioned as far upriver as Gorges, now known as Cider Mill Creek. The entire tract was three miles wide and extended inland for six miles. The final division, made the same year, mentioned only the dwellings of Henry Donnell, at Lobster Cove, Henry Lynn, on the south side of Gorges Creek, and the farmhouse of William Hook, in Scotland Parish.

At the date of division of the patent the following transfers of title had occurred:

Patentees December 1, 1631	Assignees March 2, 1631-2	Distributees November 11, 1641
Ferdinando Gorges.		Ferdinando Gorges.
Walter Norton.		Edward Godfrey.
Thomas Coppin.	Seth Bull.	Robert Thompson.
Samuel Maverick.		Samuel Maverick.
Thomas Graves.		Elias Maverick.
Ralph Glover.		Gyles Elbridge.
William Jeffrey.		William Jeffrey.
John Bursley.		John Bursley.
Joel Woolsley.	Dixie Bull.	Humphrey Hook.
Robert Norton.		William Hook.
Richard Norton.		Thomas Hook.
George Norton.	Matthew Bradley.	Lawrence Brindley.
Robert Rainsford.	John Bull.	William Pestor.‡

The outermost lot, situated on the eastern bank of Agamenticus River at York Harbor, was occupied by Nicholas Davis until

‡ Me. Doc. Hist., 4-421; Me. Hist. Col., 2-2, 327.

his death. The point lying east of the Davis homestead was acquired by John Alcock, who also died there and gave the premises the name of "Farmer Alcock's Neck." Adjoining this neck at Lobster Cove was the home and fishing establishment of Henry Donnell, who asserted that he had been a resident in this vicinity in 1631.

On the river above the Davis lot was a tract occupied about a year by George Newman, of Bristol, who conveyed it with the dwelling thereon to Samuel Maverick October 31, 1634. Two years later the premises were bought by William Dixon, a servant whose passage had been paid by John Winthrop.§

The Dixon homestead lay opposite Harker's Island and Rogers' Cove. Before 1650 small houselots had been transferred from it to Richard Burgess, Sampson Anger, Richard Cadogan and George Parker. The combined area of the last three lots, which were situated in the southerly angle between the river and Meeting-House, now known as Barrell's Creek, was only five acres.*

Above the creek was Point Bollogue which was assigned to Edward Godfrey in the partition of 1641, although he had occupied it for several years. It was known as his first division and extended inland about half a mile from Henry Norton's dwelling, which stood in Hook's division, to Gorges Creek. Included in this division were the house and lot of Henry Lynn, acquired from Richard Ormsby and situated by the river on the south side of the creek.

Godfrey reserved about thirty acres at the point where his house was located, but disposed of the residue along the river to Andrew Everett and Edward Johnson, who were abuttors of Henry Norton, John Parker and Philip Adams on the east. Johnson, who previously had lived near Rogers' Cove, built a dwelling on his lot and sold the premises to Thomas, son of Henry Donnell. The grantee, like other residents of the eastern bank, improved land on the opposite side of the river which had been granted by townsmen.

Above Gorges Creek stood the house of Sir Ferdinando Gorges. Later, the locality was styled Gorges Point and Gorges Neck, but had been known to the proprietor himself as Point

§ York Deeds, 8-209.
* York Deeds, 5-96; 6-110, 123.

Christian. The buildings with about twelve acres of cleared land were conveyed to Robert Nanney in 1647, to satisfy an execution based upon a debt due him from Gorges. The premises were improved by Edward Rishworth as agent for widow Catherine Nanney until 1679, when litigation over the title resulted in an agreement by the contending parties for Governor Thomas Danforth to convey them to Jeremiah Moulton and divide the proceeds.†

On the eastern boundary of Gorges' house lot and adjoining the creek was a point of land which at an early period had been claimed by John Davis, "the smith." It is evident that this site was purchased by Ellingham and Gale about 1650, when they also acquired fifty acres from Godfrey on the lower side of the creek. The latter tract formed a part of the proprietor's first division. At any rate, the partners began construction on the point at that time and Henry Sayward had completed three mills there a few years later.

In 1653, the entire mill property had been secured by Rishworth and Thomas Clark, of Boston, in shares. In consideration of certain timber concessions from the town the new owners guaranteed operation of saw and grist mills with special privileges for citizens. Gorges Creek lies opposite Old Mill Creek and soon acquired the name of New Mill Creek.‡

The next tributary on the eastern side of York River above the new mills was Bass Creek, on the southerly bank of which land was granted to Arthur Bragdon by Maverick and Jeffrey July 11, 1637. On the upper side of this stream was a lot given to Henry Simpson by William Hook in 1639. The former had married the only daughter and the latter the widow of Walter Norton, the patentee, and the conveyance was made in settlement of the interest of Simpson's wife in her father's estate.§

Above Simpson's land was a tract conveyed to Roger Garde by Maverick and Jeffrey. It was located in Scotland Parish and surveyed July 30, 1637, by William Hook. Garde built a dwelling on the premises within two years. Only the farmhouse of Hook, farther inland, and that of Bragdon, below, were mentioned in that period.*

† York Deeds, 6-27 ; 4-43.
‡ York Deeds, 3-120 ; 4-154.
§ York Deeds, 10-173 ; 7-83 ; 6-74.
* York Deeds, 1-119.

In 1641, the present highway from York Harbor to Point Christian had been completed. This road passed through the plantation at "Scituate Fields," now known as York Village. Between this way and the eastern bank of Meeting-House Creek, within the division of William Hook, stood the homesteads of George Puddington (1640), Ralph Blaisdell (1640) and part of that of Henry Norton, whose house stood on the farther side of the creek. In 1642, Blaisdell, who had removed to Salisbury, sold his farm to Robert Knight. Norton's lot, which adjoined it on the northwest side, extended up the creek as far as the crossroad leading from the old parish cemetery in York Village to the meeting-house. The first church, built in 1636, stood in the lower angle of the creek and highway.

Early settlers who bought lots of Godfrey on the eastern side of Scituate path were Joseph Jenks, Abraham Preble, Thomas Chambers, Richard Banks, John Twisden and Henry Simpson, in the order named. All of these men except the last removed thither from their original location in Scituate, Massachusetts.

INCORPORATION OF GORGEANA.

It had been the ambition of Gorges, like that of Levett, to found the first city in New England, and the advancement of Agamenticus was encouraged with that end in view. Although its population was not much greater than that of Kittery, it was not so widely scattered and comprised a single parish. Its inhabitants were fishermen, planters and mechanics of means, some of whom were employed by the patentees and lived in large households.

March 1, 1641-2, Agamenticus was incorporated a city and named Gorgeana in honor of its patron. The first mayor, described as a tailor, was Roger Garde who could have been styled, more accurately, a linen draper. The charter directed his election. There is no evidence that he assumed the position.

May 10, 1643, when Massachusetts and New Hampshire plantations had combined for government, a disparaging allusion to the new municipality was made in these words: "Those of Sir Ferdinando Gorge his province, beyond Pascataquack, were not received nor called into the confederation because they ran a different course from us both in their ministry and civil administration; for they had lately made Acomenticus (a poor village) a corporation and had made a taylor their mayor, and had entertained one Hull, an excommunicated person and very contentious for their minister." Joseph Hull had become pastor of the new city that year.†

The new metropolis did not prosper. Hull left the parish in 1645. It soon lost many influential citizens, including Garde, Lynn, Puddington and Simpson, all of whom died within the first four years. Thomas Gorges had returned to England and Richard Ormsby removed to Boston. Such defections were chiefly responsible for the failure of Gorges to develop Gorgeana into the leading commercial and industrial center of the North.

In 1648, Nathaniel Norcross assumed the spiritual direction of the parish, but he did not remain long in the service, either because of general dissatisfaction with the prospect or on account of more alluring proposals from western towns.

In the meantime, Gorgeana had assumed the name of Bristol, from the similarity in its form of government to that of the English municipality and because that English city was principal residence of its patrons, but rising feelings of unrest soon paved the way for Massachusetts intervention. November 22, 1652, its inhabitants, some willingly and some by coercion, signed the official act of submission to the Bay Colony.‡

YORK
1653

Possibly, at that juncture, a change of government may have been in the interest of all concerned.

† Winthrop, 2-100.
‡ Mass. Col. Rec., 4-119.

Pioneers

ALCOCK, JOHN, lived in the house of George Burdett as his farm manager, 1640; removed to the east side of York River; died 1671-5; widow Elizabeth; children Elizabeth (Banks), Hannah (Snell), Job, born 1638, John, Joseph, born 1634, Lydia (Dummer), Mary (Twisden), born 1632, Samuel and Sarah (Giddings, Herrick).

BAKER, JOHN, planter at Boston, 1630; removed to Newbury and thence to York, 1639; Cape Porpoise, 1653; wife Rebecca; child Sarah (Nason), born 1640.

BANKS, RICHARD, planter from Scituate, 1640-1643; bought land from Thomas Gorges at Yerk before 1643; died 1692; widow Elizabeth Alcock; sons John and Joseph.

BARNARD, BARTHOLOMEW, carpenter at Old Mill Creek, 1636-1647; Boston, 1651; married Jane Loxton, a widow, 1664; died 1672; children, by former wife, Matthew and Richard.

BARRETT, JOHN, planter, 1642; living at Wells with wife Mary, daughter of Edmund Littlefield, 1647; bought his house of Edward Rishworth, who removed to York; died 1662; widow, aged 45, and son John survived.

BARTON, EDWARD, planter at Salem, 1639; Marblehead, 1643; York, 1650; married Mary, daughter of Thomas Crockett; fisherman at Exeter, 1657; Cape Porpoise, where he died, 1671; children probably Benjamin and Edward, of Cape Newagen.

BLAISDELL, RALPH, tailor at York, 1637; removed to Salisbury, 1642; Lynn, 1649; died 1651; widow Elizabeth; children (the last two born in Salisbury): Henry, born 1632, Sarah, Mary (Stowers, Sterling), born March 5, 1641-2, and Ralph.

BRADBURY, THOMAS, born at Wicken Bonant, England, 1611; steward for Gorges at York, 1634-6; married Mary Perkins, of Ipswich, and removed to Salisbury; associate Massachusetts justice; died March 16, 1694-5; widow Mary; children, born at Salisbury, Wymond, April 1, 1637, Judith (Moody), October 2, 1638, Thomas, January 28, 1640-1, Mary (Stanyan), March 17, 1642-3, Jane (True), May 11, 1645, Jacob, June 17, 1647, William, September 15, 1649, Elizabeth (Buss), November 7, 1651, John, April 20, 1654, Ann, April 16, 1656, and Jabez, June 27, 1658.

BRAGDON, ARTHUR, born 1598; planter at York, 1636; died 1678; widow Mary; child Arthur.

BULL, DIXIE, merchant of London; merchant, trading eastward from Dorchester, 1632; became a pirate, robbed Pemaquid and escaped to England late in the year by way of the French settlements at Port Latour.

BURDETT, GEORGE, clergyman at Salem, 1634; Dover, 1638; York, 1639; returned to England from Pemaquid, 1641.

BURGESS, RICHARD, planter at York Harbor, 1640-3; Scituate, 1646; York, 1651; in the employment of John Davis, 1659; died after 1674, probably unmarried.

CHAMBERS, THOMAS, planter at Scituate, 1638; land at York, 1640.

CHAPMAN, FLORENCE, described as "late of Agamenticus" August 23, 1647.

COLLINS, ROBERT, laborer, York, 1647-1650; employe of John Alcock; Salem, 1651; Ipswich, 1660; Haverhill, 1679; died June 17, 1688; widow Hester (Fowler); children Philip, Hester, born April 18, 1658, Robert, born March 15, 1659-60, Nathaniel, born June 18, 1662, Elizabeth, born January 16, 1665.

CORNISH, RICHARD, laborer at Dorchester, 1640; servant of George Burdett at York that year; wife Catherine executed for his murder, at York, 1644.

CURTIS, THOMAS, planter at Scituate, 1632; York, 1640-3; bought land of Thomas Gorges; died 1684-1704; children Abigail, Ann, Benjamin, Dodivah, Elizabeth, born 1639, Hannah (Jenkins), Job, Joseph, born 1653, Lydia, Samuel, born at Scituate, 1659, Sarah, Rebecca and Thomas.

DAVIS, JOHN, born 1605; blacksmith at York, 1642; Winter Harbor, 1654; wife Catherine; lived on Batson's Neck at Cape Porpoise at the time of First Indian War; described in deeds as "Doctor John"; sold land at York, 1699; died in Portsmouth; son John, born 1627.

DAVIS, JOHN, born 1619; planter at Ipswich, 1639-1651; married Mary Puddington at York, 1649; York, 1652; deputy governor of Maine, 1681; died 1691; widow Mary; children Mary (Weare) and Sarah (Penwell).

DAVIS, NICHOLAS, born 1595; came with wife Sarah from Stephney Parish, England, in the "Planter," March 22, 1634-5; Woburn, 1640; York, 1650; died 1667-1670, at York Harbor; first wife died, 1643; survived by widow Elizabeth; daughter Mary married George Dod, of Boston; no other issue.

DAVIS, WILLIAM, servant of Thomas Gorges, 1640-3; may have been related to John or George, of Sheepscot; trader at Nequasseag, 1654; died 1660; widow Margaret, married Richard Potts and sold the estate at Kennebec, 1661.

DIXON, WILLIAM, cooper and servant of John Winthrop, who paid his passage; York, 1636; died 1666; widow Joan; children Anna (Brawn), James and Susanna (Frost).

DONNELL, HENRY, born 1602, fisherman; York, 1631; occupied Jewell's Island; died 1680; widow Frances, daughter of John Gouch, of York; children Henry, Joseph, Margaret, Samuel, born 1645, Sarah and Thomas.

DUTCH, OSMOND, mariner of Bridport, England; Dorchester, 1632; York, probably with Walter Norton, 1633; later, employed by William Hook, was found guilty of "undutifull departure from his service with a boat"; fishing partner with Thomas Millard and Maurice Thompson at Cape Ann, 1639; wife Grace; died 1684, aged 100 years; children Robert, born 1621, Esther, born 1639, John, born 1646, Hezekiah, born March 29, 1647, and Mary, born 1649.

EDGE, ROBERT, born 1610; planter, in the "Hopewell," 1635; York, 1650; wives Eleanor and Florence.

EMERSON, JOSEPH, clergyman; removed from Ipswich to York. 1648; Wells, 1653; married Elizabeth, daughter of Edward Bunkley, December 7, 1665, and removed to Mendon; died at Concord January 3, 1680; widow married John Brown, of Reading; children Edward, Joseph and Peter.

EVERETT, ANDREW, planter, 1646; died 1662; widow Barbara; son Job.

FOOTMAN, THOMAS, planter at York, 1640-8; Durham, 1648; died 1667; widow Catherine married William Durgin; children John and Thomas.

GARDE, ROGER, planter at York, 1637; died 1645, while first magistrate and registrar for York County; brother John of Boston; wife in England.

GORGES, THOMAS, cousin of Sir Ferdinando, at York, 1640-3; died at Heavitree, England, October 17, 1660; child Thomas.

GORGES, WILLIAM, nephew of Sir Ferdinando, at York, 1636-8; steward for young Ferdinando, then but four years old.

GOUCH, JOHN, planter, 1640; Cape Neddock, 1644; Wells, 1653; died 1667; widow Ruth; children Elizabeth (Austin), Frances (Donnell), James, John and Mary (Weare).

HARKER, JOHN, at Plymouth, 1637-1640; married Dorothy, widow of Robert Mills; bought house of Allen Yeo on Stage Island in York River, 1647; house claimed by Godfrey, 1648; living at York, 1674; child John.

HOOK, WILLIAM, son of Humphrey, mayor of Bristol, England, came to York by way of Port Latour in May, 1633; removed to Salisbury June 1, 1640; died 1653; widow Eleanor, previously widow of Walter Norton, proprietor of York; children William, Humphrey and Jacob, born September 15, 1640.

HOWELL, RICE, land owner at Gorgeana; sold lot on the south side of Agamenticus River to Abraham Preble February 17, 1651-2; Dover, 1653-7.

HULL, JOSEPH, born 1595; clergyman, came with his wife Agnes from Weymouth, England, March 20, 1634-5; Yarmouth, 1641; York, 1643; died November 19, 1665; children Benjamin, Dorothy, Elizabeth (Hurd), Grissel, Joanna (Bursley), Joseph, Naomi, born 1640, Reuben, Ruth, Temperance and Tristram.

HUNTER, LEONARD, land owner at York, 1641.

INGLEBY, JOHN, sawyer sent to York by Gorges, 1634; granted "Point Ingleby" and marsh on the south side of York River; admitted to the church at Boston, unmarried, November 6, 1641; wife Ruth; the eldest of three sons christened John was born in Boston April 30, 1649; others born there were William, October 7, 1655, Ebenezer, December 13, 1656, and Peter, March 8, 1658-9.

JENKS, JOSEPH, planter at Gloucester, land owner at York, 1642; may have married Hannah, daughter of Thomas Curtis.

JOHNSON, EDWARD, born 1593; planter and magistrate with Weston's Colony at Wessaguscus, 1622; Pascataqua, 1623; York, 1636; died, 1683; widow Priscilla, born 1617; children Benjamin, Deborah and Harmon.

JONES, THOMAS, tailor taxed for York meeting-house, 1636; killed in Boston Harbor July 27, 1640, by the explosion of the "Mary Rose"; probably Thomas of York, 1647-1651, was a son.

JONES, WILLIAM, tailor, from Canterbury, England; Bloody Point, 1640; Dover, 1642; York, 1644; ordered to return to his wife in England.

KNIGHT, ROBERT, born 1596; came to York by way of Pemaquid, 1633; planter at Mill Creek on the west side, but later lived on the east side of York River; died in Boston, 1676; children Daniel and Margaret (Redman), servants of Thomas Gorges, 1640-3, Joanna (Young) and Richard, of Boston.

MAVERICK, SAMUEL, merchant of Charlestown and Noddle's Island; bought the house of George Newman at York, 1634; wife Amias Cole (Thompson); sold the house at York to William Dixon.

NEWMAN, GEORGE, came to York with William Hook, 1633, by way of Pemaquid; resident of Pemaquid, 1640; died 1651.

NORCROSS, NATHANIEL, son of Jeremiah, born in London; degree at Cambridge, 1636; clergyman at Salem, 1639; Watertown, 1643; Exeter, 1646; York, 1648; returned to England, 1650; died at St. Dunstan's August 10, 1662; widow Mary.

NORTON, HENRY, planter at Boston, 1635; York, 1642-1652; died 1657-9; widow Margaret; children Elizabeth (Stover) and George.

NORTON, WALTER, planter at Charlestown, 1630-1; patentee of York, 1631; living at York, 1633; killed by Indians that year in Connecticut River; widow Eleanor married William Hook; only daughter Jane married Henry Simpson and Nicholas Bond, of York.

ORMSBY, RICHARD, born 1607; planter at York June 28, 1641; wife Sarah; Salisbury, 1645; died at Rehoboth June 30, 1664; children (the last two born in Salisbury) John, Thomas, born November 11, 1645, Jacob, born March 6, 1647-8.

PARKER, GEORGE, came from Marblehead to York, 1648; died 1663; widow Hannah; children John, born 1645, and a daughter who married Peter Bass.

PIERCE, JOHN, mariner of London and Wapping, who removed from Noddle's to Champernoone's Island, 1648; fisherman who bought Barnard's land at Mill Creek from Rishworth, 1656; wife Eleanor; estate administered, 1697; children Jane (Bracey), Joseph, Mary (McIntire) and Sarah (Jones, Mattoon).

POWELL, MICHAEL, fisherman at Hingham, 1641; Salisbury, 1647; York, 1649; had had early business relations with Humphrey Hook, of Bristol; wife Abigail; children, born in Hingham, Elizabeth, June 10, 1641, Dorothy, July 2, 1643, Michael, October 12, 1645, and Elizabeth and Margaret, January 14, 1648-9.

PREBLE, ABRAHAM, planter at Scituate, 1639; married there Judith Tilden; York, 1642; deceased 1663; children Abraham, born at Scituate, 1642; Rachel, born 1643, Joseph, Stephen, Nathaniel, born 1648, John, Benjamin, Sarah and Mary.

PUDDINGTON, GEORGE, son of Robert and Ann, of Tiverton, England, and brother of Robert, of Pascataqua; Tiverton, 1631; planter at York, 1640; died 1647; widow Mary married John Davis, of York, 1649; children Elias, Frances, John, born 1636, Mary and Rebecca.

RAYNES (Rane), FRANCIS, agent for Thomas Gorges at York, 1643; merchant at Kittery, 1645; Dover, 1649; York, 1652; died 1693-1706; widow Eleanor; children Francis, John, Nathan, Nathaniel and four daughters, who married Diamond, Mathews, Mendum and Woodman.

ROGERS, CHRISTOPHER, servant of Sir Ferdinando Gorges; given land at York by Thomas Gorges, 1640-3; living there 1645.

ROGERS, JOHN, born 1613; planter at York, 1640; named as alderman in York town charter, 1641.

SAYWARD, HENRY, came from England, 1637; mill-contractor at Hampton, 1642; Portsmouth, 1650; York, 1658; died 1679; mills at York, Cape Porpoise and Yarmouth; widow Mary; children Hannah (Preble), James, born 1667, John, Jonathan, Mary (Young, Bray) and Sarah.

SIMPSON, HENRY, planter, 1638; married Jane, only daughter of Walter Norton; died 1647; widow married Nicholas Bond; only child Henry, born 1644.

SMITH, JOHN, born 1612; miller, who arrived at Boston with the colonists of the Plough Company, May 26, 1632; apprenticed to John Wilson for five years; servant of John Alcock at York, 1640; married Joanna Wannerton and removed to Casco Mill, 1646; Cape Neddock, 1652-1685; children John and a daughter who married John Jackson.

SQUIRE, JOHN, planter at York, 1640-2; either he or Nicholas appears to have married a daughter of Benjamin Barnard and left a son Barnard Squire, born 1631 and resident later at Berwick, where he had land granted in 1652.

SQUIRE, NICHOLAS, planter at York, 1640-2.

STOVER, SYLVESTER, fisherman at Cape Neddock, 1649; died 1687-1690; widow Elizabeth, daughter of Henry Norton; children Dependence, Elizabeth (Hunnewell), George, John, born 1653, and Josiah.

TWISDEN, JOHN, born 1610; planter at Scituate, 1638-1640; York, 1640-8; died 1680; widow Susanna; children John, born 1634, and Samuel.

WARD, JOHN, son of Nathaniel, born in Haverhill, England, November 5, 1606; clergyman, receiving degrees at Cambridge, 1626, 1630; Ipswich, 1639; York, 1641; Haverhill, 1641; wife Alice Edmunds; died December 27, 1693; children Elizabeth, born April 1, 1647, Mary, born June 24, 1649.

YOUNG, ROWLAND, planter at York, 1637; married Joanna, daughter of Robert Knight; died 1685; children Mary (Moulton), Robert, Rowland, born 1648, and Samuel.

CAPE NEDDOCK RIVER

This river is situated about two miles east of York River. The meaning of its Indian name is lost.

May 4, 1637-8, Edward Godfrey with Gyles Elbridge and Humphrey, Thomas and William Hook, all of Bristol, England, procured from the Council of Plymouth a grant of 1500 acres on both sides of the stream. This concession was obtained by Godfrey during the winter following his citation by George Cleave before the Court of Star Chamber in London. In 1641, this tract was bounded easterly by another of 5000 acres which had been conferred upon Thomas Gorges.*

The western bank offered a sheltered haven for fishing boats both within the river and at Short Sands. William Ham and John Lander were the first fishermen to utilize the latter location. After the removal of these men to Pascataqua the place was appropriated by John Ball, Michael Powell, Sylvester Stover and Thomas Way, who formed a partnership for fishing and secured title from the proprietors July 3, 1649.

Weare Point, on the eastern shore, was purchased from William Hook October 18, 1644, by John Gouch and his brother-in-law Peter Weare, both of "Gorgeana," who subsequently made the premises their homestead.

Fishermen who live at Cape Neddock village and "porgy trawlers" from Gloucester and the westward still continue to seine for herring and ground fish near the mouth of this river. The locality is noted as a favorite summer resort.

* York Deeds, 8-120, 122.

OGUNQUIT RIVER

This river, sometimes called Negunquit and situated about four miles east of Cape Neddock River, formed the original boundary between Agamenticus and Wells. In 1637, adherents of Ann Hutchinson were disarmed by the Massachusetts authorities on account of their Antinomian tendencies and withdrew to Exeter, where they began a distinct settlement under direction of John Wheelwright. The commonwealth, however, was not satisfied with this arrangement, in spite of the fact that it had established its own bound house at Hampton the year before the religious controversy had arisen; under pretext of patent right, it absorbed New Hampshire June 2, 1641, and less than four months later constrained the harassed colonists at Exeter to seek a new asylum beyond the Pascataqua, where sentiment was favorable to the Church of England and the Gorges administration was less obtrusive.

Between Cape Neddock and Cape Porpoise was a large, unsettled district, which offered good advantages for agriculture and fishing, and there the Wheelwright converts concluded to found their parish. With this object in view, the first requisition for Maine lands was directed to Thomas Gorges, then deputy governor of the province, September 27, 1641, by Edward Hutchinson, Nicholas Needham and Wheelwright, all of Exeter.

While it was generally supposed that John Stratton, the early patentee of Cape Porpoise, might claim some interest in the territory under consideration, the deputy governor was receptive. March 4, 1641-2, he secured from Sir Ferdinando Gorges a personal concession of 5000 acres situated on the western bank of Ogunquit River; this grant may be regarded as an emolument of office, and the only recorded conveyance of any part of it was that of 200 acres to Edmund Littlefield and John Wadley on the west side of "Obumkegg" River November 20, 1645.*

From the unappropriated land on the eastern bank of Ogunquit River he assigned to the petitioners an extensive tract April 17, 1643. Three months later the deputy governor delegated to

* York Deeds, 1-2, 13.

Henry Boade, Edward Rishworth and Wheelwright full authority to allot homesteads at Wells, where settlement had already begun on the eastern side of Ogunquit River.†

Wheelwright selected his farm on Ogunquit Neck, and many years later the widow of John Barrett, who was a daughter of Edmund Littlefield, testified to the location of ancient fences which her husband had constructed about the Wheelwright homestead as early as 1647.‡

That year Wheelwright, a clergyman of more than ordinary ability and rectitude, removed to Hampton, where he had been offered a pastorate. Later, he returned to England and his Maine plantation drifted under the expanding influence, of the Massachusetts Government. The act of submission was executed by residents of Wells July 4, 1653.§

Thomas Gorges died in England in 1660. By the terms of his will the remnant of his land at Ogunquit descended to his son Thomas, who made his residence in Wells and, in subsequent attempts to regain possession of his patrimony, became involved in much unsatisfactory and expensive litigation.

† York Deeds, 1-28 ; 1-2, 5, 9 : Bell's Wheelwright. 45.
‡ York Deeds, 2-102.
§ Mass. Col. Rec., 3-409.

WELLS RIVER

This estuary which ebbs and flows for a long distance in an easterly direction behind Wells Beach and enters the sea about five miles from the mouth of the Ogunquit, is supplied with fresh water by a large inland brook. While the locality was attractive, early settlement was deferred because the avenue of approach from the sea to the mainland was not convenient.

At the first fall above the point where the river enters the salt marshes Edmund Littlefield and his elder son Francis, who were commorant in Exeter in 1639, built a sawmill and acquired title to the premises situated on both sides of the stream from Sir Ferdinando, through his agent Thomas Gorges July 14, 1643, on the eve of the latter's departure for England. The Indian name for that part of the river was Webhannet.*

The first planters in Wells, also known as Preston, lived upon the line of the present state highway in the following order from west to east: Edmund and Francis Littlefield, Ezekiel Knight, George Haborne, Edward Rishworth, William Wentworth, William Wardell, John Wadley and John Gouch. Between Wardell's lot and that of Wadley was a tract of land reserved by the town for municipal purposes.

There were also a few settlers about Drake's Island, which was named after Thomas Drake. October 21, 1645, Yorkshire Court granted Stephen Batson ten acres of marsh on the western end, bounded by the sea and Wells River. John Cross lived on the island.†

Other pioneers who did not retain their real estate in Wells were William Cole, Godfrey Dearborn and Philemon Pormort. The last person was an educated Englishman, whose passage was paid by the town in consideration of his services as a teacher.

Parts of the district are still occupied by lineal descendants bearing the same names as their pioneer ancestors, but none of the posterity of Dearborn, Haborne, Rishworth or Wardell is now represented in that vicinity.

* York Deeds, 1-2, 10, 11.
† York Deeds, 1-2, 13.

On account of its beaches, sand dunes, winding river and open marshes, Wells is destined to become a leading Maine summer resort.

Pioneers

AUSTIN, SAMUEL, innkeeper at Dover, 1649; sold estate and removed to Wells, 1650, when he married Elizabeth, daughter of John Gouch; after the death of his first wife he married Sarah, daughter of Edward Starbuck and widow of William Storer, of Dover; her children acquired the Storer garrison at Wells; the pioneer married again Sarah Bosworth, of Hull; Charlestown, 1678-1700; no known issue.

CROSS, JOHN, born 1584; original settler at Hampton October 14, 1638; Exeter, 1639; Dover, 1640; Preston, 1643; killed by Indians at Wells, 1675; widow Frances; children John, Joseph and Rebecca (Backus).

DRAKE, THOMAS, born 1629; Wells, 1652; Westcustego, 1664; no family record; deceased in 1678.

HABORNE, GEORGE, born 1592, glover; emigrated from Stepney and sailed from London in the "Abigail," 1635; Exeter, 1639; Wells, 1643-1650; removed to Hampton and died, 1654; widow Susanna, born 1589, married Thomas Leader, of Boston; children Rebecca, born 1625, and Anne, born 1631.

KNIGHT, EZEKIEL, planter at Ogunquit with wife Ann, 1643; sold house there, 1645; married Mary, widow of Valentine Hill, after 1662; died 1687; children Ezekiel and Elizabeth (Wentworth).

LITTLEFIELD, EDMUND, arrived with his family in the "Bevis," 1638; planter at Exeter, 1639; Webhannet, 1643; died December 11, 1661; widow Annis; children Anthony, Elizabeth (Wakefield), Francis, born 1619, Francis, the younger, Hannah (Cloyce), John, Mary (Barrett, Page, Ladbrook), born 1617, and Thomas.

PORMORT, PHILEMON, married at Alford, England, October 11, 1627, Susanna, daughter of William Bellingham; teacher at Boston, 1634; wife died December 29, 1642; he removed to Preston, 1649; wife Elizabeth, 1656; Boston, 1679; children, born in various places, Elias, Elizabeth (Norden), Lazarus, February 28, 1635-6, Anna, April 5, 1638, Pedajah, June 3, 1640, Bathsheba, 1647, and Martha, June 16, 1653.

RISHWORTH, EDWARD, of Lincoln, England, born 1617; attorney at Exeter, 1639; married Susanna, daughter of John Wheelwright; Preston, 1643; York. 1646; died 1690; children Edward and Mary (Sayward, Plaisted), born at York, January 8, 1660.

SANDERS, JOHN, planter at Ipswich, 1635; Hampton, 1639; Wells, 1643-5; Cape Porpoise, 1653; died 1670; widow Ann; children Elizabeth, Goodwin, John, Sarah (Bush) and Thomas.

SPENCER, JOHN, son of Thomas and Penelope (Jernegan), of Kingston-on-Thames; legatee of his uncle John Spencer, of Newbury, 1637; juror at Wells, 1646; sister married John Treworthy; died in Jamaica, 1652-6; estate administered by uncle, Daniel Pierce.

THING, JONATHAN, born 1621; carpenter at Ipswich, 1645; Preston, 1647; Hampton, 1650; died 1674; widow Joanna; children Elizabeth, Jonathan, Mary and Samuel.

WAKEFIELD, JOHN, planter at Salem, 1637; New Plymouth, 1640; Preston, 1648; Drake's Island. 1652; removed to Scarborough; died February 15, 1674-5; widow Elizabeth, daughter of Edmund Littlefield; children Henry, James, John, Catherine (Nanney), Mary (Frost) and William.

WARDELL, WILLIAM, planter at Boston, 1634; disarmed, 1637; Exeter, 1639; Preston, 1649-1656; wives Alice, Leah and Elizabeth Jellet, to whom he was married December 5, 1656; children, born in Boston, Meribah, May 14, 1637, Usal, April 7, 1639, Elihu, November, 1642, Mary, April 5, 1644, Leah, December 7, 1646, and Abigail, April 24, 1660.

WENTWORTH, WILLIAM, born 1616; planter at Exeter, 1639; Preston, 1645; Dover, 1650; married Elizabeth Canney; died March 15, 1696-7; widow Elizabeth Knight; children Benjamin, Elizabeth (Sharp, Tozer), born 1653, Ephraim, Ezekiel, Gershom, John, Paul, Samuel, born 1641, Sarah (Barnard), Sylvanus and Timothy.

WHEELWRIGHT, JOHN, born 1599; clergyman, graduated from Cambridge College, 1618; married November 18, 1621, Mary, daughter of Thomas Storre, of Bilsby, England; arrived at Boston May 26, 1636; Exeter, 1639; Ogunquit, 1643; Hampton, 1647; England, 1656; died at Salisbury November 15, 1679; widow Susanna, sister of Edward Hutchinson; children Catherine (Nanney), born 1629, Elizabeth (Parsons), Hannah (Checkley), John, Mary (Lyde, Atkinson), Rebecca (Maverick, Bradbury), Samuel, born 1638, Sarah (Crisp), Susanna (Rishworth) and Thomas.

WHITE, JOHN, laborer, arrived 1635; Wells, as employe of John Richards, 1643; Preston, 1645-1653.

MARYLAND RIVER

This stream still called Little River, but better known by its tributaries, Maryland River and Branch Brook, is situated nearly in the coastal center of the town of Wells, which was first called Preston. The stream enters the sea about one mile east of Wells River. Its Indian name was Neapskessett.

April 1, 1639, Richard Vines gave John Wadley, of Saco, permission to select a homestead anywhere along its borders, since the region was then an unbroken wilderness.*

Such a concession may have implied that the recipient was either a friend, or a creditor, of the Steward General.

The first permanent settler on the western bank was Henry Boade, who came thither with Wadley from Saco and settled at the mouth of the river. In 1648, he assured Governor Winthrop of his legal status and that of other early residents in Stratton's Plantation in these words: "We were sett into our possessions first by Mr Craddock's agent who bought ye pattent of Stratten, secondly by Mr Thomas Gorges." This agent of Cradock was either Thomas Mayhew or John Jolliff. This farm became the property of William Symonds, of Ipswich.†

Wadley soon claimed a large area in the heart of the town and was not disturbed in his pretensions until 1647, when Robert Booth, as employe of George Cleave, undertook to define the western boundary of Lygonia. Cleave in turn was agent for Rigby who had acquired the rights of two of the original members of the Plough Patent four years before.

Henry Boade, who was particularly interested in the issue, since he preferred the political supremacy of Massachusetts to that of the English nobleman, advised Winthrop concerning the results attained by Booth: "He measured and came short of our towne 3 miles; there was one told him he would give him a quart of sakk to measure in such a man John Wadloe who dwelleth in ye middell part of our towne; he goeth back againe & he reacheth all our towne only 2 houses."‡

* York Deeds, 1-2. 11.
† York Deeds, 1-84.
‡ Mass. Hist. Proc., 22-157.

The first survey was made in 1647 and Cleave began to assign lands that year. The second measurements were made during the following summer. Wadley, however, was not satisfied with the encroachments and sought a new title from the natives with whom he was on friendly terms. October 18, 1649, he succeeded in securing a deed of the entire town of Wells, then styled Preston, from Chabinock, an Indian proprietor. This sagamore's name meant "Squirrel" in his own language, and the size of the tract conveyed, which extended from Ogunquit to Kennebunk River, must have afforded exercise for some of his accredited attributes. The next year Wadley disposed of his interest in all of the territory west of the Neapskessett River to his son Robert, but continued to occupy the premises during his lifetime.§

Between this river and the Mousam was a section bought by John Sanders, of Hampton, from Thomas Gorges in 1643, on the same day the Littlefields purchased their properties at Webhannet.*

In 1660, the land which had been occupied by Sanders for many years was referred to by Wadley, in a deed to Daniel Epps, of Ipswich, as "the towne."†

§ York Deeds, 3-65.
* York Deeds, 1-2, 12 ; 1-142.
† York Deeds, 1-126.

CAPE PORPOISE RIVER

Although no settlement was in existence at Cape Porpoise when Christopher Levett "coasted" from Pascataqua to Cape Newagen in 1623, the name of that headland had been known by English navigators before the issuance of the Simancas map in 1610. Sagadahoc colonists, who had spent a night at Cape Elizabeth, also visited the locality of Cape Porpoise.

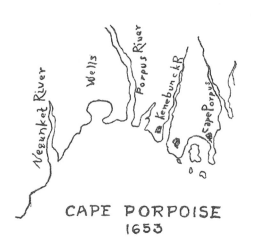

CAPE PORPOISE 1653

The first proprietor of Cape Porpoise was John Stratton, of Shotley, England, who was the son of John and Ann (Dearhaugh) Stratton, born in England in 1606.

After his father's death and the settlement of the paternal estate the son left England for America. As he was afterwards associated with Matthew Cradock in a business way in Massachusetts, it is probable that he landed at Salem with John Endicott September 6, 1628. For several years he was engaged in stock raising—presumably for Cradock who had a ranch at Medford. According to Winthrop cattle and kettles were then mediums of exchange.*

It would appear that he returned to England with Isaac Allerton before November 16, 1631, in the *White Angel* which docked at Bristol. December 2, after some solicitation by Allerton and possibly by Vines, he secured from the Council of Plymouth a grant of 2000 acres of land lying at Cape Porpoise.

* Mass. Hist. Proc., 5-126.

As a consideration for this concession in Maine, it was recited that Stratton had resided in New England for three years previous to its issuance and had expended 1000 pounds sterling in transporting cattle and providing attendants to manage them. Winthrop had secured beef from a London dealer of same name. Since no cattle had been imported into Maine before 1633, his operations must have been conducted elsewhere.†

For more than a month after he had obtained his grant of Cape Porpoise Stratton and Ralph Fogg were engaged in an attempt to audit Allerton's accounts with the London partners and the Colony of New Plymouth.‡

From other testimony of Stratton it appeared that he returned to Massachusetts in the *White Angel* with Allerton in the spring of 1632 and transshipped for the Eastward.

In a subsequent deposition, taken at Salem in 1640, the following paragraph relating to the incident was preserved: "John Stratton of Salem in New England gent aged about 34 years sworne saith that his mother Mris Anne Stratton in or about the moneth of December in the yeare of our Lord 1631 delivered unto this deponent at Dedham in Essex in the presence of Ralfe Fogge and this deponents sister Elizabeth Thorndike" two specialties and that "he lost the said specialtyes wth other writings & goods by the casting away of a boate at Cape Porpis in America about ten yeares since."§

It would appear that Stratton took a companion with him to his destination, since before September 4, 1632, Cape Porpoise was inhabited by Reynold Jenkins, an Indian trader. The account stated that "One Jenkins, late an inhabitant of Dorchester, and now removed to Cape Porpus, went with an Indian up into the country with store of goods to truck, and, being asleep in a wigwam with one of Passaconamy's men, was killed in the night by an Indian, dwelling near the Mohawks' country, who fled away with his goods, but was fetched back by Passaconamy."*

Jenkins may have been one of those to whom the New Plymouth historian alluded in his chronicles of 1632, when he claimed that Allerton "sells trading comodities to any yt will buy * * * but * * * what he could not sell, he trustes; and sets up

† N. H. State Papers, 1-45.
‡ Bradford, 2-184.
§ Lechford, 185.
* Winthrop, 1-89.

a company of base felows and makes them traders, to rune into every hole."†

The custom of trading with the Indians in the interior through the agency of native guides was an early one. John Winter at Richmond Island employed some of his men in this hazardous service.

The landing place of Stratton when he arrived from England and the location of Jenkins at the cape disclosed an intention to settle in the harbor, near the present village of Cape Porpoise.

Since the patent was lost in the boat wreck, a memorandum of the proposed grant is all that now defines the marine boundary of the concession. In the record of the Council of Plymouth it was described as "butting upon ye south side or border of ye River or Creeke called by the name of Cape Porpus, and on ye other side Northwards" (from the) "Creeke mouth of Cape Porpus, into the south side of the Harbours mouth of Cape Porpus aforesaid."‡

The stream, once called Cape Porpoise River by mariners of the Seventeenth Century, is now known by its original Indian name of Mousam, and the sea frontage of Stratton's grant extended from the mouth of that natural boundary to the harbor of Cape Porpoise near Redding's Island.

After the death of Jenkins, Stratton may have withdrawn from his exposed position at Cape Porpoise to the security of an island lying before Old Orchard Beach, subsequently known as Stratton's Island, but he did not remain there long.

He left the vicinity in 1633. The anonymous "Relation," accredited to Walter Neal, mentioned the premises of John Stratton at Cape Porpoise as "forsaken" at the time of the writer's departure from New England in the summer of that year.§

Furthermore, a court record dated March 25, 1636, contained the following decree: "It is petitioned pr Mr. Godfrey that an attachment might be of one Brase Kettell now in the hands of Mr. Edward Godfrey, wch was belonging to Mr. John Stratten, of a debt deu now 3 yeares from Mr. Stratten to him Soe Stratten may harbour the said Kettell to be answerable to the sut of Mr. Godfrey against next Court to shew cause for not pament or the Kell to be condemned."

† Bradford, 2-188.
‡ Am. Ant. Col., 1867-100.
§ N. H. State Papers, 17-491; Appendix F.

From Maine Stratton had removed to Salem where his widowed mother was living. There he was censured by the magistrates in 1637 and later in the year fined for loaning a gun to an Indian for four days.*

Upon his arrival at Salem the proprietor of Cape Porpoise had become associated with the business interests of Matthew Cradock and sold him that part of his territory which lay between the Mousam and Kennebunk rivers. In 1639, according to Lechford, he conveyed the remainder to Hugh Peters and Richard Saltonstall.

The second settlement at Cape Porpoise was known as Stratton's Plantation, and there appeared to be sufficient families in the vicinity to maintain a separate parish for religious observances for as early as April 26, 1641, Thomas Jenner while clergyman at Saco had received a request from "the inhabitance of Stratens plantation and from those of Caskoe, to be a meanes to helpe each of them to a godly minister." It was then impossible for him to comply, but he may have conducted occasional services in both communities during his long period of incumbency as a religious instructor in the district.†

PIONEERS

BARTLETT, NICHOLAS, guard of Charles Second; fled to Cape Porpoise, 1650; bought land of Cleave at Machegonne, 1651; Ipswich, 1659; Salem, 1688.
BUSH, JOHN, arrived in May, 1635; planter at Cape Porpoise, 1647; died 1670; widow Grace married William Palmer.
HAMMOND, WILLIAM, born in Slymbridge, England, 1597; servant of Edward Winslow at Dorchester, 1632; Cape Porpoise, 1645; wife Benedictus, sister of the wife of John Gouch; died 1702; children Jonathan, born 1644, and Joseph, born 1647.
JENKINS, REYNOLD, trader at Dorchester, 1630; killed by Indians while trading inland from Cape Porpoise, in September, 1632.
LOOMAN, JOHN, planter 1648-1652; removed to Weymouth with wife Ann; daughter Margaret married Griffin Montague.
MERCER, THOMAS, Salem, 1637; Cape Porpoise, 1643-1652; Sheepscot, 1653-1675; Newbury, 1676; Sheepscot, 1683-9; died at Salisbury February 5, 1688-9; daughter Lydia (Stanwood), born 1657, left children born in Gloucester, and another daughter married William Wilcott.
MONTAGUE, GRIFFIN, carpenter at New Plymouth, 1635; Exeter, 1638; Cape Porpoise, 1653; died 1672; widow Margaret Looman; son John died young.
MOORE, RICHARD, born 1620; planter at Salem, 1642; Cape Porpoise, 1647; Wells, 1653; Black Point, 1665; wife Bridget; living 1671.

* Mass. Col. Rec., 1-191. 201.
† Hutchinson's Col., 112.

REDDING, THOMAS, fisherman at New Plymouth, 1637; married Eleanor Penny July 20, 1639; removed to an island in Cape Porpoise Harbor; Saco, 1653-7; Westcustego, 1665; died 1673; widow Eleanor; children John, born 1654, Ruth (Donnell) and a daughter who married John Taylor.

SINGLEMAN, HENRY, planter at Salem, 1641; land abutted that of Morgan Howell, 1648.

STRATTON, JOHN, born 1606; planter from Shotley, England; patentee of Cape Porpoise December 1, 1631; arrived 1632, with Allerton; Salem, 1637-1640; will, 1640; daughter Ann (Lake).

TROTT, SIMON, planter at New Plymouth, 1634; married Mary, daughter of Stephen Batson; lived on an island off Cape Porpoise; wigwam of "Goody" Trott at Cape Porpoise, 1666; children John and Mary (Brookhouse).

SCOTT, RICHARD, born at Glemsford, England, 1607; shoemaker at Boston, 1634; married Catherine, daughter of Edward Marbury, English clergyman; Providence, Rhode Island, 1637; follower of Ann Hutchinson and Anabaptist, 1638; house at Cape Porpoise, 1643; died at Providence, 1681; children John, Mary (Holder), Patience (Beere) and Richard.

CAPE PORPOISE

Far gray headland, faintly glowing,
    In a purple haze of sea,
Whence the surging waves, inflowing,
    Fade like shadows in thy lee;
Where the sea-gulls in the glamour
    Scale the cliffs and skirt the shore,
Mingling notes of plaintive clamor
    With the breakers' ceaseless roar.

Every fisherman and sailor
    Pays his homage as thy due,
Whether in the darksome gale or
    When the skies and seas are blue;
Far, far out, receding never,
    Like a sentinel you keep
Watch and ward—perhaps forever—
    Day and night, across the deep.

KENNEBUNK RIVER

About two miles east of Mousam River is another which was famous at an early date for its sheltered anchorage and the abundance and excellence of its native timber. The stream itself was known to the natives as Kennebunk. Although included in the premises granted to Stratton in 1631, it was subsequently recognized as the eastern boundary of Wells. All early settlers as far west as Neapskessett River held dual titles from Cradock and Gorges and were accounted residents of Wells when they took the oath of allegiance to Massachusetts in 1653. Many of the original pioneers in the vicinity came from Saco, among whom were Ambrose Berry, Joseph Bowles, Morgan Howell, John West and Roger Willine.

Titles on the westerly side of the river sprung from Wadley, or grants from the town after 1650. The names of the grantees on the seashore were Anthony Littlefield, Daniel Pierce and John Buckland. Their allotments extended eastward in the order named from the Mousam to the Kennebunk. Inland from Buckland's lot was that of John Cheater. None of them may have lived on their concessions, since the last three were residents of Newbury.

In 1660, John Wadley, of Wells, who about a decade earlier had bought all of the territory between Ogunquit and Kennebunk rivers of Chabinock, sold his interest east of Neapskessett River to Daniel Epps, of Ipswich, but excepted from the conveyance the farm of John Sanders on the latter stream and those of Buckland, Cheater, Pierce and Symonds, situated between the Mousam and Kennebunk.

On the other bank of Kennebunk River near the mouth was the farm of William Reynolds who was living there as ferryman in 1647 and had been assigned a homestead of 200 acres by Yorkshire Court.

Roger Willine came to Richmond Island in 1637, as a boy in the employment of Trelawney; part of his wages was paid to his mother in England by his employer. June 30, 1637, he was the boatman who rowed the witnesses up the Presumpscot River above Arthur Mackworth's house, where John Winter took possession of the second Trelawney concession.

He remained at the island until 1639 and soon after must have removed to Cape Porpoise, where "hee was one of the first Inhabitants," according to the statement of John Bush, who subsequently acquired a part of his real estate by purchase. In 1648, his land was bounded on the east by that of Morgan Howell.*

Howell was another original settler who had occupied a house on premises which were conveyed to him by Thomas Gorges July 18, 1643. Five years later his building was described as "the ould house." It may have been the dwelling of Richard Scott, the shoemaker, who was living in Boston in 1634.

In 1637, at the time of the religious controversy with Ann Hutchinson, some of her adherents who were related by marriage were banished from the commonwealth; others withdrew from sympathetic motives. Among the latter was Scott, who had married Catherine Marbury, a sister of the evangelist.

He removed first to Providence, Rhode Island, but later took up his abode at Cape Porpoise with the Wheelwright associates from Exeter. In 1643, his house at the latter place was seized upon execution and transferred to John Richards, who had obtained a judgment that year for a consignment of wooden "moulds" (lasts), previously made and sold to the defendant.†

Howell's land was bounded northerly by that of Henry Singleman, of whom but little is known. Neighbors living east of Howell were Griffin Montague, previously of Brookline, and Simon Trott and Thomas Redding, who hailed from New Plymouth. The last two names are still perpetuated in those of islands near Cape Porpoise Harbor, upon one of which the latter had lived before his removal to Saco. John, son of the latter, described the paternal location at Cape Porpoise as three islands "formerly in ye Possession of my father Thos Reding who did live on ye great Island & managed a fishing Trade there."‡

Trott married Mary, daughter of Stephen Batson and the wigwam of "Goody" Trott was mentioned in 1666.§

* York Deeds, 2-94.
† 4 Mass. Hist. Col., 7-343.
‡ York Deeds, 9-187.
§ York Deeds, 2-81.

An early industry at Stratton's Plantation, in which Adam, son of Governor Winthrop, was concerned was cutting masts and treenails, which were shipped from Cape Porpoise or Kennebunk River directly to England.*

Submission to Massachusetts was effected July 5, 1653, and the list of subscribers disclosed the absence of some of the names of the first settlers as well as the inclusion of new ones."†

* Aspinwall, 8.
† Mass. Col. Rec., 3-414.

The sea forever rends the shore;
The shore forever bars the sea;
The rock-bound coast forevermore
Insures all human destiny.

BATSON'S RIVER

This stream, sometimes erroneously called Cape Porpoise River, is situated about three miles easterly from Kennebunk River. The territory, claimed by Rigby as part of the original Lygonia Patent, was allotted by George Cleave as his agent.

Early settlement on the western side was begun by Stephen Batson from Saco, after 1642. This peninsula, called Batson's Neck, lay inland across the reach from Montague's Neck. It was sold to Thomas Mercer, who in turn transferred the premises to John Helson, of Saco, and after the transaction in 1652 removed to Sheepscot. Helson resided at Cape Porpoise for several years, but subsequently conveyed his homestead to John Davis, the blacksmith from York, and Ferdinando Hoff, in equal shares.*

Between the land of Davis and the river was situated a large tract first owned by Anthony Littlefield, who had purchased it from Gorges. About 1650, Littlefield had removed to Wells and his lot, known as Barton's Neck, was occupied by Edward Barton. The recital in a later deed disclosed that the old dwelling had been remodeled by the new owner. The farm comprised 300 acres.

* York Deeds, 10-25.

LITTLE RIVER

The most significant thing about the history of this stream is the fact that it once marked the boundary between the original towns of Cape Porpoise and Saco. The land on the western bank was held by John Bush under a title from Rigby. His deed was dated September 20, 1647, and Richard Moore and Gregory Jeffrey were adjoining owners, under conveyances from the same proprietor.

On the opposite bank in Saco the land was purchased from Vines by John Smith, of Saco, July 18, 1643, with the island at the mouth of the river, afterwards called Smith's or Long, but now known as Timber Island, which was occupied very early by William Hammond, who came from Scituate and had been in the service of Edward Winslow in 1632.*

The Smith tract with the island was owned subsequently by John Lee and Ralph Tristram, of Winter Harbor, but, in 1653, became the property of William Scadlock of Saco.†

* York Deeds, 3-74.
† York Deeds, 1-58.

WINTER HARBOR

Inviting haven in a craggy shore,
    Misnamed for some uncalendared event,
Where ancient mariners withdrew before
    A wild, inhospitable continent.

Far icy torrents from the Crystal Hills
    Descend a vagrant pathway from the sky,
Through overarching forests, noisy rills
    And placid pools where mirrored landscapes lie.

Twin cities now perpetuate the site
    On which a solitary wigwam stood,
And radiant streets illuminate at night
    What once was but a dark and pathless wood.

With verdant slopes made friendly by the plough
    And gleaming vistas of the white-capped sea
The Fancy paints no Winter Harbor now,
    But rather, respite from inclemency.

SACO RIVER

Saco was the Chouacoet of Champlain in 1605. By Smith it was called Sowocotuck, by Rocraft Sawquatock, by Dermer Sowaquatocke, by Levett Sawco, by the Council of Plymouth Swanckadock and by Winthrop Sauco—all in the space of fifteen years. The pronunciation is best expressed in the form "Sawco."

In 1618, Edward Rocraft, alias Stallings, with "his owne Company," was engaged by Sir Ferdinando Gorges to go to Monhegan Island, where they were to meet Thomas Dermer from Newfoundland and "keepe the Coast that Winter quarter, being very well fitted both with Salt, and other necessaries for his turne."

The party was transported in a fishing vessel which belonged to Gorges and was provided with a pinnace; these would have been adequate for all purposes, but Rocraft confiscated a French bark, which he found fishing and trading in a creek near the island. At the end of the fishing season he sent most of the captured crew to England, in the vessel in which he had arrived.

Rocraft was disconcerted at not finding Dermer at Monhegan Island and, after the departure of Gorges' vessel, decided to go to some of his friends in Virginia, where he had lived several years before.

The reason for his leaving New England contrary to specific orders has been explained diversely by the different parties concerned.

Smith, who had been associated with Rocraft in a similar venture three years before, and the Council of Plymouth, which was interested in his discoveries in a general way, based their conclusions upon letters from the explorer himself or reports of his confederates. Accordingly, they assert that some of his companions had planned to seize the bark and engage in a buccaneering expedition along the coast.

Rocraft claimed that he discovered and defeated their plot, but instead of executing the mutineers, as he described them, he "resolved to put them a shoare, thinking by their hazard, that it was possible they might discover something, that might advance the publike; and so giving them some Armes for their defence, and some victuall for their sustentation, untill they knew better how to provide for themselves, hee left them a place called Sowaguatock."*

In order to obtain the correct version of what really happened it is necessary to consult the account of Gorges who had employed Rocraft to remain in New England during that winter and furnished him with a company "of purpose hired for the service."

In the words of Gorges, "Captain Rocraft, being now shipped and furnished with all things necessary, left the coast, contrary to my directions, and went to Virginia, where he had formerly dwelt; and there falling into company with some of his old acquaintance, a quarrel happened between him and another" (William Epps) "so that before he could get away he was slain."†

The brief record of Rocraft on this occasion indicated that he, like many other military men of his time, had an impetuous and ungovernable temper. The account of the "mutiny" proved that all of those involved, who were also employes of Gorges, were not really guilty of any serious offence in the opinion of their leader, but were permitted to spend the winter in the vicinity of Monhegan Island as agreed with their employer. They had access to the pinnace which Rocraft did not need because he had commandeered the French bark.

Furthermore, Richard Vines, who was also a servant of Gorges, must have been one of the men left by Rocraft at Saco in 1618. He was a physician of integrity, versed in botanical science, who was dispatched in Gorges' ship during the most critical stage of the plague, which included the three years from 1617 to 1619, and was also hired "to stay there the winter quarter." In 1617, this vessel, instead of going to New England, sailed late in the season to Newfoundland and, in 1619, when Dermer did reach Monhegan Island in search of Rocraft, he did not leave any of his men there for the winter because he had too few to defend it.

On the other hand, he had encountered the "mutineers" upon arrival in the country. According to the report of the council, "They remayned not long" (at Saco) "but got from thence to Menehighon, an Iland, lying some three leagues in the Sea, and fifteene leagues from that place, where they remayned all that Winter, with bad lodging, and worse fare, yet came all safe home *save one sickely man, which dyed there,* the rest returned with the

* Purchase, 19-275.
† Me. Hist. Col., 2-29.

Shippe wee sent for Rocrafts supply and provision, to make a Fishing Voyage."‡

Smith, in recounting the other misfortunes of Rocraft and Dermer, with whom he had endured captivity in the hands of the French corsairs in 1615, alluded to the general effect of the plague

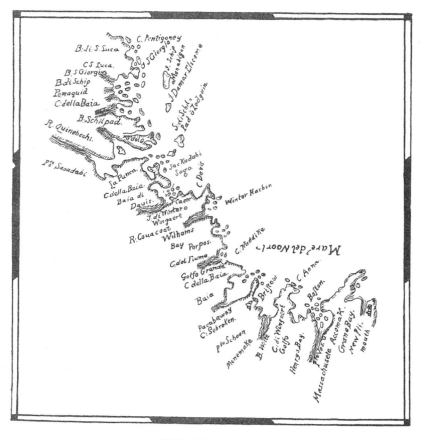

DUTCH MAP, 1631

upon the abandoned remnant of Rocraft's party and to the same fatality referred to by the council. His statement was: "Where I have seene one hundred or two hundred Salvages, there is scarce ten to be found, and yet *not any of them,*" (Rocraft's survivors at

‡ Purchase, 19-276.

Monhegan Island), *"touched with any sicknesse but one poore French man that died."*§

The fact that Vines and his companions were compelled to lie "in the cabins" (wigwams) "with those people that died," who were Indians, reflected the unusual emergency in which they found themselves at the approach of winter in the fall of 1618. And yet Gorges related of his servants that "not one of them ever felt their heads to ache while they stayed *there*. And this course I held some years together."*

In the last sentence Gorges must have referred to the employment of Rocraft, Dermer and Vines in 1618, 1619 and 1620 at Monhegan, and of others in 1622 at Damariscove.

Rocraft was killed in Virginia in the spring of 1619 and the sojourn of Vines and the other "mutineers" at Saco gave rise to the later name of Winter Harbor, for it is evident that there could have been no occasion for leaving anyone there for "discovery" at that time if it had been inhabited previously. An ancient map of Maine, engraved in 1631 or 1632, has perpetuated the name of "Winter Harbor," as the English equivalent for Sawaguatock.†

On his way south in 1619, Dermer left Tisquantum, whom he had brought from Newfoundland during the previous year and proposed to employ as an interpreter in New England, with some friendly Indians who had survived the plague at Saco, and sailed for Virginia where he arrived in November. During the transit he had noted the ravages of disease in the extinct native villages along the coast.

In 1624, Christopher Levett discovered two rivers at Saco which he believed had never been seen by any Englishman.

THE SECOND OCCUPATION.

Two years after the visit of Levett Winter Harbor must have been occupied, temporarily at least. The evidence is meager but convincing. It is derived from widely divergent sources and largely from the testimonies of persons who had been summoned to testify in litigation between George Cleave and Robert Trelawney over the title to the site of the City of Portland. In that controversy the identity of the "River of Casco" as the east-

§ Smith's Trav. & Works., 2-747.
* Me. Hist. Col., 2-24.
† N. Y. Doc. Hist., Frontispiece.

ern boundary of the Trelawney grant became the paramount issue. Winter, as agent for the defendant, described his affidavits, which were the only ones preserved in the case, as "the evidences heare of such as did most frequent that place" (Casco) "since the first discovery thereof."‡

Cleave won the first decision, but Trelawney appealed from the verdict as contrary to evidence. Thomas Gorges, Henry Jocelyn and Richard Vines were then the justices of the court of last resort. In their final determination in 1642, the opinion of the inferior tribunal was reversed and the rescript declared that Presumpscot River was the only one in Casco Bay of sufficient importance "Ever to have been Called Casco river" by the "relation of ye Antient Inhabitants & Natives."§

The first witness in point of antiquity was William Gibbons, of Saco; he had known Presumpscot River to be styled the "River of Casco" since 1623. Obviously, this planter was the agent of Levett, who was reported by his principal to have been resident in New England in 1627. He also appears to have been the brother of Edward Gibbons, of Boston, whose administrators subsequently disposed of the Saco estate.

Three other witnesses, classed by the court as "Antient Inhabitants" at the Eastward, were John Cousins, of Casco, Peter Garland, of Dover, and John Mills, of Scarborough. Each deponent had known and frequented "the river which runs by Mr. Arthur Mackworthes house." It had been recognized by them and their associates as "Casco River" for fourteen years before 1640.*

In a later deposition, relating to Pejepscot, Cousins was much more specific. His statement, made in 1683, contained the following pertinent information:

"Testimony of John Cousins, aged about Eighty Seven years, being summoned maketh oath, having lived in ye Province about Fifty-five or 6 yrs, about two years at Sauco & the rest of my time at Casco bay, & I well remember yt Mr. Thomas Purchase went from Sauco to Pejepscot which lies in Casco Bay near ye Falls of Dammas Coggan river & settled himself, & there built an house, planted & possessed a considerable tract of land wch extended as far as Maquoit to ye Westward & bounded by the river & Nacussett

‡ Me. Doc. Hist., 3-233.
§ York Deeds, 8-244.
* Me. Doc. Hist., 3-231, 239.

on the East, of wch Lands the said Mr Purchase took his first possession in the year One thousand Six hundred & twenty-eight."†

The two depositions of Cousins, taken 43 years apart but plainly corroborative, prove that a settlement was begun at Saco in 1626, from which Purchase and the affiant removed to Casco within two years. Other members of the temporary settlement at Saco, who were indicated by collateral references, were Richard Bradshaw, Peter Garland, John Mills, John Oldham and Richard Vines.

A main reason for the allotment of 1500 acres of land "above the hedd of Pashippscot" to Captain Bradshaw was specified as "the charge he had been at in his liveing there some yeares before" 1631. His concession adjoined that of Purchase.‡

Mills was a witness to the illicit trade between Thomas Wright's agent and the Indians before 1630.

In 1626, Oldham sailed from Saco ("Canada") to Virginia as merchant of a trading vessel. There was little cargo, as the freight had been sacrificed in transit near the Shoals of Cape Cod. Bradford mentioned the vicissitudes of the voyage which occurred the year after Oldham had been ejected from New Plymouth. At that time this eastern trader was a most aggressive competitor of that colony in Indian trade. His ship arrived at Hampton Roads October 2, where it was unladen at the mouth of the James River, because it had just weathered a severe storm and was reported to be "very lekie." The name of the bark was the "Happy Entrance."§

The first plantation at Saco was one of those referred to by the historian of New Plymouth in 1628, when he described the settlers as "the planters of Pascataway & other places to ye eastward of them."*

Saco appears to have been abandoned in 1628, when all of the original pioneers except Cousins and Garland are known to have returned to England. In June, Oldham with Morton as his prisoner sailed from the Isles of Shoals, and soon after Vines was paid to use his influence in England in obtaining a patent of Cushnoc for New Plymouth. Bradshaw sued for a grant at Pejepscot and Mackworth for a tract on Presumpscot River, where he had had possession many years before 1635. Mills returned with Winter to Richmond Island after a sojourn in the Old Country.

† Pejepscot Papers, 491a.
‡ Am. Ant. Col., 1867-98.
§ Bradford, 2-130 ; Min. of Va. Council, 1-121.
* Bradford, 2-149.

February 12, 1629-30, the Council of Plymouth granted the locality about Winter Harbor to Oldham and Vines and described the tract as four miles in width along the seashore and eight miles in length toward the interior. Upon the same day another concession of the same dimensions, situated upon the easterly side of Saco River and styled East Saco, was granted to Thomas Lewis and Richard Bonython.

Oldham had resided in the country about six years before the date of his grant and there was no mention of previous services performed for the council by either grantee. The subsequent home of Oldham was at Watertown.

The close association of Isaac Allerton and Sir Ferdinando Gorges in the first attempts to colonize Maine was accountable for the statement attributed to James Sherley, but dictated by Allerton himself, just one week after the Saco grants, to the effect that the latter had the "cheefe" of the council for a friend.

Early in 1630 Allerton and Vines had made arrangements with Thomas Wright, a wealthy merchant adventurer of Bristol, England, who owned the *Swift* of Bristol, to transport passengers and provisions to Saco and Casco, where they were to begin plantations for Vines and Wright respectively. Stephen Reekes, of Poole, master of this vessel, was instructed by the owner to discharge his passengers and relade upon the Maine coast with "fishe and trayne oyl" for Saint Michael's, one of the Azores or Western Islands. To avoid capture by enemy privateers to the southward, Reekes was advised to take advantage of his slight knowledge of the French language and assume French names for himself and his ship.

The *Swift* reached the coast in midsummer. The approximate time of arrival was indicated by the certificate of seizin, dated June 25, 1630, when Richard Vines took possession of the premises at Saco in the presence of Thomas Wiggin, Thomas Purchase, Isaac Allerton, Stephen Reekes, Nathaniel Waters and John Wright, a kinsman of Thomas Wright, of Bristol.

William Blackstone, William Jeffrey and Edward Hilton had been designated to give possession for the council, but the first two, who were remote residents of Massachusetts, and the last, who then lived in New Hampshire, were absent.†

Nathaniel Waters, master of the *Return*, of Millbrook, England, had fished and traded on the coast in 1627. Subsequently,

† York Deeds, 1-2, 7.

fishermen from Millbrook were employed at Richmond Island by John Winter. A master of the same name was trading at Pemaquid in 1647.

Captain John Wright was on his way eastward as factor for his brother Thomas, of Bristol, who proposed to establish a trading post in the house at Casco which had been acquired from Levett. He had also been employed by Allerton to convey supplies in his shallop to Edward Ashley at Penobscot and to assist in securing a cargo of fish and train oil for the *Swift*, in the vicinity of Pemaquid.

Purchase was interested subsequently in the settlement of the plantation at Pejepscot on Casco Bay.

Allerton who was a witness at Saco had come from England that spring with William Peirce in the *Lyon*. Peirce had landed Ashley at Penobscot and proceeded westward to Salem, where Allerton had transshipped in a shallop for Pemaquid, June 12, expecting to encounter the *Swift* at the Eastward.

In 1628, Vines had accepted a retainer from Allerton to assist him in obtaining from the Council of Plymouth a patented right at Cushnoc for Plymouth Colony, and he was still agent for Gorges and "interested in the discovery and seizure" of the eastern country. The grant of Cushnoc had been issued just a month before, and that at Penobscot, in which Allerton had an interest, was granted a month after, that to Oldham and Vines at Saco.

There is no doubt that possession was taken at Cushnoc and Penobscot during the same month, but the written evidence is not available.

The transportation of Oldham's goods to Pascataqua in the *Warwick* earlier in the year may have reflected a disagreement between the patentees on the west side of Saco River. At any rate Oldham's interest in the eastern plantation was acquired subsequently by Vines.

After his passengers had been landed at "Sacho and Cuscoe" Reekes followed the instructions of his employers and changed his name to Peter Alley and that of his ship to the *Saint Peter*. How far he was successful in securing a cargo of fish and oil among the English fishermen at the Eastward has not been disclosed. However, England was then at war with France, and while he lay at Damariscove Captain Thomas Witherly arrived from Pascataqua in command of the *Warwick* and in possession of British letters of marque and made a prize of the *Saint Peter*.

After their return to London Reekes confessed his deception in Witherly's presence at the house of Captain John Mason in Fenchurch Street.‡

The settlers who came to Saco with Vines in 1630 appear to have been Ambrose Berry, Henry Boade, George Cleave, John Cousins, Theophilus Davis, George Frost, Thomas Purchase, John Parker, William Scadlock and John Wadley. Some of these were assigned lots of one hundred acres each on the western bank of the river above Biddeford Pool and others settled subsequently in Casco Bay. Two removed, seven years later, to Cape Porpoise.

The consideration for the grant to Bonython and Lewis on the east side of the river recited previous expenditures of personal funds "to take a vew of New England in America," and a decision made by the latter and "his Assotiates to plant there." Their first colony came from Bristol in the *White Angel* in 1631. This vessel had been purchased that spring from Robert Aldworth, a Bristol proprietor of Pemaquid, for the London partners of Plymouth Colony. Like the *Swift*, which had failed in a similar project the year before, this ship was intended to convey passengers and supplies to New England and to relade there with fish and train oil for Spain, where the vessel and cargo were to be disposed of outright.§

Allerton was in charge, and his bill of lading contained cattle and goods, consigned chiefly to settlers in Massachusetts by Richard and Thomas Southcoat and William Vassal. Some of the freight was taken on the credit of John White, a clergyman of high standing in Dorchester, England, who had been one of the founders of Salem Colony.

The *White Angel* had been provided by Allerton and Richard Andrews, John Beauchamp, Timothy Hatherly and James Sherley, the London partners of Plymouth Colony, to convey supplies to Edward Ashley at Penobscot. Aside from this special service for the most easterly English settlement, this ship brought colonists and provisions for Saco. Shipments of more than twenty-four tons of corn and oats were made by George Way, of Dorchester, to Thomas Purchase and Boston consignees. This grain was freighted from Padstow, in Cornwall, to Bristol, to be ground into meal, and thence to Barnstable, to be shipped on the *Friendship;*

‡ N. Y. Gen. & Biog. Rec., 47-253.
§ Bradford, 2-179.

when that ship failed of passage, its cargo was transported back to Bristol and reshipped on the *White Angel.**

June 28, 1631, Edward Hilton, of Dover Point, delivered possession of the premises on the eastern side of Saco River to Thomas Lewis, in presence of James Parker, George Vaughan, Henry Watts and Thomas Wiggin.†

Other settlers who disembarked at Saco appear to have been John Bonython, Francis Robinson, Thomas Southcoat, Richard Tucker and Henry Warwick.

There is proof that these settlements of Vines and Lewis were the first permanent ones on the Saco River. In a letter to Winthrop, dated August 4, 1645, Richard Vines stated that the right of Alexander Rigby to the Province of Maine was based upon the "Plough Patent, which was desarted 13 years past," and declared that "If there come order, either from King or Parliment, for the establishing of Mr. Rigby in that patent, we will submit to it, soe far forth as they doe not intrench upon the liberties of Saco, (for *our Patents wear granted and possest a yeare before* that, and you knowe that all grants run, except before excepted)."‡

The Plough Patent was granted June 26, 1630, and its first colonists, on account of the barren aspect of the premises at Sagadahoc River, proceeded forthwith to Massachusetts where they appeared July 6, 1631, in search of a better location.§

In fact, during the same week that possession was taken by Lewis at East Saco, the Plough Company, as the Sagadahoc colonists were styled collectively, "desarted" the Plough Patent, "never settling on that land."**

The sentiment for exclusive proprietorship prevailed for many years upon the banks of the Saco River, although the influential Sir Alexander Rigby, assignee of the rights of two members of the Plough Company, undertook with varying degrees of success to superimpose his unpopular patent upon the older franchises of the original proprietors, both at Saco and Cape Porpoise.††

At the time of his discharge as manager for Plymouth Colony in 1631, Allerton had "expended, and given to Mr. Vines and others, aboute 543 li. ode money," to obtain inside influence with the Council of Plymouth in securing Cushnoc patent. In the quaint

---
* Bradford, 2-189 ; Mass. Arch., 100-8, 9.
† York Deeds, 2-110.
‡ 4 Mass. Hist. Col., 7-354.
§ Winthrop, 1-58.
** Mass. Hist. Proc., 21-232.
†† Mass. Hist. Prc., 22-157.

phraseology of Sherley that concession required the outlay of "no small sume of money * * * for * * * many locks must be opened with ye silver, ney, ye golden key."

Upon discovery that Barnstable merchants had consigned trading goods to Saco planters during that year, he too became interested in the eastern trade. The next spring, owing to former business relations with Vines, he became associated with him as a "consort" in commercial ventures along the Maine Coast, where he supplied him with merchandise. The New Plymouth historian alluded to Vines, or Dixie Bull, or both, in his complaint that Allerton had instructed his partners "to rune into every hole, & into ye river of Kenebeck, to gleane away ye trade from ye house ther, aboute ye patente & privilege wherof he had dasht away so much money" for that colony.‡

July 23, 1632, when Vines landed at Cape Elizabeth to deliver seizin of the Trelawney grant to Winter, Allerton was present as an attesting witness. Both were returning homeward from an eastern coasting trip on that occasion, and Thomas Cammock, who conversed with them at some length, reported that the best Indian trade was to be found near the "Scotts' Plantation" (Annapolis Royal).

The next year Vines erected a wigwam at Machias and left a few employes there to trade with the natives, but within a week two of his men were killed by the French, who took the others eastward with all of their merchandise and dispatched them from Port Latour to France. Nearly all of the trading goods captured belonged to Allerton and, as his financial condition had already become critical otherwise, he disposed of the *White Angel,* which he had employed for three years in fishing and trading along the coast, together with the season's cargo of fish and beaver, in Spain.§

In 1634, an English trader from Saco was killed by Indians in the interior. At that date the trade along the coast had been much reduced. In the spring of that year John Winter wrote to Trelawney from Richmond Island that no native had visited his vicinity for a long time for, said he, "no Indian lives nearer unto us then 40 or 50 myles, except a few about the River of Salko, for the planters here abouts, yf they will have any bever, must go 50 or 60 miles Into the Country with their packes on their backes * * * I sent a man this yeare 2 voyages into the Country to put away

‡ Bradford, 2-166, 184, 188.
§ Bradford, 2-190.

som goods with the Indians * * * and I was faine to give an Indian to go his pilot In the Country more than I got."*

The trade on the coast had been intercepted by the houses which had been established in the interior upon the rivers. During this year Gorges began his principal settlement at Agamenticus with the assurance that the proximity of Saco, where his "servant" Vines had been settled for some years, would mean a material advantage. September 10, he gave him a commission to dispose of lands within his province. Several tracts of land were thus conveyed by Vines to various private owners.

Agriculture was the principal occupation at Saco, but clapboards had already been provided for shipment August 6, 1634, when the *Pide Cow* sailed thither from Pascataqua to secure a return cargo. The industry had been fostered by Vines on the western bank of the river. Edward Trelawney, whose headquarters were at Richmond Island, reported that there was a ready market for the product at Malaga, Spain.

April 25, 1635, the Council of Plymouth apportioned all of the territory situated between Pascataqua and Sagadahoc rivers to Gorges and November 26, following, renewed the patent at Winter Harbor to Vines, in severalty. The action indicated that Oldham had consented to relinquish his proprietary interest in favor of his more active partner. After his title had been perfected, Vines encouraged the production of lumber in his settlement. With that object in view he approved the formation of a partnership between Peyton Cook, of Saco, and Richard Williams, of Boston, to operate at Winter Harbor.

The company was formed in October, 1635, with the understanding that all business should be conducted upon a share basis. Edward Trelawney, of Richmond Island, was interested in the venture and arranged with Matthew Cradock, of London, to take the entire output.

Williams came from Boston to Saco about New Year's Day and secured the services of Thomas Williams and John Smith, then employes of Vines. The proprietor was entitled to one-half of the profits to reimburse him for the timber required. About a dozen men were employed in the undertaking and the food problem became serious. Then Williams died and his estate was not fully administered by Yorkshire Court for many years.

* Me. Doc. Hist., 3-461.

The first session of the proprietary court was held at the house of Richard Bonython at Saco, March 25, 1636, which was about one month after the death of Richard Williams. The commissioners presided in the following order: Richard Bonython, William Gorges, Thomas Cammock, Henry Jocelyn, Thomas Purchase, Edward Godfrey and Thomas Lewis. The communities represented were Kittery, York, Saco and Brunswick.

The creditors of Williams were found to be James Cole, Peyton Cook, John Love, Thomas Lewis, Thomas Mayhew as agent for Cradock, Hugh Mosier, John Parker and Henry Warwick. The estate was declared to be insolvent, but Mayhew, who lived at Medford upon the Cradock plantation, undertook to continue the business in the interest of his patron who was the largest creditor. Accordingly, provisions were dispatched to Saco from Medford.

Vines, too, was a large creditor and insisted upon reimbursement of part of his claim. Under the date of May 20, 1636, he received the following letter from Mayhew:

"Sir: Wn. yr shipp comes to take Clapboards, if you want you may take soe much of mine, but by all meanes lett him take after hee hath those yt belongeth unto you as well those of the shorter sort as others, else I shall bee left unsorted: as for pvisions I will send wt. I can pr the first yt comes. I have taken course for the 200 lbs. of bread and a baill of beife to goe by Mr. Allerton if hee can take it in, if not I shall come with ye other goods & what else I have yt. hee shall desire."†

Twelve days later Thomas Babb arrived at Saco with the ship which Vines had chartered to transport his clapboards to market. The tale was taken by John Jolliff, another agent of Cradock, who delivered enough stock on the account of Vines to make him a debtor of the estate. The unsold balance of the clapboards was inventoried and distributed to all creditors on an insolvency basis, so that Cradock became a substantial loser.‡

Another important industry at Saco was sponsored by merchants of Dorchester, England, in 1636, when they laid the keel for a ship to be employed in transatlantic service. Very little is known about the project except that the construction was placed in charge of Clement Greenway, an experienced master, who had made a fishing trip to Saco that summer and kept a few employes in the country during the winter.

† York Ct. Rec., 1-83.
‡ Me. Doc. Hist., 3-88.

This was the first large sailing craft to be begun in Maine after the completion of the *Virginia* at Sagadahoc in 1607. It was launched from Winter Harbor, which is a peninsula situated on the west side and at the mouth of Saco River, between the open sea and Biddeford Pool. For many years the place was called Parker's Neck, because it had been monopolized first by John Parker, of Bideford, England, who erected a dwelling and fishing stages at the point. After Parker's removal to Sagadahoc the land was taken by Robert Jordan, in satisfaction of an execution against Vines, and conveyed to Roger Spencer, of Boston, who lived there for several years.

The first Maine colonists were faithful to the tenets of the established church of England and for this reason there was not much fellowship between them and the Massachusetts settlers. Places for religious services were provided at York and Saco as early as 1636. The first meeting-house at the latter plantation was located at Church Point, on the west side of the river and about midway between the falls and Biddeford Pool. The site is now unmarked, but the locality was indicated upon an ancient plan of the division made for the heirs of Bonython and Lewis.

CHURCH POINT, SACO RIVER

May 24, 1636, Richard Gibson arrived at Richmond Island where he had been engaged as pastor under the patronage of Robert Trelawney. Soon after his advent, his services were secured for occasional engagements at Saco.

At the latter parish a ministerial tax was assessed upon all of

SACO RIVER 179

the male inhabitants in the district, to provide for Gibson's support. While, during the same year, some of the York parishioners did object to paying their ecclesiastical charges, there appeared to have been no dissension at Saco.

The amount committed to the bailiff for collection was large for that period and the list included the names of planters on both sides of the river. All proprietors and their assigns were taxed in proportion to their several interests in the realty. The salary at Richmond Island was paid by voluntary contributions from Trelawney and his fishermen.

Since this may be regarded as the first tax of any kind ever levied in the Province of Maine, it is subjoined without abbreviation as it has been preserved on the first page of the Province Records.

Parish Tax for Richard Gibson, pastor at Saco, September 7, 1636:

Captain Richard Bonython,	03	00	00
Richard Vines,	03	00	00
Thomas Lewis,	03	00	00
Henry Boade,	02	00	00
John Wadley,	01	00	00
Thomas Williams,	02	10	00
Robert Sankey,	01	10	00
Theophilus Davis,	01	10	00
George Frost,	01	10	00
Clement Greenway,	01	00	00
John Parker,	01	00	00
John Smith,	01	00	00
Samuel Andrews,	01	00	00
William Scadlock,	01	00	00
Robert Morgan,	01	15	00
Henry Warwick,	01	00	00
Richard Hitchcock,	01	10	00
Thomas Page,	01	00	00
Ambrose Berry,	01	00	00
Henry Watts,	01	10	00
Richard Foxwell,	01	10	00

During the summer of 1638 the new ship built at Saco by English merchants of Barnstable and put into commission by Greenway, who had been appointed master, was wrecked off the Irish

Coast before it had completed its first voyage. John Richmond, a merchant of Bandon Bridge, Ireland, was a passenger on the ill-fated vessel. These two survivors returned to Saco the following year, but the infant industry lapsed.

After Gorges had acquired a royal title to Western Maine in 1639, he made a second attempt to establish a legal forum in the district and a new tribunal for the province of New Somerset was convened at Saco June 25, 1640. The records of that court furnish many interesting facts.

During the latter year Thomas Jenner was chosen pastor of the plantation to succeed Gibson, who had removed to Pascataqua about New Year's Day. This pastorate continued for six years.

In 1642, the exploration of the White Mountains by Darby Field, an Irishman of Dover, excited the general interest of Maine planters, who were still concerned with the possibilities of fabulous profits in the wilderness of Laconia. Field's exaggerated accounts of the discovery of diamonds and "muscovy glass," with the encouraging report that "The sea by Saco seemed as if it had been within 20 miles," induced "divers others to travel thither" about the last of August, among whom were Thomas Gorges and Vines.

The reader is indebted to the first "History of New England" for the only story of the adventure now extant, which is appended.

"They went up Saco river in birch canoes, and that way, they found it 90 miles to Pegwagget, an Indian town, but by land it is but 60. Upon Saco river, they found many thousand acres of rich meadow, but there are ten falls, which hinder boats, etc.

"From the Indian town, they went up hill (for the most part) about 30 miles in woody lands, then they went about 7 or 8 miles upon shattered rocks, without tree or grass, very steep all the way. At the top is a plain about 3 or 4 miles over, all shattered stones, and upon that is another rock or spire, about a mile in height, and about an acre of ground at the top. At the top of the plain arise four great rivers, each of them so much water, at the first issue, as would drive a mill; Connecticut river from two heads, at the N.W. and S.W. which join in one about 60 miles off, Saco river on the S.E., Amascoggen which runs into Casco Bay at the N.E., and Kennebeck, at the N. by E. The mountain runs E. and W. 30 or 40 miles, but the peak is above all the rest. They went and returned in 15 days."§

§ Winthrop, 2-89.

In 1643, John Winter at Richmond Island mentioned Saco planters who had exchanged their surplus supplies of grain with him. His list included William Gibbons, Richard Hitchcock, Thomas Jenner, John Lee, Francis Robinson, Richard Vines, Henry Warwick and Thomas Williams, all of whom had been residents on the river for several years.

September 30, 1645, during Jenner's pastorate, Vines sold his patent of Saco to Robert Childs and during the following spring emigrated with some of his friends to Barbadoes, where he was engaged in tropical farming and renewed the practice of medicine as his original profession. He died on his farm in 1651, only a few years after the decease of Gorges. Many of the present land titles in Biddeford may be traced to leases granted by him and confirmed later by the town.

DIVISION OF LAND IN BIDDEFORD.

According to tradition Vines and his associates landed originally upon Fletcher Neck, where there were fishing stages. That locality, then known as "Winter Harbor," is now recognizable as the favorite summer resort of Biddeford Pool. On an ancient British map of the "Province of Mayne," dated 1655, six dwellings were depicted upon the western bank of Saco River, one of which may have been intended to represent that constructed to shelter the employes of John Parker, the Bideford fishmonger. In early days his peninsula was styled "Parker's Neck."

About the northerly quadrant of Biddeford Pool were located the pioneer homes of Robert Booth, Ralph Tristram, Richard Hitchcock and Thomas Williams. The dwelling of the latter was mentioned in 1636. The land between that of Williams and Saco River was acquired in 1647 by Richard Cummings, who conveyed it to Walter Merry.

The next habitation on the river was occupied by Henry Boade, before 1636, but it was transferred to James Gibbons and Thomas Mills by Vines in 1642. Boade had removed to Wells.

Like that of Boade the rest of the lots upriver were eighty rods in width and extended for 200 rods westward. The next four house lots were assigned, in the order named, to Robert Sankey, Joseph Bowles, Samuel Andrews and William Scadlock. The last two settlers resided upon their lots in 1637. Sankey died before

1642 and his title was acquired successively by John Wright and John Bouden. Bowles conveyed his estate to Roger Hill and withdrew to Wells. Andrews died in 1637 and his widow, who had married Arthur Mackworth, of Casco, sold her interest to Peter Hill, father of Roger; the premises were subsequently occupied by John Helson and William Dicer. Scadlock retired to Little River on the west side of the town and disposed of the Saco farm to Richard Seeley, a mariner of the Isles of Shoals.*

Above the main settlement a large section of the wilderness had been reserved for the grandson of Gorges, of the same name. Apparently, such a concession had been made at an early date. In 1642, an interior lot containing one hundred acres and bounded southerly by land of "Ferdinando Gorges decd," easterly by Saco River and northerly by Smith's Brook, was assigned by Vines to Ambrose Berry.†

That same year another homestead of equal dimensions, situated above the brook, was conferred upon John Smith, who like Thomas Williams, had been a "servant" of the proprietor. The easterly boundary of the last premises was defined as the river and "Church Point," where, obviously, the first meeting-house in the province had been located.‡

Beyond an intervening strip of virgin forest which terminated at West's Brook was a house and clearing leased by Vines to John West in 1638. Previously, it had been held under temporary leaseholds by Samuel Andrews and Thomas Cole in succession. The locality was known as "West's Point," and the building was described as "a mansion." Between the point and Saco Falls is situated Cow Island which was given to West by the town long after his settlement in the vicinity.

There is no direct evidence to disclose the exact spot on which the proprietor lived. At the falls is situated Indian Island, which was made the subject of controversy by Joan, wife of Vines, and Lewis and Bonython at the first session of Saco court in 1636. A temporary decree authorized the defendant to plant and cultivate what space she required for domestic purposes until her husband could return from England and the title be determined. Many years later the disputed premises, known as Bonython's Island and comprising part of the present City of Saco, were equally

* York Deeds, 3-124; 1-33, 42.
† York Deeds, 7-181.
‡ York Deeds, 2-10.

divided between William Phillips, successor of Robert Childs and Vines, and John Bonython, son of the Saco proprietor. In 1643, Vines assured Governor Winthrop that he had been compelled to travel two miles to reach home after attendance at the local court. Seven years earlier the New Somerset tribunal had convened at the house of Richard Bonython in East Saco. Later sessions had been conducted in the dwelling of Thomas Williams at Winter Harbor. Church Point was near the center of population and it is probable that after the completion of the meeting-house all public hearings were held there. The distance of the site of that building from Saco Falls and the fact that his wife had planted Indian Island as a matter of convenience and safety during the season when her husband was absent, clearly point to the conclusion that the dwelling of Vines stood near the westerly end of Saco Bridge above the falls.

DIVISION OF LAND IN SACO.

The ancient map disclosed six buildings distributed for four miles along the river in "East Saco." The coastal tract was occupied by William Gibbons, who must have been a near relative of Major Edward, of Boston.

In the Casco controversy between Cleave and Trelawney the Saco planter testified that he had known Presumpscot River since 1623. This statement qualified him as one of the party of Robert Gorges, which had arrived late in that year and visited the Eastern Country during the winter. He was mentioned as commorant at Saco from 1636 to 1652, but not afterward, while Edward Gibbons, who had been engaged in eastern trade for many years, died in 1654, leaving a large estate.

The next year John Richards, who had just disposed of his land at Sagadahoc to Clark and Lake, was living near Blue Point in Saco. Obviously he was acting as an agent for Edward upon the estate of the deceased William Gibbons, since two years later he with the other administrators of the Boston merchant conveyed the Saco premises to Henry Warwick. The real estate was then described as a tract of 400 acres which extended eastward from the mouth of Saco River to Goosefair.§

The next dwellings appear to have been those of John Wadley and Edward Robinson. The latter and Francis, presumed to be a

§ York Deeds, 6 80

son on account of his minority at the time of settlement, may have been employes of Bonython.

About four miles from the mouth of the river was a plantation of fifty acres which had been assigned to Thomas Page. It lay nearly opposite Church Point and was bounded by two creeks, the most southerly being still known as "Nichols' Brook." Page and his wife died suddenly in 1645, leaving only minor children. His descendants disposed of their interests in the original tract nearly one hundred years later.*

Above Page's Plantation was the dwelling and cultivated land of Richard Bonython and beyond that, opposite the falls, stood the house of Thomas Lewis. It is apparent that all of the proprietors at Saco anticipated that their principal revenue would be derived from the manufacture of lumber, agriculture and the Indian trade, rather than from deep-sea fishing on the coast.†

MASSACHUSETTS SUPREMACY.

Massachusetts colonies had secured no control in Maine before 1652. This is best illustrated by an incident that occurred at Saco two years before. In the spring of 1650, Richard Seeley "did steale his fathers boat" and with Thomas Wallen induced the wives of Thomas Mills and Thomas Warner to abandon their homes at Winter Harbor and proceed with them to New Plymouth. Upon arrival at their destination Seeley, whose father Richard operated at the Isles of Shoals at that time, and Wallen, who was also commorant within Massachusetts territory and amenable to punishment by the colony, were sentenced forthwith by the local magistrates and immediately "comitted to ward," while the others were remanded to Winter Harbor where they resided. The elder Seeley, whose name was spelled "Carle," subsequently lived near Winter Harbor in Biddeford.‡

July 5, 1653, the inhabitants on Saco River submitted to the Massachusetts regime.§

In one of Maverick's descriptions of the Eastern Country, dated July 26, 1665, the only municipalities mentioned for the old Province of Maine were Kittery, York, Wells, Saco, Scarborough and Falmouth. These were "all built by the seaside and five or

* York Deeds, 3-42 ; 12-69.
† York Deeds. 3-94.
‡ Plymouth Col. Rec., 2-205.
§ Mass. Col. Rec., 3-412.

six miles long at least," although they had "but 30 houses in them, and these very mean ones." Another list dated September 5, that year, enumerated only twenty-six houses in the Eastern Country beyond Sagadahoc River.*

Settlements were continued at Saco River until after the first

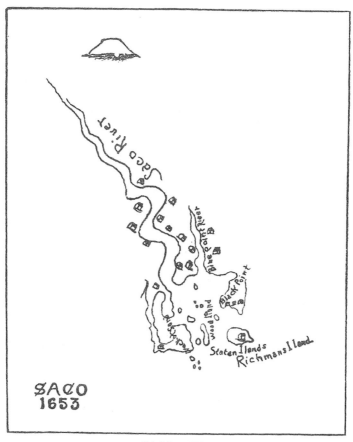

SACO, 1653

outbreak of the Indian Wars, when the English planters were driven westward as far as Wells. The devastation at this point was almost complete. Hubbard's account, made soon after the event, stated that the savages had burned all of the houses at Saco

* Sainsbury's Col. Pap., 2-213.

which were situated "above the Fisher-mans Stages" near the mouth of the river.

In 1708, a fort was built upon Parker's Neck, at the expense of Massachusetts government, to provide protection for the few remaining settlers against the raids of the Northern Indians. This fortification, located upon the point below Biddeford Pool, was named Fort Mary.

SACO ISLANDS.

Gibbons Island is a small island of ten acres lying east of Parker's Neck. It was assigned to James Gibbons and was included in the first division outlined by Bonython and Foxwell.†

Wood Island lies east of Parker's Neck near the former island and contains thirty acres. It was named for the density of its primeval forest.‡

PIONEERS

ANDREWS, SAMUEL, born 1598, arrived with his family from Stephney, England, in the "Increase," 1635; Saco, 1636; died 1637; widow Jane, born 1605, married Arthur Mackworth; children Jane (Neal), born 1632, Elizabeth (Purchase), born 1633, James, born 1635, and Philippe (Felt).

BALL, RICHARD, brother of John; fisherman at Salisbury, 1651; Winter Harbor, 1653; Cape Porpoise, 1655; Kittery, 1667; Dover, 1668.

BATSON, STEPHEN, planter, 1637-8; Cape Porpoise from Saco, 1642; died at Wells, June 30, 1676; widow Elizabeth; children Elizabeth (Ashley), John, Margery (Young), and Mary (Trott, Brookhouse, Clay).

BERRY, AMBROSE, planter, at Saco, 1636; Cape Porpoise, 1642; married Ann Bully, 1654; died 1661; children Ambrose, of Boston, 1686, and Hannah (Chase).

BOADE, HENRY, planter, at Saco, 1636; cousin of John Winthrop; removed to Kennebunk, 1637; died January 16, 1657-8; widow Ann.

BONYTHON, RICHARD, patentee of Saco, 1631; died 1653; widow Lucretia; children Elizabeth (Cummings), John, born 1648, and Susanna (Foxwell).

BOOTH, ROBERT, born 1602, clergyman; Exeter, 1644; Saco, 1647; died March 14, 1672-3; widow Deborah married Thomas Ladbrook; children born in various places, Mary (Pennell), September 30, 1627, Eleanor, February, 1634, Simon, May 10, 1641, Martha, April 12, 1645, Robert and Rebecca, July 25, 1655.

BOWLES, JOSEPH, born 1609, planter; Winter Harbor, 1640; Cape Porpoise, 1648; died 1678; widow Mary; children Elizabeth (Locke, Pitman), Joseph, Mary (Frost), Mercy, Rebecca, Samuel, Sarah (Chadbourne) and Thomas.

CLEAVE, GEORGE, planter, 1630; Spurwink, 1631-3; Casco (Portland), 1633; wife Joan; died 1666-1671; only daughter Elizabeth (Mitten).

COLE, JAMES, Salem, 1631; Casco, 1636; Sagadahoc, 1654-1672.

†York Deeds, 15-10.
‡ York Deeds, 17-15.

SACO RIVER 187

COLE, THOMAS, planter, 1640; land adjoined Batson's, 1641; Pemaquid, 1669.

COLE, WILLIAM, born 1580; planter at Exeter, 1639; Saco, 1640; constable at Wells, 1645; wife Elizabeth; died 1663; son William, born 1627, removed to Sheepscot before 1665.

COOK, PEYTON, merchant at Saco, 1635; living, 1684.

COUSINS, JOHN, born 1594; Saco, 1630-2; Casco, 1634, as an employe of Brown and Mackworth; Cousins Island at Westcustego, 1639; died 1685; only authority that there were settlers at Saco, 1627.

DAVIS, THEOPHILUS, planter, 1636-7.

EDMUNDS, ROBERT, servant of Matthew Cradock, 1635; Sagadahoc, 1687.

ELKINS, THOMAS, born 1595; planter at Boston, 1634; Saco, 1640; died 1664-7; children Christopher and Thomas.

EVANS, GRIFFITH, planter, 1636.

FERNALD, JOHN, surgeon, 1637-1640; widow Joanna, 1660.

FOXWELL, RICHARD, born 1604; trader at Dorchester, 1633; Saco, 1634; Scarborough, 1638; died 1677; widow Susanna, daughter of Richard Bonython; children Esther (Rogers), Eunice (Cutts), John, born 1639, Lucretia (Robinson), born 1642, Mary (Norton), Philip, born 1651, Richard, Sarah (Curtis) and Susanna (Ashton).

FROST, GEORGE, planter, 1635-7.

GARDINER, CHRISTOPHER, gentleman at Boston, 1630; Saco, 1631; returned to Bristol, England, 1632.

GIBBONS, JAMES, planter, born 1614; sailed from London in the "Increase" April 13, 1635; Saco, 1637; wife Judith, daughter of Thomas Lewis; Barbadoes, 1662-1692; children, born at Saco, James, March 19, 1648, Elizabeth (Sharp), April 25, 1652, Thomas, November 23, 1654, Charity, January 5, 1656, Rebecca, January 30, 1657-8, Rachel (Edgecomb), October 23, 1660, Hester, August 16, 1664, Anthony, October 14, 1666.

GIBBONS, WILLIAM, mariner, knew Presumpscot River, 1623; mentioned at Saco, 1638-1652.

GRANT, FERDINANDO, employe of Thomas Williams at Winter Harbor, 1640.

GREENWAY, CLEMENT, mariner of Barnstable at Saco, 1635-8; master of the ship built at Saco and launched, but lost off the Irish Coast, 1638.

HALEY, THOMAS, arrived 1637; Saco, 1640; wife Mary, daughter of John West, died 1658; children Ann, Lydia, Samuel and Thomas.

HELSON, JOHN, one of Cradock's fishermen at Boston, 1631; Winter Harbor, 1652; had built a house near Church Point, 1671; deceased 1686; widow Joanna, daughter of Henry Warwick; children Ephraim, John and Samuel.

HITCHCOCK, RICHARD, born 1608; planter in Massachusetts, 1634; Saco, 1636; died 1671; widow Lucretia, daughter of Thomas Williams; children, born at Saco, Jerusha, November 28, 1653, Thomas, February 20, 1655-6, Lydia (Plaisted), November 30, 1658, Rebecca, August 20, 1661, and Ann and Margaret, September 25, 1664.

HOGG, PETER, employe of Clement Greenway, 1635-7.

HOW, ANTHONY, fisherman, 1637.

HOWELL, MORGAN, planter, 1637; Cape Porpoise, 1643; died 1666; child John, born at Saco, June 16, 1642.

HURD, THOMAS, planter, 1640.

JENNER, THOMAS, clergyman at Weymouth, 1636; Saco, 1640-6; Norfolk, England, 1650; children Thomas, born 1628, and two daughters, mentioned in his correspondence.

LEE, JOHN, planter at Boston, 1639; Salem, 1641; Saco, 1642; had live stock at Cape Porpoise, 1647; son-in-law of John White at Sheepscot, 1664 to 1677, when he removed to Scituate.

LEIGHTON (Layton), JOHN, planter at Kittery, 1645; Layton's Point, Biddeford Pool, 1653; wife Joanna; removed to a farm bought of Thomas Atkins at Sagadahoc, "near 30 years" before 1678; child John.

LEWIS, THOMAS, Saco proprietor, 1631; had deceased with wife Elizabeth, 1639; children Elizabeth (Heywood), Judith (Gibbons), born 1627, and Mary (Gibson).

MILLS, ROBERT, planter, 1637; died at York, 1647; left a claim for wages long due from Vines at Saco; widow Dorothy married John Harker June 30, 1647; son James and three other small children.

MILLS, THOMAS, native of Exeter, England; Wells, 1653; wife Mary, a daughter of John Wadley, was at Bristol, England, that year; died 1681; children Martha, born at Bristol January 8, 1653-4, married James Smith and Christopher Grant, Elizabeth (Cloyce) and Sarah (Cloyce).

MORGAN, ROBERT, born 1602; sailed from Gravesend, England, June 20, 1635, in the "Philip"; Saco, 1636; Pemaquid, 1640; had land from Clark and Lake at Woolwich before 1665; living 1673; wife Mary.

MOSIER, HUGH, planter; arrived at Boston June 12, 1632, in the "James"; Casco, 1640; died 1660; widow Rebecca; children Elizabeth (Lane), James and John.

NANNEY, ROBERT, born 1613; merchant who sailed from Lombard Street, London, April 18, 1635, in the "Increase"; Saco, 1635; Dover, 1640-1651; Boston, 1662; died in Boston August 27, 1663; given execution against Gorges' house at York for former services; widow Catherine, daughter of John Wheelwright, married Edward Naylor; children, besides those who died young, Samuel, born 1659, Mary, born 1661, and Elizabeth, born 1664.

NEWLANDS, ANTHONY, planter, recognized as a resident of Maine, 1643; evidently a brother of Jeremiah, of Ipswich; Salisbury, 1651; Ipswich, 1659.

OLDHAM, JOHN, planter and trader at Plymouth, 1623; on the Maine Coast, 1626; removed to Watertown, with the first settlers; killed at Block Island by the Indians in July, 1636.

PAGE, THOMAS, born 1606; tailor from All Saints Stayning; sailed from London in the "Increase" June 20, 1635; wife Elizabeth, born 1607; Saco, 1636; both parents died in 1645, leaving children, born in England, Thomas, 1633, Catherine, 1634; born at Saco, Christopher, George, born 1641, Mary and Sylvester.

PARKER, JOHN, of Bideford, England; first mate of the "Mayflower" at New Plymouth, 1620; Saco, 1630; Damariscove, 1645; Sagadahoc, 1648; died 1661; widow Mary; children Thomas, John, born at Saco, 1634, and Mary, born 1637, and married to Thomas Webber, of Charlestown.

PENWELL, WALTER, fisherman; son of Clement of Newton Ferrers, England; sailor with Ambrose Bouden on the "Margery," 1643; Saco, 1647; Biddeford, 1653; dead, 1682; widow Mary, daughter of Robert Booth: children Walter, born December 1, 1649, Mary, born March 12, 1652-3, Deborah, born December 30, 1654, Sarah, born August 2, 1661, and Susanna, born March 29, 1669.

PURCHASE, THOMAS, born 1577; planter at Saco from Dorchester, England, 1631-2; Brunswick, 1633; wife Mary Grove died in Charlestown, 1654; died at Salem, May 28, 1678, aged 101; widow Elizabeth; children Elizabeth (Blaney), Jane (Elkins) and Thomas.

RICHMOND, JOHN, merchant, 1637, from Bandon Bridge, Ireland; Richmond Island, 1638; wrecked in the new ship of Barnstable, built at Saco, 1638; on the Maine Coast, 1639.

ROBINSON, EDWARD, planter, 1640, seems to have been father of Francis.

ROBINSON, FRANCIS, born 1618; employe of Thomas Lewis at Saco, 1631; merchant at Barbadoes, 1650; Saco, 1667.

ROGERS, THOMAS, planter at Saco, 1638; Old Orchard, 1662; killed by Indians at Biddeford October 13, 1675, and his house at Saco burned the next day; children John, Richard and Thomas, born January 12, 1658-9.

SANKEY, ROBERT, born 1605; sailed from London June 20, 1635, in the "Increase"; fisherman and constable at Saco, 1636; died 1640-2.

SCADLOCK, WILLIAM, planter at Biddeford, 1636; removed to Cape Porpoise section later; died 1662; widow Eleanor married Stephen Kent, of Newbury, May 9, 1662; children John, Rebecca, Samuel, born 1643, Sarah (Gannett), Susanna and William.

SMITH, JOHN, born 1591; carpenter and member of the Company of Lygonia; arrived at Boston July 7, 1631; Saco, 1636; wife Ann in England; living 1687.

SMITH, THOMAS, son of Simon and Martha, of Stephney and London, England; Saco, 1640; Cousins Island with John Cousins, 1645; died 1652-8; daughter Judith married Richard Tozer of Berwick.

SMITH, WILLIAM, born 1588, brother of Richard, of Westchester, England; Saco, 1636; York, 1640; died at Scarborough, without issue, March 6, 1675-6.

TRISTRAM, RALPH, planter at Winter Harbor, 1644-1654; deceased 1679; children, born at Biddeford, Samuel, February 2, 1644-5, Benjamin and Nathaniel, July 10, 1650, Rachel, August 23, 1653, Ruhama, December 16, 1655, Freegrace, October 7, 1661, and Ruth, August 10, 1664.

VINES, RICHARD, physician and patentee of Saco, arrived from England in June, 1630, in the "Swift"; sometime a servant of Gorges; Barbadoes, 1646; died at Saint Michael's, 1651; widow Joan; children Belinda (Parasite), Elizabeth, Joan (Ducy), Margaret (Ellacott) and Richard, born at Clerkenwell, 1626.

WADLEY, JOHN, planter, 1635; Wells, 1639; died, at Biddeford, February 15, 1674; widow Margaret; children Mary (Mills) and Robert.

WALTON, JOHN, carpenter, arrived 1635; Saco, 1636; Portsmouth, 1644; wife Mary; died at Portsmouth, 1657; widow Ebel, of Plymouth, England; child John, born 1635.

WARNER, THOMAS, Boston, 1639; fishing partner of William Batten; Saco, 1647; Cape Porpoise, 1653; died 1658; widow Catherine, married John Searl November 26, 1661; child Thomas, born in Boston, 1658.

WARWICK, HENRY, planter on the east side of Saco River, 1636; died 1679; widow Jane; children Joanna (Helson, Tenny) and John.

WATTS, HENRY, born 1604; fishmonger from England; arrived at Saco in the "White Angel" in June, 1631; fowler at Scarborough, 1639; married the widow of George Barlow, before 1670; living in 1687.

WAY, GEORGE, fisherman at Winter Harbor, 1650; came to New Plymouth with Richard Carle and Thomas Wallen, in a boat belonging to the former's father; sent home.

WEST, JOHN, born 1588; planter at Salem, 1636; Saco, 1637; Wells, 1659; died 1663; widow Edith; children Ann and Mary (Haley).

WILLIAMS, RICHARD, contractor at Boston, 1635; died in March of the next year while manufacturing clapboards at Saco, in partnership with Peyton Cook.

WILLIAMS, THOMAS, Boston 1631-4; Saco, 1636; indebted to Cradock at Saco, 1636; may have married Ann, widow of Thomas Wannerton, of Pascataqua, as his second wife; children Jerusha (Hull) and Lucretia (Hitchcock).

WISE, THOMAS, planter, 1636-9; in partnership with Hugh Mosier at Casco, 1640; Casco, 1668.

SCARBOROUGH RIVER

This stream, called Oriscoage by the Indians and Blue Point River by the English settlers, enters the sea at its confluence with the Nonesuch—about six miles northeasterly from the mouth of Saco River. The first European resident on the western bank was Henry Watts, a fishmonger, who removed from Saco to Pine Point in 1633. Three years later Richard Foxwell secured five hundred acres above that point, then styled Blue Point, from his father-in-law Richard Bonython, whose patent for Saco included the district.

The homesteads of Foxwell and Watts were contiguous. That of the latter contained only an hundred acres and, in 1639, other tracts of the same dimensions had been selected, in the order named, along the shore to the westward by Nicholas Edgecomb, Hilkiah Bailey and George Dearing. Subsequently, the widow of Dearing married Jonas Bailey, and the last two lots were combined in one farm.

William Smith, of Casco, testified in later years that, when he first visited Blue Point in 1640, the only plantations then established on that side of the river were those of Dearing, Edgecomb, Foxwell and Watts. Wilmot, wife of Nicholas Edgecomb, came to Richmond Island as a "covenant-servant" and, according to her own statement, removed to Scarborough at the time of her marriage in 1641. George Barlow and Edward Shaw settled on the eastern bank of Scarborough River, but much later.

Submission to Massachusetts was effected by this and the Casco plantations July 13, 1658.*

STRATTON'S ISLANDS.

These two diminutive islets, lying before Old Orchard Beach—about two miles south of Scarborough and three miles west of Richmond Island—took their name from John Stratton, either because he was wrecked there in 1632, or lived there until the next year. Stratton could not have made a reasonable claim to the premises

---

* Mass. Col. Rec., 4-296

because they were not included in his patent of Cape Porpoise. They contain about twelve acres.

In 1637, the islands were only inhabited by fishermen, who had left the service of Winter at Richmond Island. Seven boats were employed there constantly under the supervision of Andrew Alger, a former servant of Winter. His associates were John Billings, Oliver Clark, Alexander and William Freathy, William Ham, Narias Hawkins, John Lander and John Symonds.

Alger and his men were still living on the larger island in 1645, after it had been conveyed to Cammock by Gorges. Some of his earlier partners soon departed westward or returned to their English homes, but he removed to Saco and thence to Dunstan, on the mainland.

NONESUCH RIVER

The original English name for the stream that unites with the Oriscoage from the northward and enters the sea at Pine Point was Black Point River. "Strattons Yslands" were described as "lying neare" and "abutting upon Bla: Poynt" to the south. The pioneer on the west bank of Nonesuch River was John Mills, who had been an employe of John Winter at Richmond Island. He was located at Whinnock's Neck in 1638, when attorneys of Trelawney and Goodyear required him to attorn as tenant of the proprietors.

In 1651, the territory situated between Scarborough and Nonesuch rivers—although previously comprised in the second grant to Trelawney and Goodyear and seized by their agents July 12, 1638—was purchased from the Indians by Andrew Alger and his brother Arthur, then of Saco. The tract acquired by them was afterwards called Dunstan in honor of the English town of their nativity. The dwelling of Andrew was situated in the interior on the western bank of Nonesuch River, adjoining that of Arthur Alger. Later, lots below these were occupied by Andrew, Elizabeth, John and Matthew, children of the former. The daughter married John Palmer, born in 1640.*

October 12, 1675, the Alger settlement at Dunstan was attacked by the Indians and among the fatalities Andrew Alger was killed during the conflict and Arthur died two days later at Marblehead, whither he had been transported on shipboard with other refugees from the Eastward. No person by the name of Alger was stationed at Scarborough a year later.†

Between Nonesuch and Spurwink rivers was a tract, containing 1500 acres, which was granted by the Council of Plymouth to Thomas Cammock November 1, 1631, in consideration of the facts that he had lived "for this two yeares last past" in New England and had there "Inhabited planted & built In the Countrey of New England aforesayd some convenient housing, & for that hee hath ventered him selfe, hazarded his life, & expended severall somes

* York Deeds, 2-113 ; 13-102.
† Me. Hist. Col., 3-110.

of Money in the more ample discovery of the Coast & Harbours of those parts, & is for the aeffecting of soe good a worke minded to undergoe the further Charge of settleing him selfe, his family & freinds in those Parts."‡

The two years' residence of Cammock in New England, alluded to in the patent, was the period of his service for the Laconia Company, in association with Jocelyn and Neal at Pascataqua, where he was rewarded later for his "Charge and Desertful endeavour" with a conveyance of the land at Eliot which he had recovered from William Hilton.§

After a stormy passage Cammock arrived from England April 22, 1632, and landed, apparently, at Jewell's Island, where he was injured by a fall from the fishing stage of George Jewell, master of an English vessel. Three months later the invalid was visiting Richmond Island, where he reported that, owing to his disability, he had been unable to complete a house.

Under the date of October 18, 1632, Cammock arrived in Massachusetts Bay from Pascataqua, in company with Edward Godfrey. They brought sixteen hogsheads of Indian corn, in Captain Neal's pinnace, to be ground at the windmill in Watertown.

When the order for dismissal of the employes of the Laconia Company was issued in England December 5, of that year, Neal was instructed to allot land to the principal employes in consideration of their services for the proprietors at Pascataqua. Cammock was instated by Neal in the Hilton tract at Eliot.

The Pascataqua pioneer took possession of his concession at Black Point May 23, 1633. Delivery was made by Neal in the presence of Abraham Shurt, Richard Smith and John Winter, and described a tract "bounded to the Southward with the Bay of Sacoe, on the Westward with bla: Poynt River, To the Eastward with the small brooke Called Spurwinke." A confirmation by Sir Ferdinando Gorges, dated March 15, 1640-1, specified that Stratton's Islands were to be part of the premises.*

When Cammock built the first house at Black Point is not definitely known, but it was standing on the easterly side of Nonesuch River opposite Blue Point in 1638.

In the summer of that year John Jocelyn, a versatile writer for the times, with his father Sir Thomas, of Kent, Cammock and

‡ York Deeds, 2-84, 87.
§ York Deeds, 1-3, 1.
* York Deeds, 2-84.

NONESUCH RIVER

other passengers shipped for New England on the *Nicholas* of London. During the voyage the narrator mentioned Martin Ivy and Thomas Jones, two of the boys who had been engaged by Cammock to work on his plantation at Scarborough. Their vessel first sighted Newfoundland.

Four days down the coast Cammock left the ship and "went aboard of a Barke of 300 Tuns, laden with Island Wine, and but 7 men in her, and never a Gun, bound for Richmonds Island, set out by Mr. Trelaney of Plimouth." Later in the season Winter alluded to this vessel as the *"Samuel* of Aveiro."

The *Nicholas* continued its course to Boston. July 12 Jocelyn sailed with his father for Black Point—a distance estimated at 150 miles—and two days later arrived at his destination, accompanied by his brother Henry from Pascataqua.

Their advent was announced by Winter in these words: "Mr. Joslins father is now Com over, & another of his sonnes with him, & doth purpose to live their with him: the live all yett with Captaine Cammocke before he have fitted him selfe with a house." From this observation it appears that Jocelyn, who had just removed thither from Newichawannock, had not resided upon his grant long enough to have completed a habitation of any kind.†

Excerpts from Jocelyn's narrative of his first voyage to New England are roughly descriptive of frontier conditions at that time at the Eastward.‡

On one occasion, in August, he "hapned to walk into the Woods, not far from the Sea-side" where, "near half a mile from the house," he encountered "a piece of ground over-grown with bushes, called there black Currence * * * they being ripe and hanging in lovely bunches." These were known to later settlers as whortleberries. While he was satisfying his appetite he "heard a hollow thumping noise upon the Rocks approaching" and "presently * * * a great and grim over-grown she-Wolf" appeared.

In the language of the narrator, "I began presently to suspect that she had fallen foul upon our Goats, which were then valued (our she Goats) at Five pound a Goat; Therefore to make further discovery, I descended (it being low water) upon the Sea sands, with an intent to walk round about a neck of land where the Goats usually kept. I had not gone far before I found

| Mc. Doc Hist., 3-140.
‡ Mass. Hist. Col., 3-3, 226.

the footing of two Wolves, and one Goat betwixt them, whom they had driven into a hollow, betwixt two Rocks, hither I followed their footing, and perceiving by the Crowes, that there was the place of slaughter, I hung my piece upon my back, and upon all four clambered up to the top of the Rock, where I made ready my piece and shot at the dog Wolf, who was feeding upon the remainder of the Goat."

In the month of May "within a stones throw" of the house, the writer killed "above four score Snakes." Some of these were, in his own words, "as big as the small of my leg, black of colour, and three yards long, with a sharp horn on the tip of their tail two inches in length."

"About 4 of the clock in the afternoon" of September 24, after his arrival in the country, "a fearful storm of wind began to rage, called a Hurricane." Jocelyn said, that the "impetuous wind that goes commonly about the Compass" in such cases, "began from the W. N. W. and continued till next morning, the greatest mischief it did us was the wracking of our Shallop, and the blowing down of many tall Trees, in some places a mile together." While the language is archaic, the accounts are interesting.

John Jocelyn left Black Point for England by way of Boston in the *Fellowship*, George Luxon master, September 23, 1639; he did not return until after twenty years had elapsed.

Sir Thomas Jocelyn, who had been chosen a local commissioner by Gorges in 1639, left the country with his son before he had received notification of his appointment.

Henry Jocelyn remained at Scarborough, where a grant of 1000 acres, situated upon the inland margin of the Cammock tract, had been conferred upon him. Vines claimed that such a concession had been made to him before any of the patents were executed by the Council of Plymouth in that vicinity. The grantee occupied a part of his territory and leased and conveyed lots from it to his brother Abraham Jocelyn, Andrew Heifer, Philip Hingston, John Libby and Anthony Row. The district bordered upon Libby's River.

When Cammock died in the West Indies in 1643, he had already devised his holdings in Maine to his widow Margaret and his former business associate Jocelyn in equal shares. Subsequently, the joint legatees were married and continued to reside upon the estate at Black Point. A part of their farm is now known as Prout's Neck. July 16, 1666, Jocelyn sold the premises, with 750 acres of his own which had never been alienated, to Joshua Scottow, a Boston merchant, and removed to Pemaquid.§ In December, 1676, a ship was sent from Massachusetts to the Eastward to remove the surviving Englishmen. The Indians had depopulated the "whole country, driving away all Christians from the ffishing Islands as well as Continent as farre as Black point, which they tooke, and burnt and destroyed all houses Eastward."*

Pioneers

ALGER, ARTHUR, born 1625, brother of Andrew; Scarborough, 1651; wounded by Indians at Dunstan, October 12, 1675; died two days later at Marblehead; widow Ann married Samuel Walker of Woburn.
BAILEY, HILKIAH, employe or tenant of Richard Foxwell at Blue Point, 1640; last mentioned, 1645.
BARLOW, GEORGE, clergyman at Exeter, June 5, 1639; Saco, 1649; owned land at Dunstan; widow Sarah married Henry Watts, 1670; children may have included George, who died at Plymouth, 1684.
BOUDEN, AMBROSE, mariner, had a dwelling on the west side of Spurwink River, opposite Robert Jordan's house, thirty years before 1676; died 1679; children Ambrose and John.
BOUDEN, JOHN, son of Ambrose; fowler at Black Point, 1640; Saco, 1671; married Grace, widow of Nicholas Bully; children, born at Scarborough, Hannah, July 9, 1653, Lucy, June 25, 1660, John, July 15, 1671, and Nicholas, January 19, 1673-4.
BURRAGE, BENJAMIN, farmer at Spurwink House, 1639-1640.
BURRAGE, JOHN, of Thorne Combe, Devonshire, England; farmer at Spurwink House, 1639-1640; removed to Blue Point; died 1663; widow Avis married Thomas Hammett; son William, born at Scarborough, 1648.
HICKFORD, JOHN, butcher from Cheapside, England, 1637; Saco, 1640; returned to England.
JOCELYN, JOHN, brother of Henry, arrived at Black Point from England by way of Boston, July 14, 1638; returned to England. 1639; came back, 1660; no issue; wrote an account of his two visits to Maine.
JOCELYN, THOMAS, born 1650, father of Henry and John, came with the latter to Black Point, 1638; described as an "auncient knight"; returned to England, 1639; children, by Elizabeth Tirrell, Ann (Mildmay), Benjamin, Dorothy (Brewster), Edward, Elizabeth (Neile), Frances (Vincent) and Thomas; by wife Theodora, Henry. Theodora and Thomazine.
SHAW, EDWARD, planter at New Plymouth, 1632; Blue Point. 1640; Saco, 1645; Scarborough. 1658; wife Jane; deceased 1662; child Richard.
TUCKER, RICHARD, born at Stogumber, England. 1594; planter at Spurwink, 1631; wife Margaret. daughter of Nicholas Reynolds and sister of Mary, wife of Arnold Allen; Casco. 1633; merchant at Great Island. 1653; drowned 1679; daughter Mary (Hoskins).
WEEKS. OLIVER. employe of George Cleave at Spurwink, 1633; employe of Winter at Richmond Island, 1634-1643; Saco, 1650.

§ York Deeds. ?-6
* Doc. Rel. to N. Y., 3-255.

SPURWINK RIVER

This stream is situated about three miles east of Scarborough River and was styled a brook by early mariners. Prout's Neck and Scarborough Beach intervene between the two rivers. The Spurwink was made prominent in local history by George Cleave and Richard Tucker, who built a small house near its mouth on the eastern bank in 1630.

The first habitation became the subject of much subsequent litigation and was finally acquired by the owners of Richmond Island. Although they obtained possession by virtue of their grant from the Council of Plymouth in 1631 and took control two years later through the agency of John Winter, the real ownership was in dispute for more than thirty years.

The history of Spurwink River during the colonization period is identified with that of its island port near the mainland, with which it is connected by a bar at low water.

RICHMOND ISLAND.

This oblong islet, which lies near the point of Cape Elizabeth, is only three miles in perimeter and contains about 200 acres of land.

It was known to early Dutch navigators as "Wingardes Eylant" and to the Italians as "Winter or Wingert" Island. The name was derived from the German word "Weingut," meaning vineyard. The place was so named on account of the profusion of wild grapes found there by the discoverer.

In 1607, Richmond Island was the unnamed seagirt refuge visited by Sagadahoc colonists when they "overshot" the mouth of the Sagadahoc River in their western course from Saint George.

May 29, 1623, the island with the mainland opposite was drawn by the Duke of Richmond, in the great lottery of New England territory. It afterwards assumed his name.

Late in that same year Christopher Levett found it to be uninhabited by Europeans, but he described the locality as an ideal resort for fishermen. His statement was that "There hath been more fish taken within two leagues of this place this year than in any other in the land."*

April 11, 1627, John Burgess, master of a fishing vessel, which was called the *"Annes"* and hailed from Westleigh, England, made his will while lying sick "in Richman's Island" in New England. The will was probated in a British registry May 24, 1628, and disposed of marine equipment.†

By some the name of "Richman's Island" has been presumed to have been derived from its connection with John Billington, or Woodman, as he was styled by the author of the New English Canaan. Woodman was an early discoverer of valuable slate deposits, as he supposed, on the northerly end of the island, but his dream of monopoly and wealth induced him to commit murder for which he was executed in Massachusetts in 1630.

The first occupant of the island was Walter Bagnall. His death occurred there October 3, 1631, after a New England residence of seven years. He had lived at Mount Wallaston in 1624, but sought this lone island in 1628. As a member of Thomas Morton's household at the time of the latter's arrest he was banished from Massachusetts and later referred to in the following statement: "Some of ye worst of ye company were disperst."‡

Bagnall was the individual to whom Morton alluded when he remarked, "A servant of mine in 5. yeares was thought to have a 1000.p. in ready gold gotten by beaver, when hee dyed."§

The death of Bagnall was described as a murder committed by an "Indian Sagamore, called Squidrayset, and his company, upon one Walter Bagnall, called Great Watt, and one John P—, who kept with him. They, having killed them, burnt the house over them, and carried away their guns and what else they liked." To this report was added, by way of description, "This Bagnall was sometimes servant to one in the bay, and these three years had dwelt alone in the said isle, and had gotten about £400 most in goods. He was a wicked fellow, and had much wronged the Indians."**

Squidrayset, according to Levett, was living at the first fall in Presumpscot River in 1624. Obviously, the companion of

* Me. Hist. Col., 2-83.
† Waters' Gen. Glean., 1-2.
‡ Bradford, 2-162.
§ N. E. Canaan, 70.
** Winthrop, 1-62.

Bagnall was John Peverly, whose name was preserved in a list of servants sent to New England by Captain John Mason between 1622 and 1635; the first of these colonists settled in Massachusetts. William Wood asserted that Bagnall's family, perhaps alluding to Peverly only, was killed at the time of the early evening massacre, and there has always been some conjecture as to what became of the gold. It was asserted that the savages took what else they wanted, but the redistribution of the money by them was never detected by the English traders. Morton assumed that it was confiscated by the Massachusetts authorities, but disposed of the mystery with the expression, "whatsoever became of it." In 1855, however, an earthen jar, containing coins and a seal ring with the initials "G. V.," was uncovered by the ploughshare on a northerly slope of the island.†

December 2, 1631, which was about two months after the decease of Bagnall, the Council of Plymouth issued a grant of Richmond Island, together with 1500 acres on the mainland opposite, in his name, but there is no record of any assertion of title by his heirs in after years.

CAPE ELIZABETH.

George Cleave claimed to Sir Ferdinando Gorges, as chief proprietor, that he was the original settler at Spurwink River, where he had been "lawfully seized" of a certain tract of land for seven years before 1640. The claimant had held his premises "by virtue of a promise made unto him" by Gorges himself. He supplemented his plea with the reminder that the "promise was made unto me for my encouragement before my coming into this Country, in any place unposessed, as is to you well knowne."‡

This statement disclosed the fact that Cleave had been one of the original pioneers of Gorges, who had come to Saco in the *Swift* in 1630 and chosen the site for his home at the mouth of the Spurwink River, where he had built a habitation that year. Richard Tucker formed a partnership with him the following year and they occupied the premises jointly. It was during the first year of their association that Sir Christopher Gardiner visited their establishment and by way of trade secured a warm-

† Me. Doc. Hist., 3-6.
‡ Me. Doc. Hist., 3-206.

ing pan and fowling piece for which his host, Thomas Purchase, was held to be accountable in a subsequent court proceeding.

December 1, 1631, when the Council of Plymouth granted the mainland at Cape Elizabeth to Robert Trelawney and Moses Goodyear, merchants of Plymouth, it was generally understood that the right of the Duke of Richmond in that territory had lapsed for failure to proceed with colonization. Goodyear was a son-in-law of Abraham Jennings, of Plymouth, who had operated formerly at Monhegan.

A few months after the issuance of their patent the Plymouth proprietors executed an agreement with Thomas Pomeroy and John Winter, both of Plymouth, to take legal possession for them. Their tract extended along the coast from Cammock's boundary at Spurwink River to the Presumpscot, then called Casco River, and included "the Bay and River of Cascoe," with the mainland opposite the island formerly occupied by the pioneers of Levett in Casco Bay.§

Trelawney insisted that Levett had lost his previous rights at Casco by failure to comply with the seven-year period of occupancy required of proprietors in the earlier grants, and asserted that a patent of the same premises abandoned by Levett had been promised to him by the council two years before it was finally issued.

April 17, 1632, Winter arrived at Richmond Island from England as attorney for the proprietors and July 21, following, took possession of the mainland from Richard Vines of Saco. At the same time he requested Cleave and Tucker to vacate their house at Spurwink. A letter written by Trelawney to Gorges after April 2, 1637, alluded to that patentee's previous occupation of the concession in these words: "I have issued out £3900, & have binne these 7 yeares almost on itt."*

Winter returned to Plymouth in midsummer, but he left Andrew and Thomas Alger and John Baddiver in charge of the house at Richmond Island, where they were engaged subsequently in felling and sawing timber by hand, as well as in fishing.

Meantime, events of a startling nature were transpiring at the Eastward. About the time of Winter's departure a French buccaneer raided Plymouth plantation at Castine while its man-

§ Me. Doc. Hist., 3-1.
* Me. Doc. Hist., 3-103

ager was absent at the westward. In the same raid the marauders captured Dixie Bull with his ship and trading goods. Bull and his crew hailed from Dorchester, Massachusetts, but hovered constantly about the Northern Coast, or as Winthrop expressed it "kept about the east." The victims of this outrage were convinced that their misfortunes were traceable directly to some suggestion or complicity on the part of the planters at Pemaquid. They assumed that Shurt was envious of their coastal trade, which was conducted wholly by means of a small shallop.

Adopting the same tactics which they had supposed were used at Pemaquid, Bull and his sympathizers formed a coalition with the northern French planters and raided Shurt's trading house.

There were persistent rumors that the piratical crew proposed to sack Dorchester itself, where the magistrates had incurred their early ill will. Even Richmond Island was mentioned as a point of attack because one of Trelawney's men had offended in some way, probably during Bull's eastern passage that spring.

But the winds proved unfavorable for their plans, and they were detained so long beyond Casco Bay that Captain Neal of Pacataqua started in pursuit with two pinnaces, two shallops and about forty men. He encountered a long spell of adverse winds at Pemaquid, and failed to apprehend the pirates, but on his return in December he "hanged up" an Indian, called Black Will, who was supposed to be "one of those who had there murdered Walter Bagnall."†

March 2, 1632-3, Winter came back from England with Peter Hill, John Mills and John Wilkinson, prepared to remain through the winter. Thomas Alger and John Baddiver embarked for home on the return of their ship *Welcome* July 15, 1633.

Although Neal had ordered Cleave and Tucker to quit the premises at Spurwink they still persisted, in spite of the fact that the captain was recognized then as governor of the whole district from the Merrimac to Sagadahoc River.

During July and August a house was built on the island for Trelawney's employes. This building was described as forty feet long, eighteen feet wide, and fitted with bunks for summer fishermen. Winter reported to Trelawney, "We have made a pallasatho about our house of 15 foote high, & mounted our

† Winthrop, 1-99.

ordinance" (two small cannon) "in platt formes with in our pallasatho for our defence from those that wish us harme heare."‡

The dwelling at Spurwink was abandoned by Cleave and Tucker in the fall of 1633, and under the date of June 18, 1634, Winter wrote to his principals in England: "At the maine we have built no house, but our men lives in the house that the old Cleves built, but we have fitted him som what better, and we have built a house for our pigs."

Writing in the same letter, Winter said: "I have an Intent, God willinge, to Com home for England the next yeare, and I think so will all our Company that ar heare with me." The permanent residents at Cape Elizabeth at that time, including Oliver Weeks, who had left the employment of Cleave to serve Winter, were six.§

April 26, 1635, Narias Hawkins came to take supervision of the plantation and the old company returned to England, as predicted by Winter. The new company was composed of John Billings, Oliver Clark, Sander (Alexander) Freathy and his brother William, William Ham, Narias Hawkins, John Lander and John Symonds.*

Under the date of August 10, 1635, Richard Mather, who came from the Eastward, on his way from England to Massachusetts, noted in his daily memoranda: "When we came within sight of the island, the planters there (or rather fishers, for their chief employment was fishing,) being but two families, and about forty persons, were sore afraid of us, doubting lest we had been French, come to pillage the island, as Penobscote had been served by them about ten days before."†

The inhabitants of Black Point and Richmond Island were loyal to the established church of England and signs of any dissension among the factions represented in the western colonies were matters of general interest at the Eastward at that time. There politics and religion masqueraded under the same banner. The Wheelwright controversy was one in which Massachusetts authorities were fearful of criticism in those neighboring communities where political sentiment was favorable to the Gorges administration.

‡ Me. Doc. Hist., 3-31. 48.
§ Me. Doc. Hist., 3-32.
* Me. Doc. Hist, 3-97.
† Young's Mass. Chron., 471.

As an illustration, April 17, 1637, Edward Winslow reported to Governor Winthrop: "The last news is this whereat I am most grieved That all the late differencs betw. mr Wheelwright & yor selves in Church & Court are in writing at Richmunds Ile where" (Edward) "Turlany shewed" (Myles Standish) "six sheets of pap full written about them."‡

The sequel of the Massachusetts contention was a bloodless one, in which the Wheelwright adherents were deprived of their arms and ammunition and left helpless in case of Indian assault. Fortunately, the natives were then at peace with the settlers.

Mills operated by water power were not an early convenience. The first saw pit, in which vertical saws were driven by man power, was mentioned at Kittery Point in 1637. July 10, 1639, Winter reported that there was no gristmill east of Massachusetts Bay.§

Shipbuilding at Richmond Island was begun at an early date. The bark *Richmond,* finished there in 1639, was freighted at Casco with clapboards for England, whence it never returned to this country. The ship *Richmond,* completed two years later, was retained by Trelawney in foreign commerce.

An early settler at the mouth of Spurwink River on the western bank was Ambrose Bouden, whose title was derived from the Cammock estate. He was an English sea captain who had conducted several fishing enterprises at Richmond Island, before 1643, in the interest of Trelawney. In 1640, his son John had distinguished himself at Scarborough as an expert fowler. At that time the house built by Cleave on the opposite side of the river was occupied by John and Benjamin Burrage, farmers employed by Winter to manage Spurwink plantation.

Pioneers

ALGER, ANDREW, born 1610; employe of Winter who arrived April 17, 1632; returned to England and came back in the "Speedwell," April 26, 1635; Stratton's Island, 1636-1645; bought Dunstan from Indians, 1651; killed by them on his own premises October 12, 1675; widow Agnes, born 1621; children Andrew, Elizabeth (Palmer, Austin), born 1644, Joanna (Oakham, Mills), born 1650, John, born 1640, Matthew and Mary (Ashton), born 1648.

ALGER, TRISTRAM, fisherman, arrived February 13, 1636-7, in the "Hercules"; returned to his wife in England after 1641.

ALLEN, WILLIAM, fisherman, arrived from Millbrook, England, May 10, 1638, in the "Fortune"; went back to England two months later.

‡ Mather's N. E., 287.
§ Me. Doc. Hist., 3-172.

AMORY, JOHN, cooper, arrived from Chudleigh, February 13, 1636-7, in the "Hercules"; returned to his wife in England the next year.
ANDREWS, EDMUND, blacksmith, from Yealmpton, England, 1642-5.
BADDIVER, JOHN, laborer, employed by Trelawney to hold possession at Cape Elizabeth during the winter of 1632-3; returned to England July 15, 1633, in the "Welcome."
BAGNALL, WALTER, trader at Mount Wallaston; Richmond Island, 1628; killed by Presumpscot Indians October 3, 1631.
BAILEY, JONAS, born 1607; planter, 1634; Scarborough, 1641; wife Elizabeth; died at Saco, 1664; widow Eleanor, who had previously been the wife of George Dearing and John Jackson.
BEST, EDWARD, fisherman, arrived from Millbrook, England, May 10, 1638, in the "Fortune"; returned to England two months later.
BILLINGS, JOHN, fisherman, arrived April 26, 1635, in the "Speedwell"; Stratton's Island, 1636; Kittery Point, 1639; died 1646; widow Elizabeth married Richard Thomas; son John, born 1635.
BONE, THOMAS, fisherman, arrived from Saltash, England, February 13, 1636-7, in the "Hercules"; sailed for Newfoundland July 19, 1638, in the "Samuel."
BUCKNELL, ROGER, fisherman, 1638-9; left a wife in England.
BUNT, GEORGE, fisherman, 1639-1641.
BURGESS, JOHN, master of a fishing vessel called the "Annes," who was taken sick at the island and made his will April 11, 1627; died at Westleigh, England, 1628; widow Joanna Bray; children John, Robert and William.
CANNAGE, MATTHEW, fisherman, 1634; fatally injured at his house on Monhegan by Gregory Castle in 1654.
CHAPPLE, ANTHONY, fisherman, returned to England in the "Fortune," 1638.
CHAPPLE, WILLIAM, fisherman, returned to England July 8, 1637.
CLARK, ANTHONY, fisherman, 1639; returned to England, 1641.
CLARK, OLIVER, fisherman, arrived April 26, 1635, in the "Speedwell."
COBB, PETER, fisherman, 1639.
CUMMINGS, RICHARD, born 1603; fisherman, 1635; Isles of Shoals, 1645; married Elizabeth, daughter of Richard Bonython; died 1678; children Elizabeth (Foxwell) and Jane (Jose).
DEARING, GEORGE, carpenter, 1637; Scarborough, 1640; died soon and his widow married John Jackson and Jonas Bailey; son Roger, born 1646.
DUSTIN, THOMAS, born 1605; fisherman; arrived March 2, 1632-3, in the "Hunter"; Kittery, 1640; died 1678; widow Elizabeth; son Thomas, of Haverhill.
EDGECOMB, NICHOLAS, born 1592; fisherman, 1637; married Wilmot Randall; Scarborough, 1641; Casco, 1658; died 1681; widow survived; children John, Mary (Page, Ashton), born 1642, Christopher, born 1643, Joanna (Elkins, Pyncheon), born 1649, Michael, born 1651, and Robert, born 1652.
EDMUNDS, HENRY, fisherman; arrived from Millbrook, England, May 10, 1638, but remained only two weeks.
EDWARDS, WILLIAM, fisherman, drowned, 1637.
FIELD, RICHARD, fisherman, 1637; returned to England, 1641.
FISHCOCK, EDWARD, boatmaster, 1634; returned to England, 1637.
FREATHY, ALEXANDER, fisherman, arrived in the "Speedwell" April 26, 1635; Stratton's Island, 1636; returned to England, 1638.
FREATHY, WILLIAM, fisherman and brother of Alexander, arrived 1635; Stratton's Island, 1636; York, 1640-1671; widow Elizabeth; children Joan (Holmes), John and Samuel.
GARLAND, JOHN, born 1621; mariner, 1639; died at Hampton January 4, 1671; widow Elizabeth.

GAUDE, MARK, fisherman, arrived from Saint Johns, England, May 10, 1638, in the "Fortune," and returned soon after.
GIBSON, RICHARD, clergyman, arrived from England in the "Hercules" May 24, 1636; married Mary, daughter of Thomas Lewis; Portsmouth, 1639; Isles of Shoals during the summer of 1642; returned to England that year.
GILL, ARTHUR, shipwright, 1637-8; Boston, 1639; died in England, leaving family in this country; widow Agnes; children, born in England, Frances; born at Boston, John, November 16, 1639, Thomas, October 12, 1644, and Nathaniel.
GILL, PETER, fisherman, 1633; returned to England, 1634.
GOUCH, WILLIAM, fisherman, 1641-3.
GULLET, PETER, fisherman, arrived May 24, 1636, in the "Fortune"; died October 2, 1636; widow in England.
HAM, WILLIAM, fisherman, arrived from England in the "Speedwell," April 26, 1635; Stratton's Island, 1636; died at Portsmouth January 26, 1672-3; daughter Elizabeth (Cotton).
HAMMOCK, THOMAS, fisherman, 1638-1643; married Avis, widow of John Burrage; died in Scarborough, 1676.
HAMMOND, PENTECOST, fisherman, 1637-1641.
HANCOCK, HENRY, carpenter, 1638-1640.
HATCH, CHARLES, apprentice of Clement Penwell, of Newton Ferrers, England; wife in England, 1634-1641; died 1653.
HATCH, PHILIP, brother of Charles; fisherman; arrived from England in the "Hercules" February 13, 1636-7; servant of Nicholas Ball at York, 1650; died 1674; widow Patience; child Philip, born 1651.
HAWKINS, NARIAS, overseer, arrived from England in the "Speedwell" April 26, 1635; headquarters at Stratton's Island, 1636; left for England, 1639; master of the "Star" next year; wife in England.
HEARL, WILLIAM, fisherman, 1638-1640; died at Portsmouth, 1690; widow (Beaton); child Sarah (Cotton).
HEIFER, ANDREW, fisherman, arrived from England in the "Fortune" May 24, 1636; Kittery, 1640; wife in England; died at Black Point April 14, 1661.
HEMPSON, JOHN, fisherman, arrived in the "Hercules" from England February 13, 1636-7; remained until 1641.
HEWETT, NICHOLAS, fisherman for only ten days, 1642.
HILL, PETER, fisherman, arrived with Winter March 2, 1632-3; removed to Saco; died August 29, 1667; only son Peter, born 1635.
HINGSTON, PHILIP, fisherman, from Holberton, England, 1639-1643; Saco, 1653; deceased 1662; widow Margaret married George Taylor; children Philip, Meribah and Sarah.
HOLE, or HOWELL, JOHN, fisherman, arrived from England in the "Hercules" February 13, 1636-7; merchant at Kittery, 1671-1690; died at Barbadoes; widow Elizabeth; son John, born 1633.
HOSKINS, JOHN, fisherman, 1634.
HUMPHREY, JEREMIAH, servant of Robert Jordan, 1648.
HURD, ARTHUR, fisherman, 1634.
JENKINS, REGINALD, born 1608; surgeon, arrived from England with Winter March 2, 1632-3; bought a house at Eliot of John Newgrove, 1650; wife Ann; children Jabez, Mary, Philadelphia, Sarah and Stephen.
JOPE, SAMPSON, fisherman, 1637-9; wife in England.
JOY, RICHARD, carpenter, 1641.
KING, THOMAS, carpenter, arrived from Stonehouse, England, with Winter March 2, 1632-3; services hired from Nicholas Longworthy; built the house at Richmond Island, 1633; returned to England.
LAKESLEY, JOHN, fisherman, 1641-3.

LANDER, JOHN, fisherman, arrived from England in the "Speedwell" April 26, 1635; Stratton's Island, 1636-8; Kittery Point, 1639; died 1646; probably drowned with Billings, who was his fishing partner.

LAPTHORNE, STEPHEN, fisherman, 1637-1640; returned to his wife and children in England, 1640.

LISSEN, THOMAS, fisherman from Plymouth, 1639.

LIBBY, JOHN, born 1602; fisherman, arrived from England in the "Hercules" February 13, 1636-7; died 1683; widow Mary; children Abigail (Fickett), Anthony, Daniel, David, Hannah (Fogg), Henry, James, Joanna (Bickford), John, born 1646, Mary (Slaughter), Matthew, Rebecca (Brown), Samuel and Sarah (Tidy).

LOPEZ, JOHN, servant of Winter, drowned, 1637.

LUCAS, WILLIAM, fisherman, 1637-1641.

MADDIVER, MICHAEL, fisherman, 1640-3; married Agnes, widow of Richard Carter, of North Yarmouth; died 1669; children Joel and Catherine (Marr).

MARTIN, FRANCIS, son of John, former mayor of Plymouth; Casco gentleman, 1640; daughter Mary executed in Boston, 1646, on the charge of destroying her illegitimate infant.

MARTIN, RICHARD, fisherman, arrived from England in the "Hercules" February 13, 1636-7; married Dorothy, widow of Benjamin Atwell; died at Falmouth January 14, 1672-3; daughter Lydia (Corbin).

MATHEWS, NICHOLAS, fisherman, 1639-1640.

MELLIN, WILLIAM, fisherman, 1638-1642.

MILLS, EDWARD, fisherman, arrived from England in the "Hercules" February 13, 1636-7; returned to England, 1640.

MITCHELL, PAUL, sailor, from Sheviock, England, 1637; wife in England, 1643; drowned in Massachusetts on a fishing cruise November 18, 1653.

NYLE, RICHARD, fisherman, arrived from England in the "Hercules" February 13, 1636-7.

OKERS, ROWLAND, fisherman, 1634.

PEVERLY, JOHN, one of Weston's men who came from Mount Wallaston, 1628; killed by Indians at Richmond Island October 3, 1631.

ROBERTS, JOHN, fisherman, drowned, 1637.

ROGERS, GEORGE, fisherman, 1637-8; servant of Thomas Gorges, 1640-3; Portsmouth, 1651; deceased that year; children Benjamin and four girls.

SAMPSON, THOMAS, brewer, 1637; returned to a wife in England.

SARGENT, STEPHEN, carpenter, arrived from England in the "Fortune" February 13, 1636-7; returned to England, 1640; back again, 1641; drowned at the Isles of Shoals, 1649.

SATERLEY, ROBERT, fisherman, arrived from England in the "Fortune" February 13, 1636-7; wife in England.

SAUNDERS, ROBERT, of Plymouth, fisherman, 1639-1640.

SHEPERD, THOMAS, fisherman, arrived from England in the "Hercules" February 13, 1636-7; returned to England, 1642.

SHORT, TOBIAS, servant of Winter, 1639-1643.

STEVENS, BENJAMIN, husbandman, arrived from Landrake, England, in the "Hercules" February 13, 1636-7; returned to wife in England, 1641.

SYMONDS, JOHN, born 1615; fisherman, arrived from England in the "Speedwell" April 26, 1635; Stratton's Island, 1636; Kittery, 1641; married Welthen, widow of John Goddard; died at Salem, 1671; children unknown.

TOWNSEND, HENRY, fisherman, 1634.

TREBY, EDWARD, fisherman, 1639-1642.

TRELAWNEY, EDWARD, of Bake, son of Robert, mayor of Plymouth, and brother of Robert, the patentee; arrived in the "Speedwell" April 26, 1635; returned to England, 1637; died 1643; widow Mary; children born in England, Anne (Toms), 1616, Eulalia, 1617, Elizabeth, 1619, Mary, 1621, Katherine, 1623, Dorothy, 1625, and Robert.

VINION, JOHN, fisherman, arrived from England in the "Hercules" May 24, 1636; returned to England, 1641.

WHITE, NICHOLAS, fisherman, arrived from England February 13, 1636-7, in the "Hercules"; House Island, 1661; Maquoit, 1662; died 1668-1671; widow Margery married William Haynes, of Scarborough; children Daniel, Margery and Samuel.

WILKINSON, JOHN, arrived from Plymouth March 2, 1632-3, in the "Welcome"; Saco, 1640; Scarborough later; dead 1666.

WILLINE, ROGER, fisherman, 1637; arrived from England in the "Hercules"; one of the first settlers of Cape Porpoise, 1641; Pemaquid, 1672; no record of his death.

WINTER, JOHN, arrived from Plymouth, England, April 17, 1632, on a fishing voyage; returned from Richmond Island that year and came back to the island March 2, 1632-3, with a few fishermen who had consented to "stay over" winter; wife Joan left at Plymouth, 1634; went back to Plymouth in 1635 and brought his wife the next year; died 1645; children John, Sarah (Jordan) and Mary (Hooper), who remained in England.

FORE RIVER

This important adjunct to Portland Harbor was known to the natives as Capisic River. In 1631, the western shore, known as Cape Elizabeth, was granted to Trelawney and Goodyear. The first settler on that side of the river was Michael Mitten, who married Elizabeth, only daughter of George Cleave. In 1637, the latter, as land agent for Gorges in his county of New Somerset, gave Mitten a lease of Peaks Island, which lies opposite the mouth of the river.

The tract on the eastern shore was called Machegonne by the Indians and settlement was begun there, in the fall of 1633, by Cleave and his partner Richard Tucker, who removed thither from Spurwink River. According to a deposition of Henry Jocelyn, Cleave and Tucker were the first European occupants on the site of the City of Portland.

In 1636, Cleave who had become solicitous for his legal rights at Casco went to England, where he held conferences with Gorges himself and January 27, 1636-7, purchased from him the entire point situated between Fore and Presumpscot rivers. This tract had been called by the natives Machegonne, but it was renamed Stogumber, in honor of the English town of Tucker's nativity.*

While in London Cleave had retained Thomas Morton to advocate the nomination of Gorges as royal governor of all New England, and Cradock, former governor of the Massachusetts Bay Colony, was asked to contribute to the expense of the campaign under a pretext that such an appointment would be beneficial to the interests of his colony.†

Although Gorges was appointed July 23, 1637, he never became active because the Massachusetts members of the commission declined to serve on account of their conviction that the interests of Gorges in Massachusetts and Maine were inimical to their own.

Cleave, however, fortified in his own mind for the purpose,

* York Deeds, 1-95.
† 4 Mass. Hist. Col., 6-127.

returned to Maine with the intention of summarily ending the controversy which had arisen between himself and Trelawney as to his titles at Spurwink and Machegonne.

By virtue of their deed the proprietors of Machegonne took seizin of the premises from Arthur Mackworth June 8, 1637. They had already occupied that point for about four years. Nevertheless, only twenty-two days later the rival proprietors of Cape Elizabeth, who had procured an extension of their former grant, took constructive possession as far east as Presumpscot River. On that occasion Richard Vines acted as attorney for the Council of Plymouth and Mackworth was one of the subscribing witnesses. Other influential planters who favored the title of Trelawney and Goodyear to Machegonne were Edward Godfrey, of York, Thomes Purchase, of Pejepscot, and John Winter, of Richmond Island.

On account of their political prominence in the district and because of their open opposition to his claim of ownership at Casco, Cleave at once cited all but Mackworth to appear in London, before a session of the court of Star Chamber to be holden October 11, 1637. At the hearing the complaint was dismissed for jurisdictional defects and resulted in the assessment of court costs against Cleave.

June 25, 1640, Cleave began litigation anew in a session of the Maine court which had been reorganized by Thomas Gorges. He proposed to establish his title over the rival claim of Trelawney, who on account of the death of Goodyear upon March 26, 1637, was sole owner at Casco by right of survivorship.

At the time of the suit the plaintiff alleged continuous occupation of the disputed premises for seven years. The defendant, who was represented by John Winter, asserted proprietorship by virtue of his original grant from the Council of Plymouth, which had defined his eastern boundary as the "River of Casco." Possession had been taken by the latter June 30, 1637.

During the trial testimony was introduced by Trelawney to prove that the Presumpscot was the "River of Casco" referred to in his grant.

The jury consisted of Arnold Allen, John Baker, Henry Boade, Thomas Cammock, William Cole, Richard Foxwell, Arthur Mackworth, Thomas Page, Francis Robinson, James Smith, John West and Thomas Withers. Some of the panel resided on the western side of the county. Mackworth should have known the facts, for he was represented as in possession of land on the easterly bank of the Presumpscot for "many yeares" before 1635.

Winter maintained that his witnesses had frequented Casco Bay before the plaintiff had occupied any part of the premises, but charged that the statements of members of the jury were secretly considered in its deliberations, and that none of the jurors had known Casco "above 5 or 6 yeares at the most." This time limit, when compared with the testimony of Arthur Brown, who was the defendant's witness and an associate of Mackworth, is significant, for the deponent testified that he had lived at Presumpscot but six years before the trial. Only seven years previously Neal had found the place deserted.‡

The decision, which was criticised by Godfrey as contrary to evidence, was to the effect that Fore River was the true Casco and that all of the land east of that boundary belonged to Cleave.§

An appeal from the verdict was taken to Godfrey, Gorges and Vines, who reviewed the entire case on or about July 29, 1642, and reversed the preliminary decision by finding that the Presumpscot was the "River of Casco" and the true eastern boundary of Trelawney's territory.

But the victory of the defendant was short-lived. The next year Cleave returned to England to obtain further relief. There he faced a dubious outlook. While chiefly instrumental in securing for Gorges the governorship of the Northern Colonies six years before, he could expect no immediate help from that source. The British government was in a state of war. His former patron, then over seventy years of age, had resumed active military service at the request of his sovereign, and his New England affairs were being neglected.

As an alternative course he sought an alliance with Sir Alexander Rigby, an influential member of Parliament who was concerned with the foreign policies of the realm.

As a theme of mutual preference Cleave directed the attention of the statesman to the possibilities of the New World. He even advocated the purchase of the Lygonia patent which had been in existence for a dozen years, although its owners had accomplished

‡ Me. Doc. Hist., 3-208, 233, 246, 273.
§ Me. Doc. Hist., 3-240.

nothing in the way of settlement. Some of patentees had died in the interim, and the concession was described by Vines as having lapsed into "an ould broken title."*

Rigby was easily convinced that acquisition of the defunct patent of Lygonia would increase his political prestige by a revival of royal interest in the Province of Maine. April 7, 1643, the transfer was effected. He purchased the shares of two surviving patentees for trifling considerations.

Cleave, on the other hand, was advised by Rigby to present his grievance to Parliament and in order to obtain consideration was directed to file a petition endorsed by a substantial number of the residents of New Somersetshire.

The document was alleged, owing to the exigencies of the occasion, to have been fabricated in London by the complainant himself. Upon it were exhibited the names of thirty-one planters commorant in the settlements of York, Wells, Cape Porpoise, Saco, Scarborough and Casco Bay. It was presented to Parliament upon the day following Rigby's acquisition of Lygonia. The accompanying address asked for a commission to review the adverse decision of Godfrey and Vines.

The efforts of Cleave were successful and April 28, 1643, the commission was ordered. It consisted of John Winthrop and Edward Gibbons of Boston, Henry Boade of Wells, Arthur Mackworth of Casco, and Thomas Morton, who was then in England.†

When the warrant reached this country it was forwarded to Casco to secure the depositions of Godfrey and Vines with such other evidence as they might be able to offer. The Boston members would not serve, and Mackworth refused to act as magistrate on account of what he considered technical defects in legal procedure. He also disclaimed his signature on the preliminary London petition. Andrew Alger, William Hammond, Francis Robinson, John Smith, John Wadley, Henry Watts, Peter Weare, John West and John Wilkinson, followed suit later.

The other men who made no protest were John Alcock, John Baker, Bartholomew Barnard, Joseph Jenks, Edward Johnson, Henry Lynn, George Puddington and Henry Simpson, of York; Henry Boade, of Wells; Ambrose Berry and William Reynolds,

---

* 4 Mass. Hist. Col., 7-353.
† Brit. Proc., 1-143.

of Cape Porpoise; John Bonython, William Cole, George Frost, Anthony Newlands, Thomas Page and William Smith, of Saco; and Arnold Allen, Michael Mitten, William Royal and Richard Tucker, of Casco.

As an alternative course the appellant then administered suppletory oaths to two of his colleagues who could be induced to attest the genuineness of the entire petition. Such action gave Vines sufficient reason to complain to Winthrop that the whole proceeding had been fraudulent from the beginning.

Thus far the controversy had netted but little advantage to either party and the status of Machegonne remained unchanged save for a confirmation of the title by Rigby May 23, 1643.‡

That statesman proceeded to outline a form of government for his part of New Somersetshire between Wells and Pejepscot and appointed Cleave "deputy president" with authority to dispose of his lands. Fortified by his new commission the deputy organized a rival regime, defined the territory of the province and executed leases of extensive tracts.

January 23, 1643-4, a court was convened at Casco on the same day as that at Saco. Both factions became belligerent, but finally were induced to await further instructions from Parliament.

During the armistice Cleave and "about thirty" of his supporters appealed to Winthrop for protection against the Gorges administration and requested membership in the confederation of Massachusetts colonies, which had been formed during the previous year.

A month later Vines appeared at Boston with a letter signed by all of Gorges' commissioners and "between 20 and 30" other inhabitants of the province. The figures indicate that the total census of adult planters in New Somersetshire at that time was only about sixty.§

The ownership of Maine real estate was destined to become more complicated. While control of the local government was in doubt and title to the site of Portland was being litigated, new claimants began to encroach upon Capisic lands in the interior. July 12, 1649, Squidrayset, sagamore of Presumpscot, conveyed 2400 acres of the territory situated between Fore River and

‡ York Deeds, 1-94.
§ Winthrop, 2-155.

Amuncongen (Westbrook) to Francis Small, the Indian trader. These premises were acquired subsequently by John Phillips. Other adverse interests were imminent at any stage, for Indian deeds, properly executed, were recognized by the General Court.*

As agent for Rigby interests Cleave sold a house lot on the western side of Fore River, above Long Creek, to Joseph Phippen, a fisherman who had an interest in the establishment at House Island. This deed was dated September 30, 1650, and described an hundred acres which must have been bounded on the south by the early homestead of Michael Mitten.

Cleave made sales, during the same year, from his own tract on the other side of the river to his son-in-law, in 1651, to Nicholas Bartlett, of Cape Porpoise, and May 20, 1658, to his grandson Nathaniel Mitten. At the last date he had disposed of the remaining land along the shore, with two exceptions, as far as Presumpscot River.†

He was facing old age and financial ruin from prolonged litigation with powerful opponents and September 26, 1659, assigned his homestead and contiguous real estate to John Phillips, of Boston. This action was taken none too soon, for within a few months Robert Jordan, successor to the Trelawney estate, brought a counter suit for the recovery of Machegonne.

Original documentary evidence was produced at the trial and as a consequence the plaintiff obtained a favorable verdict. The defendant had already arrived at the level of pitiable destitution. Even the couch to which the aged and infirm wife of Cleave was confined was taken in satisfaction of a paltry execution.

* York Deeds, 20-108.
† York Deeds, 6-3 ; Me. Hist. Col., 1-72.

THE CABIN AT CASCO

Far-faring seamen
Coasted the cape lands
And threaded the channel
That led to a harbor
And islet surrounded
By beautiful landscapes.

On this far islet
In the lone harbor,
Rough-hewn from the forest
And fashioned from fir trees,
They builded a structure—
The cabin at Casco.

Vessels returning
Over the ocean,
Receded from vision
Beyond the horizon
And left there undaunted
This household of toilers.

Often came thither
Indian sachems,
Who lived on the mainland,
To truck with the planters
In furs of the beaver,
And otter and moose skins.

Wives from the homeland
Lived not at Casco;
No voices of children
Awakened the clearing,
But cries of the sea-gulls
And surge of the breakers.

Oft in the evening,
Dreaming of Yuletide,
They heard in the distance
From over the water
Faint chiming echoes
From belfries of Devon.

Summers and winters
Gazing to seaward,
They looked for their comrades
To follow them thither,
But vainly they waited
While none came to join them.

Barnstable sailors
Fishing and trading,
Strayed into their clearing
And drank to their prospects,
But forthwith departed
At end of the season.

Then came a morning,
Never forgotten,
When incoming vessels
Brought word to recall them
Once more to their country
And arms of their loved ones.

Over the rooftree,
Where they had sojourned
In far-away Casco,
To welcome the stranger,
They left their loved ensign,
The banner of England.

Time had passed onward.
Immigrants later
Reclaimed the lone harbor.
Where once stood a cabin
To-day stands a city—
The City of Portland.

But the fair islet
Still forms a bulwark,
A sentinel guarding
The river and haven,
Where gulls in the water
Still sport with the surges.

VIEW OF PORTLAND

PRESUMPSCOT RIVER

Indefinite allusion to the region about Casco Bay is to be found in the account of a Sagadahoc colonist which was discovered among the private papers of Sir Ferdinando Gorges after his decease.

That writer described a visit to the coastal section west of Sagadahoc. His party consisted of Captain Raleigh Gilbert and fourteen others who "sailed by many gallant islands, and * * * were constrained to remain that night under the headland called Semeamis" (Cape Elizabeth).

After reaching Richmond Island and spending part of the next night there, they retraced their course homeward on August 30, 1607. Between Semeamis and Sagadahoc River was situated "a great bay" in which they encountered "many islands, so thick and near together" that they could not "well discern to number them."*

While Purchase ascribed the authorship of the anonymous document to James Davis, there is even stronger internal evidence that it was the work of Robert Davis. Whichever it may have been, the explorer's name was assigned to the headland of Cape Elizabeth and to Casco Bay, as late as 1631, when designations of "Cape Davis" and "Baia di Davis" were conspicuous on Italian maps.

Captain John Smith examined the coast of Casco carefully in 1614, using a boat of shallow draft to enable him to approach the mainland at all points. His reproduction of the Indian name for that locality was Aucocisco, although he christened it Harrington Bay.

Christopher Levett was a native of York, England. May 5, 1623, the Plymouth Council granted to him 6000 acres of land in New England which was not defined by metes and bounds. As the early patentees were not even familiar with natural boundaries in the New World, it was understood that the land was to be chosen from territory not then occupied by Englishmen and that surveys were to be made and recorded with the council. In those days sea captains, accustomed to the use of nautical instruments in navigation, were generally skilled in engineering. Levett had been engaged for several weeks after his arrival in the country in surveying a similar tract for David Thompson at Pascataqua, although he never completed the undertaking on account of its magnitude. The task was rendered almost impossible because of the presence of the virgin forests.

Levett came to Pascataqua by way of the Isles of Shoals and lived with Thompson in the new house at Little Harbor until his men, who had reached the eastern fishing grounds in "divers" ships, had arrived at his rendezvous. These employes were Englishmen who had worked on the fishing vessels until the end of the season and had arranged previously to remain through the winter with Levett.

After exploring the coast of Maine as far east as Cape Newagen Levett returned to Quacke, where he had decided to found a city by the name of York in honor of the English municipality of that name.

* Mass. Hist. Proc., 18-106.

The narrative of the settlement at Quacke, written by Levett himself in 1624, contains internal evidence that his house was located upon an island, to and from which Indians passed "over the harbor" in canoes. Samuel Maverick, who must have seen the post many times and may have lodged there, asserted that Levett had a patent for 6000 acres of land at Casco, "which he tooke up in this Bay neare Cape Elizabeth," where he "built a good House and fortified well on an Island lyeing before Casco River."†

Levett himself located "Quacke" about "two leagues to the East of Cape Elizabeth," and described it as "a Bay or Sound betwixt the Maine and certaine Ilands which lyeth in the sea about one English mile and halfe * * * going up within the Ilands to the Cape of Sagadahock" (Small Point). His final comment was, "After many dangers, much labour and great charge, I have obtained a place of habitation in New England, where I have built a house, and fortified it in a reasonable good fashion, strong enough against such enemies as are those Savage people."‡

The testimonies of William Gibbons, who had known the river before any house was built at Casco, and of other persons who had frequented it soon after, proved beyond question that the Presumpscot was known originally, and for many years after discovery, as Casco River. Its identity was determined, in 1642, by justices Godfrey, Gorges and Vines. The name "Chasco" was given to the Presumpscot on the earliest extant map of the province before 1655.§

The statement of Maverick was made about five years after the ancient map was engraved, and the site of Levett's fortified dwelling must have been on Mackworth's Island, which lay before the mouth of the Presumpscot River and contained about forty acres of tillable land. A year before Maverick issued his statement, in a second suit between Cleave and Robert Jordan, who had succeeded to the title of Trelawney, the same issue was again raised, and the Presumpscot was judicially determined to be the "River of Casco." The decision must have been known to all planters at the Eastward as well as Boston traders like Maverick.

† Mass. Hist. Proc., 21-232.
‡ Baxter's Levett, 105.
§ Me. Doc. Hist., 3-231. 239. 246. 250 ; Jenness' Eng. Doc.

Heretofore, the assumption that Levett's habitation stood upon House Island was based upon the belief that Fore River was the original Casco, and that the name of House Island implied a particular significance in itself. But that islet was settled after 1640 by some of Trelawney's discharged fishermen, of whom Nicholas White was one. Before that date Winter and his assistants had lived upon Richmond and Stratton's islands.

MACKWORTH'S ISLAND, CASCO BAY

Levett, who was a surveyor as well as sea captain of experience, placed his location "two leagues to the East of Cape Elizabeth" and within a bay a mile and a half wide. The eastern limit of such measurement must have been the house at Casco, which as a fortified post was intended to become the nucleus of a great English seaport, to be called York. Directly opposite his station were situated the 6000 acres—near, but not at, Cape Elizabeth and in Casco Bay.

A strong inducement for the selection of this site at the mouth of the river was the proximity of an Indian village, which located only a few miles upriver at the first fall in the Presumpscot, attracted many influential sagamores. The only experiments undertaken at Casco by Levett were with planting and trading. Before settlement on the premises he had examined the general character of the soil on both sides of Presumpscot River.

The proprietor of the house at Casco intimated that, during his sojourn at the post, Thomas Weston, without license from the council, had intercepted his legitimate trade with the natives by weekly incursions upon a neighboring river and, when ordered to desist, had threatened to assault him in his own house.

"At this place," said Levett, writing in Casco in 1624, "there fished divers ships of Waymouth this yeare." Other casual visitors at Quacke during that spring were a sea captain who had fished at Cape Ann, Robert, son of Sir Ferdinando Gorges, and Indians from miles around, some of whom he had met at Pascataqua.

When Levett was about to leave the country in midsummer, as indicated by his ignorance of local conditions after July, all the sagamores of Northern New England assembled to bid him farewell. Those named were Chief Sadamoyt, of Penobscot; Robinhood (Manawormet), of Sagadahoc; Runacwitts (Opparrunwit), of Pentucket (Haverhill, Massachusetts); Squidrayset (Skedraguscett), of Presumpscot; Cogawesco, of Casco and Quacke; Samoset (Somersett), of Pemaquid; and Passaconway (Conway), of Pennacook (Concord, New Hampshire).

He sailed for England in one of the fishing vessels at the close of the fishing season which ended with June, 1624, leaving at the house at Casco ten of his men—the same number taken to Pascataqua by Thompson the year before. Save the fishing plantation at Monhegan Island there appears to have been no other English establishment in Maine at the time of his departure.

Nothing is known of the history of the Casco colony during the following year, but there must have been fishermen in the harbor that summer. In the fall of that year Edward Winslow from New Plymouth must have passed the island on his way to Kennebec River to trade corn for furs with the Indians.

In 1626, Thomas Morton may have tarried at the house at Casco on his voyage eastward, where he secured the spring beaver trade at Kennebec to the detriment of Plymouth Colony. This same year Peter Garland, John Cousins and John Mills were fishing in the locality. Some years later Morton remarked: "I have seene in one Harboure, next Richmond Iland, 15 Sayle of shipps at one time, that have taken in them dryied Codds for Spaine and the Straights."*

In 1627, John Winter was in the harbor with the *Consent* from Plymouth and commanded a fishing crew which seined for bait in Presumpscot River. When he cited the fact in 1640, none

* N. E. Canaan, 86.

of the men who had then worked for him were living in Maine. The nature of their work did not detain them in the country. He was authority for the statement that "4 ships of Weymoth did fysh at Casco that yeare," of which the masters were Arthur Guyer, William Lash and Henry and Joseph Russell, and that their crews were "divers others about Plymoth and Barnestable."†

In June, 1627, plainly alluding to Morton, Bradford deplored the fact that the unconscionable dealings of some of the baser European traders with Maine Indians, in that and the preceding year, had made it dangerous for the English to remain in the East "after the fishermen are gone."

Levett mentioned no one who was resident at Casco, although in one of his letters to Sir John Coke, written November 17, 1627, he was on the point of instructing his "servants" who still remained in New England "to come away wth there shippes that ar now going to fish there," if his plan to fortify the eastern coast should fail. He had already recommended Casco as a permanent base for a naval police patrol and described conditions similar to those reported by Bradford:

"The tyme of danger is from the begininge of June to the last of January or therabouts All wch tyme there is no English shipps uppon that coste ffor the fleet of ffishermen doe comonly arive there in January and ffebr: The fishinge contenewes untill the begininge of May and by the ende of that month comonly they dept.

"The maner of the ffishermen is to leave there shallops in the Contry untill the next season every shipe in that harbor where they fish. There may be of them in all about 3 or 400 and if they want there botts they may easily be pvented.

"If an enemy should come it is likly that they will put into the first harbor they make for it is dangerous lyinge longe for shipps uppon that coste wthout extraordynary good pilotts. The coste beinge full of depe bayes broken islands and souncken rocks. Now they can come into no harbor but they shall fynde botts for the transportinge of there men alongst the costes to any place they desier wherin is the greatest danger for they cannot march by lande And it is not like that there will come any great flett to take up many harbors *the planters beinge in all not above 300.*

† Me. Doc. Hist., 3-250; Mass. Hist. Proc., 47-188.

"The first thinge wch I conseve fitt to be done is that all men be comanded at the end of there voyage to bringe all there shallops into one harbor and there to have them untill the next yeare And the fittest harbor I conceve to be quacke (but by me in my discovery named Yorke) beinge the most princepall in the Contry and in the mydst of all the fishinge."

June 9, 1628, all of the New England plantations "wher any English were seated" contributed to the expense of deporting Morton, who had ranged the whole coast and been convicted of trading arms and ammunition with the Indians.‡

It is significant that Casco, Richmond Island, Monhegan and Penobscot, some of the oldest settlements in Maine and situated in the center of the exposed district, were not named. The positive inference is that the house at Casco had been abandoned at the return of the fishing ships earlier that season.

It is obvious that the dream of Levett, to make Casco a commercial center and the principal New England port of entry, was not to be realized. And so terminated the first European occupation of Casco Bay, where had been located, in the words of Levett, "the Land which was granted me by Pattent and made choyce of before any other man came there."§

THE SECOND OCCUPATION OF CASCO.

According to a claim of George Cleave, the first permanent settler of Casco, the house and island of Levett at Quacke were sold by the latter to Thomas Wright, the merchant of Bristol. This transaction was effected late in 1628 after the premises had been abandoned by Levett's men.

The new owner must have done some trading at Casco during 1629 because complaints were made before John Endicott and his associate justices that Wright was forwarding contraband articles which were sold by his agent at the Eastward.

At that time Endicott, who had arrived September 8, of the previous year, was chief executive of the Salem administration, and he continued to have special jurisdiction as late as 1633, when about twenty-two of his "lawes" had been submitted to the lords to be approved for use within his district.*

‡ Bradford, 2-161.
§ Baxter's Levett, 107.
* 3 Mass. Hist. Col., 9-257.

May 27, 1629, only ten days after the date of execution of the Wheelwright deed at Squamscott and early enough to have been dispatched on the outgoing ship in which Oldham had arrived, Endicott wrote a letter to his company in which he complained of the unlawful commerce of "former traders to those parts" with the Indians and recommended that some action be taken. The complaint does not disclose the name of any transgressor. His communication was referred by the company to a subcommittee in England.

While, throughout New England, the sale of arms and ammunition to the Indians was regarded as adverse to English interests in event of hostility and had been prohibited by royal edict, the French who lived in fortified camps in Nova Scotia were not bound by British edicts. Some had made fabulous profits from unrestricted barter, not only by extortion, but because the natives recognized the superiority of the new firearms and soon became so proficient in their use that the fur supply was increased automatically.

Wright was not long in discovering that contraband articles were most coveted by the warlike eastern tribes and brought the best returns in beaver skins. Accordingly, when forwarding supplies to Casco in the spring of 1630, he included a large consignment of lead, powder, shot and rapier blades, which were used as darts to kill beaver.

From what transpired it is obvious that this prohibited merchandise was freighted on board the *Lyon* in the custody of Levett, although passengers and provisions were shipped a few weeks later directly to Casco on the *Swift* which belonged to Wright. When the cargo of the *Lyon* was overhauled at Salem the contraband was exposed.

It is evident that the latter vessel was the one implicated for it was the only ship in Salem Harbor when the *Arbella* arrived on June 12. Winthrop had been chosen governor before leaving England. Upon his advent in the country he had superseded Endicott as chief executive and was the proper official to consult with relation to laying an embargo upon contraband.

Levett appeared on the same day as a passenger with William Peirce in the *Lyon* and both held an early conference with the new governor which lasted for some time. There is no doubt that his responsibility as master of the vessel induced Peirce to have the matter decided forthwith. In fact, he had been lying in the harbor for several days. The *Lyon* had been one of the first of the Winthrop fleet to reach New England that summer. The other, called the *Mary and John*, had discharged at Hull May 30.

Peirce, however, had arrived at Salem by way of Penobscot, whither by previous agreement with Sherley in England he had promised to "bend" his course in consideration of a share in the future profits of Edward Ashley from the eastern Indian trade. After that factor and his "five or six" subordinates with their goods had been landed at Machabitticus, the main cargo, to be delivered in Massachusetts, still remained on board. The principal consignee was the London Company which had chartered the vessel. The company's freight was to be unladen on the premises selected by Winthrop and his associates. The rest of the cargo, which belonged to Christopher Levett and Thomas Wright, was to be discharged at Salem.

Another conferee with Winthrop at Salem was Isaac Allerton, who had returned from England with Peirce and was interested in the ventures of Wright at Casco, as well as Ashley's at Penobscot.

There is still extant in Suffolk files a very ancient document, undated, unaddressed, unsubscribed and heretofore unpublished. Although a scrap, it contains an allusion to early eastern affairs. No particular importance has been attributed to it, but it must have related to the visit of Levett to Winthrop. Comparisons with other specimens of the handwriting of Roger Conant point unmistakably to him as its author. He had been recognized as the founder of Salem and its official monitor for four years.

The note was written in an advisory capacity and a careful transcription is appended. Who Wright's servant was cannot now be determined, but the offence must have been committed at Casco during the previous year.

"The Planters Complayned against Mr. Wright for sending peces, and other prhebyted comodityes to trayd wth the Indyans.

"To this John Milles hath sworne before Capt: Endycott and the rest who were joyned in Counsell wth him, that he saw Wrights servant trucke a fowlinge pece wth the Indyans.

"Allso Christo: Levett will take oth that Wright dyd so send, pieces raper blayds &c by him to so trayde wth the Indyans, and allso that he said to him that he had sent these things to be trayded to the Indyans, and would doe so again in spite of any should say nay to it.

"If for these things you please to make stay on his goods, I Conceve it is fitt that order be given to Captain Endycott to deliver to Capt: Levett and the Company, what er they shall make appeare belongs to them, and to detayne the rest beinge all Wright's goods."†

A deposition of John Mills, taken for the Trelawney case in 1640, disclosed that he had frequented Casco Bay and Presumpscot River for fourteen years before the trial. While some of the jury were charged with remarking that they would as soon believe a dog or an Indian, in this instance at least the witness had had the opportunity to be informed.

The disposition of Wright's consignment was not reported, but a decision must have been made before July 7, when the *Lyon* which had been freighted with live stock for Boston consignees had been unladen at Charlestown and sailed for Salem. Two weeks later Peirce had contracted with Charlestown authorities to return to Bristol at once for more supplies for the colony, which was in straitened circumstances.‡

Servants of Wright came to New England in the *Swift* in the early summer of 1630 and occupied the deserted "house at Casko." The inmates mentioned were Thomas Alger and Edmund Baker, of Newton Ferrers, and Nicholas Rouse, of Wembley, England, where all were living ten years later.§

Another planter who was interested in the settlement of Casco was Arthur Mackworth. At an early date he had acquired title to land on the eastern side of Presumpscot River, known as Mackworth's Point, "by good Deed from the Indian Natives & Sr Ferdinando Gorges." The tract was called "Newton" and the owner's dwelling stood opposite the "house at Casko," which was located on Mackworth's Island.*

Captain John Wright, brother of the new owner at Casco and master of Ashley's shallop, who was to act as agent for his rela-

† Suffolk Court Files, 26366.
‡ Savage's Winthrop, 1-448.
§ Me. Doc. Hist., 3-251.
* York Deeds, 16-26.

tive also, was present at Saco when the first colonists took possession. Thomas Purchase, the subsequent patentee of Pejepscot, was in the company with Wright when possession was taken by Vines.

Wright's colonists did not remain long at Casco. The chief reason may have been the confiscation of his trading goods. Massachusetts magistrates argued that they had greater concern for the safety of the Eastern Country than those of New Plymouth on account of their proximity to the district and because their commerce was conducted in trading vessels rather than fortified stations.

By 1630, Levett had disposed of the residue of his interest in Casco territory to the Merchant Adventurers of Plymouth and had formed a trading partnership with John Boggust and Henry Lauson at Agawam (Ipswich).

Soon after September 9, of that year, he embarked for England in the *Gift* of which John Brock was master. This vessel reached Bristol in November, but Levett had died during the voyage and was buried at sea. His personal effects had been administered and were delivered to his widow at that port January 22, 1630-1.†

John Winthrop, who had sent letters in the custody of the deceased passenger, and William Peirce, who as master of the *Lyon* had encountered Brock before December 1 in Bristol Harbor, complained that the mail on board the *Gift* had been opened without license. At that time both Massachusetts colonies did not hesitate to tamper with private correspondence, if by such means they could discover the political or business relations of unaffiliated planters.

Within three weeks after the departure of Levett Massachusetts Bay Colony ordered the abandonment of his plantation at Agawam and began prosecutions against Boggust, John Goalsworth and others for intoxication and doubtful misdemeanors. As a consequence most of the evicted tenants left the country and the colony took charge of the partnership property.

June 14, 1631, news of the death of Levett had been reported in Massachusetts for on that day the following court decree was issued by Endicott and a majority of the other influential planters associated with him in the council at Salem:

"It is ordered, that the constables of the sevall plantacons shall give notice to the creditrs of Capt. Levett, John Boggust & Henry

† Baxter's Levett, 76.

Lauson, to be att the next Court, to make pfe of their debts, that they may receive satisfaccon for the same, soe farr as their goods will afford."‡

Evidently, there was no dividend left for English claimants after the distribution of the estate to the creditors in New England, for, nearly two years later, the widow of Levett, then living in Exeter, England, requested Winthrop "to call for Captayne Endicotte and Mr. Conant to examine them" about some goods of Levett's which belonged "unto her & her children."§

Maverick was authority for the statement that the patent at Casco had been sold to "Mr Seeley Mr Jope and Company of Plimouth," known as the "Merchant Adventurers," of whom Moses Goodyear was a member.*

For many years the Merchant Adventurers had been interested in trade at Newfoundland and, incidentally, had become somewhat conversant with conditions on the Maine coast. The fishing and trading facilities at Casco were generally known in England, but the attention of Goodyear and his partner had been directed specially to that section and they determined to obtain a patent with definite boundaries.

November 1, 1631, the mainland from Spurwink to Casco River was granted by the Council of Plymouth to Robert Trelawney and Moses Goodyear, merchants of Plymouth. The former patentee maintained later that the claim made by Cleave, that his land had been "formerly granted to one Levite, & by him to one Wright," pertained only to the house and island in Portland Harbor. Trelawney also asserted that, so far as the mainland was concerned, the original patentee "never tooke that as parte of his pattent, but an Iland in that baye of Cascoe, and besids his pattent was Under a Condition to plante & inhabite within 7 yeares, which he never did, soe that if itt were parte, itt is forfaited longe since, & nowe by Pattent granted to mee & others."†

Under the date of June 14, 1632, John Wright, brother of the grantee, in company with Abraham Shurt, of Pemaquid, was reported to have been wrecked by an explosion at Pascataqua, in which his shallop and cargo were lost and one of his mariners was killed. The lading consisted of English commodities of consider-

‡ Mass. Col. Rec., 1-80.
§ 5 Mass. Hist. Col., 1-118.
* Mass. Hist. Proc., 21-232 ; 5 Mass. Hist. Col., 1-501.
† Me. Doc. Hist., 3-102.

able value which had been left at Castine for Massachusetts consignees. Wright died many years later at Agawam and there was no subsequent reference to him in Maine unless he was the owner of the Sankey lot in Biddeford.

July 21, of the same year, Thomas Alger and his associates had removed from Casco to Richmond Island, where they assumed charge of the premises for Trelawney during the first winter. The house at Casco was again abandoned.‡

The next spring Governor Neal had occasion to go eastward as far as Pemaquid and he paid a visit to Black Point May 23, where he served peremptory notice upon Cleave and Tucker to vacate Spurwink which was claimed by Trelawney and Goodyear as a part of their territory. When Neal delivered the precept he gave the tenants the privilege of remaining on the premises until harvest.

Neal, who sailed from Boston for England August 15, 1633, stated in the "Relation" that "Cassica" was "at my Cominge away forsaken."§

Henry Jocelyn deposed, years afterward, that Cleave and Tucker were the first occupants of the tract of land which lies between Fore and Presumpscot rivers, known as Machegonne.*

The actual date of removal from Spurwink is not known, but June 25, 1640, Cleave alleged that he had been in possession at Machegonne "for these seaven yeares and upward." He must have meant that he had improved it by planting.†

Hence, the first permanent settlement of Portland must have taken place in September or October, 1633. Oliver Weeks, an employe of Cleave, assisted in transporting the household goods from Spurwink in a boat which had been borrowed from Winter at Richmond Island.

The records of the first session of court in Maine contained an account of a suit by William Royal against Cleave, which indicated that the plaintiff, who was a carpenter and had come to Massachusetts in 1629, had worked upon the buildings at Casco for the defendant and been debited with six weeks' "diet." Another employe was George Taylor.‡‡

March 30, 1635, Arthur Mackworth secured title to Mackworth's Island and the point at Menickoe from Gorges as chief

‡ Me. Doc. Hist., 3-244, 17.
§ N. H. State Papers, 17-491.
* Willis' Portland, 28.
† Me. Doc. Hist., 3-208.
‡‡ Essex Rec., 2-25.

proprietor of the district. It had been in the possession of the grantee for "many yeares" and was to be called Newton. It is significant that some of the tenants in "the house at Casko" in 1630 hailed from Newton Ferrers, England. Thomas Morton, who was a subscribing witness to this conveyance in England, obtained from Gorges—probably at the same time—a deed of the Clapboard Islands and 2,000 acres of the mainland adjacent.§

The location at Casco had begun to elicit favorable comment. Captain John Underhill, in his history of the Pequot War, published in England in 1638, alluded to the advantages of this part of Maine in the following comment: "Casko hath a famous bay, accommodated with a hundred islands, and is fit for plantation, and hath a river belonging to it, which doth afford fish in abundance, fowl also in great measure. So full of fowl it is, that strangers may be supplied with variety of fowl in an hour or two after their arrival, which knew not how to be relieved before. Because the place in general is so famous, and well known to all the world, and chiefly to our English nation (the most noblest of this Commonwealth), I therefore forbear many particulars which yet might be expressed."*

At the time of Underhill's account the most famous fowler in Casco Bay was Benjamin Atwell, who was located on Martin's Point on the west side of Presumpscot River. There is no doubt that this professional hunter was attracted to the locality because of the abundance of fish and wild fowl in that river. One of his customers was Winter, who required large quantities of provisions for his employes at Richmond Island.

Next to the homestead of Atwell, along the shore to the westward, was a lot occupied by Hugh Mosier and Thomas Wise, previously of Saco. All land on the west side of the Presumpscot, including that of Atwell, Mosier and Wise, had been acquired from Gorges by Cleave and Tucker, who then lived on the point at Machegonne within the present limits of Portland. At the same time Arthur Mackworth had a dwelling upon land bought from the same proprietor on the eastern bank of the Presumpscot. He also owned the island before the mouth of that river.

In the dispute between Cleave and Trelawney in 1640, testimony was introduced to prove that the Presumpscot was the "River of Casco." The affiants, who were described as those who

§ York Deeds. 1-2. 1 ; Mass. Hist. Proc., 58-163.
* 3 Mass. Hist. Col., 6-14.

"did most frequent that place since the first discovery thereof," were William Gibbons, John Mills, Henry Watts and Arthur Brown, who had "known" that river since 1623, 1627, 1631 and 1634, respectively. John Cousins and Peter Garland, mariners, had also "known and frequented" Casco Bay for fourteen years. Other persons, who were then living in England and did not testify, were Ambrose Bouden, of Holberton, John Taylor, of Jalme, and Bennett Wills, of Plymouth, who had fished with Winter in the Presumpscot thirteen years before the trial.

While the jury decided in favor of Cleave, the supreme court of appeal reversed the decision and reported that it had been clearly

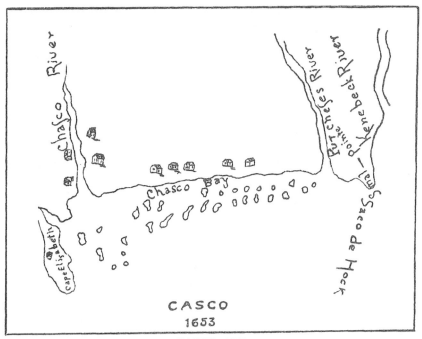

CASCO, 1653

proven "by ye relation of ye Antient Inhabitants & Natives" that the Presumpscot had "Ever been Called Casco river."†

In spite of the adverse ruling Cleave, as deputy for Rigby, still continued to control the eastern situation. For a time his dictatorship was unopposed. None of the Lygonia patentees had settled at

† Me. Doc. Hist., 3-322; York Deeds, 8-244.

Casco. Even Stephen Bachilor, who had contemplated service there as pastor in 1630, did not regard the field an attractive one when he was invited to assume the same position fourteen years later.‡ After the submission of Casco to Massachusetts, in 1658, the old issue involving the identity of the "River of Casco" was raised in a new tribunal.

Then the contending parties were Cleave and Robert Jordan, who upon the decease of Winter had become the successor of Trelawney. The old decree of the justices was reaffirmed the next year, and Cleave again lost every vestige of title to Machegonne, which had been conferred upon him by dual peers.

When Maverick, in 1660, described the location of Levett's house as an island "lyeing before Casco River," he must have been familiar with the result of the prolonged litigation. However, there is other proof that Mackworth's Island was the site of Levett's house in Casco Bay.

An ancient deed definitely described the situation of "Old Casco," which was then more than a matter of tradition. It lay "Over Against" Hog Island "in Casco Bay in ye town of falmouth * * * on ye Northeast Side of ye Coming in to Portland." The date of this conveyance was 1719, which marked the beginning of the period of resettlement of the Eastern Country. At that time the only English building left standing to the eastward of Black Point was a fish house upon Damariscove Island.§

The earliest mention of Portland as the name for Falmouth occurs in Waldron's report of the eastern expedition against the Indians, preserved by Hubbard in his account of the early wars with the natives and published in 1677.

THE FIRST ISLANDS OCCUPIED IN CASCO BAY.

Mackworth's Island contains about forty acres and was first occupied by Christopher Levett in 1623. It was given later to Arthur Mackworth by Gorges, with part of the mainland.

Cushing's, early known as Andrews, Bangs and Portland, Island contains 215 acres. There was a house upon it in 1668. Seven years later the place became a refuge for some of the inhabitants of Casco Bay who had escaped from the Indians on the mainland.

‡ 4 Mass. Hist. Col., 7-101.
§ York Deeds, 9-186

House Island contains twenty-four acres. It was occupied at an early date by Sampson Penley and Nicholas White. An old house, acquired from the inhabitants, in 1661, by George Munjoy, was sold by his widow in 1683.

Pond, also called successively Michael's, Palmer and Peaks, Island contains 717 acres. Michael Mitten leased the premises from Cleave, as agent for Gorges, December 28, 1637.

Great Diamond, originally called Great Hog, Island contains 360 acres. It was granted to Cleave and Tucker January 27, 1636-7.

Long Island contains 800 acres. It was occupied by John Sears from Massachusetts in 1646 and sold by him in 1655.

Jewell's Island contains about 100 acres and lies on the outer rim of the Casco archipelago. The first known occupant was George Jewell who found it a safe and convenient fishing port. It was provided with stages and flakes. A mariner who gave his name to the northern sound was George Luxon, a fishing master from Barnstable. Before 1660 the place was utilized by Henry Donnell, the veteran fisherman of York.

Lower Clapboard Island contains about thirty acres and lies about a mile off the Falmouth shore near the eastern line of the town. It was claimed by Thomas Morton in his will of 1643, but was occupied by the Felt family before 1663.

Great and Little Chebeague Islands contain 300 and fifty-seven acres, respectively. The larger island was sold by Cleave to Walter Merry, of Boston, September 18, 1650.

Upper Clapboard Island contains about forty acres and lies in Cumberland. Morton claimed it in 1643, but it was first improved by Thomas Drake in connection with his plantation at Prince Point. It is now known as Sturdivant Island.

PIONEERS

ALGER, THOMAS, trader, living in "the house at Casko," 1630; Richmond Island, 1632-3; returned to England in the "Welcome" July 15, 1633; Newton Ferrers, England, 1640.

ATWELL, BENJAMIN, fowler at Presumpscot, 1640; widow Mary married Richard Martin of Scarborough; son Benjamin.

BAKER, EDMUND, trader, living in the house at Casco with Alger, 1630; Newton Ferrers, England, 1640.

BROWN, ARTHUR, merchant and partner of Arthur Mackworth at Presumpscot, 1634-9; Winnegance (East Boothbay), 1640-1; York, 1642.

GARLAND, PETER, mariner, knew Presumpscot River, 1626; Malden, 1634-8; Dover, 1640; Boston, 1654; died at sea in the south; widow Elizabeth, born 1599; son John, born 1622.

LEVETT, CHRISTOPHER, born at York, England, 1586; married Mercy, daughter of Robert More, 1608; mariner, built a house in Casco Bay, 1623; England, 1624-9; sold Casco plantation to Thomas Wright, of Bristol, 1629; Salem, 1630; embarked for England in the "Gift" in September, 1630, but died and was buried at sea; widow Frances in Exeter, 1633; children by former wife, Sarah, born 1610, Rebecca, born 1612, Mary, born 1613, Jeremiah, born 1614, and Edith.

MACKWORTH, ARTHUR, merchant, had had possession at Presumpscot "many years" before 1635; partner of Arthur Brown; married Jane, widow of Samuel Andrews, as his second wife, 1637; died 1657; children, by first wife, Rebecca (Wharf) and Sarah (Adams).

MILLS, JOHN, planter, knew Presumpscot River, 1626; arrived at Richmond Island with Winter March 2, 1632-3; Spurwink, 1638; deceased 1664; widow Sarah; children James, John, Mary and Sarah.

MITTEN, MICHAEL, fowler at Diamond Island, 1637; married Elizabeth, daughter of George Cleave and settled on Fore River; died 1661; widow married Peter Harvey; children Ann (Brackett), Elizabeth (Clark), Martha (Graves), Mary (Brackett), Nathaniel and Sarah (Andrews).

MOSES, JOHN, born 1616; apprentice of Cleave and Tucker at Casco, 1639-1646; wife Alice, 1648; wife Ann, 1667; Little Harbor, 1648-1686; children Aaron and Sarah.

MUNJOY, GEORGE, son of John of Abbotsham, near Bideford, born 1627; mariner at Casco, 1647, when he removed to Boston; sister Mary, wife of John Sanders, of Braintree; died 1681; widow Mary (Phillips) married Robert Lawrence and Stephen Cross; children John, born April 17, 1653; George, born April 21, 1656; Josiah, born April 4, 1658; Philip, Mary, Hephzibah, Pelatiah and Gershom, baptized at Dorchester, in 1662, 1665, 1673 and 1675, respectively.

PHIPPEN, JOSEPH, son of David and Sarah; seaman at Hingham, 1637; wife Dorothy Wood; Falmouth, 1650; Salem, 1655; died in July, 1687; children, born at Hingham, Joseph, August, 1642, Mary, March 5, 1643-4; born in Boston, Sarah, February 4, 1644-5, David, February 11, 1646-7, Joseph, April 30, 1649, and Elizabeth, June 10, 1652.

ROUSE, NICHOLAS, trader, living in the house at Casco with Alger, 1630; Wembley. England, 1640.

TAYLOR, GEORGE, born 1608; employe of Cleave and Tucker at Casco, 1635; married Margaret, widow of Philip Hingston, after 1662; deceased in 1686; son Andrew.

WILLS, BENNETT, fisherman, at Presumpscot with Winter, 1627; trading at Richmond Island, 1643.

ROYAL RIVER

This stream flows through Yarmouth, about eight miles east of the Presumpscot, and was known to the natives as Westcustego.

In 1640, all of the territory extending westerly from the bank of Royal River, as far as Broad Cove, was in possession of John Phillips, the Welshman. About that date Phillips conveyed the western section adjoining the cove to George Felt, of Charlestown, who secured a confirmation of his title from Thomas Gorges in 1643 and continued to occupy the premises for more than forty years.

Phillips was a millwright and constructed on Pumgustuck Falls in Yarmouth the first sawmill in Eastern Maine. The mill was completed about 1645. A deed of land situated at York, dated June 8, 1646, disclosed the names of early residents near "Casco Mill." Those mentioned were John Smith and his wife Joan, as grantors, and Richard Carter, John Jackson, and William and Phebe Royal, as available witnesses.*

Soon after the sale to Felt the next lot to the eastward was acquired by Thomas Drake and transferred to Richard Martin; it contained sixty acres and was known subsequently as Martin's Plantation. The residue of the land between that plantation and Royal River was purchased by Richard Carter about 1646 and sold to John Maine six years later. The extremity, now known as Parker's, was formerly called Maine's Point.†

Before 1665 Westcustego had been defined as a township by Sir Ferdinando Gorges and fifteen years later, at the close of the First Indian War, Maine's Point was approved as a site for the new village of North Yarmouth.

About a mile above the mouth of Royal River the Chusquisack enters it from the northeast. The principal fall on that tributary was styled "Susqussugg," which was merely another way of spelling the same word. By early visitors the stream was called "North," or "Cousins," River.

The first English owner of the tract situated in the northerly angle between the two branches of the Westcustego was William

* Aspinwall, 15; York Deeds, 1-32.
† York Deeds, 12-316; 9-221.

Royal, from whom it derived its present name. He was originally from Charlestown and had assisted George Cleave in the construction of his buildings at Machegonne. The concession comprised about 250 acres and title to the premises, now known as Brown's Point, was confirmed to Royal by Thomas Gorges March 27, 1643. The grantee did not then reside upon that site.

In the spring of 1674 Robinhood and his colleagues in the vicinity conveyed to Thomas Stevens a large section of the virgin forest, two miles wide and extending from the first fall at Pumgustuck to the head of Royal River. The district was said to have contained 100,000 acres. That same year Stevens transferred the entire plot to Bartholomew Gedney and Henry Sayward, who erected mills at Pumgustuck, now Yarmouth village, and cleared stumpage areas for cultivation and pasturage on both sides of the stream above their buildings.‡

About two miles inland from its junction with the Westcustego the Chusquisack branches and forms a "neck" of marsh and upland upon which was located the early home of John Cousins as its first English settler. He had lived at Winter Harbor in 1627, but after two years had withdrawn to Casco Bay, where for many years he was engaged in stock raising and trading with the Indians. In 1637, he was ordered by Saco Court to make restitution to an eastern sagamore whom he had circumvented in trade. His actual location in Casco Bay was not definitely indicated. At that time Arthur Brown and Arthur Mackworth, who resided at the mouth of Presumpscot River, were instructed to enforce the decree. The monitors, who had been operating as a partnership for three years, may have been responsible for the acts of Cousins as an employe and benefited by his extortion.

The trader was living at Chusquisack in his own right as early as 1639. In 1645, he and Thomas Smith were interviewed there by George Cleave, who as a magistrate of Rigby was anxious to secure incriminating evidence against Robert Nash, the Boston merchant. The gist of the offence was that that coaster had dispensed an unusual allowance of intoxicants at Richmond Island and elsewhere at the Eastward and, in consequence, had been honored by the fishermen at his departure with an ovation becoming an emperor. It appeared later, however, that in firing the salutes whole hogsheads of his own gunpowder had been consumed.

‡ York Deeds, 2-190.

An early tenant of Cousins was Richard Bray, who February 21, 1650-1, acquired a half interest in part of "Cousins Place" and Cousins Island. Both settlers maintained stock ranches on the island and rafted their winter provender from marshes upriver. At the beginning of the First Indian War the Cousins mansion was attacked by the natives and partially destroyed. The owner was seriously wounded in one of his hands and forced to seek refuge in the western country. Hannah Hazelton, who had known the pioneer as a neighbor and the landlord of her father, Richard Bray, deposed long after the decease of elder generations that Cousins had been entertained in the Sayward home at York, where he recovered from his injuries. In 1679, at the close of the war, he conveyed all of his eastern real estate to Mary Sayward.§

In his deed of the premises at Chusquisack, made just before his death, the pioneer described his homestead as a tract of 300 acres, situated on the west bank of "Susgussugg" River and known as "Cousins Place." The location was near that of Royal, and his buildings consisted of a "mansion" and stock barn.

The nearest neighbor of Cousins on the south was Thomas Redding who had sold his land at Winter Harbor in 1657 and removed to the eastern bank of Royal River, where he acquired 200 acres and remained until his decease.

Between the last settlement and the sea was the original Casco residence of William Royal, occupied in 1640, and confirmed by Thomas Gorges three years later. Before his door was an island of about twenty acres, which he sold in 1658 with his dwelling and the adjoining curtilage to James Lane, of Malden, and retired to Brown's Point, where he built another habitation just below Pumgustuck Falls.

Lane's Island still perpetuates the fact of ownership by that ancient family. The ancestor was killed by Indians at Casco before 1681, when his widow had married Henry Kenny. His children were Ann (Bray), Elizabeth, Henry, Job, John, born in 1652 and died at Gloucester January 24, 1737-8, and Samuel. Some of the descendants remained at Casco during the later period of Indian warfare. Subsequently, they removed to Cambridge and their interests in eastern real estate were mentioned in Middlesex registry.

Adjoining Royal's eastern boundary was another tract of 200 acres which had been conveyed to Arnold Allen, of London, by

§ York Deeds, 12-273 ; 8-233.

Thomas Gorges in 1643. The grantee was a brother-in-law of Richard Tucker.*

In 1646, Allen's only child had been apprenticed to Thomas Dexter, a wealthy farmer of Lynn. The arrangement was made by Cleave and Tucker against the wishes of Mary, wife of Arnold and mother of the minor, who was reported to have been kept in a destitute condition of servitude. Cleave became abusive and with a natural inclination to dictate and the added advantage of his superior position as a magistrate attempted to intimidate the parents with the unfounded accusation that the mother had performed criminal abortion at Casco. The testimony adduced not only injured the reputation of the magistrate but lessened the prestige of the Rigby administration.†

There is more than a suspicion that Hope Allen, afterwards a currier of Boston, was the son of Arnold. Before the latter's plantation at Casco were two islands, both of which he owned at an early date. One of these contained ten acres and was known as "Arnold"; the other, comprising fifty acres, was called "Hope Island"; both were conveyed to John Mosier in 1673 and are now designated Great and Little Mosier. In later years, perhaps as a consequence of previous relations, Cleave and Tucker granted to Hope Allen a large allotment of real estate at Machegonne.‡

After the consummation of his purchases from Allen, Mosier enlarged his holdings at the Eastward, for when he disposed of his entire estate to Joseph Nash in 1683 it comprised three hundred acres and abutted upon the western bank of Harrisicket River. The later chain of this title passed through Gilbert and Nathaniel Winslow, Job Otis and William Thomas to Offen Boardman, to whom, in 1734, Arnold's original rights was assigned by the proprietors of North Yarmouth.§

There were no English settlers upon the eastern bank of Harrisicket, or nearer it than James Smith at Maquoit, until after the submission of Casco to Massachusetts in 1658.

COUSINS ISLAND.

This island, very irregular in form, is situated about a mile southerly from Royal River and contains 1,346 acres. It was pur-

* York Deeds, 1-2, 3.
† 4 Mass. Hist. Col., 7-362 ; Aspinwall, 246.
‡ York Deeds, 16-104 ; 1-120.
§ York Deeds, 13-279

chased from Vines by John Cousins April 8, 1645, and confirmed by Cleave, as agent for Rigby, June 22, 1647.*

One-half of the premises were sold by Cousins to Richard Bray three years later, but, in 1688, the island was confirmed to Vines Ellacott, grandson of Richard Vines. At the latter date it was called "Hog Island," which was the name by which it was first known to English fishermen. The logical conclusion is that the place was an early resort for dressing and curing fish and that the waste was fed to pigs and poultry which in turn were consumed in the country or carried away at the end of the season.†

PIONEERS

ALLEN, ARNOLD, planter on the east side of Royal River, 1637-1647; wife Mary, daughter of Nicholas Reynolds and sister of Margaret, wife of Richard Tucker, was living in London, 1637; child may have been Hope, who served apprenticeship with Thomas Dexter, of Lynn.

BRAY, RICHARD, tailor, bought half of Cousins Island, 1651; Boston, 1678; wife Rebecca; children John, Mary, Nathaniel and Samuel, both killed at Casco by Indians, 1678, and Hannah (Freathy, Hazelton), born 1660.

FELT, GEORGE, born 1601, planter at Charlestown, 1633-9; Casco, 1640; Mystic, 1643; Casco, 1667; died at Malden, 1693; widow Elizabeth, daughter of Prudence Wilkinson; children Aaron, Elizabeth (Larrabee), born 1640, George, born 1651, Mary (Nichols), twin of Elizabeth, and Moses.

MAINE, JOHN, born 1614; planter on west bank of Royal River, 1648; married in 1649 Elizabeth, born 1623; died in Boston March 27, 1699; children Hannah (Felt), Priscilla (Carroll), Rachel (Carlisle), Sarah (Atwell, Batten) and Thomas.

MORTON, THOMAS, gentleman, with Weston's colony at Mount Wallaston, 1622; trader on Kennebec River, 1626-7; deported to England, 1628 and 1630; will made in England described estate opposite Clapboard islands, 1643; died at York, 1646; widow Grace Miller.

PHILLIPS, JOHN, born 1607; Welsh millwright at Casco, 1642; bought land on the Presumpscot River from Cleave, 1650; removed to Kittery, 1675; died there before 1701, when his estate was administered by Rowland Williams, a nephew, who was the only relative in New England.

ROYAL, WILLIAM, carpenter, sent to Charlestown, by the London Company, 1629; Casco, 1635; married Phebe Green, of Boston; Westcustego, 1643; died at Dorchester June 15, 1676; widow died July 16, 1678; children Isaac, John, Joseph, Mary, Mehitable, Samuel and William, born 1640.

SEARS, JOHN, born 1613; Charlestown, with wife Susanna, 1639; Woburn, 1641; scalemaker at Long Island, Casco Bay, 1646; wife died at Woburn August 29, and he married November 20, 1677, Hester Mason; she died August 14, and he married November 2, 1680, Ann Farrar; died at Woburn October 5, 1697.

* York Deeds, 3-52.
† Me. Doc. Hist., 6-408.

BUNGANUCK RIVER

With the interchangeable consonant of the Indian language the name of this stream was first known as Pugamuganunug River, which meant "The Brook with High Banks." It flows into the western side of Maquoit Bay about eight miles east of Royal River.

On the westerly bank the land was occupied by James Smith from Salem as early as 1639. Above this tract was a lot adjoining the river which was occupied two years later by Alexander Thwayts. Smith, however, like Thwayts, removed to Woolwich after a few years, and his premises at Maquoit, acquired by Richard Potts, were conveyed to Thomas Haynes April 20, 1675, when the eastern boundary was defined as Smith's Brook.*

The territory between Bunganuck and Sagadahoc rivers was included in the patent from the Council of Plymouth to Thomas Purchase and George Way, of Dorchester, England, June 16, 1632. In 1683, John Cousins testified that the former patentee took possession at Pejepscot, "which lies in Casco Bay near ye falls of Dammas Coggin," in 1628. Fifty years later a fortification located upon the same premises and situated at the point at Brunswick Falls was known as Pejepscot Fort. Mare, now Mere, Point was fenced at the isthmus by Purchase and furnished pasturage for colts which he undertook to breed for commercial purposes.

In 1639, the home of Purchase was visited, during his absence, by Robert Sankey, sheriff for the Eastern District, who distrained some of his property, and, again during his absence in the same year, by James Smith, of Maquoit, Arthur Brown and Robert Shute, of Winnegance, and Robert Norman, of Pemaquid, who took from the premises forty-four moose skins, which were the property of Abbagadusset, sagamore of Kennebec River. A complaint, filed against the trespassers in Massachusetts two years later, contained the information that the safety of the property and family of the Pejepscot merchant had been jeopardized by the lawless act of the pilferers, for the sagamore held Purchase accountable. In 1643, although he had made full reparation for the loss, the house and patent of Purchase were destroyed by fire.

* York Deeds, 4-19; 10-89

Thomas Redding, who had lived previously at Cape Porpoise and Saco, where he had disposed of his lot in 1657, occupied Mare Point Neck "for many years * * * by sufferance of Mr. Purchas."†

In 1661, Nicholas White, who had just disposed of his interest in House Island in Casco Bay, removed to Mare, then known as Sandy, Point and built a dwelling on the outer extremity.

On the shore of the bay, between Bunganuck River and Maquoit Creek and about four miles from Brunswick Falls, a tract had been acquired from the patentee at an early date by his relative, Robert Jordan. When the latter retired to Richmond Island to manage his wife's patrimony, he left Thomas Haynes in charge of the farm in the interest of his minor son of the same name; the change of residence took place in 1641.‡

Pioneers

JORDAN, ROBERT, son of Edward, of Worcester, born 1613; clergyman living with his relative Thomas Purchase, 1639-1640; married Sarah, daughter of John Winter and removed to Richmond Island, 1641; died at Newcastle, 1679; children Dominicus, Jedediah, Jeremiah, John, Robert and Samuel.

LEWIS, GEORGE, planter at New Plymouth, 1637; employe of Purchase at Pejepscot, 1646; wife Ann; died at Casco, 1682; children George, Hannah (Darling), John, Mary (Wilkins, Lewis), born at Back Bay, 1653, Philip, eldest son, born 1646, and Susanna (Cloyce).

SMITH, JAMES, planter, Salem, 1636; Maquoit, 1639; bought Tuessic of Robinhood May 8, 1648; died 1660; widow Elizabeth married Richard Hammond, who was killed by Indians August 13, 1676; children Elizabeth, Herediah, of Beverly, James, Mary and Samuel, who was killed with his stepfather.

THWAYTS, ALEXANDER, planter; arrived from London April 6, 1636; Boston, 1640; Maquoit, 1641; Winneganset Creek, 1649; Swan Island, 1665; widow Ann; children Alexander, Ann (Hodsdon), Elizabeth, John, Jonathan, Lydia, Margaret, Mary and Rebecca.

† Me. Hist. Col., 3-329.
‡ York Deeds, 10-211.

NEW MEADOWS AND PEJEPSCOT RIVERS

Early references to the locality indicated that Pejepscot was the Indian name for the district about New Meadows River. On the oldest provincial map of Maine now extant it was inscribed as "Purcheses River" and marked the natural waterway leading inland to his pioneer domicile near its head.

The first allusion to Pejepscot may be found in the account of settlement of Sagadahoc Colony August 22, 1607, only a few days after its selection of a site for Fort Saint George. On that day Captain Popham set sail in a shallop for the "ryver of Pashipskoke." His interest in the district indicated that he had had access to information secured by some previous explorer.

At Pejepscot the colonists had interviews with Skidwaros and Nahanada whom they had left a few weeks before at Pemaquid, where the English claimed "They do make thear abbod." Apparently, both sachems possessed unusual warlike proclivities. These Indians advised Popham that they had just been engaged in native warfare with Sasanoa and had killed his son in a recent conflict. The English exploring party arrived home the day after its departure. It could not have gone farther than Merry Meeting Bay.

September 5, following, Dehanada and Skidwaros, with about forty men, women and children in nine canoes, rowed into the mouth of Sagadahoc River to visit Fort Saint George while on their way home from the westward. It was customary for the natives to transport an entire village by boat whenever the fishing, planting or hunting seasons required.

The first territory allotted by the Council of Plymouth at Pejepscot was conferred upon the Earl of Arundel July 22, 1622. Its marine boundary was defined as extending "from ye Southermost poynt of Peshippscott East 12 miles in a straight Lyne as the Coast lyeth on ye Sea shoare." The tract extended for thirty miles "upp into the Mayne Land due North," and included Monhegan, as well as all other islands and havens directly seaward.

Pejepscot Point was identical with Small Point and most of the tract must have been situated on the easterly side of Sagadahoc River.*

February 18, 1622-3, Richard Bashrode, or Bradshaw, a merchant of Dorchester, England, petitioned the Council of Plymouth, by his attorney William Derby, that "either himselfe or some one of his Associates might bee admitted a patentee." Since it was their purpose "to Settle a plantacon in New England," they also "prayed to have Lycence granted unto them to send forth a Shippe for Discovery and other Imployments in New England for this yeare, which the Councell ordered accordingly."

The large group of associates which Derby represented was known subsequently as the "Dorchester Merchants" and included in its membership Thomas Purchase and George Way, both merchants of Dorchester. John White, a distinguished clergyman and neighbor of Way, was one of the most enthusiastic adventurers in the enterprise, who furnished funds and pledged his credit to finance the early colonization of Massachusetts.

These merchants immediately undertook to establish a colony which, according to Captain Smith, had been begun, before the spring of 1624, beside that of New Plymouth at Cape Ann. The whole project was discontinued four years later, when the new London Company purchased all former rights in the old combination and March 19, 1627-8, procured from the Council of Plymouth the patent which furnished a foundation for Massachusetts Bay Colony.

Some of the adventurers in the old organization became members of the new one. Among these was George Way. Purchase, however, did not affiliate, but before 1628, when the Dorchester Company of which he was a member dissolved, he had directed his attention to the region lying eastward of Cape Ann.

It is not known when he first came to New England, but he had been a servant of Charles First soon after the accession of that monarch to the English throne in 1625 and, according to John White, clerk of the Dorchester Merchants, was supposed to be residing at Dorchester, England, in 1627.†

The year when Pejepscot was first occupied by Purchase has been derived from the recital in a subsequent deed of the premises

---

* Am. Ant. Col., 1867-64.
† Me. Hist. Col., 3-331; N. E. Hist. Gen. Reg., 61-278.

from his heirs. In that document the event is represented to have occurred in the third year of Charles First. The date in the deed was based upon the deposition of John Cousins who had testified long afterward that "Mr Purchase took his first possession in the year One thousand Six hundred & twenty-eight, & hath made improvement of sm ever since, untill he as well as many others were forced out of their Interests by the late Indian Wars, till which time the said Mr Thos. Purchase hath ever peacebly enjoyed the premises without molestation. And ye Depont. did always understand & it was generally so taken by us the Inhabitants of Casco Bay that Mr. Purchase had a Patent right for his Interest by him so long & peaceably possessed, & further saith not."‡

The earliest reference to Purchase in any New England record was under the date of June 25, 1630, when in company with Captain Stephen Reekes he had subscribed his name as a witness to the certificate of seizin of the Saco patent. Apparently, he had arrived on the coast that spring as a passenger in the *Swift* from Bristol.

The day after possession was taken at Saco, a grant of the Sagadahoc region, called Lygonia, was issued by the Council of Plymouth in England. That concession has been styled "The Plough Patent," from the name of the vessel in which its first colonists were transported, and extended for forty miles westward along the shore from Sagadahoc River to Cape Porpoise and for twenty miles inland. The tract included part of that which had been assigned to Sir George Calvert by the Council of Plymouth in 1622 and lay within the civil jurisdiction of that section of Maine which had been conferred upon Gorges and Mason later in the same year. The island of Seguin, also known as Sutquin to the English and Schillpad, from its resemblance to a frog, to the Dutch, had been given to Calvert in addition to the mainland.

When Purchase took possession, all previous rights in Pejepscot territory appear to have lapsed for unoccupancy. He still had business relations with New Plymouth and was found in company with Isaac Allerton, in the summer of 1630, at Saco. In August, of that year, he contracted with Allerton for a shipment of provisions from England.

November 18, following, the latter was in Bristol and William

‡ York Deeds, 4-16.

Peirce reported that he had freighted "a ship to depart from Barnstable very shortly." This was the *Friendship* which had been hired to transport merchandise and undertake fishing in New England for Plymouth Colony.§

The provisions billed to Purchase consisted of oatmeal and wheat. Some of this grain was conveyed in George Way's bark from Padstow, in Cornwall, to Bristol, to be milled; thence it was transferred to Barnstable for shipment in the *Friendship*, but was taken back to the *White Angel* at Bristol when the former vessel failed to make its first passage.

Although the *White Angel* had been procured by Allerton to transport supplies to Edward Ashley at Penobscot, it was laden with live stock for Massachusetts and mixed freight for several parties in New England. A large part of the cargo was shipped upon the credit of John White, the clergyman of Dorchester, England, who had been clerk of the Dorchester Merchants and was then a prominent member of the London Company as its successor. In December, 1630, a payment was made by White on account of his general bill of lading and May 20, 1631, a bill of exchange was issued by George Way for the proportionate expense of his shipment which had been forwarded to Saco for the use of Purchase.*

Since Allerton's ship contained some freight consigned to the eastern settlements at Saco, Pemaquid and Penobscot, it was delayed at the Eastward until June 28, 1631, and did not arrive at Boston Harbor with the cattle until July 22.†

Thomas Wiggin claimed that, early in the fall of the same year, Purchase went from the eastern part of New England where he then lived to Massachusetts and there married Mary Grove—a youthful member of the family of Sir Christopher Gardiner. At any rate, that knight, who had arrived in the country early in the previous year, and possibly in the same ship with Purchase, accompanied the bridal pair to the Maine wilderness.

During his sojourn in the family of Purchase, either at Saco or Pejepscot, Gardiner was alleged to have borrowed a warming pan and bought a gun on credit from Richard Tucker of Spurwink. Consequently, Yorkshire Court, many years after the departure of the knight from the country, held his host accountable

§ 5 Mass. Hist. Col., 1-196.
* Mass. Arch., 100-9.
† Winthrop, 1-59.

for the full value of both items. The instance illustrates the necessity for the modern statutes against frauds.

Late in the fall of 1631 a shallop belonging to Henry Way, of Dorchester, failed to return from a voyage to the Eastward. Investigation disclosed that the Indians had killed the son and three employes of the owner of the vessel.‡

A second shallop, sent to recover the first, was wrecked at Agamenticus and two of its crew were drowned.

Henry Way had a son who bore the same name as that of the partner of Purchase at Pejepscot; both Ways had been residents of Dorchester, England, and acquired real estate in Dorchester, Massachusetts; they appear to have been brothers and this voyage to the Eastward may have had some direct relation to their mutual affairs.

November 1, 1631, the Council of Plymouth granted to Richard Bradshaw a tract of land lying "above the hedd of Pashippscot, on ye north side thereof (not formerly granted to any other)." The consideration for the issuance of this concession was stated to have been "the charge he had been at in his liveing there some yeares before, & for yt he purposed to settle himselfe there with other his friends & servants."§

A letter from the Plough Company in England to its associates in Massachusetts, dated March 8, 1631-2, referred to its relations with Bradshaw and Sir Ferdinando Gorges in the following paragraph:

"Wee have had much ado abought our patten, and that there was one Bradshaw that had proquired letters patten for a part as wee soposed of our fformer grant, and so wee think stell, but he and Sir Fferdinando think it is not in our bouns. He was ffrustrat of his ffurst purpose of cuming over, but is now joyned with 2 vere able captens and marchants" (John Winter and Thomas Pomeroy, captains, and Robert Trelawney and Moses Goodyear, merchants) "which will set him over, and wee sopowse will be ther as soun as this shipe, if not befor. Weè can not posible relat unto you the labur and truble that wee have had to establishe our former grant; mane rufe words wee have had from Sir Fferdineando at the ffurst, and to this houer he douth afferm that he never gave consent, that you should have aboufe forte

‡ N. E. Prospect, 68.
§ Am. Ant. Col., 1867-98.

mills in lenkth and 20 millse in bredth, and sayeth that his one hand is not to your patten if it have anne more * * * Wee can proquer nothinge under his hand, but in our heringe he gave order unto Mr. Aires to wright unto Capten Neyle of Pascatoway, that Bradshew and wee maight be bounded, that wee mayght not truble ech other, and hath given the Capten comand to serch your patten, what it is you have under my lords hand and his."*

Although Bradshaw may have lived previously at Salem or Cape Ann, under the administrations of the Dorchester Merchants and London Company, it is evident that he had not then located any definite territory in Maine. He may have been stationed at Pejepscot with Purchase before the date of the foregoing letter. If he came to Richmond Island with John Winter, he arrived in the country April 17, 1632, or just before the letter reached Massachusetts.

It is obvious that there was a difference of opinion as to the projection of Bradshaw's patent in Maine. Gorges, who had a map which delineated the earlier allotments, was convinced that it was too far inland to conflict with the twenty-mile limit of the Plough Patent.

Neal, who laid out the bounds in 1632, soon after described the patent as comprising the "Northeast side of Peckipscot River." The tract contained 1500 acres and extended two miles to the eastward of the head of Pejepscot River and one mile inland.

In spite of the clear description of the grant itself, George Cleave undertook, many years later, to base his title to a house and land at Spurwink River upon Bradshaw's proprietary right to territory in the Pejepscot region. He alleged that Neal gave the patentee possession of land at Spurwink which was "inherited" afterwards by his partner Richard Tucker.†

But the house at the mouth of the Spurwink River, near Richmond Island, was constructed by Cleave several months before the concession was made to Bradshaw by the Council of Plymouth, and was then recognized as the only building on the mainland within the bounds of the grant to Trelawney and Goodyear. Cleave had based his right upon a mere promise of Gorges.

However, Bradshaw disappeared completely from New Eng-

* 4 Mass. Hist. Col., 7-93.
† Me. Doc. Hist., 3-207.

land records and no claim was asserted subsequently, by him or his heirs or assigns to any part of the district.

June 16, 1632, Purchase and Way, who were related by marriage, procured from the Council of Plymouth a grant "of certaine Lands in New England, called the River Bishopscott and all that Bounds and Limitts the Maine Land, adjoining to the said River to extend two myles: from the said River Northwards four myles, and from the house there to the Ocean Sea."‡

After issuance the original document of title was deposited, for safe-keeping, with Sir Francis Ashley, of Dorchester, who had been recognized as the official head of the Dorchester Merchants.§

From the description contained in the patent itself it is plain that the house built by Purchase and Way had already been erected near Brunswick Falls at the head of navigation. While the concession extended to the seashore in Casco Bay, it did not include Merryconeag or Small Point.

The tract occupied by the pioneer had been cultivated by him before his patent was granted and his location was favorable for Indian trade. There were no competitors and he had easy access to Androscoggin and Kennebec rivers.

During 1632 Purchase returned to England with his young wife, who like Sir Christopher Gardiner, her former employer, had been decreed to banishment from the country by Massachusetts magistrates. The doughty knight had evaded his inquisitors at Pejepscot for several months, but reached Bristol unexpectedly with the fishing ships about the middle of August. As the trip usually took two months, he may have sailed in July. It may be assumed that the host and his wife took passage in the same vessel.

November 26, of that year, Gardiner was given proprietary rights in New England by the Council of Plymouth, and Purchase was present at Dorchester, England, the following spring, for April 22 he executed certain "articles of agreement" with George Way. According to the heir of Way, the agreement related to a division of their patent in Maine, but permanent possession was not taken at Pejepscot until forty years before the First Indian War, or about 1635.*

‡ Sainsbury's Col. Pap., 1-152.
§ Me. Hist. Col., 3-330.
* York Deeds, 4-18.

One of the early occupations at the plantation was raising colts, which were yarded upon a peninsula then known as Mare, now Mere, Point in Casco Bay. An employe on the premises was George Lewis.†

In the summer of 1636 Purchase appeared at the house at Newichawannock, then occupied by agents of the widow of Captain John Mason. There he sold a "great boat" to John Treworthy, who had arrived that spring from Dartmouth, England. Later, he instituted a suit against the purchaser for damages occasioned by his failure to keep the terms of the sale and complained that the delinquency of Treworthy had detained his three employes at Newichawannock and interfered with the harvesting of the hay crop at the Eastward, so that his live stock suffered for want of provender.‡

Purchase was zealous in his attempts to maintain his vested territorial rights at Pejepscot. This was shown in more than one instance. September 20, 1633, Captain Thomas Young, of London, had been granted a special commission to explore the uninhabited parts of America. It was the broadest delegation of powers ever conferred by Charles First upon any individual. He was given full authority to provide a fleet, discover and trade in the country, establish fortified posts, seize vessels and dispose of prisoners summarily, at his discretion.§

What transpired in Maine was disclosed by Maverick in an interesting bit of early history. He described the results in these words: "One Captaine Young and 3 men with him in the Yeare 1636 went up the" (Sagadahoc) "River upon discovery and only by Carying their Canoes some few times, and not farr by Land came into Canada River very neare Kebeck Fort where by the French, Capt Young was taken, and carried for ffrance but his Company returned safe."*

Later, Young complained that he had been misled by the advice of Purchase, whom he had met at Pejepscot or Sagadahoc, but there seems to have been no basis for such charge since the latter could not have been expected to be familiar with interior conditions of the country at that time. So far as known, the London explorer was the first European to trace the Kennebec

† Me. Hist. Col., 3-332.
‡ Lechford, 153.
§ Hazard, 1-338.
* Mass. Hist. Proc., 21-232.

River back to its source and reach the Saint Lawrence River through the deserted reaches of the intervening wilderness.
Purchase was in a peculiar position of disadvantage. While by virtue of his patent he was in possession of a comparatively small area, his extensive sea and river boundaries were exposed to the constant danger of trespass by strangers. His only abutter was Bradshaw, who was described in an English deposition, dated May 5, 1637, as a seafaring man, aged 41; his residence was at Saint Margaret's, Westminster, at that time; his rights at Pejepscot appear to have been absorbed by Purchase.†

July 3, 1637, Sir Ferdinando Gorges assigned to Sir Richard Edgecomb, of Mount Edgecomb in Devonshire, 8000 acres of land described as "lying between Sagadahock and Casco Bay." This concession had always been known to planters as Small Point, but was called Pejepscot Point by early navigators. It was bounded northerly by the premises of Purchase and Way.‡

It has been claimed that the transaction between Gorges and Edgecomb represented a full settlement of debts due the latter at that time. Sir Richard died March 23, 1638-9. It is not known that he ever visited New England or made a survey at Small Point, which was anciently described as situated "near the lake of New Somerset, fifteen miles from Casco Bay." The lake alluded to is now known as Merry Meeting Bay.

Eighty-one years after the date of the original grant to the nobleman, Nicholas Edgecomb, supposed to be an heir of the English proprietor, undertook to define the location and establish the rights of other heirs-at-law in the tract at Small Point. Much of that territory had already been sold by the natives.

Because of the sharp tactics of his nearest competitors Purchase became involved in financial straits. Although he was a commissioner in the administration of Gorges, he sought protection from his former colleagues outside the province. John White, of Dorchester, England, who had been a partner with George Way as one of the Dorchester Merchants, appealed to Governor Winthrop in these words:

"My neighbor, Mr Way of this place, who hath ben an hearty freind to N. Engl., hath servants in the Bay who as it seems are not soe indifferently respected in their lott as they ought to be.

† N. Y. Gen. Biog. Rec., 47-76.
‡ Me. Doc. in Eng. Arch., 89.

They desire to open their case to you, & I know you will doe them right."§

There is no doubt that this reference was made to Purchase and Way and their associates who were established early at Salem and Dorchester and first directed their affairs at the Eastward from those points.

Under date of May 10, 1639, Winthrop alluded in his history to a letter in which "One Mr. Ryall, having gotten a patent at Sagadahoc out of the grand patent, wrote our governour and tendered it to our government, so as we would send people to possess it."*

Later events show that the grant to which Royal referred was that obtained by Purchase at Pejepscot, which was situated within the Sagadahoc Country. It is apparent that the proponent named had been selected by Purchase to make the first overtures of sale to the Massachusetts government. He had been an early resident of Charlestown and was intimate with the Bay magistrates.

The first offer was rejected, but July 22, following, Winthrop accepted the original proposition and secured from Purchase all of his territory at Pejepscot, except a few hundred acres, then in different stages of cultivation, and whatever additional forest land the grantor might wish to reclaim in seven years. Massachusetts was thereby invested with the right of civil control and colonization.†

The Pejepscot Papers, so-called, contain many depositions which were taken for the purpose of determining the actual location of Purchase's house.

The pioneer built three dwellings during his sojourn at Pejepscot. The first one was mentioned as a monument in the river boundary from the mouth of the Androscoggin to the sea. That river terminated in a "precipice" at Brunswick and the Pejepscot extended from that point to Merry Meeting Bay. The original grant to Purchase was two miles wide on each side of the Androscoggin and maintained that width to the "Ocean Sea," where he claimed four miles of coast line.

In November, 1639, New Plymouth abandoned Cushnoc and Pejepscot became the frontier. Unfortunately, the Indians were

§ 5 Mass. Hist. Col., 1-253.
* Winthrop, 1-304.
† Mass. Col. Rec., 1-260.

not the only "neighbors" who disturbed the tranquillity of Purchase. Late in that year Robert Morgan, of Pemaquid, James Smith, of Maquoit, and Arthur Brown and Robert Shute, of Winnegance, abstracted forty-four moose skins from the house at Pejepscot, where they had been left for safe-keeping by Sagamore Abbagadusset of Kennebec. Rather than endanger the lives of his wife and children, Purchase reimbursed the Indian for the confiscated property.‡

By 1640 the Pioneer of Pejepscot had determined to remove all of his personal property beyond jurisdiction of the Province of Maine. Many frivolous suits had been instituted against him in an unfriendly court where he had formerly undertaken to administer justice to others. The political faction of Cleave, as well as that of the adherents of Vines, was hostile.

John Winthrop, who had accepted jurisdiction over the district of Pejepscot for his colony, was informed by Vines that he had heard "that Mr. Purches had carried away his cattell and other goodes, for the Massachusetts, and was intended to fetch away the rest with all speed."

During the absence of the proprietor Maine magistrates sent their marshal, Robert Sankey, from Saco to Pejepscot to obtain security for his appearance at court. The officer found only Robert Jordan, a minister who kept the house when the proprietor was away from home. He was a relative of Purchase who had lived in the country for two years. There was but one house at Pejepscot at that date, and after an attempt to obtain recognizance from the "neighbours," who were apparently indifferent, the marshal carried away 120 yards of Indian beads, called wampumpeag, as a pledge.§

August 3, 1640, recognizance was given by Purchase and Jordan for the appearance of the former at the next session of court. At that time one of the most serious charges preferred against the respondent was in the nature of a criminal action brought by Captain Thomas Young in the name of the King of England. The complainant claimed that the Pejepscot proprietor had interfered with his efforts to explore the country about Kennebec River in 1636, when he had penetrated the wilderness as far as Quebec and was captured by the French.

‡ Lechford, 219.
§ 4 Mass. Hist. Col., 7-339.

The explorer had returned too late from captivity in France to enter his action against Purchase in the first Yorkshire Court which had ceased to function in 1637. Evidently he had been waiting four years for an opportunity to bring his suit in a local forum.

In this connection Vines had advised Winthrop: "At that present tyme I received a letter, with a greate complaint, from Capt: Thomas Young, how that Mr. Purches had endeavored to hinder his discoveries by many" (misleading) "suggestions, and he feares, to the overthrow of his designes, promising to produce many witnesses to prove it; and desired justice from our Court, for that the wrong was offred within our Province."*

The disposition of this case is not preserved in Maine records, but it may be presumed that the relief was inconsequential, if the action was prosecuted to the final stage of recovery.

September 9, 1640, Robert Knight, William Gibbons, William Royal and Robert Shute, Indian traders, testified in the court at Saco that the scales used by Purchase for weighing furs bought from them were not reliable. From a record of the case it appeared that Arthur Mackworth, who lived at the mouth of Presumpscot River in Casco Bay, was a strong competitor in the wholesale fur industry.

In 1641, George Way died at his residence on North Street, in Dorchester, England. He left a widow Sarah and a son Eleazar. In the will he mentioned his friends William Derby and John White, who had been associated with himself and Purchase at Cape Ann in 1622. He disposed of a houselot at Dorchester, Massachusetts, and the proceeds of merchandise which had been consigned to Roger Clap, Henry Cogan, Thomas Ford and Stephen Taylor, at Dorchester and Salem. He owned cattle and corn in New England, but gave his "plantation, houses, land and ground in New Beshipscot," which he claimed as a partner of Thomas Purchase, to his son. It would appear that the first wife of Purchase had been a sister of the testator.†

The name "New Pejepscot" implied an older location, which had been established by the patentees nearer the sea. There is some indication that the first truck house was built at Maquoit. In 1643, after the prolonged period of litigation with his neighbors, the house then occupied by Purchase was destroyed by fire

* 4 Mass. Hist. Col., 7-338.
† N. E. Hist. Gen. Reg., 43-151.

and his patent was burned with it. The pioneer constructed a small temporary structure near the old site, but later built a substantial stone house above Brunswick Falls.‡

This building marked the initial bound of Sagadahoc patent as defined by Cleave in 1648. At that time Henry Boade, of Cape Porpoise, complained to Winthrop about the unfairness of that survey in these words: "He cannot come neere us if he begin to take his measure according to his pattent wch is at Sakado-hec river the South west syd of yt; but he began at Mr Purchas's house at the river called Mengipscott river."§

Purchase was too powerful an antagonist to be ignored.

Trade with the Indians was never conducted according to any well defined code of ethics by Europeans. William Hubbard, who came from England to Ipswich in 1635, described the business relations between the settlers and natives in his narrative of the Indian Wars of New England published in 1677. On account of his careful research, intimate connection with the colonists and obvious sincerity as a writer, he is entitled to full confidence. The State of Maine alone owes him an incalculable debt.

While Hubbard did not indicate definitely whom he meant in his use of the initial, the identity of the Pejepscot planter, who was then living, is apparent in the following sentence:

"The more sober and prudent of the Indians have always most bitterly complained of the Trading of strong Liquor in our English, as well as in the French and Dutch, whose ordinary Custome is first to make them, or suffer them to make themselves drunk with Liquors, and then to Trade with them, when they may easily be cheated both in what they bring to Trade, and in the Liquor itself, being one half or more nothing but Spring Water, which made one of the Amonoscoggin Indians once complain that he had given an hundred pound for Water drawn out of Mr. P. his well."

About 1654 Purchase acquired from the Indians extensive additions to his land at Pejepscot. The deed is lost but the native grantors acknowledged his title many years later. One of these was known as Derumkin, who may have been a lineal descendant from Mentaurmet, father of Robinhood, alias Manawormet, and

‡ Me. Hist. Col., 3-330 ; Pejepscot Papers.
§ Mass. Hist. Proc., 22-157.

grandfather of Natahanada, Ramchock and Tussuck, all early residents on Kennebec River.*

The Purchase tract was bounded on the west by Bunganuck River and on the east by the Sagadahoc. It was defined on the south side by Casco Bay, Merryconeag and Small Point. The former peninsula was described as that "Necke of Land Called Mereconege, lying over against an Ysland Called Sebasco, alias Sequasco Diggin in Casco Bay in the province of Mayne" which was "bounded at the head or upper end with ye plaines, of pejipscott, or land late belonging to or claimed by Mr Purchass, & on all other parts & sides * * * by the sault water."†

Small Point, which adjoined Sagadahoc River and had been granted to Sir Richard Edgecomb originally, passed eventually to English settlers through the medium of Indian conveyances.

To the northwestward the Pejepscot tract then ran "into the main land above twenty miles, four miles on each side of a small river, called Andros Coggan river, which by a precipice empties itself into the westernmost branch of Bay of Kennibeck."‡

Purchase reared a family upon the Maine plantation, but his second wife died in Boston January 7, 1656, and there is evidence that his family was then resident there.

After the Indians had plundered the home of Purchase in September, 1675, his family fled with him to the westward as far as Presumpscot River, where the English settlers were marooned on an island in Casco Bay for several weeks. From this refuge, known as Andrews' Island, the surviving heads of the respective households directed an appeal for help to the Massachusetts government. This petition was not dated, but it bore the signatures or marks of Thomas Skillings, Thomas Purchase, Francis Neal, Abraham and Jonathan Adams, Elizabeth Harvey, Edward Barton, Dorcas Andrews and William Phillips.§

In answer to the appeal a vessel was sent to Casco "to bring off" the refugees. Purchase removed at that time to Lynn, where he died May 11, 1678, aged 101 years.

After twenty-six years of litigation by the devisees of Way to recover possession of the patentee's interest at Pejepscot, his son Eleazar Way sold his father's share, as established by judg-

* York Deeds, 4-14.
† York Deeds, 3-127.
‡ Me. Doc. in Eng. Arch., 89.
§ Suffolk Court Files, 26061.

ment of court, to Richard Wharton October 10, 1683. The heirs of Purchase disposed of their rights in the eastern plantation to the same grantee two years later.

A subsequent decision of the Massachusetts courts extended the Pejepscot tract from Brunswick Falls to Maquoit and from Merry Meeting Bay to Small Point Harbor. This territory was confirmed to Wharton, who maintained that the original proprietary grant had been enlarged by Indian concessions to Purchase about thirty years before.

An early settler at Small Point was John Parker, previously of Saco, who bought the point and Stage Island, lying in the river to the eastward, from the natives in 1648. The deed was lost.

New Damariscove Island lies off the Pejepscot shore. It contains 1000 acres and was settled by a mariner named Richard Potts in 1663, when he was in the employment of Clark and Lake at the Eastward. His wife Margaret was the widow of William Davis, an early settler at Woolwich. In 1676, while he was fishing from a boat near the mainland, his wife and children on the shore were captured, and some of them killed, by the Indians.

IMPERIAL KENNEBEC

Majestic River of the North,
   Surging from the heart of Maine,
   Turning backward not again,
But ever trending boldly forth—
   Ever bearing to the sea
   Thy tribute to immensity!

So, too, fares forth the State's new blood
   From each vale and mountain side,
   Hopeful, fearless and untried,
To mingle with the world at flood—
   Falling, rising evermore,
   But always facing to the fore.

Flow on, Grand River of the State!
   Deep and strong and confident
   That in future you were meant
To seek and emulate the great,
   Merging till the end of time
   In tuneful tides, full and sublime.

SAGADAHOC RIVER

The Old Empire of Moashan or Mawooshen.

Maine once contained a vast Indian monarchy which extended, coastwise, from the Saco to Union River, a distance of 120 miles, and into the northern wilderness for 150 miles. This district, known as Moashan, was bounded on the west by Epistoman, on the east by the country of the Tarratines and on the north by a great wood called Senaglecounc.

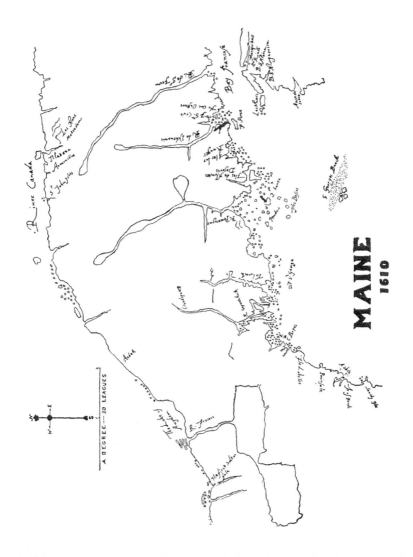

It was described in an indefinite way by Richard Hakluyt, who had obtained his information from discoveries of Bartholomew Gosnold in 1602, Martin Pring in 1603, George Waymouth in 1605, Pring, again, in 1606 and the Sagadahoc colonists in 1607 and 1608.

The district was represented by Gorges as "in a manner dreadful to the beholders, for it seemed but as a desert wilderness, replete only with a kind of savage people and overgrown trees." Captain Smith reported: "It is a Countrie rather to affright then delight one; and how to describe a more plaine spectacle of desolation or more barren I knowe not."

The form of government was monarchical and the ruler was styled Bashaba. He lived upon the Penobscot River in the vicinity of the present city of Bangor and his village was the famous Norumbega visited by Spanish mariners.

Examination of Hakluyt's geographical description of this kingdom disclosed the large rivers, the number of dominant lords, known as sagamores, the names of their villages and their military census. A condensed outline of the main statistics has been appended.

River.	Village.	Sagamores.	Wigwams.	Men.
Shawakotoc (Saco),	Crokemago.	—	—	—
Ashamahaga (Wescustego),	Agnagebcoc,	Maurmet and Casherokenit,	70	240
Sagadahoc, Kennebec,	Kenebeke,	Apomhamen,	80	100
	Ketangheanycke,	Octoworthe,	90	330
	Naragooc,	Cocockohamas,	50	150
Sebasticook,	Massakiga,	—	8	40
Androscoggin,	Amereangan,	Sasuoa and Scawas,	90	260
	Namercante,	Octoworokin,	40	120
	Buccawganecants,	Baccatusshe,	60	400
Aponeg (Sheepscot),	Nebamocago,	Mentaurmet,	160	300
	Asshawe,	Hamerhaw,	80	70
	Neredoshan,	Sabenaw,	120	100
Apponick (Damariscotta),	Appisham,	Abochigishic,	—	—
	Mesaqueegamic,	Amniquin,	70	80
	Matammiscowte,	Narracommique,	80	90
Apanmensek (Pemaquid),			—	—
Apanawapeske (Muscongus),	Meecombe,	Aramasoga,	50	80
	Chebegnadose,	Skanke,	30	90
Ramassoc (Saint George),	Panobscot,	Sibatahood,	50	80
Pemaquid ("Penobscot"),	Upsegon,	Bashabes,	60	250
	Caiocame,	Maiesquis,	—	—
	Shasheekeing,	Bowant,	—	—
Quibiquesson (Union),	Precante,	Asticon and Abermot,	50	150
Totals,			1238	2930

An examination of the list of names for the rivers will disclose the fact that the early colonists regarded the Penobscot as the River of Pemaquid.

Claim has been made by historical writers of note that this account of the empire of Moashan is purely mythical. While it may seem fantastic, it was derived from real and reliable sources and has value. Its descriptions of the nine rivers are unmistakable. Their widths, depths and comparative lengths will always remain unchanged. The distances between carrying places represented the leisurely stages and circuitous routes followed by Indian hunters and are merely relative. The inclusion of the larger lakes and islands makes the identities of these rivers absolutely certain.

The actuality of persons and their locations, in some cases, has been substantiated by extrinsic evidence. Illustrative of this assertion, such chieftains as Sasuoa, Mentaurmet (father of Robinhood), Sabenaw, Amniquin, Bashabes and Asticon were mentioned by Champlain and contemporary colonists at Sagadahoc.

On the other hand, Shawakotoc, Sagadahoc, Kenebeke, Naragooc, Pemaquid and Panobscot are easily recognizable as the modern names for Maine places.

That the territory of Moashan terminated at Saco River at the westward and did not include Saint Croix River at the eastward, is apparent from the clear identity of the former and from the fact that the inhabitants on the banks of the latter belonged to a different tribe and gave it their name. By the first French settlers the Saint Croix was called "The River of the Etechemins."

There is no doubt that the census was compiled by Hakluyt or some of his correspondents from undisclosed sources.

THE FIRST COLONY.

The voyages of Bartholomew Gosnold in 1602 and of Martin Pring in 1603 were directed by the patrons of American colonization, Henry, Earl of Southampton, Thomas, Earl of Arundel, Sir Ferdinando Gorges and their associates, with the settlement of Maine as the sole object.

No English mariner visited the coast in 1604, but in 1605 George Waymouth, under instructions from the same promoters who had sent Gosnold and Pring, surveyed Saint George's River and seized five Indians, named Tahanedo, Amoret, Skidwaros, Mannedo and Assacomoit, whom he conveyed to England.

The interest created by examinations of these savages, some of whom were secured and interviewed by Gorges, induced the members of the council to dispatch two vessels the following year. Funds for the enterprise were advanced by private subscription. However, only the expedition sponsored by Chief Justice John Popham reached its destination.

Gorges claimed subsequently that the results attained by Pring in that voyage were the most satisfactory he had ever known.

Encouraged by favorable reports of the explorers and by the extravagant accounts of the Indians, the Council of Virginia, under the supervision of Popham and Gorges, dispatched the *Gift of God* and the *Mary and John* with about 120 settlers from London and Western England. These ships sailed May 31, 1607, and arrived in safety.

The names of some of the colonists were:

George Popham, president; Raleigh Gilbert, admiral; Edward Harlow, master of ordnance; Robert Davis, sergeant-major; Ellis Best, marshal; James Davis, captain of Fort Saint George; Gome Carew, chief searcher; Richard Seymour, clergyman; John Davis, Robert Eliot, John Goyett, Thomas Hanham, Henry Harlow, John Hunt and Edward Popham.

There is ample proof that in their efforts to select a favorable location for settlement these colonists first retraced the coastal trails of George Waymouth. In fact, both vessels, after wide divergence in storms at sea, met at Saint George's Island, which they identified by the cross which had been erected by the Bristol navigator two years earlier. Every subsequent movement of both divisions indicated full knowledge of the previous excursions of the explorer. Twice by boat they visited Pemaquid where Waymouth had captured his Indians: once by way of New Harbor Creek and later by sailing around Pemaquid Point itself.

They detected the mouth of Sagadahoc River by the presence of Sutquin or Seguin, an island of forty acres, lying before it to seaward. They rowed up Pejepscot and Kennebec rivers and traversed Casco Bay to the westward as far as Richmond Island and Cape Elizabeth, which they reported to be a headland suitable for natural fortification.

August 19, Sagadahoc Colony was founded auspiciously within the present town of Phippsburg. Settlement was begun in the midst of the great wilderness of Moashan, in the Province of Sabenaw, then one of the lords under Bashaba. The spot chosen was a peninsula situated on the west bank of Sagadahoc River near its mouth. It was described plainly by two writers who appear to have obtained their information from the same quarter.

In his description of Moashan Purchase mentioned the great island of Sagadahoc, now Georgetown, in connection with the river of that name. Concurrently, he noted the incommodious situation of Sabenaw, or Hunnewell's Neck, which was represented as a "small Iland" lying "in the verie entrance of this river," and added "from the West of which Iland to the Maine, there is a Sand that maketh as it were a bar, so that that way is not passable for shipping: but to the Eastward there is two fathoms water."

From the usage of similar terms and, in some cases, from literal adoption of words in his text, it is probable that Purchase may have had personal interviews with the anonymous writer of our only extant "Relation" of the founding of Sagadahoc Colony. In fact, an annotated copy of the historical treatises of the former ascribes the unknown authorship to Captain James Davis, the colonist.

At any rate, the "Relation" alluded to the Fort of Saint George as "our plantation whch ys at the very mouth or entry of the Ryver of Sagadehocke on the West Syd of the Ryver beinge almoste an Illand."

In this wild, unexplored and desolate region the founders of the first northern plantation attempted to establish themselves in a fortress, impregnable so far as the aborigines were concerned. It was named Fort Saint George in honor of the Patron Saint of England.

Its strategic position for control of the whole river was criticised subsequently by the French, upon the assumption that the river delta rendered it ineffectual for defence against the outside world. Its natural surroundings, form, material of construction, and the arrangement of buildings within it, disclosed a special effort to guard against the uncertain dangers of the interior. Its strongest ramparts faced the unexplored continent. The only avenue of escape led across an uncharted sea.

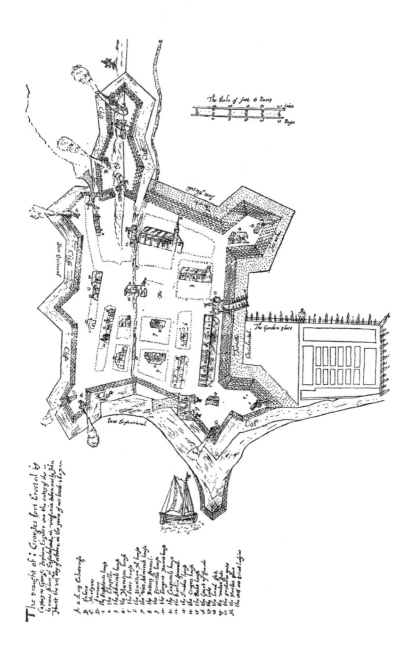

A plan of Fort Saint George was protracted by John Hunt at Sagadahoc October 8, 1607. Presumably the fortification was not then completed, but the sketch was taken to England by the engineer.*

William Strachey, who wrote an account of the trials of the colony, claimed that fifty houses were completed within the fortified enclosure. Some writers have disclaimed his statement, but an examination of the structures outlined in the plan discloses a series of tenements in each barrack.

Some fishing, lumbering and exploration was done during the first autumn, and the keel of the bark *Virginia* was laid by English mechanics in the first shipyard on the American continent.

On the shore overlooking Atkins Bay was written by President Popham the first Latin correspondence composed in New England. It remains a distinct tribute to the high social standing of the colonists and to the classical trend of English institutions of learning. It was prepared December 13 and dispatched two days later with a returning vessel to the king of England.

Only forty-five adventurous spirits were left in the country at that time. The ensuing winter was unusually severe, yet only the aged president succumbed to its rigors. His successor was Raleigh Gilbert. The storehouse with all its provisions was burned.

With the advent of spring, Robert Davis returned with one vessel and supplies, but he brought, also, the depressing news that Chief Justice Popham and Sir John, brother of Raleigh Gilbert, had died in England during the winter.

During the summer of 1608, some planting was undertaken and the fishing continued, but under dangerous circumstances.

Pierre Biard, a French priest, who visited the abandoned Fort Saint George three years later, asserted that its occupants had not remained upon friendly terms with the natives during Gilbert's administration; that the Indians had become insolent and massacred three boatloads, consisting of eleven men, while they were on the fishing grounds during the last year of their sojourn.†

Biard's account was more than a mere tradition. His version of 1611 corresponded with the story of the same event as recounted by the Indians in the vicinity more than a century later.

Discouraged by many reverses, the Sagadahoc pioneers at

* Brown's Genesis U. S., 1-190.
† Jesuit Rel., 2-45.

last bade farewell to Sabenaw in November, 1608. When they returned to England they took the pinnace *Virginia* with them, as the only valuable product of their industry in the New World.

It may be true that Chief Justice Popham, President Popham and Sir John Gilbert might not have perpetuated this colony if they had lived, but without their abiding support it was doomed. Cold, fever, war, conflagration and starvation could penetrate the strongest barriers.

After unpleasant experiences with a northern climate some of the Sagadahoc planters sought the southern colony the next year.

May 20, 1609, James and Robert Davis sailed from Plymouth in the pinnace *Virginia*, which was then the property of Sir George Somers. The pinnace reached its destination, but Somers was wrecked in another vessel in the Summer Islands. He subsequently became a prominent member of Virginia Colony.

The claim has been made that the settlement at Sagadahoc River was never deserted. It has been cited as proof that, in 1614, Captain John Smith found a ship, belonging to Sir Francis Popham, stationed in the mainland opposite Monhegan, "that had there such acquaintance, having many yeares used onely that porte, that the most parte there, was had by him."

The business of Sir Francis Popham was described by two contemporary writers.

Sir Ferdinando Gorges, in commenting upon this subsequent action of his colleague, said "The President was to return to settle the state his brother had left him; upon which all resolved to quit the place, and with one consent to away, by which means all our former hopes were frozen to death; though Sir Francis Popham could not so give it over, but continued to send thither several years after in hope of better fortunes, but found it fruitless, and was necessitated at last to sit down with the loss he had already undergone."‡

Smith, discussing the same subject, said: "Yet Sir Francis Popham sent divers times one Captaine Williams to Monahigan onely to trade and make core fish, but for any Plantations there" were "no more speeches."

The depressing effect of abandonment of the first colonization project was described as follows: "The arrivall of these people

‡ 3 Mass. Hist. Col., 6-56.

here in England, was a wonderfull discouragement to all the first undertakers, in so much as there was no more speech of setling any other Plantation in those parts for a long time after: only Sir Francis Popham having the ships and provision, which remayned of the Company, and supplying what was necessary for his purpose, sent divers times to the Coasts for Trade and fishing; of whose losse or gaines himselfe is best able to give account * * * Our people abandoning the Plantation in this sort as you have heard; the Frenchmen immediately tooke the opportunitie to settle themselves within our limits."§

If this last statement of the Council of Plymouth were not sufficient proof of the termination of the Sagadahoc enterprise, such preliminary abstracts from reliable sources prepare the mind for the conviction that the real sequel of the whole matter was that briefly stated by an anonymous contemporary writer. At any rate, it was given full credence by Purchase, the historian, during the decade immediately following the abandonment of the project and he, if not the author himself, incorporated an almost literal copy of it into his own story of the rise and fall of the first Maine settlement.

The original account of the denouement, after reciting the outlook, concluded with these words: "Wherefore, they all embarked in this new arrived ship, and in the new pinnace, the *Virginia,* and set sail for England. And this was the end of that northern colony upon the River Sachadehoc."*

It only remained for Samuel Maverick, who visited the spot in 1624, to give the situation a delicate touch of pathos: "Three leagues distant from Damerells Cove is Sagadahocke at the mouth of Kenebeth river, on which place the Lord Pohams people setled about fiftie yeares since, but soon after deserted it, and returned for England; I found Rootes and Garden hearbs and some old walles there, when I went first over, which shewed it to be the place where they had been."†

The first northern colony had failed.‡

The immediate encroachment of the French upon territory claimed by the English nation was the occupation of Mount Desert Island, which was terminated by Sir Samuel Argal from Virginia in 1613.

§ Purchase, 19-271.
* Mass. Hist. Proc., 18-110.
† Mass. Hist. Proc., 21-232.
‡ Thayer's Sagadahoc Colony, 87.

While there were no more English plantations undertaken in Maine for many years, there were many fishing ships which visited the coast annually after the return of the Popham Colony and it is more than probable that during the summer months some of the seaworn crews were quartered comfortably upon Monhegan, to cure fish and trade with the natives, or each other, when conditions would permit.

SAGADAHOC, LYGONIA, OR PLOUGH PATENT.

From the time of organization the Council of Plymouth had favored some plan to found a public colony on the Sagadahoc. Although one attempt to gain a foothold had been futile, the opinions of mariners and some of the survivors of the old colony were favorable to that design. Besides, some of the larger cities of England were overcrowded with worthy citizens who were unable to procure a satisfactory livelihood. While they were unaccustomed to agriculture, they were anxious to improve their conditions under any plan that appeared to be operative.

June 26, 1630, the council granted a large tract of land in the Maine wilderness to a company composed of prospective English husbandmen. The names of the patentees, all of whom lived in London, were: John Crispe, John Dye, Thomas Juppe, John Robinson, Nathaniel Whetham, Henry Fowkes, Brian Kipling, John Roach, Grace Hardwin, Daniel and Roger Binckes.

The patent was lost, but an abstract shows that it embraced an area forty miles square, lying on the south side of Sagadahoc River, within territory granted to Sir Ferdinando Gorges and Captain John Mason in 1622, but unoccupied at that date. Even the grantors were not positive as to the premises conveyed. The description was so indefinite that it could never be explained, but was thought to include two large islands which lay sixty miles inland in the Kennebec River.

Thomas Jenner, in discussing the subject with Winthrop a few years later, remarked: "Now Sacadehock River is a certaine & sure place for one terme of its bounds, but the Ilands are doubtfull, which they are, or wher they are: & more over ther possession was first taken * * * Sacadehock river reacheth but to Merry Meeting, & then its branched into Begipscot, & Chenebeck, & is no further cald by the name of Sacadehock."§

§ 4 Mass. Hist. Col., 7-360.

Some of the patentees admitted to their associates, "Wee can not posible relat unto you the labur and truble that wee have had to establishe our former grant; mane rufe words wee have had from Sir Fferdineando at the ffurst, and to this houer he douth afferm that he never gave consent, that you should have aboufe forte mills in lenkth and 20 millse in bredth, and sayeth that his one hand is not to your patten if it have anne more."

Although the need of so large an area was explained to be that "the grettest part of it was not habetable, beinge rocke, wer no man could life," Gorges debated that it would have included other plantations already granted, if it had comprised more than twenty miles in width on the coast.

Another disturbing element was the grant to Richard Bradshaw which the Plough Company, as the Sagadahoc patentees were styled collectively, believed to be contained within its boundaries, although Gorges and Bradshaw himself thought otherwise.

Pemaquid was also presumed to be involved on the easterly border, concerning which the company decided March 8, 1631-2, that "This conterfers" (controversy) "must be ended between your sellfes and such guferners of them of Pimequed as they have apointed."

Captain Walter Neal was designated by Gorges to decide the true location of the Sagadahoc Patent and that of Bradshaw. As he later defined the limitations of Pemaquid between the Damariscotta and Muscongus rivers, it may be assumed that the easterly boundary of Sagadahoc was fixed at the Damariscotta margin by a previous decision.*

The first colonists sent over by the Sagadahoc patentees refused to settle at Sagadahoc, where they appear to have had some controversy with the occupants of Pemaquid.

Under the date of July 6, 1631, the following account of their arrival in Massachusetts was noted: "A small ship of sixty tons arrived at Natascott, Mr. Graves master. She brought ten passengers from London. They came with a patent to Sagadahock, but, not liking the place, they came hither. Their ship drew ten feet, and went up to Watertown, but she ran on ground twice by the way. These were the company called the Husbandmen, and their ship called the *Plough*. Most of them proved familists and vanished away."†

* 4 Mass. Hist. Col., 7-93.
† Winthrop, 1-58.

The names of the planters who remained in Massachusetts were John Crispe, John Smith, John Dye and John Kirman. Bryan Binckes and Peter Johnson removed to Virginia. The affairs of the company were adjusted by bankruptcy proceedings.‡

The writer of the anonymous relation dismissed the subject in 1635 with the significant remark, "Sagadehock was never planted." Maverick, writing many years later, was even more emphatic, when he asserted that the members of the Plough Company abandoned their patent, "never settling on that land."§

July 7, 1643, two surviving members of the company sold their interests in Lygonia to Alexander Rigby, an influential English nobleman, who claimed that all of the country occupied by planters as far west as Cape Porpoise was within his jurisdiction.*

However, the new proprietor recognized the superior rights of Purchase at Pejepscot and by excluding that area extended his own tract farther west. Nevertheless, Purchase was not satisfied with his allotment and, in 1654, secured additional territory from the natives. The deed is lost, but the tract comprised all of the land situated between Sagadahoc River and Maquoit and as far inland as Merry Meeting Bay and Brunswick Falls.†

Before 1650 native conveyances in Maine had been infrequent, but thereafter the same premises at Sagadahoc were sold and resold with utter disregard for prior rights.‡‡

THE PARKER FAMILY.

A grandson of John Parker stated that the immigrant was a native of Bideford, England, but the date of his birth is unknown. In 1765, a grandnephew John Phillips testified, "That Sagadahock had the name of Parkers Island given it for one Thomas Parker, who, as the deponent was informed, was the mate of the first ship that came from England with the Plymouth People * * * and father to Thomas Parker who * * * lived on Parkers Island: That John Parker, brother of the last Thomas Parker, lived opposite to Arrowsic Island, on the Western Side, which side was called Kennebec Side." The witness was mistaken with regard to the name of the immigrant who was John and not Thomas Parker.

‡ Mass. Col. Rec., 1-89.
§ N. H. State Papers, 17-491; Mass. Hist. Proc., 21-232.
* Winthrop, 2-256.
† York Deeds, 4-14.
‡‡ Appendix G.

June 14, 1659, John Parker, the son of the immigrant, acquired from Robinhood a tract of land six miles in length situated on the western bank of Sagadahoc River, between Parker's Head and Winnegance Creek. The grantee was represented in this deed as "the first of the English Nation that began to subdue the sayd tract of Lands, & undertake In the fishing trade." This was another case of mistaken identity, for the father was engaged in fishing at Damariscove Island when the son was but eleven years of age. The son deposed in 1684 that he was "aged about fivety yeares."§

These statements afford some ground for uncertainty, for both Sagadahoc and New Plymouth colonists sailed from Plymouth.

If the elder Parker were a seaman on the *Gift of God* or *Mary and John* in 1607, it may have been more than a mere coincidence that this mate afterwards purchased the site of Fort Saint George from the natives. When he bought the fort he also obtained title to Stage Island, which contained about eight acres covered with fishing stages.

However, it is plain that in his allusion to "the Plymouth People" Phillips meant those who had sailed from Plymouth in the Mayflower September 8, 1620, and sighted their first land at Cape Cod, where Christopher Jones, the master, "and his mate, and others experienced in fishing," took note of the whales and species of fish near the coast. While in the country Jones sent out several expeditions "to see where fish could be got" for his cargo.*

There is a tradition that Parker was the fisherman who spent a winter on the southern end of Parker's Island at Georgetown in 1629 and combined with the colony of Vines at Saco the next spring.

The birthplace of the younger John Parker must have been at Biddeford, in 1634, and his sister Mary was born there three years later. These children, with their mother Mary and her eldest son Thomas, composed the entire family of the immigrant, whose home was located on Parker's Neck at Biddeford Pool, then called Winter Harbor—on the outer point described in the Province Map before 1653 as a "Neck of Land." Here the immigrant maintained a dwelling and a fishing stage for some years.

In 1636, he was interested in the clapboard industry and be-

§ York Deeds, 4-16, 17; 2-13.
* Mourt's Rel., 2, 26.

longed to the church society at Biddeford, where he contributed to the ministerial fund for the support of Richard Gibson, who was pastor at Winter Harbor and Richmond Island.

In 1645, Parker's Neck was acquired from Vines by Robert Jordan who had secured an execution for debt against the patentee in favor of the estate of John Winter.

Parker withdrew to the Eastward, and that same year his hearsay evidence was incorporated by George Cleave, as magistrate, in that of Henry Watts, the fishmonger of Black Point. The full text of this testimony contained the statement that "John Parkar of Dammarills Cove affermath that Robert nash being with him gave & sould so much Sack to his men that nash himselfe and parkars me'n we'are all so drunke for severall dais togethar that his men Could not goe to Sea in the prime tyme of fishing whereby the said parkar & his Company lost 40 or 50 pownds."†

Three years after this incident "John Parker Senr of Sacatyhock" bought from Robinhood as local sagamore "a Tract of Land on the Easter Side of Sacaty hock being an Island commonly called by the name of Sagosett alias Chegoney by the Indians." The first deed of the premises, known as Stage Island, was lost, but the sale was confirmed subsequently to Mary, widow of the grantee. In the same transaction Parker had acquired Small Point and the ancient site of Fort Saint George, which were transferred by his heirs to Thomas Clark and Thomas Lake.‡

As a consequence, forty-one years after the first settlement Parker became sole owner of the plantation occupied by the first colonists at Sabenaw, or Sabenoa, as the last native owner was known.

February 27, 1650-1, he bought from Robinhood "the Island Called Rasthegon lying by Sacittihock Rivers Mouth." The island has since been called Georgetown and contains about 18,000 acres.§

May 23, 1654, the immigrant with other colonists on the Sagadahoc took allegiance to Plymouth Colony. At that time his son John was living at Arrowsic. This island, which contains about 4,100 acres, had been acquired from Robinhood by

† Me. Doc. Hist., 4-6.
‡ York Deeds, 11-139; 14-140.
§ York Deeds, 10-252.

John Richards in 1649. In disposing of it in 1654 Richards excepted "one hundred Acres of landes Lying upon ye said Island formerly sold unto John Parker whereon hee hath erected a dwelling howse." When Parker sold the premises in 1657, he was described in the deed as a "seaman."*

An antedated copy of the immigrant's will, made October 31, 1661, was deposited with the files of Lincoln County. He bequeathed forty pounds in money to each of the three children, including Mary who had just married Thomas Webber, and the residue of his estate to his widow. The family relationships are plainly defined in a later transaction.†

Parker's Neck at Winter Harbor was acquired by Roger Spencer from Jordan before 1660. At that early date the place was described as "one fishing stage & house & Necke of Land wron the stage standeth, which is commanly knowne & Called by the name of Parker's Necke." In 1700, Joseph Webber, son of Mary (Parker) Webber, then living in Charlestown, sold his interest in premises defined by him as "one Neck of land called Parkers Neck lying in Saco within ye Province of Maine."‡

From these conveyances it is obvious that descendants of the early immigrant persisted in claiming interests in his old location at Winter Harbor, although the courts had disregarded all such collateral titles to family ownership many years before Parker removed to Sagadahoc.

PIONEERS

ATKINS, THOMAS, fisherman at New Plymouth, 1640; at Atkins' Bay with wife Elizabeth, 1647; deceased 1680-6; children Abigail (Washburn), Ann (Clark), Elizabeth (Davis), born 1645, Esther (Pike), Margaret (Hackett), Rachel (Drake, Barry), Rebecca (Hall), Ruth (Haskins), Sarah (Gurney) and Susanna (Green).

DOLE, WILLIAM, Woolwich, 1650-1665; children John, born 1654, and William, born 1656; the family removed to Salem.

GENT, JOHN, a fisherman at Salem, 1642; trading at Pemaquid, 1647; died at sea, 1661; widow Elizabeth bought land east of Mason's Neck from the Indians, 1663; she was driven from Sheepscot by the Indians, 1677, and married George Speare, of Boston; they returned to Sheepscot, then called New Dartmouth, 1683; children Elizabeth, who married John, son of James Phipps and had John, born 1668, Mary (Mason, Allen) and Thomas, born 1642.

HOPKINS, JOHN, Woolwich, 1647-1654.

---

* Plymouth Col. Rec., 3-58 ; Suffolk Deeds, 2-44 ; Lincoln Deeds, 1-19.
† York Deeds, 10-152.
‡ York Deeds, 1-113 ; 6-144.

THE VALE OF CUSHNOC

With distant murmurs from the fall
    And music of a thousand rills,
    With breeze along the serried hills
And forest echoes over all;
With salmon leaping to the sun
    And wild deer drinking in the glade,
    With wood duck glinting in the shade,
A day at Cushnoc had begun.

But eagles homing one by one
    And shadows growing in the stream,
    And daylight passing gleam by gleam,
Betoken that the day is done.

A cabin marks the terraced shore
    With smoke arising through the trees,
    With hunters resting at their ease
And beagles romping at the door.
And when at last the dusk comes on—
    The master whistles to his dogs,
    Piles high the open hearth with logs
And dreams of home until the dawn.

KENNEBEC RIVER

The colonists of New Plymouth first became interested in the resources of Maine in 1622, when from necessity they were compelled to seek supplies from the fishing vessels which came to Monhegan and Damariscove islands. In the words of Governor Bradford, they thereafter "knew ye way to those parts for their benefite."*

In 1624, the colony sent the *Little James* to Pemaquid to fish and trade, but it was wrecked in that harbor by a severe storm, and three of its crew were drowned. Late in the summer this ship was repaired and sent home, for the season was too far advanced to use it again that year.

After the harvest of 1625 Edward Winslow was sent with a shallop forty or fifty leagues to the Eastward and up the Kennebec to trade with the natives. He exchanged a cargo of corn raised by the Plymouth planters for seven hundred pounds of beaver and other pelts. Winslow's Rocks near the City of Bath were discovered upon this or a subsequent trip.†

Although Massachusetts colonists claimed to have instituted the practice of intercepting the Indian trade by use of the inland waterways, Gorges was the first to adopt it, seven years before, when he instructed Richard Vines to seek the natives in their own haunts. Furthermore, Thomas Weston resorted to this method at Casco, the year before Winslow's expedition on the Kennebec, and Christopher Levett alluded to it as the scheme of an "evill member" in his harbor.

Near the end of 1626, according to the ancient style of reckoning, the plantation at Monhegan, which had belonged to merchants of Plymouth, was discontinued. At that time the entire stock of unsold merchandise, including articles salvaged from a French bark which had been wrecked at Sagadahoc in the spring, was bought in equal shares by Plymouth Colony and David Thompson. The price paid was one thousand pounds, a part of which was promissory notes. The goods bought by the colony were intended for trade with the Indians in the vicinity.

* Bradford, 2-90.
† Bradford, 2-138.

It remained for Thomas Morton to anticipate the agents of New Plymouth on the "Kynyback River," where "his boate had gleaned away all before they came."‡

In June, 1627, Governor Bradford complained that "Besides the spoiling of the trade this last year, our boat and men had like to have been cut off by the Indians, *after the fishermen were gone*, for the wrongs which they did them, in stealing their skins and other abuses offered them, both the last year and this."§

The price paid by Morton for his injudicious interference with colony's trade on the Kennebec was expulsion from the country in 1628, when he was accused of many imaginary misdemeanors as a pretext.

Late in the fall of that year the colony delegated Isaac Allerton its agent "to procure a patente for a fitt trading place in ye river of Kenebec." The reasons advanced for this action were that New Plymouth had been the first to engage in trade on that river and might be excluded therefrom "by the planters at Pascataway & other places to ye eastward of them, and allso by ye fishing ships, which used to draw much profite from ye Indeans of those parts." In fact, some competitors had already threatened to secure proprietary rights on the river.*

The "other places to ye eastward" of Pascataqua, to which allusion was made in the quotation, must have included French settlements.

The procedure followed by Allerton to procure a patent was expensive and protracted. James Sherley, the London agent for the colony, complained later that "many locks must be opened with ye silver, ney, ye golden key" and that the grant for New Plymouth and Kennebec was no exception to the rule, since it was obtained "with no small sume of money."

Allerton first sought the advice and influence of Richard Vines, who as "servant" of Sir Ferdinando Gorges, then president of the Council of Plymouth, could act for him in the capacity of a friend at court.

To this end, in 1628, he advanced £30 to Vines and more to others.†

As there were several petitions before the council for private grants in New England, as well as an enlargement of the terri-

‡ N. E. Canaan. 149.
§ Mass. Hist. Col., 3-57.
* Bradford, 2-149.
† 3 Mass. Hist. Col., 1-199.

torial area of New Plymouth, it was deemed advisable, for all concerned, to take a general view of the premises. For this purpose a common fund was raised by the petitioners in 1629 and Allerton contributed £50 for the colony's proportion.

The exploratory expedition may have been present at Squamscott May 17, 1629, when Vines and his associates, who were interested in settlements at Pascataqua, Saco and Penobscot, witnessed the deed from the Indians to John Wheelwright.

Owing to his intimacy with Vines and the expenditure of more than £500, Allerton finally secured the favor of the council, for according to Sherley he had become an intimate friend of Gorges and obtained "all that Mr. Winslow desired in his letters to me, & more also."

The grant at Cushnoc was not issued until January 13, 1629-30, and was mentioned as just made, but not confirmed, in Sherley's letter to Bradford, dated March 19, following. As this letter was dictated by Allerton he must have been conversant with the contents.

The account of Bradford, written nearly twenty years afterwards, was misleading wherein it was claimed that a patent for Cushnoc was brought to this country by Allerton before 1630, since that writer later asserted that "ye patent came to above 500 li. and *yet nothing done in it but what was done at first without any confirmation.*"‡

After the issuance of the patent a house was erected at Cushnoc on the Kennebec. The site was identical with that of Fort Western, within the present area of the City of Augusta and "in ye most convenientest place for trade." The commander of this post was John Howland, a member of Plymouth Colony, who continued there for several years with a few assistants, known as the "family." The stock in trade consisted of corn, coats, shirts, rugs, blankets, biscuit, peas and prunes.§

The business at Cushnoc was conducted by a partnership, consisting of the leading members of the New Plymouth plantation and Richard Andrews, John Beauchamp, Timothy Hatherly and James Sherley, merchants of London. This association had assumed the debts of the colony, four years earlier, in exchange for the exclusive privilege of trading within its jurisdiction.

‡ Bradford, 2-166, 187.
§ Bradford, 2-157.

This same year the partners established the trading post under supervision of Edward Ashley on their new grant at Penobscot.

John Alden took possession at Cushnoc, but the tract was never fully defined. It was situated so far inland that the boundaries were uncertain. Although visited by Waymouth in 1605, all that the grantees knew of the wilderness had been obtained

FORT WESTERN, AUGUSTA

from vague reports of the Indians or from their own incursions to parts of it by way of the river.

According to the natives and early explorers, Sagadahoc River terminated at Merry Meeting Bay, where the Kennebec became an eastern tributary. Cushnoc grant comprised a tract fifteen miles in width on each side of the latter stream, extending inland from the mouth of Cobbosseecontee River in the City of Gardiner to the Falls of Negaumkeag, or about six miles above the City of Augusta.*

Cushnoc trading post at the head of tide in the Kennebec River was intended, like that of the Laconia Company at Newichawannock, to dominate inland traffic with the natives through control of a great navigable waterway. With the use of wampumpeag as a medium of exchange the colony soon diverted the entire trade with the interior tribes from the "fisher-men and in a great part from other of ye stragling planters."

Allerton, however, after his dismissal from the service of the

* Ford's Bradford, 2-176.

colony and the loss of Ashley in 1631, formed "a company of base felows * * * to rune * * * into ye river of Kenebeck, to gleane away ye trade from ye house ther."†

The company employed by Allerton must have been composed of passengers or members of the crew of the *White Angel*, who were described by Bradford as "such a wicked and drunken company as neither Mr. Allerton nor any els could rule." The later fatal consequences in the Hocking incident, when the colony undertook to defend its exclusive trading privilege at Cushnoc Falls, led to the general arraignment that "To the Eastward they cut throats for beaver."

Although the post at Cushnoc had been surrounded by a strong palisade and was kept guarded to prevent invasion, an early attempt was made there to kill Governor Winslow. An Indian concealed himself in a tree near the enclosure, and only the early retirement of his intended victim to the security of the barracks defeated his purpose.

In 1632 and 1633 the *White Angel* was on the coast fishing and trading.

In April, 1634, John Hocking, with two men and a boy, "belonging to ye plantation of Pascataway, wente with a barke and comodities to trade in that river" (Kennebec) "and would needs press into their limites; and not only so, but would needs goe up ye river above their house (towards ye falls of ye river), and intercept the trade that should come to them."‡

In spring, the Indians were wont to come down from the hunting and trapping areas about the numerous lakes and streams above that point.

John Howland and John Alden, both magistrates of Plymouth Colony, were present at the time. Howland was commander of the post and Alden had just arrived with a boatload of supplies for opening the season.

Hocking was advised to depart on the ground that he had trespassed there the year before and such action on his part did not represent the sentiment of his plantation at Pascataqua. After refusal to comply Howland, John Irish, Thomas Savery, William Reynolds and Moses Talbot attempted to cut the vessel adrift. In the struggle which ensued Talbot and Hocking were

† Bradford, 2-188.
‡ Bradford, 2-199.

shot and instantly killed. John Alden, of Plymouth fame, did not participate in the action, but was arrested and imprisoned by officials of Massachusetts Bay Colony.§

While during the earlier years Maine trading privileges had proven valuable, the volume of business at Cushnoc gradually diminished until it became unprofitable on account of the cost of supervision. At first the trading had been managed by Bradford and other ambitious members of his colony, of whom Allerton was one, under the terms of the general lease, dated September 30, 1627, and limited to six years. The employes were members of the colony who were referred to collectively as "the family."

After the expiration of the first lease, trading rights on the Kennebec were relet at decreasing rates, but December 1, 1640, no one had been trading at Cushnoc for more than a year and the post was deserted. There had been no bidders when the previous lease had expired in November, 1639.*

In 1641, the trading house was reoccupied under the supervision of Thomas Willett, who formerly had had supervision at Penobscot. The next year Winslow, who had selected the original site for the station at Cushnoc twelve years before, made an official inspection of the place. Winslow's visit may have been occasioned by the advent of a few Massachusetts colonists on the lower reaches of the Sagadahoc, where the acquisition of Pejepscot by their colony had induced them to locate.

Eight years later Christopher Lawson appeared in the vicinity. After some negotiation with the natives he secured valuable tracts at Swan Island and Waterville, where he was maintained by his employers, Clark and Lake, at an expense of more than £100 per year, and monopolized the native trade.

March 8, 1652-3, at the suggestion of Bradford, Edward Winslow filed a petition in England which sought further concessions in Maine. It was alleged in the declaration that "for many years the plantation had had a grant of a trading place in the river Kennebec, but not having the whole of the river under their grant and government, many excesses and wickednesses have been committed, and the benefit for trade and furs, one of the greatest supports of their plantation, had been taken from the

§ N. E. Hist. Gen. Reg., 9-80.
* Plymouth Col. Rec., 2-2.

inhabitants of New Plymouth." The petitioners asked for a patent for the whole Kennebec region.†
The request was granted and May 23, 1654, the straggling Sagadahoc settlers as well as those on the Kennebec submitted to the civil jurisdiction of Plymouth Colony. The family at Cushnoc, then in charge of Thomas Southworth, was composed of employes from New Plymouth, registered previously as "covenant servants" or freemen who were not required to resubmit. Like employes at the trading post, the independent settlers at Sagadahoc hailed from Massachusetts, Western Maine, or Pemaquid plantation.

Competition from Clark and Lake soon made the sale of the patent feasible, and October 27, 1661, Antiphas Boyce, Thomas Brattle, Edward Tyng and John Winslow purchased all Maine rights of Plymouth Colony for £1400.‡

After the sale, the premises at Cushnoc returned to the solitude of former ages. Trade on the river was gradually reduced because of the extinction of local Indians by tribal wars, disease and the development of a general sentiment which proved adverse to English interests. The animosity of the eastern Indians for Maine colonists became apparent in their first war of 1675, but did not culminate until a year later.

August 13, 1676, the savages closed in upon the unsuspecting settlements. The principal points of attack were the house of Richard Hammond at Woolwich and the mill settlement of Clark and Lake at Arrowsic. At the latter location "six several Edifices are said to have been there erected," besides other dwellings situated within a mile.§

The result was a series of massacres in which Captain Lake was killed. The river was abandoned by all planters and it became unsafe for any English settler to remain on the upper banks of the Kennebec.

These uncertain conditions prevailed at Cushnoc until 1754, when the influence of its owners and their desire to develop it led to the construction of a line of frontier forts on the river at Richmond, Augusta and Winslow. Fort Halifax, situated in the easterly angle of Kennebec and Sebasticook rivers on the last location, was built on the site of an ancient Indian stockade.

† Sainsbury's Col. Pap., 1-376.
‡ York Deeds, 9-226.
§ Hubbard's Wars, 2-42.

THE DAWN OF CHRISTIANITY ON THE KENNEBEC.

The first religious ceremony on the river was performed at or near Sabenaw by Sagadahoc colonists in 1607.

Twenty-three years later the "family" of New Plymouth employes at Cushnoc conducted occasional services, after the manner of their colony, at the trading post. The Indians, however, do not appear to have been favorably impressed.

Sagamores of the Upper Kennebec, who had formed commercial relations with French colonists on the Saint Lawrence River, became interested in the Catholic faith. At their urgent request Gabriel Druillettes was induced to penetrate the wilderness of Central Maine at an early date. At Quebec the object of the mission was described as an attempt to teach the natives "the path to Heaven."

Maverick assigned a different motive to the visit. He claimed that Druillettes, "a Gentleman and a Fryer," came down the Kennebec "from Kebeck to us in New England to desire aide from us agst the Mowake Indians" who were deadly enemies.

The story of this priest's hardships was thrillingly told by Jerome Lalemont in the *Jesuit Relations.*

He left Sillery August 29, 1647, accompanied by Indians and encountered almost insuperable difficulties from the start. He traversed the whole length of the Kennebec in company with a savage who was familiar with the resorts of the Abenaki Indians.

At Cushnoc he was well entertained by the English captain, John Howland. Later he visited Acadia and on his way thither was received cordially at "seven or eight" English settlements along the coast. A list of these places probably included the plantation of James Smith near Winslow's Rocks, and that of Bateman and Brown at Woolwich, as well as Cape Newagen, Winnegance, Corbin's Sound, Damariscove, Pemaquid and Monhegan. At Pentagoet he found a colony of Capuchin monks.

The Superior of this "little home" was styled "Father Ignace, of Paris." The inscription on a copper plate, which was unearthed at Castine many years ago, proves that a chapel was begun at or near the French fort at Penobscot at an early date. A translation of the legend, perforated in abbreviated Latin, reads as follows:

"1648, June 8, Brother Leo, of Paris, in Capuchin mission, laid this foundation in honor of our Lady of the Sacred Hope."

Upon his return to the Kennebec he was conducted to a spot, situated about three miles above Cushnoc, where the Indians had already built a small chapel of boards and surrounded it with a village of fifteen large wigwams. Druillettes remained there about three months, during which time thirty of the natives were baptized.

The evangelist left Maine May 20, 1648, after paying another visit to the Cushnoc trading post, to which Howland, who had spent the winter in New Plymouth and Boston, had just returned. The account did not mention any other employes of the partners, nor imply that the station had been occupied since that fall.

Not long after the departure of the French missionary the Indians induced some English carpenters with mercenary motives to erect a fort at Pigwacket as a protection against the Mohawks. This improvised refuge was enclosed with a palisade of logs and contained a rude chapel. It was situated in Fryeburg on the Saco River and was called Narrakamagog Fort. Similar buildings were constructed by the French at Norridgewock.

The first Protestant society on the Kennebec was organized at Bath by Robert Gouch, of Salem, in 1660, when he purchased a large frontier tract of Robinhood as dominant sagamore of that district. All of the English, however, were expelled by the Indians fifteen years later.

In 1693, a new Indian fort was erected on the Kennebec at Arreseguntecook which was situated about one day's journey above Norridgewock. Phonetic spelling has evolved the word "Amiicungantoquoke" with the meaning, "banks of the river abounding in dried meat."

April 11, 1700, according to Romer, there were but three Indian fortresses in Maine, in each of which could be found a French chapel and two priests. The locations were at Narrakamagog, Norridgewock and Arreseguntecook.*

Employes

HOWLAND, JOHN, arrived at New Plymouth in the "Mayflower," 1620; agent for the colony at Cushnoc, 1630-4; wife Elizabeth, daughter of John Tillie; died February 23, 1672-3; children, born at Plymouth, John, February 24, 1626, Deborah (Smith), Desire (Gorham), Elizabeth (Hicks), Hannah (Bosworth), Hope (Chipman), Isaac, Jabez, Joseph, Lydia (Brown) and Ruth (Cushman).

* Me. Doc. Hist., 10-49.

IRISH, JOHN, servant of Timothy Hatherly from Clisden, England, 1629; employe of Plymouth Colony at Cushnoc, 1634; Duxbury, 1637; received there land "due for his service," 1644; died at Bridgewater, 1677; widow Elizabeth; children Elias and John.

REYNOLDS, WILLIAM, employe of Plymouth Colony at Cushnoc, 1634; Duxbury, 1637; married Alice Kitson August 30, 1638; Salem, 1640; Kennebunk River, 1647; died 1675-9, when his heirs obtained land by reason of former service to the colony; children Job, John, born 1651, Mary (Langley), Samuel and William.

RICHARDS, JOHN, employe of Plymouth Colony at Penobscot and Cushnoc, 1630-8; had employe's grant, 1637; Saco Court, 1640-3; bought Arrowsic from Indians, 1649; owed an account to Thomas Richards, of Weymouth, 1650; freeman at Sagadahoc, 1654; sold Arrowsic to Clark and Lake that year; described as "Old Richards" of Kennebec, 1656; owed Plymouth Company at Kennebec for merchandise, 1659.

TALBOT, MOSES, employe of Plymouth Colony at Cushnoc; killed below the falls in Augusta in April, 1634.

PHIPPS POINT, NOW OWNED BY GOVERNOR WILLIAM TUDOR GARDINER

SHEEPSCOT RIVER

The Indian name for this river was Aponeg. Its present name was derived from the words "sheep's cote," which type of cot or shelter was conspicuous along the shores, when the principal occupation of eastern pioneers was sheep raising.

In 1606, the chief of the province was Mentaurmet, father of Robinhood, who subsequently disposed of all his lands to the English. The considerations for the conveyances were so small compared with the extent of the tracts that James Stilson, who was related to John Brown of Pemaquid, maintained that the Eastern Country was "settled by people without purchase."

The first conveyance of Robinhood was executed in 1639, when he sold to Edward Bateman and John Brown, of Pemaquid, the whole of the present town of Woolwich, then called Nequasseag, extending from Kennebec to Sheepscot River.

Soon after their purchase the grantees sold Phipps Point, situated on the westerly side of the latter river, to James Phipps and John White. The site is still known as the birthplace of Sir William Phips in 1651.*

The residue of Nequasseag above Phipps Point upon the Sheepscot side was acquired later, through mesne conveyances, by Thomas Clark and Thomas Lake of Boston.

In 1662, Thomas Cleves and John Tucker, fishermen at Cape Newagen, obtained from Robinhood leases of two tracts situated above Phipps Point on the western bank at Couseagan. These grantees were engaged in their work upon the coast during the fishing season and did not reside upon the premises. After four years Cleves sold his lot to a Boston merchant. At that time it was bounded northerly by land at Wiscasset, bought from the Indians by George Davis December 15, 1663.†

The next tract above Nequasseag was sold to Nathaniel Draper, of Damariscove River as he was styled, March 6, 1662-3, by Indians. It extended for six miles along the river bank, above and below the falls, and for five miles into the interior.‡

* York Deeds, 17-190 ; Lincoln Deeds, 9-99.
† Me. Hist. Gen. Rec., 7-20 ; Suffolk Court Files, 139279.
‡ York Deeds, 12-188 ; Me. Hist. Gen. Rec., 6-477.

This territory had been appropriated before its purchase by English planters who had settled at Sheepscot with Draper. Some of these may have come from older Sagadahoc plantations. Two of the earliest were Robert Allen and Thomas Mercer, of whom the latter came thither from Cape Porpoise and secured one hundred acres of the Draper tract just above the falls.

Descendants claimed that Draper had possessed his land at Sheepscot for thirty-five years, when he was killed there in the Indian massacre of 1689. Computation fixes the date of his settlement at 1654, or about fifteen years after Bateman and Brown arrived at Nequasseag.‡

The first Draper dwelling was located opposite the lower point of Dyer's Neck; a later one stood about a mile above the falls. Whether the pioneer was the son of another person of the same name who was a member of the crew of the *Falcon*, chartered by Thomas Pell, of New Haven, is not known, but that early trader had been engaged in the exchange of northern deer and bear skins for southern tobacco when he died in Virginia April 27, 1647, and, although survived by "kindred," he bequeathed his unpaid wages to David Selleck, a Boston soap boiler.§

Robert Allen, for whom Allen's Falls were named, may have come to Maine from Massachusetts to avoid persecution by the magistrates. In 1660, he affirmed at Bristol, England, that he had known John Brown, then of New Harbor, for seventeen years. Brown, however, had sojourned at Nequasseag from 1639 to 1654, and removed beyond Pemaquid to New Harbor soon after the latter date. Since Allen described himself as a resident of Sheepscot, the proximity of the residences of Allen and Brown accounted for their prolonged acquaintance, although the former appeared to have been more closely affiliated with Pemaquid plantation.

While Cleves and Tucker were early residents at Cape Newagen on the easterly side of the Sheepscot, the whole Boothbay shore, for seven miles, was owned by Henry Curtis, of Beverly, under a title from the Indians secured January 20, 1666-7. This tract contained 9,000 acres.†

Above Boothbay was a whole township acquired from the

‡ Mass. House Journal, 1731-87.
§ New Haven Rec., 1-451.
† Me. Hist. Gen. Rec., 7-18.

natives December 15, 1664, by George Davis who lived upon a part of it within the present limits of Wiscasset village.†

Above Back River was Mason's Neck, which had been acquired from the natives by John Mason January 20, 1652-3. The southerly extremity of this land was bought by John White, of Sheepscot, who sold half to Philip Bendall July 10, 1664, and Bendall conveyed it to Robert Scott the next year. Above the White premises was another tract bought from Mason by William James and transferred to Thomas Gent.‡

The next lot above Mason's Neck lay beyond the falls and on the eastern bank opposite Nathaniel Draper's house and was bought from the Indians January 3, 1662-3, by Elizabeth, the widow of John and mother of Thomas Gent.§

Eastward of the farm of Thomas Gent was the location of that of William Cole and farther inland on the river was Nassomeck, purchased from the Indians by William Dyer February 11, 1662-3, and styled "Dyer's Neck."*

July 26, 1665, Samuel Maverick as commissioner for New York wrote to Sir Henry Bennett: "Upon three rivers, the East of Kennebeck, Shipscot and Pemaquid, are three plantations—the greatest has not above 20 houses—and they are inhabited by the worst of men; they have no Government, and have fled thence from punishment; for the most part they are fishermen, and share in their wives as they do in their boats."††

In spite of the unfavorable report the commissioners were instructed to require submission of the inhabitants of the Eastern Country. Damariscotta was not mentioned at that time and its few residents were combined with those at Sheepscot. The meeting was called at the house of John Mason September 5, 1665. As James Phipps had deceased before 1654 his name did not appear in this list of freemen. From the number of subscribers it is evident that Sheepscot, the largest of the three eastern plantations, contained only fourteen dwellings. ‡‡

Previous to the Indian Wars Sheepscot had become a prosperous farming and grazing community. On the night of August 13, 1676, the natives attacked the home of Richard Hammond at Woolwich and a few hours later captured the garrison at Arrow-

† York Deeds, 2-8.
‡ York Deeds, 20-86 ; Me. Hist. Gen. Rec., 6-476.
§ York Deeds, 20-96.
* York Deeds, 15-225, 227.
†† Sainsbury's Col. Pap., 2-313.
‡‡ Sullivan, 287 ; Appendix H.

sic. A girl who was living in the Hammond household and John Dole, a boy employed at Arrowsic, evaded the savages, crossed the intervening rivers and apprised the settlers at Sheepscot and Damariscotta of the danger.

As a consequence both settlements withdrew to Cape Newagen the next day. Subsequently, the inhabitants on the eastern bank withdrew to Massachusetts. Hubbard reported that "Those of Shipscot taking this Warning escaped away as soon as they could, leaving their Cattel and their Dwellings as a Prey to the Indians."

The records of Scituate recite the names of the principal planters and divulge the importance of their individual losses. The refugees were described as "Strangers from Shipscot River" who were in need of municipal aid. The following property was listed as destroyed at the Eastward:

"Mr." (William) "Dyer left all behind him, who sowed 16 bushells of wheat, planted a bushell and a half of Indian corne, sowed 9 bushells of peas, left 56 hed of Cattell, 30 swine, and household goods, and tackling for a plow and carte."

"John White, and John Lee his son in law, sowed 10 bushells of wheat, planted 2 bushells of Indian corne, 5 bushells of peas, 17 hed of Cattell, 16 swine, one horse."

"Philip Bendall sowed 9 bushells of peas, 5 or 6 of wheat, 16 hed of Cattell, 6 swine."

"Widow" (William) "Cole, 2 oxen, cowes, 2 heifers, sowed 6 bushells of wheat, planted 3 bushells of Indian corne."

Others who abandoned the east bank of the Sheepscot were Elizabeth, widow of John Gent, and her son Thomas, who escaped to Boston. At a meeting in the latter town six years later some of these eastern refugees voted to return to their deserted farms at "New Dartmouth." They proposed to build a fort on Gent's, otherwise known as "The Great Neck," and surround it with homesteads in close formation.

By the terms of the compact Walter Phillips was required to surrender all claim to the site of the new village or submit to the general restrictions prescribed therein. So far as known, the superior rights of Phillips were derived from Indian deeds. He did not subscribe his name to the settlement contract.

The new pioneers, providing live stock and provisions for

* Hist. of Scituate, 402.

the undertaking, began the plantation at Sheepscot in 1683. Some of the old settlers had deceased and were represented by children or widows.

The plantations of Sheepscot and Damariscotta were again deserted on the same fatal day in August, 1689. At that time the northern Indians killed several members of the planters' families, among whom were William Dyer and Nathaniel Draper. The attack on Sheepscot garrison was recounted many years later by a daughter of the latter.

Her version of the incident was preserved by Mary Varney, of Boston, who testified that she had heard Esther (Draper) Roberts "tell of her living in Fort or Garrison where they were surrounded by the Indian Enemy and were affraid of going from Fort or Garrison least they should be made captives. She then ventured without with two pails to get some water, and saw a number of Indians, one of whom was going to fire at her, when she heard others say repeatedly 'no shoot Esther Draper,' in consequence of which she safely got in to her place of security, where she, with other females, dressing themselves in men's apparel, assisted the only two men that were then with them in defending their Garrison surrounded by the Enemy, who were doing their best to subdue it."

After the death of Draper his widow married Robert Scott, whose wife appears to have been killed in the same tragedy. Scott's child Samuel was then but a year old, as appears from the record of his decease at Wrentham, Massachusetts, dated November 6, 1755, when he was in his sixty-eighth year.

Pioneers

ALLEN, ROBERT, deposed at Bristol, England, 1660, that his residence was Sheepscot and that he had known John Brown, of New Harbor, for seventeen years.

CURTIS, HENRY, planter, bought the westerly half of Boothbay, amounting to 9,000 acres, from the Indians January 20, 1666-7; living there 1672-4; children Henry and John, born 1655.

DAVIS, GEORGE, mariner at Lynn, 1650; bought Wiscasset from the Indians, 1663; wounded by the natives at Arrowsic, while on a fishing trip eastward, 1676; only child William.

DYER, WILLIAM, planter at Boston, 1637; wife Mary executed for her religion, 1660; bought land from the Indians at Sheepscot, 1663; killed by natives in August, 1689; children Christopher, the eldest, John, born 1648, and Mary, who married Samuel, son of Joseph Bowles, of Cape Porpoise.

MASON, JOHN, born 1619; arrived in the "Philip," which sailed from Gravesend, England, June 20, 1635; married Mary, daughter of John and Elizabeth Gent; planter on Mason's Neck, which he bought from Robinhood, 1652; died 1665; widow married John Allen of Charlestown; children James and Mary (Manning).

PHIPPS, JAMES, gunsmith, bought Phipps Point from Bateman and Brown after 1639; died 1651-4; widow Mary married John White; the best known members of her first family were Anne, James, John, Margaret, Mary, and Sir William born February 2, 1650-1.

SCOTT, ROBERT, born 1634; planter opposite the Oyster Beds at Damariscotta, 1665; Gloucester, 1677; New Dartmouth, 1683; married Esther, widow of Nathaniel Draper, 1690; the only child, by a former marriage, was Samuel, born 1688.

WHITE, JOHN, partner of James Phipps, who married his widow; died on the premises at Sheepscot after the first Indian war; the survivors of his eight children were Peter, born 1653, John, born 1655, Benjamin and Philip, born 1662, and Sarah (Lane).

WHITE, JOHN, planter on the east side of Sheepscot River; the records of Scituate, where they took refuge in 1676, described the conditions of the abandoned farms of himself and neighbors at the Eastward; John Lee was a son-in-law and Lydia, his only grandchild, married Thomas Leaworthy.

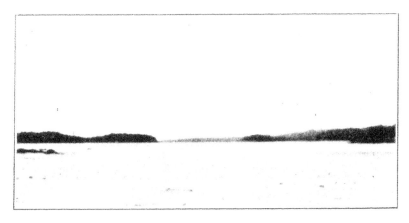

DAMARISCOTTA RIVER, BELOW NEWCASTLE

DAMARISCOTTA RIVER

The Indian name of this river was Apponick, as described in the geographical description of Moashan. In his account of the first settlement of Sagadahoc, Purchase mentioned a visit to the country of Amniquin. That chief did not hesitate to strip his person of valuable furs in exchange for a few worthless articles of English merchandise. The river was called Tamescot in the narrative, but the similarity of names is apparent.

That there were no early European settlements on this stream in the interior was indicated by the lateness of the Indian conveyances. The territory on the easterly side, which was granted to Robert Aldworth and Gyles Elbridge in the Pemaquid patent February 29, 1631-2, was not defined by Walter Neal until May 27, 1633. The title passed through John Elbridge to his brother Thomas and finally lodged in Nicholas Davison, of Charlestown, September 3, 1657.*

The first settlers moved up from Pemaquid and over from Sheepscot. The peninsula, known as Buckland's or Bucknell's Neck, located on the easterly side of Corbin's Sound, now called Johns Bay, comprised two farms which belonged to George Bucknell.†

John Taylor, aged 16, came from Gravesend, England, in the *Philip* June 20, 1635, in company with John Mason and Robert Morgan, who settled in the vicinity.‡

According to affidavits of John Allen, John Brown, Thomas Gent and Robert Scott, the Taylor homestead at Damariscotta had been in the settler's possession for at least fifty years of his lifetime. Subsequently, Thomas Gent married Sarah, one of Taylor's daughters, and occupied a part of it.§

Taylor lived above "Salt Water Falls" in Newcastle and may have settled there in 1635. However, the land occupied by him was absorbed later by a greater tract which Walter Phillips bought from the Indians February 15, 1661-2. The grantee was born in 1619, had lived at Pemaquid and then at Winnegance

* York Deeds, 18-112 ; Suffolk Deeds, 3-50.
† Me. Hist. Gen. Rec., 8-180.
‡ Hotten, 94.
§ York Deeds, 16-112.

(East Boothbay) that "he might be near the sea." His final location was below the first fall in the town of Newcastle.*

In 1639, there were living at or near Winnegance Arthur Brown, Henry Champney, Walter Phillips, Richard and Robert Shute and John Taylor.

June 2, 1651, Taylor and Nathaniel Draper were described as residents upon "Damiriscove River." This might mean Pemaquid. Draper had been living at the latter place in 1649; but he may have served elsewhere as agent for English merchants. He removed to Sheepscot in 1654 and bought his homestead there from the Indians in 1662.†

In 1665, the land on the westerly side of the river at Winnegance was owned by Edmund Arrowsmith and Henry Champney, both originally of Pemaquid.‡

That same year John, son of the immigrant Brown, took up his residence in Damariscotta below the fall. He was born in 1635 and had lived with his father for thirty years at Pemaquid, Woolwich and New Harbor.§

On the river above the Brown homestead was that of Robert Scott, who was born in 1634 and married the widow of Nathaniel Draper after 1689.

Above the farm of Scott, and adjoining the Oyster Mounds, were five hundred acres of land bought from the Indians by Sylvanus Davis June 14, 1659. The witnesses to this transaction were Edward Bateman, Edward Hall, Thomas Kimball, Walter Phillips, Philip Swadden and John Taylor. The tract was sold subsequently to Thomas Kimball, who lived there a few years and afterwards conveyed it to Phillips.**

Many years later John Pierce deposed that the families of Brown, Gent, Phillips, Scott and Taylor were the only ones living at Newcastle and Damariscotta in 1665, and these planters all took the oath of allegiance at Sheepscot that year.††

The river was abandoned soon after the outbreak of the first Indian war of 1675, and the refugees retired to Massachusetts where they, with many others from the Eastern Country, were admitted as freemen of the Commonwealth.‡‡

* York Deeds, 18-2, 235.
† Suffolk Deeds, 1-24; Aspinwall, 205, 209.
‡ Me. Hist. Gen. Rec., 7-16, 18.
§ York Deeds, 20-85.
** York Deeds, 16-113, 208.
†† York Deeds, 18-281.
‡‡ Essex Rec., 6-399.

DAMARISCOVE ISLAND.

From his reference to the name of Damerill's Cove, in 1614, it is obvious that Captain John Smith may have known something about the discovery of the place which has been lost to later generations. Humphrey Damerill was a master mariner of prominence, who died in Massachusetts, or at sea, in 1654. He may have been one of Smith's seamen who had discovered that haven. The Indian name for Damariscove Island, which lies near the mouth of Damariscotta River, was Agguahega and its area comprises about 200 acres.

The island is situated about three miles southerly of Linekin Neck and is usually visible from that point. Near its center it is nearly cut in two. On account of the uninviting aspect of its ledges and the absence of forest trees, the place presented a decidedly bleak and inhospitable appearance to strangers, but its proximity to the mainland and to the neighboring fishing grounds made it an attractive resort for all of the early mariners who were unable to obtain adequate stage room at Monhegan. Its harbor, facing the southeast quarter, was not so well sheltered in case of sudden emergencies as were those at Cape Newagen and Winnegance, but its convenient access to and from the sea offset its other disadvantages to some extent.

During the long period of European visitation, Damariscove had only occasional inhabitants who were mainly dependent upon the fishing industry. The surrounding islands were not mentioned in any of the early accounts of the locality.

In the early administration of foreign affairs the Council of Plymouth undertook to impose rigid restrictions upon fishing and trading on the New England Coast. The plan adopted included registration and the collection of a privilege tax for every British vessel bound thither. The volume of commerce could not have been large, for April 25, 1621, a parliamentary debate relating to the freedom of the seas disclosed that "The English, as yet, little frequent this" (region), "in respect of this prohibition; but the Dutch and French * * * who come, and will fish there, notwithstanding the colony."§

Yet, it was not uncommon for vessels to evade custom officers, and one of these ships was that of the London merchant, Thomas Weston, who was later accused of dispatching it to the Northern

§ Brit. Proc., 1-35.

Coast without license, in 1621. At that time Weston was financially interested in the settlement of New Plymouth.

It was plain that the establishment of trading centers in the New Country would soon render the scheme of the council inoperative and for that reason the members of that organization could not have been expected to be particularly anxious to advance western colonization.

The first plantation at New Plymouth was the result of private enterprise and May 2, 1621, it was claimed in parliament that Sir Ferdinando Gorges and Sir John Bowser had not settled "one man there" (in America), "in theis 70 years." Not only was this charge undisputed, but the following year arrangements were made to begin immediate colonization; presumably, from fear that otherwise the charter itself might be annulled.

Since it was common knowledge that but few natives then inhabited "the Coast, for two hundred Leagues together" Leonard Peddock was dispatched by the council "to dyve into the bowels of the Continent" and "search and finde out what Port, or Place, is most convenient to settle our mayne Plantation in, where wee meane to make the Residencie of our State and Government."*

At the same time the Virginia Company sponsored an expedition by Thomas Jones, master of the *Discovery*, who provided the major part of the requisite funds.

Meantime, Weston was not idle. Divorced from his self-serving but unsatisfactory connections with Plymouth Colony, he undertook to found a private settlement in Massachusetts. With this intent he formed a partnership with John Beauchamp, another London merchant associated with the first colony, and they sent over a fishing vessel called the *Sparrow,* in which were "six or seven" advance agents prepared to explore the Northern Coast and select a favorable site for a settlement.

The *Sparrow* sailed from London and arrived at the Eastward in May, 1622, but owing to poor anchorage and stage accommodations at Monhegan withdrew to Damerill's Cove.†

This harbor, which lies within the southern end of Damariscove Island, was called "Dambrell's Cove in Canada" by Virginians and afforded a safe and convenient refuge for deep-sea fishing craft.

When Phineas Pratt, one of Weston's agents, landed in the

* Purchase, 19-283.
† Bradford, 2-72.

cove the number of vessels in the vicinity had increased to about thirty, but none of the mariners were familiar with the coast of New England. This is apparent from the predicament of Pratt, who sought a pilot to navigate a boat to the southward.

The agent's description of the situation follows: Thomas Weston "sent forth a ship for ye settleing a plantation in the Massachusetts Bay, but wanting a pilote we Arived att Damoralls Cove. The men yt belong to ye ship, ther fishing, had newly set up a may pole & weare very mery. We maed hast to prepare a boat fit for costing. Then said Mr. Rodgers, Master of our Ship, 'heare ar Many ships & at Munhigin, but no man yt does undertake to be yor pilate; for they say yt an Indian Caled Rumhigin undertook to pilot a boat to Plimoth, but thay all lost thar Lives.' Then said Mr. Gibbs, Mastrs Mate of our ship, 'I will venter my Live wth ym'."‡

The incidental remark of Rogers, to the effect that "heare ar Many ships" (at Damariscove) "& at Munhigin, but no man yt does undertake to be yor pilate," substantiated the statement of Captain Smith, made the same year, that "all these Ships, till this last yeare, have bin fished within a square of two or three leagues, and not one of them all would adventure any further."§

The outcome was that Pratt, with six companions and a few hardy sailors, set their course for Massachusetts in an open boat with John Gibbs, mate of the *Sparrow,* as volunteer guide. After some examination of the Isles of Shoals and Agawam at Cape Ann, they selected Wessaguscus as the place for Weston's settlement and began construction of the community buildings.

About the first of July the *Charity,* in command of William Reynolds, and the *Swan,* from London, reached their rendezvous at New Plymouth. The former vessel landed about fifty passengers for the Wessaguscus plantation and proceeded to Virginia with others. Thomas Morton, a barrister from Clifford's Inn and not a mechanic, remained at Patuxet while new buildings were being erected. The *Swan* was left in the country to trade from New England to Virginia for the benefit of Weston's Colony. At the close of its season the *Sparrow,* which had been fishing and trading with fishermen and Indians at Damariscove, was sold by Weston, with its cargo, in the Southern Colony.

‡ 4 Mass. Hist. Col., 4-477.
§ Purchase, 19-311.

Other vessels on the coast of Maine during that spring were the *Bona Nova, Discovery* and *Marmaduke,* in command of John Huddleston, Thomas Jones and John Gibbs, respectively. The *Charles, George, Gift of God, James* and *Warwick,* names recurrent in New England annals, were also engaged in transatlantic service for the Virginia Company that year.*

Nearly all of the other ships dispatched to Virginia with colonists relied upon the northern fishing industry for return cargoes and insisted upon a natural right to operate at Monhegan in spite of emphatic protests by Gorges and his colleagues, who claimed a monopoly of the island as their "usuall fishing place."

Damariscove was made a settlement by Gorges in 1622. Proof may be found in an undated letter written by John Pory at Damerill's Cove to the governor of Virginia late in that year. The document, which contains a dozen internal clues to the location of the writer, represents the third example of extant correspondence composed by Englishmen on the Maine Coast. Only the letters of George Popham at Sagadahoc and John Huddleston at Monhegan are known to have antedated it.

At Damerill's Cove the writer encountered John Gibbs, who had completed at least one other voyage that season from the Eastward to New Plymouth. He produced as an authority on fishing conditions the same "John Gibbs (who this summer hath passed 5 or 6 times betweene this place" (Damariscove) "and New Plymmouth." He quoted the report of the mate of the *Sparrow,* to the effect that "a man cannot cast out a hooke at anie ledge at sea in that distance, but he shall draw up goodlie fish at pleasure." The fishing had been proven to be just as good to the "East and North" of the island, but to the south of New Plymouth, where the Virginia Company was anxious to obtain information, some uncertainty prevailed.

While William Vengham, an English mariner of experience in Southern Waters, was skeptical that there was good fishing in that quarter, a Flemish pilot, who had been engaged by Sir Samuel Argal to navigate a pinnace into Hudson River, was convinced that codfish were plentiful for at least twenty-five leagues beyond Martha's Vineyard.

Upon the authority of Gibbs, Pory asserted that "divers meane to fish the next yeare more toward the south-west," a de-

---

* Purchase, 19-143.

cision that led to the first experiments at the Isles of Shoals in 1623.

However, the most important part of the ancient text is the following excerpt:

"Besides the plantation of New-Plymmouth in 41 degrees and ½ and that other in Massachusett in 42 or thereabouts, there is a third in Canada at Damrells Cove in 43 and 45 minutes at the Cost of Sir Ferd: Gorge, consisting of some 13 persons who are to provide fish all the yeare with a Couple of Shallops for the most timelie loading of a ship.

"And to keepe that Iland to be fearmed out in Sir Ferdinandos name to such as shall there fish, and least the French or the Salvages should roote them out in winter, they have fortified themselves with a strong pallisado of spruce trees some 10 foote high, haveing besides their small shott, one peece of ordinance and some 10 good dogs. Howsoever they speed, they undertake an hazardous attempt, considering the salvages have beene this yeare (as those to the north use. to be by the French) furnished in exchange of skinnes by some unworthie people of our nation with peeces, shott, powder, swords, blades, and most deadlie arrow heads, and with shallops from the French, which they can manage as well as anie Christian, as also their peeces, it being an ordinarie thing with them to hitt a bird flying. And how litle they are to be trusted here as well as in Virginia, may appear by the killing latelie of the maister of a ship of Plimmouth with 18 of his companie among the Ilands toward the north-east, which was the cause that the same ship lost her fishing voyage & went emptie home."†

Pory was an intimate friend of Hakluyt and may have given him valuable information relating to New England. Late in the summer he sailed "from the northern coast of Virginia," where he "had been upon some discovery," for the Southern Colony. He was a passenger on board the *Discovery* of which Thomas Jones was master. This vessel, by virtue of a commission from the Virginia Company, had proceeded to Jamestown that spring and thence to Damariscove, where some of its unsold commodities had been bought by fishermen. Pory may have accompanied the expedition from Jamestown.

On its southern course the *Discovery* touched at Wessaguscus

† Pory's Letter, 29.

and New Plymouth. At the latter place the governor, to whom Pory dispatched a parting letter, dated August 28, 1622, explained that Captain Jones had been "set out by some marchants to discovere all ye harbors" from Cape Cod to Virginia.‡

According to the report of Leonard Peddock, rival agent for the Council of Plymouth, the *Discovery* met severe reverses on the Massachusetts coast. His story, recounted in England about three months after the event, disclosed that Jones, "who was imployed by ye company of Virginia to fish upon ye Coasts of New England, hath this last yeare robbed the Natives of their ffurres, and offered to carry some of them away prisoners, but being grounded upon ye Sands, neere Capecodd, ye Savages escaped and made great exclamacon against the present planters of New England." It is evident that Jones did deport at least one native for after his return the Council of Plymouth ordered that Unipa Whinett, an Indian boy taken at Wessaguscus, should be restored to his home by a returning ship. Gorges was directed to enter a complaint with the Virginia Company.§

The council at once began to make plans to increase the Damariscove Colony by transporting more permanent settlers thither. For this purpose publicity was given to the undertaking and a few volunteers were secured. Two of these men mentioned under the date of November 30 were William Pomfrett, a distiller, and George Dugdeale, a tailor, who offered themselves "to goe for New England" with the next shipping. Pomfrett was probably the same person who subsequently lived in Dover, on the Pascataqua River.

A report of the council rendered to the king late in the year was in the nature of an answer to the recent complaint of Parliament that no progress had been made in New England colonization. It announced: "Wee have setled at this present severall Plantations along the Coast, and have granted Patents to many more that are in preparation to bee gone with all conveniencie."

The only plantations then established in New England were located at New Plymouth, Wessaguscus and Damariscove. The grant of Patuxet to John Pierce had been made upon June 1, of the previous year, and all others that year. They may be summarized in the following list:

‡ Bradford, 2-90.
§ Am. Ant. Col., 1867-74, 78.

March 9, Agawam and Plum Island to Captain John Mason.
April 20, undefined territory to John Pierce, which was surrendered.
July 24, Cape Elizabeth and Richmond Island to the Duke of Richmond; Casco and Seguin to Sir George Calvert; Pemaquid and Monhegan to the Earl of Arundel.
August 10, territory between Merrimack and Sagadahoc rivers to Gorges and Mason.
October 16, Pascataqua and Great Island to David Thompson.
December 30, Eastern Massachusetts to Robert, son of Sir Ferdinando Gorges.

After the return of the fishing fleet in 1622 the council had become convinced of the necessity of appointing a naval officer to enforce its edicts and collect license fees from the masters of fishing vessels. Accordingly, Captain Francis West was chosen temporary admiral to regulate New England commerce and January 28, 1622-3, was provided with a commission to seize Monhegan. Gorges, whose plantation was located at Damariscove, was then president of the council and approved the order which authorized forcible occupation of the "usuall place of fishing." The action is proof that the island, formerly in possession of the grand patentees, had been monopolized by fishermen.

In the last days of February, 1623, when John Sanders, successor of the deceased Richard Green as overseer at Wessaguscus, required supplies for his colony, he sought "Munhiggen, where was a plantation of Sir Ferdinando Gorges, to buy bread from the ships that came thither a fishing."

This quotation from Edward Winslow was published in London within a year of the incident and it is plain that the writer referred to the region about Monhegan, which included the plantation of Gorges at Damariscove. The use of the past tense is proof that, at the times of their visits to Damariscove and Monhegan the summer before, colonists of New Plymouth and Wessaguscus had seen the settlement sponsored by the president of the council.

In March, when the establishment at Wessaguscus had proven a failure and been abandoned entirely, the surviving planters embarked in the *Swan* for the Eastward with the expectation of meeting Weston himself and obtaining supplies, or of earning passage for England at Monhegan or Damariscove, where they anticipated the arrival of early fishing ships. They did not expect to find any surplus of provisions at the latter island.

By this time, however, Weston, disguised as a blacksmith, had reached the eastern fishing grounds with the first fleet. A little later, after some inquiry among southern traders and many mishaps, he succeeded in intercepting the remnant of his colony at Pascataqua and secured possession of his bark. After recovering the *Swan*, he obtained funds at New Plymouth and proceeded to raid Indian villages for corn, and especially Dorchester and Agawam which had been instigators of the attempt to destroy his former settlement at Wessaguscus.

In May, Admiral West arrived on the Maine Coast in the *Plantation*, accompanied by Thomas Squibbs as captain, and Joseph Stratton as master, of the *Katherine* which belonged to Lord Edward Gorges. Squibbs had been instructed by the Council to assist West in restoring order among the refractory fishermen, but his principal object was the "discovery" of Mount Desert Island and renaming it Mount Mansell in honor of his patron.

As soon as the admiral became convinced that his purposes could not be accomplished at Monhegan, where the masters were both stubborn and abusive, he released Squibbs who proceeded eastward upon his special quest. With the *Plantation* he sailed directly to Virginia and remained two months.

At the beginning of September West returned to Maine with his ship which he discharged with its crew at Damariscove, where there was less antagonism among the doughty exponents of free fishing than at Monhegan. In the exercise of his official functions it did not appear that West undertook to deal with Weston, whose fishing vessels had been libeled by the Council for nonpayment of license fees. He embarked for England in the *Katherine* soon after his advent at the Eastward, but his former crew visited New Plymouth in the *Plantation*.*

However, Weston's good fortune was not destined to last, for in the fall succeeding West's departure, he encountered at New Plymouth Captain Robert Gorges, who had then taken possession of the buildings at Wessaguscus. After some controversy Gorges, under a special order from the Council, impressed his vessel and entire crew and employed them in a voyage to Eastern

* Young's Plymouth Chron., 328, 330, 341, 342, 278.

Maine, where they were detained until spring, when the *Swan* was restored by agreement of the parties concerned.

Christopher Levett, who remained at the Eastward as late as the summer of 1624, did not allude to Damariscove that year, although he referred to Weston as an "evill member," who had threatened Gorges in his house at Casco with a dangerous weapon, and mentioned "Pemoquid and Capmanwagan, and Monhiggon" as districts which had been assigned previously to other adventurers. Four deserters from Weston's colony were entertained by him at Casco, but according to Winslow who was familiar with the sequel of that adventurer's affairs, "most of them returned" to England.

June 25, 1624, Humphrey Rastell, a merchant of London, and Captain John Wallaston, who was related by marriage to Captain John Mason, arrived on the coast with colonists en route for Massachusetts and Virginia. At Cape Ann they found new plantations of the Dorchester Merchants and Plymouth Colony, but were unable to obtain fish for food without going ashore for it. Smith reported that both plantations were just begun. As their vessel needed some repairs, Wallaston decided to transship the southern passengers and return to England from that point.

While large ships like the *Charity* and *South Phenix* were engaged in fishing at Cape Ann when the *Unity* arrived, the little bark of Weston's was selected by Rastell to carry out the terms of his original charterparty. One of his passengers was Martin Slatier, aged twenty years, who was living at Martin's Hundred February 4, 1624-5.†

Recently published minutes of Virginia Council indicate that Damariscove, like Monhegan, had become a summer trading center for eastern shipping in 1625. June 14, the *Swan*, which had spent the winter in the south, sailed for Damerill's Cove with tobacco. A large part of the cargo belonged to Virginia planters and was to be sold or exchanged upon a commission basis.

Some of the seamen employed in this voyage, who may have been members of its original crew because they were not mentioned in the census of Virginia, were Edmund Barker, William Foster, John Giles, Nicholas Hodges, Christopher Knolling and Edward Nevell, who had charge of the bark.

† Hotten, 239

The *Swan* was moored to "A stage hed" while at Damariscove and sprung a leak which caused injury to some of its cargo. Suits were instituted against Weston in the Virginian court by southern planters. Judgments were obtained by Thomas Crispe for loss of tobacco and sea biscuit; and by Robert Thresher for failure to procure servants for him in Canada, according to a previous agreement.

Weston and Rastell were in communication at this time and it is reasonable to assume that some of the unfortunate colonists at Mount Wallaston could be induced to enter servitude temporarily in order to escape from the country. Their condition was explained by Bradford in his description of the dissolution of the plantation at Mount Wallaston under the direction of Rastell.‡

An English sailor named Jeffrey Cornish visited the *Swan* at Damerill's Cove and made inquiries of its crew and other Virginian planters at the island for information about his brother, Richard Cornish, alias Williams, who, while serving as captain of the *Ambrose*, had been executed by the magistrates in Virginia upon slight evidence. Ten years later this same sailor was put ashore from the ship *James* at Milford Haven on account of intoxication.§

John Witheridge was located at Pemaquid throughout the summer of 1625 and his name was suggested as surety for some of the ambitious but impecunious factors at Damariscove. He sailed for Barnstable, England, before the departure of the *Swan* which arrived at its southern port October 8.*

In the spring of 1627, there were fishermen at Damerill's Cove who helped to salvage some of the cargo of a French ship cast away at Sagadahoc. As these commodities were sold to Massachusetts traders who were in competition with them at the Eastward, it may be inferred that the owners did not propose to remain on the coast during the ensuing winter and that no nearer factors could use them to better advantage. Furthermore, simultaneous sale of similar merchandise at the neighboring island of Monhegan, because that plantation was to be discontinued, furnished additional proof of the same intention at Damariscove.

Massachusetts patent, dated March 19, 1627-8, gave its conferees the right to fish and trade wherever its predecessors had

‡ Bradford, 2-158.
§ Young's Mass. Chron., 457.
* Min. of Va. Council, 75, 76.

exercised those privileges, and some of the former colonists had previously invaded the Sagadahoc region.

In 1630, the *Swift* was captured at Damariscove by Thomas Witherly, master of the *Warwick*. It was taken as a prize for improper registration of a British vessel as a French merchantman.

A trader who frequented Damariscove after that year was Henry Way, of Dorchester, Massachusetts, whose vessel was foundered at the Eastward in the fall of 1631. Subsequent investigation disclosed that its crew of five had been murdered by eastern Indians. A second shallop, sent to recover the first, was wrecked at Agamenticus and two more men were drowned.†

Evidently, Way was not discouraged, for October 3, 1632, Massachusetts magistrates imposed the following sentence: "It is ordered, that Nicholas Frost for thefte comitted att Damerills Cove upon the Indeans, for drunkenes and fornicacon, of all wch hee is convicted, shalbe fined Vl. to the Court, & XII. to Henry Way & John Holman, shalbe severely whipt, & branded in the hand with a hott iron, & after banished out of this pattent."‡

The penalty for returning to the patent was to be death, and two years later, when Frost brought his family from England, he settled at Kittery.

Damariscove was only a summer fishing place for those who chose to occupy it. At times, like Monhegan Island, it was deserted.

John Parker, described as "the first of the English Nation" to undertake the fishing industry in that vicinity, spent the summer of 1645 on the island. He was associated with a company of fishmongers, but his venture of that season proved unprofitable on account of the excessive consumption of intoxicants which had been provided by Robert Nash, of Boston, master of his vessel.

Two years later, Francis Knight, who was then acting as agent for the trading house at Pemaquid, mentioned store accounts with tenants at Monhegan, but none for Damariscove.

Abraham Shurt, who preceded Knight as factor at Pemaquid, stated that in 1649, when Thomas Elbridge took possession of the premises as sole heir, he cited the inhabitants of Damariscove and Monhegan to appear at court and attorn to the new landlord.

† Winthrop, 1-79.
‡ Mass. Col. Rec., 1-94.

By special arrangement at that time all tenants "continued" at the islands by "paying a Certain acknowledgement." The only person known to have been a resident at Damariscove was Thomas Phillips.§

May 18, 1672, Robert Parker owned a dwelling and "Stage Room" on the island.*

Other residents on the same date were Thomas Alger, John and Leonard Allen, John Bodwell, Richard Friend, Richard Hunnewell, William Lee, Simon Newcomb, Nicholas Osborne, Edmund Robbins, Roger Sayward, Elias Trick, John Wriford and Emanuel Whitehouse.†

As this list was compiled during the fishing season it is probable that some of the persons named were transients.

Gradually, during the subsequent years, the place lost its residential character. An early inhabitant of the locality, who "went a fishing from sd Island" of Damariscove, deposed that in 1675 there were "Seven fishing Boats that Continually used sd Place." He testified also that there were then four persons who "had been Old Settlers there," but that he never had heard "that any of the aforesd Persons ever pretended any right thereto but only Used it as a Fishing Place which they Esteemed free for any Person." The individuals mentioned by him had been former pioneers of Massachusetts.‡

In 1700, Romer reported that "Before the War there was a palisado'd Fort on Damarascove Island for defence of the Fishermen & a little higher there was another place cald Cape Newagin where the people cur'd their Fish, and two harbours where they secured their Vessels from Storms. And tho those harbours lye open to the Sea yet in case of necessity they serve turn, when the Fishermen cannot get into Kennebeck River."§§

The original fort at Damariscove, built in 1622, was a palisaded structure and may have been kept in repair for many years.

In 1686, the Colony of New York sold the island to Richard Pattistall, of Boston.**

Many years later Patrick Rogers, who in his prime had been a commanding officer at Pemaquid Fort, asserted that he had

§ York Deeds, 24-256.
* Me. Hist. Gen. Rec., 7-21.
† Suffolk Court Files, 12-1117.
‡ Me. Hist. Col., 5-237.
§§ Me. Doc. Hist., 10-49.
** York Deeds, 9-230.

lived at Georgetown in 1721, "at which time the Deponent saith there was not one house that he knew off, between Georgetown and Annapolis Royal, except one in Damaris Cove, an island to make fish on, until the time St. Georges Fort was built."†

PIONEERS

ARROWSMITH, EDMUND, planter at Winnegance as early as 1639; submitted to Massachusetts, 1665; left land at Pemaquid near New Harbor.

PHILLIPS, WALTER, born 1619; planter near Winnegance, 1647; removed to Damariscotta Falls, 1665; wife Margaret; Lynn, 1678; Salem, 1702; died 1704; children James, Jane, John, Margaret, Sarah and Walter.

SHUTE, ROBERT, brother of Richard, living at Winnegance May 31, 1641; estate administered in Suffolk County, 1652.

SHUTE, RICHARD, Indian trader near Pemaquid, January 9, 1641-2, when he witnessed Richard Pearce's deed at Broad Bay; son Richard, born 1647, at Winnegance (East Boothbay).

TAYLOR, JOHN, born 1619; sailed from Gravesend, England, June 20, 1635, in the "Philip"; planter at Damariscotta ("Damariscove") River, 1651; Newcastle, 1665; widow Elizabeth daughter of Humphrey Davie, of Boston; children Isaac, Mary and Sarah (Gent).

† Commissioners' Report, 1811-60.

THE WHITE ANGEL OF BRISTOL*

Night by night the stars trailed west
   Where the dark horizon lay;
Eastward on its homing quest
   Drove the vessel, day by day,
With full sail and straining spar
Toward the Milford lights afar.

All the summer months her crew
   Drifting with the flashing seine,
Had pursued the shadows through
   Reaches of the Gulf of Maine,
Luring treasures with their wiles
From the far, mysterious isles.

Happy fishermen were these,
   Idlers, as a last resort,
Weaving port yarns on the seas,
   Spinning sea yarns when in port,
Boasting of their feats galore
As they neared their native shore.

And while some still dreamed of home
   Or on watch at midnight posts
Longed to glimpse the flying foam
   That enwreaths the Cornish coasts,
With no warning hint nor hail
Three strange ships bore down full sail.

These were pirates of Dunkirk,
   Watching on the Northern Main
For some Englishman or Turk,
   Or the treasure ships of Spain—
Sea hawks lurking in the way
For rich merchantmen as prey.

When the gray of morning spread
   Over trackless wastes of sea
And the dawn, a golden thread,
   Ran from starboard to the lee,
Solid shot across the bow
Brought a challenge from the foe.

* Bradford, 2-179.

Bristol fishermen could fight
  And, if need be, they could die,
But they would not think of flight
  Nor submit to slavery,
When the loss of freedom meant
Slave marts of the Orient.

So their captain held his course,
  Cleared the decks and primed his guns,
Mustering his lesser force
  To dispel far greater ones;
With the hope that sunrise might
Overtax the foemen's sight.

Storms of shot shrieked up aloft;
  Mizzen sails went by the board;
Deck planks ripped abaft, but oft
  Answering guns of Bristol scored,
While the ensign masthead high,
Ever flew defiantly.

Then the foremost privateer,
  Hit below the water line,
Sank before her boats could clear—
  Ere the nearest brigantine,
Shortening her sails, could take
The survivors in her wake.

Yet the last great ship-of-war,
  Sweeping on at fearful speed,
Confident of conquest or
  Quick surrender, took the lead,
Holding both her broadsides back
For the fateful, last attack.

So the Bristol gunner fell,
  Overcome by smoke and heat,
In that fiery, choking hell
  Where the havoc was complete;
Every gun was burst save one
And the crew dead or undone.

There his mate, a Cornish lad,
   Punctured through the shoulder blades,
Fired the only charge he had
   At the murderous renegades,
Leaning on the rack beneath
With a slow match in his teeth.

And that last shot won the day,
   Fired at fifty yards point-blank
At the hull of dingy gray
   Through the walls of live oak plank
And all barriers between
To the powder magazine.

All was ended when that night,
   Far upon the Irish tide,
With no harbor lamps alight
   And no living hand to guide,
The *White Angel* once again
With full cargo drifted in.

And in Bristol port they can
   Tell the world that awful feat
Of a light-armed merchantman
   Which destroyed a full-armed fleet,
But they cannot name again
Any of its gallant men.

PEMAQUID RIVER

The earliest glimpse of Pemaquid was furnished by Rosier, June 3, 1605. Some of the Pemaquid Indians, who were first to greet the crew of Waymouth at Pentecost Harbor, induced the explorers to accompany them to their village where they claimed to have a supply of furs and tobacco for exchange.

The visitors set out in a rowboat, preceded by three canoes belonging to the natives. The canoes landed at New Harbor

NEW HARBOR

Point where their fires were visible but no commodities had been provided for trade. The English would proceed no farther and became more suspicious when the Indians attempted to guide them "up into a little narrow nooke of a river, for their Furres." This stream was New Harbor Creek from the head of which a carrying place led over the peninsula to their town on the eastern side of the harbor where Pemaquid village is now located.

The excursion ended at New Harbor, but a few days later five of the suspected Indians were seized on board the vessel at Pentecost Harbor and deported. The names of these natives have been variously spelled, but may be listed as Tahanedo, sagamore of Pemaquid in subjection to the Bashaba, Amoret, Mannedo and Skidwaros, sachems of the same tribe, and Assacomoit, a servant.

August 8, 1607, Captain Raleigh Gilbert, with thirteen prospective colonists, followed in the wake of Waymouth. Under the direction of Skidwaros, whom they had restored to his native shore, the party "rowed to the Weste in amongst many gallant Illands and found the ryver of pemaquyd to be but 4 Leags weste from the Illand" they called Saint George's. They were piloted into a "Lyttell Cove" (New Harbor) "and marched over a necke of the Land near three mills." The narrator brought the journey to a close with these words: "So the Indyan skidwarres brought us to the Salvages housses whear they did inhabitt although much against his will."

At the time of this second visit to the Pemaquid country the village was found to contain about one hundred men, women and children. The commander of the place was Nahanada, styled Tahanedo by Rosier.

Two days later, both Gilbert and Popham, with fifty men in two shallops, left their ships and sailed for the river of Pemaquid. This time, by instructions from Skidwaros, they came to the beach right in front of the wigwams at Pemaquid village. The voyage was accomplished by sailing about Pemaquid Point and ascending the river, instead of landing at New Harbor.

Nothing was gained by this visit unless the survey of the place may have made it appear unsuitable for settlement at that time. Skidwaros was lost among his people and refused to return to Pentecost Harbor. A few weeks later, in the vicinity of Pejepscot River, he was engaged with his chief Nahanada in a conflict with the Indians of Sagadahoc, where they had killed the son of Sabenaw. The whole tribe must have become extinct soon after, and the Indian village at Pemaquid, weakened by losses of war and the subsequent ravages of a universal and irresistible pestilence, must have shared a similar fate as other coastal towns of Central and Southern Maine.

Greater antiquity has been accorded Pemaquid than any other English plantation in Maine, chiefly on account of the statement of Captain Smith that, in 1614, he found a ship belonging to Sir Francis Popham in the mainland opposite Monhegan, that had "used" the same port for "many yeares."

Smith, however, stated in another connection that Popham "sent divers times one Captaine Williams to Monahigan onely to trade and make core fish," and that in 1616 Popham's ship was the only one of a dozen Maine fishing craft that returned from a prosperous voyage.*

Gorges, commenting upon the action of his former colleague after their signal failure, said that Sir Francis "continued to send thither several years * * * but found it fruitless."

While the haven frequented by Popham's crews was the inner harbor of Pemaquid where, according to Bradford, "ships used to ride" in safety before his time, the only advantage that any early visitor could have gained must have been confined to trading and fishing. There was no mention of a winter colony at that point, and the good will of the natives must have been derived from summer contacts.

July 24, 1622, Monhegan with the mainland in that vicinity was allotted to the Earl of Arundel by the Council of Plymouth. Pemaquid was not mentioned in that connection. In the fall of that year John Pory, a visitor at Damariscove, commented to the governor of Virginia upon the northern mineralogical and climatic conditions:

"They say that up the river Pemaquid there is a place of even champian countrie without anie rockes, abounding with varietie of excellent timber, and like Anquam, neerer unto Cape Anna, a levell of more beautie and largenes. Within an infinitie of rockes may be entombed abundance of rich minerals among which silver and copper are supposed to be the cheif.

"Out of these rockes do gush out delicate streames of water, which together with the temper of the aire maketh this place marveilous wholsome in summer, which is the cause I have not knowen one man sicke all the time I was there, save onlie that villaine which accused yow falselie concerning Swabber, and died aboard the Bona-nova, as he had lived, franticke. Yet is the aire too cold here for the somer, but with easterlie winde subject to fogs and mists."†

July 29, 1623, distinct interests in the mainland of New Eng-

* Smith's Trav. & Works. 2-740.
† Pory's Letter. 30.

land were assigned by agreement to proprietors of the Grand Patent. The names of the patentees were engrossed on the earliest reproduction of Smith's map to indicate the respective divisions. Council records do not mention Damariscove nor Pemaquid during this year, but two large islands near the mouth of Sagadahoc River, corresponding to Arrowsic and Georgetown, had been reserved for a public plantation.

In 1624, John Witheridge, master of the *Eagle*, a Barnstable ship owned by Melchard Bennett, had established himself at Pemaquid Harbor, where he was located by Levett. While forbidden by the council to truck with the Indians, he had been licensed to fish on the coast. According to the pioneer at Quacke, Witheridge was then so popular with the Indians that they reserved their furs and traveled long distances to seek his trade. Their preference for him was manifest as far west as Casco Bay although other shipmasters in the vicinity were as well supplied with attractive commodities.

At that time the statement of Levett, that he had heard that Pemaquid, Cape Newagen and Monhegan had been granted previously to others, must have referred to the proprietorship of the Earl of Arundel. No settlement by Europeans in any locality from Pascataqua to Cape Newagen was mentioned by him during his sojourn.‡

About the first of March, 1624, Plymouth Colony dispatched the new English pinnace, called the *Little James* and commanded by John Bridges, to a station near Damariscove, in which it was "well harbored" at "a place wher ships used to ride." Posterity is indebted to Levett for a definite location of this ship at Pemaquid instead of Damariscove. The latter place was better known to Bradford as the site of the third plantation in New England, although later in his history he alluded to the former several times by name.§

When the *Little James* arrived at its destination there were other vessels in the vicinity which had just come from England, and previous customary usage of Pemaquid Harbor must have included its occupation by ships of Sir Francis Popham, John Witheridge and other Barnstable fishermen.

Not long after its arrival a violent storm arose and "broak over such places in ye harbor as was never seene before," and

‡ Me. Hist. Col., 2-88.
§ Me. Hist. Col., 2-99.

drove the *Little James* upon great rocks where it sank with its cargo of provisions and salt. The account, which follows, indicated that the pinnace had been anchored beside the shore ledges and not near any wharf or fishing stage. The narrative is that of Altham.

"Upon the 10th of Aprill, 1624, hapned a greate storme and some of our cables that we were mored withall gave way and slip of on the place they were made fast to ashore and soe the winde and sea being very high drave our ship a shore upon rockes where she beate. In the mean time being night the master and Company arose and every man shifted for them selves to save life, but the master going in to his cabin to fetch his whishell could not get in to any boate aboute the ship the sea brake soe over the ship and soe by that meanes before a boat could come the ship overset and drowned him and the other two and the rest that were got into our shallops that hung about the ship had much a doe to recover the shore your cosin for one for the ship oversettinge pich her maineyard in to one boate where were 6 or 7 of our men and soe sunke her for thoes that could then swim got to the shore with much hurt the rest that could not swim were drowned, and soe before the next morninge our ship was quite under water sunke and nothing to be sene save only the tops of her masts some times for the sea did rake her to and fro upon the rocks."

In this casualty the master and two of his crew, Peter Morrett and John Vow, went down with their ship. The ship's boat and four shallops or fishing dories, one of which had been borrowed, were destroyed, and the season's catch was reduced to 1000 fish.

Later in the summer, at the expense of the colony, Emanuel Altham, Captain Cook of Barnstable and the masters of English fishing vessels in the vicinity salvaged the hull and rebuilt the pinnace, but it was then too late to accomplish anything at the Eastward. The *Little James* returned to England where it was libelled for debts.*

If, as claimed by Levett, Witheridge enjoyed a monopoly of the Indian trade at Pemaquid as early as 1624, he appears to have supplanted Captain Williams, the agent of Popham, in the esteem of the natives, for he had no local competition as far as Sagadahoc.

* Bradford, 2-108, 129 ; Mass. Hist. Proc., 44-182.

As for Richard Williams, alias Cornish, then captain of the *Ambrose*, his fate was sealed in Virginia, late that year, when he was tried and executed by local authorities. The following spring the captain's brother "Jeffery" Cornish boarded the *Swan* at Damariscove to ascertain the particulars from members of that vessel's crew who had been present at the trial and execution. For disclosures made to him on that occasion Edward Nevell and another seaman later lost their ears before the southern tribunal.

Cornish declared that he would be the death of the governor of Virginia "yf ever he came for England." The presence of this sailor at the Eastward at that early date, and within sight of Pemaquid Harbor, warrants the belief that he had visited the locality in company with his brother on previous voyages. Ten years later this same individual was put ashore at Milford Haven, where he had been engaged in a quarrel with other seamen.†

For a long period after its discovery all of Northern New England was known by such names as Norumbega, Virginia, Canada, Muscongus and Pemaquid. Captain Smith claimed the credit for restoring a large part of Canada to his sovereign and suggesting its present name. He asserted that visitors had "obscured it, and shadowed it, with the title of Canada; till at my humble suit, it pleased our most Royall King Charles * * * then Prince of Wales, to confirme it with my map and booke, by the title of New England."‡

March 27, 1625, when Charles First was crowned, the new name had been approved for nine years, but Virginians still continued to regard the coast of Maine and its outlying islands as a part of Canada. Since all early mariners were traders, their fishing stages on the islands were summer marts for the storage of English and Indian commodities, which in turn were exchanged for southern tobacco.

Some credit was allowed, but in 1625 Edward Nevell, as agent for Weston, refused to deliver a consignment of tobacco to Thomas Crisp, a merchant from Virginia, unless Captain Witheridge, the Dorchester factor at Pemaquid, would assume the responsibility for deferred payments. The merchandise had reached Damariscove in the *Swan*, of which Nevell was master,

† Young's Mass. Chron., 457.
‡ Smith's Trav. & Works, 2-891.

and the fact, that Witheridge returned to England at the end of the season without undertaking the obligation, proves conclusively the seasonable nature of his business.

Thomas Morton claimed that, during the years 1626 and 1627, he had "spoiled" the Kennebec trade for New Plymouth, which pretended to have a monopoly of that district by discovery. Bradford admitted the claim and complained that employes of the colony "had like to have been cut off by the Indians, after the fishermen were gone." Neither Pemaquid nor any other eastern plantation presented any grievance.

In the spring of the latter year the plantations at Damariscove and Monhegan were discontinued and the goods sold on the premises. David Thompson, formerly of Pascataqua, and Plymouth Colony were the only bidders at the auction and they combined and purchased the whole rather than compete with each other. Such a combination would have been futile if there had been other buyers.

These two islands may be regarded as the outposts of Pemaquid during that decade, but such a conclusion does not warrant the belief that the mainland was occupied throughout each year. Shurt, the pioneer of Pemaquid, took prior possession at Monhegan, for Thomas Jenner, a contemporary of veracity, declared that the first places occupied by the English, in that vicinity, were the islands.

In June, 1628, all plantations "wher any English were seated" combined to deport Morton. Since none of these was located east of Pascataqua River, such a statement implied that there were no English settlers in Maine on that exact date. The explanation is that Saco and Casco had been deserted, and Richmond Island and Castine had not been occupied by Bagnall and Ashley until later in the season.

During that year Plymouth Colony forwarded furs to Bristol in the *Marmaduke, Pleasure* and *White Angel,* of which the masters were John Gibbs, William Peters and Christopher Burkett, respectively. The last ship belonged to Aldworth and Elbridge, the merchants of Bristol who had acquired Monhegan the previous year; the latter collected freight and port fees from the colony.§

The Aldworth family, to which Elbridge was related, had

been interested in Newfoundland commerce prior to the discovery of Plymouth Rock. Like other citizens of Bristol, Aldworth and his partners had been concerned with fishing and trading in New England for five years.*

Other Bristol merchants, who were associated with Aldworth and Elbridge in western trade, were Walter Barrett, Walter Merchant, Thomas Pitt, Richard Russell, Walter Sandy, Thomas Wright and Hugh Yeo. Several of these adventurers were related by kinship or marriage. Wright was mentioned in Aldworth's will. Shurt was named as agent for Yeo in a subsequent suit.†

There is some evidence that no part of the Maine coast was occupied *permanently* before 1630. Patentees of all territory west of the Sagadahoc, who took possession that year, or later, united in the claim that their holdings consisted of "parcels of Land, where never any Christian Inhabited." Conversely, French diplomats, after an exhaustive study of the historical resources of two nations, admitted that Massachusetts Bay Colony was founded as early as 1629, but insisted that "le surplus des colonies de Nouvelle Angleterre fut établi de 1630 à 1639." It is generally conceded that the French are dependable in determining questions of fact.‡

Isaac Allerton, business manager for Plymouth Colony, was an active agent in promoting all of the first Maine settlements. In the spring of 1630, he arrived at Castine from England, in company with Captain William Peirce in the *Lyon*. At that point they landed Edward Ashley, who was to establish a trading post on that river for New Plymouth and its London associates. Both Allerton and Peirce were interested in that venture.

June 12, Peirce's vessel was at Salem and Allerton, who had just secured a patent of Cushnoc for New Plymouth, was reembarking for the East, where he expected to find the *Swift*, another Bristol ship. That vessel, which belonged to Thomas Wright, had been utilized by Allerton, Vines and the owner to transport passengers and provisions to their new plantations at Saco and Casco; its return cargo was to consist of fish and train oil. Allerton and John Wright, brother of Thomas, were both at Winter Harbor when the *Swift* arrived. June 25, their names,

---
* Young's Mass. Chron., 309.
† N. E. Hist. Gen. Reg., 8-140 ; Waters' Gen. Glean., 2-1009.
‡ New Eng. Vind., 42 ; Rep. French Commission, 1751-102.

with that of the master, were inscribed on the certificate of seizin of Biddeford patent.

From Saco River Allerton and Wright, who was master of a shallop, proceeded to Pemaquid, where the former had intended to procure a return cargo for the *Swift*. However, before that vessel could be laden it was seized and sent back to England.

Abraham Shurt, agent for Aldworth and Elbridge at Pemaquid, was first mentioned September 17, 1631, when he restored the wife of James Sagamore to her home at Agawam, where she had been captured by the Tarratines during the previous month.

The patent of Pemaquid, dated February 29, 1631-2, contains conclusive proof that at that time the Council of Plymouth did not know that the mainland had been occupied by tenants of the patentees. The concession was to be located, according to its own terms, "neere ye River, Comonly called or knowne by the name of Pemaquid," and *"next adjoyning to the place* where the people or servants of the said Robert Aldworth and Gyles Elbridge are now settled, or have Inhabited, *for the space of three yeares last past."*

The tract was to be laid out compactly "both along the sea Cost as the Cost lyeth, and so up the River," so far as was necessary to provide 12,000 acres. A significant conclusion to the description was this clause: "With all the *Ileland,* Ileletts, *within the lymitts next adjoyneing the said land,* butting within the lymitts aforesaid three leagues into the maine Ocean."§

The marine limitation of that date, based upon the estimate of Waymouth or Dermer, was intended to include Monhegan as the most remote part of the district. That island was not named but was described as "the Ileland * * * next adjoyneing the said land." The coastal tract, as defined later by Neal, comprised all of the mainland between Damariscotta and Muscongus rivers.

Shurt himself, who acted for the purchasers, interposed an interim of *three years* between the time of his acquisition of Monhegan and the seizin of Pemaquid, where he was living in 1631. The period corresponds with that given in the patent and seems to cover the interval, during which he had resided on the island, as the original plantation of Aldworth and Elbridge.

There is competent evidence that the patentees regarded Monhegan as a part of Pemaquid. From Gyles Elbridge, the surviv-

§ Suffolk Deeds, 3-52.

ing joint tenant, the patent descended to his son Thomas, who came to Maine later and resided upon the premises. Subsequently, in a conveyance of Damariscove and Monhegan, this son described them as "scittuate & lying at or neere Pemmaquid."*

With the same idea in mind, Samuel Maverick, who came from England to Massachusetts in 1623, asserted many years later that colonization of Pemaquid was begun in 1625 by Alderman Aldworth, of Bristol. He also conceded in the same document, which was an obvious arraignment of the Massachusetts policy of expansion, that, if it had not been for the early establishment of plantations at Monhegan and Pascataqua by Plymouth merchants, the undertaking at New Plymouth would have failed. He did not allude to Pemaquid as an eastern plantation of dependable resources, and his errors in other instances made his statement of its antiquity, written more than thirty years after settlement, unreliable.†

A single palisaded trading house was established at Pemaquid Harbor by Shurt and his associates. In a later conveyance of a half interest in the plantation Thomas Elbridge, as sole heir to Pemaquid patent, referred to his previous sale of the other part of the premises "wth the moyty & halfe endeale of all ye house Household stuffe Cattle, or any other thinge then belonging to the said Plantacon."‡

A late inventory of the contents of this dwelling was recorded at Charlestown. It contained treatises on religion and implements of war. Besides a great Bible the books listed in the library were "The Faith and Head of the Church," "A Plea for Grace and Military Discipline" and a Book of Caveats. The ordnance consisted of four short cannon styled "chambers."§

The building itself, like other trading establishments of the period, was occupied by a few employes. The household at Pemaquid, like those at Casco and Little Harbor, could not have consisted of more than ten persons. These men hailed from Bristol or vicinity and their plantation was situated more than sixty miles, in either direction, from the frontier posts of Plymouth Colony at Cushnoc and Machabitticus.

Penobscot and Pemaquid were in exposed positions. In the early summer of 1632, while Willett and Shurt were bound west-

* Suffolk Deeds, 3-49.
† Mass. Hist. Proc., 21-231.
‡ Suffolk Deeds, 3-57.
§ Middlesex Deeds, 2-27; Suffolk Deeds, 2-68.

ward with a cargo of commodities which had been landed at the former station for reshipment to Massachusetts, the French sacked Castine.

In the fall of the same year the house at Pemaquid was "rifled" by Dixie Bull with the help of only sixteen ordinary traders, some of whom were Frenchmen from the East. Furs to the value of 500 pounds sterling were abstracted.*

These posts upon the water front had no strength to oppose invasion. This fact is apparent because threats of similar raids along the whole coast created much apprehension of impending danger as far west as Richmond Island.

There is evidence that the Bull family of London was related to that of Samuel Maverick, and the latter was one of the most enterprising merchants of Massachusetts. Both Bull and Maverick had been named as grantees in the Agamenticus patent, revised in 1632, and the vessel chartered by the pirates for the eastern voyage hailed from Winnisimet and belonged to Maverick.

Winter, of Richmond Island, reported that Bull was a trader for beaver who had "turned pirate"; that his residence was London and that he had "done much spoyle" in the country.†

Roger Clap, writing in Massachusetts, said that Bull *"went to the eastward"* to trade, turned pirate, took a vessel or two, plundered some planters thereabouts, and "intended to *return into the Bay*, and do mischief to our magistrates here in Dorchester and other places. But, as they were weighing anchor, one of Mr. Short his men shot from the shore, and struck the principal actor dead, and the rest were filled with fear and horror * * * These men fled eastward, but Bull himself got into England."‡

Announcement was made soon after by "some who came from Penobscott," that the loss of their leader "by a musket shot from Pemaquid" had effected a sudden reformation among the pirates and that they had "given another pinnace in exchange for that of Mr. Maverick, and as much beaver and otter as it was worth more."

Late in the year Bull arrived in England, where with Gardiner, Morton and Ratcliff he appeared before the royal commissioners in an attempt to repeal the Massachusetts charter, but some of his confederates went back to their Massachusetts homes

---
* Winthrop. 1-96.
† Me. Doc. Hist., 3-23.
‡ Young's Mass. Chron., 362.

—not to overthrow the government at Dorchester as intimated—but to reform.

Proof of the absence of police power in northern New England is found in the necessity for the mobilization of two pinnaces, two shallops and forty men at Pascataqua in the attempt to discipline this small band of outlaws. This fleet, "coming to Pemaquid" in December, was "there wind bound about three weeks." The expedition was unsuccessful.§

Although Bull had reached England before the return of the fleet to Pascataqua, another was dispatched after him during the following spring. This squadron was composed of a pinnace from Winnisimet, in command of Maverick himself, and other boats from Neal's and Hilton's plantations.*

While Neal was at Pemaquid he gave possession of the premises to Shurt, as agent for Aldworth and Elbridge. The certificate, dated May 27, 1633, bore the signatures of William Hook, Robert Knight, George Newman and Christopher Burkett, master of the *White Angel* which then belonged to Allerton.

In the will of Robert Aldworth, dated August 30, 1634, he said, "I give and bequeath unto Abraham Shurt, my servant, if he live till my decease and shall return to Bristol, the sum of two hundred pounds." The testator died at Bristol November 6, of that year, and Shurt, who was a merchant of Bristol, may have learned of the bequest early the next spring, because May 6, he was making plans to return in the *White Angel,* of which Christopher Burkett was master.†

The *White Angel* had had a record. In 1628, it had belonged to Elbridge and visited New Plymouth under the same master. In 1631, Isaac Allerton bought it from Aldworth, to be used in conveying provisions to Ashley at Penobscot. At that time it was renowned for having won a remarkable naval victory in a former voyage. It was replaced in the Bristol fleet by the *Angel Gabriel*. June 19, 1635, Shurt sailed from Richmond Island in the former ship, which had been repurchased by Elbridge.‡

Only three days later the *Angel Gabriel* cleared from Milford Haven for New England, in company with the *James*. The two Bristol ships must have passed in mid ocean. At any rate, while the *White Angel* arrived safely at Bristol, the *Angel Gabriel* was

§ Winthrop. 1-97.
* 2 Mass. Hist. Col., 8-232.
† Waters' Gen. Glean., 1-735 ; Essex Rec., 2-23.
‡ Me. Doc. Hist., 3-58.

wrecked, with Massachusetts passengers, during the severe storm of August 15 in Pemaquid Harbor. The fact that survivors were forced to seek shelter in their tents until they could obtain transportation to their destination proved the utter absence of lodging capacity at Pemaquid at that time.

Shurt's renewal of his covenant with the surviving patentee of Pemaquid for five years' service from November 11, 1635, may imply an extension of a former indenture with Aldworth and Elbridge, for the same term, from 1630.§

That winter he returned to Maine in the *White Angel* in company with William Cock, another early resident of Pemaquid.

During the period that followed the plantation was in a critical position, due to its nearness to the French settlements to the north. Its attitude in this respect was misunderstood. As one early writer claimed "In truth ye English them selves have been the cheefest supporters of these French; for besides these, the plantation at Pemaquid (which lyes near unto them) doth not only supply them with what yey wante, but gives them continuall intelligence of all things that passes among ye English (espetially some of them), so as it is no marvell though they still grow, & incroach more & more upon ye English, and fill ye Indeans with gunes & munishtion, to ye great deanger of ye English, who lye open & unfortified, living upon husbandrie; and ye other closed up in their forts, well fortified, and live upon trade, in good securitie."*

June 28, 1636, Shurt apprised Governor Winthrop that he had been warned of impending invasion by the French. According to his communication, an English or Scotch captive among the Frenchmen at Penobscot had encountered "a boate of ours (draylinge for mackrell)," presumably a dory belonging to the *White Angel*. The name of Shurt's informant was William Hart who reported that the French had "gone to the Eastwards to fetch more helpe to take this plantation & others." As to the means of communication the manager said: "This the master & purser of our shippe tould me: cominge hither for my lettres for England." Since his arrival in the *White Angel* that spring the vessel had been fishing in Penobscot Bay.†

At Pemaquid it was decided to await developments and de-

§ Aspinwall, 31.
* Bradford, 2-210.
† 4 Mass. Hist. Col., 6-570.

fend the place, if possible, when the occasion required—a decision made more confidently because there was little danger of an alliance between the enemy and eastern Indians. The natives about Penobscot then complained to resident Englishmen, as they had to Smith twenty years before, that they were disposed to abandon the district on account of harsh treatment by the French. In this connection Shurt observed: "It is lamentable that a handfull should insult over a multitude."

What actually transpired at Pemaquid was disclosed by Edward Winslow in a letter to Winthrop, dated April 17, 1637. That part which related to eastern affairs was worded as follows: "Concerning things Estward, Capt. Standish is returned who reporteth of the Royall entertainemt Shurt hath given Dony at Pemaquid. He saith (being commander Generall) that if he receive a Comission he must take him, onely six weeks before he will give him notice, and in lue thereof tis said Mr. Shurt hath promised him to informe him of whatever prepacon shall be made or intended against them. He further saith that if his commission be to take the Grand Bay (yorselves) he will attempt it though he should have no other vessell then a Canoe. But the English are all his friends except Plimoth: nor is he enemies to any other. Shurt hath undertaken to furnish him wth powder shot yea all manner of provisions, And to that end under a colour of gathering up some debts is come to make provisions for them till his owne ship come. Tis also reported that Sr fferdinando Gorges hath written to Saco that the ffrench here are not sett out nor allowed by the King of ffr. but a base people wch their state disclaime, & therefore stirreth them up to informe both you & us that we might joyne together to expell them. One thing more wch I had almost forgotten they have lost their Gally & a pinnase at Ile Sable & brought away their people who are at Penobscot where they have built a pinnase of threescore tunne."‡

From this letter it is apparent that the French had withdrawn all colonists at Sable Island to strengthen their position at Penobscot. On the other hand, Shurt, more concerned than ever, had formed a friendly alliance and was engaged in commerce with Aulnay.

One of the outstanding debts referred to was that of Thomas Wannerton, of Pascataqua. There had been dealings between

‡ Mather's N. E., 287.

Pemaquid and Pascataqua for several years. May 20, 1637, Shurt brought suit against the debtor to recover the balance of his account.

Between July 16 and October 8, 1638, the name of Pemaquid plantation was changed to Aldworth Town.§

January 4, 1638-9, Walter Barrett and Walter Sandy and their company at Bristol petitioned for a license to transport 180 persons to their plantation in New England, "to provide and gather up in that country a sufficient quantity of Victualls for furnishing of such Shipps and men as the Petitioners intend to keep and employ in a Fishing trade upon that Coast all the year, for which Works it hath ever been permitted to export provisions from hence." The petition further stated that the merchants of Bristol and their friends had "disbursed great charges for many years in setling of a Plantation in New England, which Plantation was by them begun long before such multitudes of people were sent as now are planted there, That those whom the said Petitioners have there already and all such as they intend now to send are regular people * * * That their Plantation is apart from all others and hath no relation to them."*

The fact that these settlers were adherents to the doctrine of the Church of England and outside the civil jurisdiction of the western governments of Gorges, Mason and Winthrop, disclosed the fishing plantation at Pemaquid as their true location.

July 21, 1639, Gyles Elbridge obtained a license to transport 80 passengers and provisions "formerly accumstomed * * * for the encreace and Support of his *fishing plantacion* in New England." These were embarked on the *Charles*, of Bristol, which belonged to "Mr. Elbridge."†

Bristol merchants were independent traders at Pemaquid and, in 1640, Hugh Yeo recovered judgment for merchandise formerly delivered to Thomas Purchase and at the same session Elbridge obtained a similar decree upon a separate account. In the suits the plaintiffs were represented by Arthur Brown, Robert Knight and Shurt himself. Brown then lived at Winnegance. Francis, brother of Robert Knight, was also involved in litigation.

February 4, 1643-4, Gyles Elbridge died at Bristol and an examination of his affairs showed that his manager at Pemaquid

§ 4 Mass. Hist. Col., 6-571.
* N. E. Hist. Gen. Reg., 8-140.
† Lechford, 180.

had never accounted in his stewardship at the plantation. Suit was begun against Shurt upon the covenant which had been executed at Bristol eight years before. The defendant removed to Charlestown, where he furnished security to John Elbridge, brother and sole legatee of the Bristol patentee, to await the verdict.

At the departure of Shurt from Pemaquid Francis Knight, with his brother's influence, secured control. In 1647, however, Thomas Elbridge, younger brother and heir of John, arrived in the country and superseded Knight in the management of his new estate. At that time the owner cited before him fishermen living at Damariscove and Monhegan and secured acknowledgement of his rights in their premises.

In the outstanding accounts for the year 1647 Knight filed an itemized statement of the transactions which had taken place between himself and John Holland, of Dorchester, who had been a trader on the Maine coast for many years. One item of debit comprised goods charged to the plantation but delivered to "Monhigon men."‡

Other persons who then lived in the vicinity of "the house" at Pemaquid were Thomas Atkins, of Sagadahoc, Edward Bateman, Elizabeth and George Buckland, John Cousins, John Gent, John Hopkins, Elias Hoskins, Robert Knight, Walter Phillips and Richard Toogood.

The purchases consisted largely of clothing, ammunition and liquor; the sales comprised bread, fish, peas and furs. Some of these provisions were delivered to Knight at "Nagausset," which fact, considered in connection with a credit for goods received from "Mr. Bateman," indicated continued business relations, begun at Pemaquid, where Bateman and Brown had formerly lived.

June 20, 1649, Nathaniel Draper was living at Aldworth Town, where he drew an order upon William Foster, of Boston, in favor of George Newman for the account of Charles Saunders, a London merchant resident in Boston. The bill was dishonored. Three days later the same person witnessed a note drawn by Francis Knight who still continued at Pemaquid. Two years later Draper was described as living upon "Damiriscove River"—evidently as a fisherman or planter at Winnegance.§

The only resident of Pemaquid who submitted to the New

‡ Suffolk Deeds, 3-100.
§ Aspinwall, 205, 209; Suffolk Deeds, 1-24.

York government in 1665 was Thomas Elbridge; he was joined by Edmund Arrowsmith and Henry Champney, of Winnegance, and George Buckland, of Corbin's Sound, all proprietors of large farms on Damariscotta River.

In 1672, Elbridge removed from Pemaquid to Marblehead, Massachusetts, and three years later to Barbadoes, leaving his

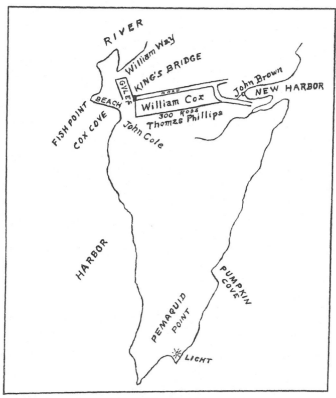

SKETCH MAP OF PEMAQUID

family, consisting of five children, in the custody of the eldest daughter at Marblehead.

He died in Spring Plantation, Barbadoes, in 1682.

At the beginning of the Indian Wars of 1675, a contemporary writer remarked that "There have been for a long Time seven or eight considerable Dwellings about Pemmaquid, which is well accomodated with Pasture Land about the Haven for feeding Cattel, and some Fields also for Tillage."*

* Hubbard's Wars, 2-7.

John Earthy, son-in-law of Gardiner, the early settler associated with Shurt at Pemaquid, was in charge at that port in 1676. Although he had tried to maintain friendly relations with the Indians, western traders directed by Major Waldron, of Dover, had seized several of the natives at Cape Sable. The captors were Henry Lawton and John Laverdure and the captives were sold at Fayal in the Azores. The eastern tribes regarded this act as an infringement of their treaty with the English.

At that time the New York government built at Pemaquid a new fort, consisting of a redoubt and outwork of pine logs fifteen feet in height, which were defended for a short time by twenty soldiers and seven cannon. Governor Andros reported that the chief commercial products of Pemaquid were fish and masts.

In 1677, Earthy and all other eastern residents had withdrawn to Salem district, where they took the oath of allegiance in various towns. After the death of his father-in-law Earthy may have returned to Pemaquid, but he was living in Boston ten years later. His family consisted of his wife Mary and daughters Abigail, Ann, Elizabeth and Mary.

The correspondence of Edward Randolph, in 1688, mentioned an interview that he had just held with William "Stuert," town clerk of Pemaquid. The name has been mistaken for that of Shurt, who, if he had been then living, would have been a centenarian.

John Brown of Pemaquid.

This pioneer was a tenant of Aldworth and Elbridge, and the alleged Indian deed given him by Samoset, of land at New Harbor, has furnished a basis for the claim that there were settlers at Pemaquid in 1625. Moreover, in 1660, Samuel Maverick asserted that Robert Aldworth, mayor of Bristol, had transported colonists to Pemaquid during the same year in which the Brown deed purports to have been dated, but the Massachusetts authority was writing long afterward and at a distance, and his allusion must have been to Monhegan, which was regarded as part of the Pemaquid premises. However, the patent issued to Aldworth and Elbridge fixed the date of their settlement at 1628.

The Samoset deed to John Brown was forged more than a century later. Two hundred years ago such a statement would have met strenuous denial, because the title to a tract of land twenty-five miles long and eight miles wide—equivalent to four full townships—was based upon the authenticity of the alleged deed. Now, neither public sentiment nor private interest requires recognition of its validity, and it is unfortunate that mention of it must be associated with the earliest period of Maine history, where its omission might be misconstrued.

Samoset, one of the supposed grantors, was the most noted Indian in New England. In 1619, he had associated with Dermer; in 1621, he had sought the acquaintance of Plymouth colonists; and, in 1623, he was a persistent attendant of Levett at Casco. Unnongoit, the other grantor, does not appear again in any relation.

Brown and his son-in-law Richard Pearce were friendly with the natives and transmitted some account of Samoset to their descendants. Depositions of Brown's grandchildren, taken more than a century later, proved that they had known many of the earliest settlers by name. With selfish motives and such an historical background it was not difficult to fabricate an Indian deed. Apparently, that was just what happened.

The Trail of Brown. The settlement at Bristol was known first as Pemaquid. The patent, issued in the spring of 1632, disclosed the year of settlement as 1628—probably at Monhegan. Legal seizin was not taken until 1633. Five years later the plantation, then a mere fishing hamlet, was called Aldworth Town.

Late in 1639, when Brown and Edward Bateman bought the whole of Woolwich from Robinhood, the grantees were described as residents of Pemaquid. Soon after the purchase they removed to their new property, upon which only an Indian house or wigwam was then standing.

In 1654, Brown was still residing at Woolwich when he signed the articles of submission to New Plymouth, which had just extended its jurisdiction down the Kennebec from Cushnoc.

In 1658, the Woolwich interests of Bateman and Brown had all been sold to James Cole, James Phipps and John White, by various conveyances. Brown's acknowledgement of his release in 1664 described him as a resident of Pemaquid, but "lately of Nequasseag" (Woolwich). In this connection the sworn statement of Robert Allen, of Sheepscot, taken at Bristol, England, February 12, 1659-60, referred to Brown as a mason of New Harbor; the deponent also testified that he had known that mechanic for seventeen years; that his father's name was Richard, of Barton Regis, and that his wife was Margaret, daughter of Francis Hayward, of Bristol, England.

The year before his deposition was given Allen had been a subscribing witness to the transfer of the islands of Damariscove and Monhegan as part of Pemaquid patent.†

The lineage of Brown's descendants was prepared by the heirs to establish their rights of inheritance in his estate at New Harbor. The families represented are subjoined.

1. Margaret, who married Alexander Gould, of Salem, about 1660. She left two daughters: Margaret, born at New Harbor in 1661, and another baptized at Marblehead November 21, 1686. The former married James Stilson and had James, John, Mary, and Margaret who became the wife of William Hilton. Gould was killed by Indians, but his widow married Maurice Champney and resided on Muscongus Island.

2. John, who was born in 1635 and lived with his father until thirty years of age, when he settled at Damariscotta Falls. He died in Framingham in 1720, leaving a son of the same name.

3. Elizabeth, who was born in 1642 and married Richard Pearce, of Muscongus. She was a stepmother of some of the following children: Richard, born in 1647, John, born in 1653, Francis, Elizabeth, wife of Richard Fulford and Samuel Martin, Margaret, William and George, born in 1666.

4. Francis, who was named for his paternal grandfather in England. He was living at Pumpkin Cove near Pemaquid in 1674.

5. Emma, who married Nicholas Denning. Her husband was born in 1645, lived at Pumpkin Cove and died in Gloucester June 9, 1725. Their children were Eliza (Paine), Nicholas, Mary (Stevens), George, Grace, Emma and Agnes.

The immigrant spent the last days of his life with his eldest son and may have died in Massachusetts. There is some evidence that his widow resided at New Harbor after his decease.

The Forgery of the Samoset Deed. Aldworth and Elbridge, patentees of Pemaquid, were wealthy merchants of Bristol, which was the paternal home of Brown's wife and, at that date, the principal port of departure from Western England. It is absurd to suppose that Brown, a mason, who substituted his mark for a signature, could obtain a native title to 120,000 acres at Pema-

† York Deeds, 17-868.

quid for the price of "fifty skins," trapped upon the premises, while two influential subjects of the British realm were only able to procure one-tenth of that area to found a city for the Crown.

Payment in clothing, ammunition or liquor would have been more in accord with ordinary trade relations, savage needs and historical precedent. There are instances when the Indians sold land and agreed to pay forfeitures with furs, but the grantors proffered them as a medium of payment rather than received them as a consideration.

The text of the alleged Samoset deed was couched in comparatively modern phraseology. Historians have pronounced the instrument the masterpiece and model of all American conveyancing, on account of its exemplary form and precision. Its perfection in these respects renders it an object of suspicion and leads to the conclusion that it was merely an adaptation of forms in existence when it was made, and not the precursor of deeds of the Seventeenth Century.

In the descriptive part nautical terms were used in defining the courses, but such terms as "North and by East" and "South and by East" belong to conveyances of later dates. Even grants by the Plymouth Council, established to cede dukedoms to New England proprietors, were limited wholly by natural boundaries and surveyed accordingly.

The names of witnesses affixed to the Samoset document are those of Matthew Newman and William Cox. The latter was a witness at Bristol in 1635, when Shurt made his agreement with Elbridge to return to Pemaquid, and the former may have been the Matthew Norman who was a witness at Pemaquid in 1640.

The chief inconsistency in the attestation was that it was followed in the line of title by another from John Brown to his son-in-law Alexander Gould, to which the same witnesses subscribed in exactly the same order, although, according to the professed dates of the two instruments, there was an interval of thirty-five years between executions. It is doubtful if this combination would have recurred if the same persons had lived together in the same house for the entire period. Moreover, Cox attested another deed of Brown's in 1671.‡

A year after the date assigned to the Samoset deed the Indian grantors were represented as having appeared at Pemaquid be-

‡ Lincoln Deeds, 5-61.

fore Shurt to confirm a written contract which they could not read, interpret or identify by any reasonable method. The capacity of the magistrate to officiate was not indicated. He was merely the Pemaquid agent of Aldworth and Elbridge, who took possession of part of the same premises for them, seven years later.

No such formula of acknowledgement was required in England by the leasehold system, nor prevailed in this country until 1641, when an order of Plymouth Colony first made it a prerequisite for registration. The laws of Massachusetts did not become effective in any part of Western Maine until after 1652, and not in Pemaquid until later.

In 1653, Shurt was a resident of Charlestown and a specimen of his clerical proficiency was recorded in Maine. The spelling of that certificate cannot be reconciled with the exquisite orthography of the Samoset formula. Three other Samoset conveyances, of 1641 and 1653, were not acknowledged at all.

No deeds certified by a magistrate were recorded in Maine registries until the decade of 1660. If comparison of this acknowledgement be made with that endorsed on the alleged deed from Brown to Gould, purporting to have been made in 1660, it will be seen that, except for necessary modifications, the forms were identical.

The Samoset deed to Brown was not presented for entry in the Book of Eastern Claims until December 1, 1720, and the affidavit of Benjamin Prescott shows that the clerk accepted the instrument after the expiration of the legislative limit and neglected to docket the entry. The usual explanation for such improper procedure is undue influence. At any rate, soon after registry the original deed had disappeared and, although the county recording office for York had been available for over ninety years, it was not until 1739 that a copy of a copy of Brown's deed was transcribed therein.

Simultaneously with the entry of the Samoset deed, the other from Brown to Alexander Gould was filed. Comparison of the two documents indicates that both were drawn at the same time and by the same person, although the latter was acknowledged before Thomas Garner. The magistrate intended appears to have been Thomas Jenner, a deputy of Massachusetts authorized to take acknowledgements of deeds.

Extrinsic Evidence. It may now be impossible to identify the perpetrator of the dual forgery, but one of the persons who presented the deeds for record is reported to have served sentence for a similar offence. The title to sixty-four square miles of territory beyond Pemaquid was an adequate motive.

In 1688, James Stilson, who had married a daughter of Alexander Gould, claimed Muscongus Island, situated near New Harbor, as a marriage portion from his wife's mother, who was the eldest daughter of John Brown. He asserted that his wife's grandfather had acquired the island from Samoset in 1652.

That date reverses the last two figures of 1625 and shows that Brown secured some deed from Samoset at about the time that he disposed of his property at Woolwich. Hence, the reason why he had made no objection to the conveyance from Samoset to Richard Pearce ten years earlier, or to that of Richard Fulford during the following year, although both tracts were included in the description of the forged document, is apparent.§

The conviction that the deed of 1625 was forged may be strengthened by collateral reference. John, the eldest son of the New Harbor pioneer, was born in 1635 and resided with his father until thirty years of age. He was living with his parents throughout the period in which the Pearce and Fulford deeds were executed. In a sworn, but unsigned, statement against his own interest, that son declared that his brother-in-law Richard Pearce had bought land within the area defined by the forged conveyance, with his father's knowledge and without any objection.

He also maintained that his father had occupied his homestead at New Harbor under a lease from Aldworth and Elbridge and had laid claim to no other tracts in the vicinity except "Somerset Island" in Broad Bay and a point called "Sawk Head" (Saquid), lying about three leagues eastward from New Harbor at the mouth of Saint George's River.*

§ Me. Doc. Hist., 6-262.
* Commissioners' Report, 1811-115.

ISLE OF MONHEGAN

Lost amid wild northern gales
Fleeting hulls and phantom sails,
Fluttering from yard and mast,
Vanish in the magic past.

Outlines of a Spanish ship
On its long swells rise and dip,
Landing in the crimson dawn,
Chests of pirate cargazon.

Here the fishermen of France
Dream of pleasure and romance—
Of Yvonnes and Juliettes—
While they mend their broken nets.

Safely anchored in its lee,
Three leagues off within the sea,
English mariners of yore
Scan the strange, uncharted shore.

On this bit of Occident,
Men of Plymouth pitch their tent;
In the cabins roughly made,
Men of Bristol ply their trade.

Thrice abandoned, desolate,
Once the threshold of a state,
Scarred by storms and worn with tides,
Gray Monhegan still abides.

MONHEGAN ISLAND.

Champlain called the island "La Nef" on account of its resemblance to a ship. Dutch mariners of the contemporary period, like Hendricksen and Jacobs, followed the lead of Champlain in their translation "Het Schip," while Smith in 1614, Brawnde in 1616, Dermer in 1619, and Piddock and Levett in 1624, spelled

THE CLIFFS, MONHEGAN

it Monahiggan, Manehegin, Monahiggon, Menhegen and Monhiggen, respectively. An Italian chart of 1631 combines both names in the legend "I. Schip ò Manabigon." No Maine name has been given more varied forms by European linguists.

The island is situated in latitude 43° 45' 53" and longitude 69° 18' 59" and contains 433 acres. Its extreme altitude is 178 feet above sea level. Its harbor is situated on the southerly side, between it and the small island of Manana.

While it might be difficult to present conclusive proof of the occasion for it, historical allusions point unmistakably to this port as the principal point of arrival and departure for British commerce with New England during the first three decades of the Seventeenth Century. While the fishing grounds in that vicinity were never considered superior to those on the Grand Banks, nor about the Isles of Shoals, Captain John Smith asserted, without qualification, that all fishing masters, before the year 1622, had confined their operations to a square area of two or three leagues about the island.

The poetical tradition that the trail of a calf in the dew was responsible for the delineation of the main thoroughfare of Boston, leads to a similar inference that the first voyage of George Waymouth dominated sentiment in Europe and, so far as English navigators were concerned, fixed the future point of contact with Northern Virginia.

In 1605, under patronage of the influential Earl of Arundel, Waymouth sailed from Bristol in the *Archangel*. He was the first mariner who had ever attempted a direct course for New England; other vessels had made the voyage by way of Spain or the West Indies. He first sighted land near Cape Cod, but turned northward to seek his objective. May 17, he erected a wooden cross on Monhegan, which, in the fervor of gratitude for a safe arrival, he named Saint George's Island.

Later he anchored his ship in the mouth of Saint George's River which he christened Pentecost Harbor. From that point he visited Pemaquid and conducted personal expeditions for sixty miles up the Sagadahoc and for forty miles up Saint George's River, where, on the bank above Thomaston, he erected a second cross. At his departure he kidnapped five Indians, one of whom was a native of Pemaquid, known as Nahanada, and withdrew to Monhegan for safety during his fishing operations.†

The Indians were left in an excited frame of mind. Only a few days later Champlain, returning from his first voyage to Malabarre (Cape Cod) toward Saint Croix, found the natives at Sagadahoc in a state of hostility toward strangers on account of the recent seizure of their chief men. He was assured that Waymouth's vessel was still anchored at the islands. It was on that occasion that the French styled Monhegan "La Nef," or "Ship Island," a name which was used afterward on many Dutch, Italian and Portuguese charts.

Monhegan was visited by Pring in 1606, and by the colonists from Sagadahoc, during the next two years.

Familiarity with the accounts of northern adventurers who had followed in the wake of the first colony, and the lack of more definite knowledge concerning the New England coast generally,

† Me. Hist. Col., 3-297.

kept the ocean route fixed, with exploratory excursions trending sometimes north, but usually south, from the terminal. As to the accumulation of maritime information, Edward Godfrey presented a petition to representatives of the dominant administration in England, in 1659, in which he claimed to have in his possession a record of "all passages" from the British Isles to America for forty years.‡

April 27, 1610, King James of England granted colonization privileges in Newfoundland to a society of English noblemen and merchants. This association was styled "The Company of Adventurers, and Planters of the Citie of London, and Bristoll, for the Colony or Plantation in New-found-land."§

Some of these patentees were identical with those who afterwards helped to colonize Maine. Among them were Humphrey Hook, and John Langton, of Bristol, and Abraham Jennings of Plymouth, whose exercise of their royal franchise brought them in close contact with French adventurers who were interested in the development of Canadian trade. The English merchants, however, were inclined to dominate the situation on the northern seas, although French mariners had been earlier visitors to that coast. According to Champlain they eventually became masters, "imposant un tribut sur la pesche du poison: la tout pour les travailler, & en fin leur faire quitter la pesche, en se rendant maistre de toutes les costes peu a peu."

Damariscove, Manana and Monhegan islands were usually associated in historical reference with the mainland of Pemaquid, or Pemacuit, as designated upon a map of 1610. July 29, of that year, Sir Samuel Argal and Sir George Somers, with two vessels from Virginia Colony, had ranged the coast as far north as Seal Island in the Matinicus group.*

Upon Argal's return southward he must have observed Monhegan. Later in the season it was sighted by Jean de Biencourt, while on his way from France to Port Royal. The French classed that island with the Metinic group, which they called "Emetenic."

In the summer of 1611, the islands at Monhegan formed a safe haven for the captains of two English fishing vessels. They found there Captain Platrier, a resident of Honfleur, who had just settled on the old French site at Saint Croix River. A ransom

‡ N. H. State Papers, 17-509.
§ Purchase, 19-407.
* Purchase, 19-80.

was exacted from him for his freedom and he was admonished not to fish or trade on the coast in that vicinity.

November 6, of the same year, Biencourt and Pierre Biard, who had been exploring the Sagadahoc River, found English fishing boats at Monhegan which had been stored there for use in the following spring. Biard reported that the English came "in the summer to fish, at this island of Emetenic," which was located by him "eight leagues from the fort they had begun building." The fortification to which he referred was Fort Saint George.†

While it has been assumed by late writers of Maine history that there was an early French plantation on the mainland at Castine, this claim is not substantiated by any accounts of the period. The real location of the first French settlement in that vicinity was upon Mount Desert Island, which was regarded as part of Norumbega or Pentagoet district. The latter was but another name for Penobscot. The presence of European settlers at the island was unknown to Virginians, who ranged and fished in northern waters, until it was disclosed to them by local Indians. If there had been a plantation in Penobscot Bay at that time, its existence would have been known to all English fishermen.

In the summer of 1613, after the French had become well established at Pemetiq, or Mount Desert, which had been named by them Saint Sauveur, Biard alluded to Damariscove and Monhegan as the "Isles of Pencoit" (Pemaquid). His words were: "Now the English of Virginia are accustomed every year to come to the Pencoit Islands, which are 25 leagues from St. Sauveur, to lay in a supply of codfish for the winter."

As soon as the Virginians had located the French settlement at Mount Desert, an immediate and successful attack was made under the leadership of Sir Samuel Argal. As a consequence the colony was entirely dispersed and some of the captives were transported to the "Pencoit islands and entrusted to English fishermen for conveyance to France."‡

In 1614, Sir Thomas Smith and the Virginia Council dispatched Captain John Smith from The Downs with two vessels and forty-five men and boys. His masters were Michael Cooper and Thomas Hunt. With his party there was an expert named Samuel Crampton, who had had previous experience in whale fishing at Newfoundland.

† Jesuit Rel., 2-31, 47.
‡ Jesuit Rel., 2-253, 263, 275.

Smith arrived about the end of April and established his headquarters in the little harbor between Monhegan and Manana. He planted a garden on the heights of the former island and was engaged chiefly with exploring the coast while his men were fishing. The only other English ship found by him in that vicinity was that of Sir Francis Popham, which was anchored in the mainland opposite the island.

The explorer had intended to keep possession of the entire district with ten of his companions, but conditions did not prove favorable for that purpose. He sailed from the island and reached England August 5, but the *Long-Robert*, commanded by Hunt, remained to complete its cargo of fish and, on the way to Virginia, kidnapped twenty-nine Indians from the vicinity of Capawick (Martha's Vineyard). All but two of these natives were sold as slaves in Spain, where Hunt disposed of his fish. One of them was Tisquantum of Patuxet.

In June, 1614, the West Countrymen, under the direction of Sir Ferdinando Gorges, sent Edward Harlow, who had been a member of the original Sagadahoc Colony, Nicholas Hobson, John Matthew and some of Gorges' relatives named Sturton, to locate and take possession of a gold mine at Capawick. They found their destination with the help of the Indians Assacomoit, Epenow and Wenape, but Epenow, who had promised to locate the mine, escaped to his relatives. The native tribes were so much incensed at the recent perfidy of Hunt that the object of the expedition was entirely frustrated.

The next year Smith was engaged by Gorges, and his associates in the Isle of Wight and Western England, to undertake the supervision of another voyage to Capawick. Accordingly, he embarked with Thomas Dermer, Edward Rocraft, alias Stalling, and fourteen others and proposed "to stay in the countrey," but pirates captured him in one of his vessels and detained him in France until December. His other vessel, in charge of Dermer, reached Monhegan in May and returned to England in August, after a prosperous voyage.

Smith's old crews of the previous year were employed by the Virginia Company, of London, and began to fish on the Maine coast in March with four ships. One went to Virginia to supply the colony, one was taken by pirates and the others reached home in six months, well freighted with fish and furs.

October 15, 1615, the Virginia Company dispatched Sir Richard Hawkins from London with two ships "to trye the Winter." According to Gorges, he "undertook by authority from the Council of the second Colony to try what service he could do them as President for that year."

Smith reported that this expedition crossed the Atlantic by way of the West Indies and did not arrive in New England until the following spring, "wasting in that time, their seasons, victuall, and healths."

He found six fishing vessels, four of which were from Plymouth, "harbourd in manehegin." The *Blessing* and *David* hailed from that western port and were in charge of Arthur Hitchens and John Winter; the *Judith* and *Trial*, from London, were commanded by William West and James Edwards; the *Nachen*, from Dartmouth, of which Edward Brawnde was master, had sighted Seguin April 20 and reached Monhegan four days later. The crew of the *Nachen* consisted of twenty-one men and the London ships were manned with forty-four men and boys.

As chief admiral of New England, Hawkins commandeered the boats which he found in the possession of Brawnde and others and with them laded one of his own vessels with fish and train oil and dispatched it homeward before the close of the season. He left the island with some of the fishing craft July 21, and the rest followed him the next day.

Gorges, who from the first had appeared to be skeptical of the outcome, dismissed the account of Hawkins' achievements in his usual perfunctory way, remarking that he had "spent the time of his being in those parts in searching of the country and finding out the commodities thereof." However, some allowance was made in the following conclusion: "But the war was at the height, and the principal natives almost destroyed; so that his observation could not be such as could give account of any new matter, more than formerly had been received. From thence he passed along the coast to Virginia, and stayed there some time in expectation of what he could not be satisfied in; so took his next course for Spain, to make the best of such commodities he had got together, as he coasted from place to place, having sent his ship laden with fish to the market before. And this was all that was done by any of us that year."§

§ Me. Hist. Col., 2-28.

Brawnde assured Smith that there were "greet voyages" to be made in New England in the fish and fur industries, but suggested that only one factor, or agent, should be permitted to control and license Indian commerce and that fishing boats were inadequate and expensive. Aside from these temporary disadvantages, he concluded that the country was good and "worthye of prayes" and the climate healthful, and that the natives, who frequented the company of the English "vere much," were harmless.*

Smith claimed that the Plymouth ships returned—one of them by way of Spain—"well fraught, and their men well, within 5 months and odde daies"; that one of those from London "returned againe into England within five months and a few dayes; the other went to the Canaries with dry fish, which they solde at a great rate, for royalls of eight, and * * * turned Pirates."†

Dermer, who had escaped from pirates when on his way to New England in 1615, sailed during the following year for Newfoundland, where he was associated with Captain John Mason, then governor of that island. His residence was located at "Cuper's Cove" on Conception Bay. The place may have been named for David Cooper, one of his acquaintances. Dermer was still living there September 9, 1616, as his letter of that date was mentioned by Purchase. While at the island he met Tisquantum, who had been captured by Hunt and sold in Spain. The Indian had been emancipated by John Slanie, of London, one of the northern patentees, who had educated him for a year and sent him to Newfoundland, hoping to profit by his knowledge of New England.

In 1617, Captain Smith formulated a new plan to settle in Maine with fifteen men, but his ships were becalmed so long at Plymouth that they sought Newfoundland instead, because the winds were more favorable for that course and the fishing in that latitude was not so far advanced.

In 1618, five vessels from London and two from Plymouth visited Monhegan "to fish and trade only." One of those from the latter port belonged to Gorges and furnished transportation for Edward Rocraft. The latter had special instructions to unite with Dermer and Tisquantum, who had agreed to come thither from Newfoundland. Rocraft's party consisted of about a dozen men who were supplied with salt and other necessaries for fishing and

* N. E. Hist. Gen. Reg., 28-249.
† Smith's Trav. & Works, 1-241.

had made a compact to remain in the country during the winter.

Captain Smith asserted, in a letter to Lord Bacon, that until that year no English ship had undertaken to fish outside "a square of two leagues" for a distance of two or three hundred leagues along the New England coast. This area—equivalent to an ordinary township, only six miles square—was situated about Monhegan. All other favorable localities had been neglected.

Although Rocraft was provided with a pinnace for coasting, he confiscated a French bark, which he found fishing and trading in a creek near the island. No doubt, his detention by French pirates in 1615, when he had planned to reach and spend the winter in New England with Smith, inspired him to take this summary action in the spirit of retaliation. After the fishing season was concluded the captive crew was dispatched to England in the vessel of Gorges, who afterwards complained of the seizure of the bark, because he was compelled by the admiralty court to reimburse its owner.

As winter approached and Rocraft began to despair of meeting Dermer at Monhegan that season, he decided to winter in Virginia, where he had lived formerly and had friends of long standing. His proposed course was in plain violation of explicit orders from Gorges. He excused his own refractory conduct in that instance with the pretext that a serious disaffection had developed among his men, and that the disloyal members had been left in the North, where they might secure valuable information in the public interest.

Some of his party, which must have included Richard Vines, objected to the proposed southern trip and were left at Saco, where they did not continue long, but withdrew to "Menehighon, an Iland lying some three leagues in the Sea, and fifteene leagues" distant. They remained on that island "all that Winter, with bad lodging, and worse fare."

The removal of the "mutineers" to Monhegan was proof that the island, bad as it might have been for food supplies, did provide some accommodation in the way of shelter and was recognized generally as the sole resort of English fishermen.

At any rate, Rocraft with a few congenial companions sought the milder climate of Virginia, where they arrived in December. April 18, of the next year, the explorer was present when Sir George Yardley, the new governor, reached Jamestown. He was killed a few days later in a duel with William Epps, an old Virginian planter, and his death was reported to the refugees at Monhegan in the following month by Captain John Ward, of Virginia.‡

According to the Council of Plymouth, Dermer did not go directly from Newfoundland to New England, where he had agreed to meet Rocraft in 1618, "at our usuall place of fishing" (Monhegan). He chose to act upon the advice of Captain Mason and visited England first in order to confer with Gorges and secure means for the undertaking. He took Tisquantum with him to London, but arrived too late to complete arrangements to proceed that season and remained there during the winter.

In the spring of 1619 he came from Plymouth to Monhegan in the fishing ship which belonged to Gorges. The crew consisted of thirty-eight men and boys. The explorer was in the employment of Gorges and his agreement required that he should reside in New England and coöperate with Rocraft. At the island he learned from the "Mutiners which hee found there," and who had lived there "all that Winter," that his predecessor had gone to Virginia.§

With the arrival of Dermer on the Maine coast it was learned that the widespread ravages of an unknown contagious disease had almost depopulated New England. This mysterious epidemic had been raging for three years, without abatement, and some of the scattered survivors were destroyed subsequently by remote hostile tribes.

Such wholesale extinction of the aborigines of New England was regarded by Dermer and his associates as a special dispensation of Providence, designed to pave the way for peaceable occupation by English planters. In correspondence with Captain Smith he was convinced, to use his own words, "that God had laid this Country open for us, and slaine the most part of the inhabitants by cruell warres, and a mortall disease."

Smith, disclosing Dermer as his informant at that time, remarked, "where I have seene 100 or 200 people" (in 1614) "there is scarce ten to be found." Relative to the conditions in Maine, he had been advised that "From Pembrocks bay to Harrintons bay" (Penobscot to Casco Bay) "there is not 20; from thence

‡ Purchase, 19-121.
§ Purchase, 19-276.

to Cape An, some 30," survivors of the pestilence. Yet, he learned that the only European who succumbed was a shipwrecked Frenchman.*

The same or a greater percentage of mortality had prevailed in Massachusetts. At the time of his advent at New Plymouth, Winslow reported that Tisquantum was then "the only native of Patuxet, where we now inhabit." That writer added that this Indian "was one of the twenty captives that by Hunt were carried away, and had been in England, and dwelt in Cornhill with Master John Slanie, a merchant, and could speak a little English."†

Dermer decided to seek Rocraft in the South and, incidentally, to attempt the discovery of a supposed passage to the Pacific Ocean. Accordingly, in May he shipped the greater part of his provisions in the *Sampson,* a vessel from Jamestown in which Captain Ward, who had been fishing for his colony at Monhegan, was ready to return to Virginia.

Dermer, however, before leaving New England, visited the island of Capawick, to investigate the report of a gold mine which had been elaborated by Epenow five years before. There he "found seven severall places digged" and "sent home" some of the earth from Monhegan, to which he had returned June 23.

Thence he coasted southward in company with four or five other members of the ship's crew who had been assigned to him by Gorges. For this voyage he utilized the open pinnace which had been abandoned by Rocraft the previous year.

Before his departure from Monhegan the vessel, in which he had arrived from Plymouth, had sailed for England with all of the "mutineers," except one who had died there. He left no one at the island because he could not spare men to defend the place. Even Tisquantum, owing to the extinction of his tribe at Patuxet and the length of the southern journey, preferred to pass the winter with some of his "Savage friends at Sawahquatooke."‡

On the trip south Dermer noted the entire extinction of native villages upon the coast and the miserable conditions of the survivors. Near Cape Cod he rescued three shipwrecked Frenchmen from Indian captors. After arrival at Jamestown in November the whole party was taken sick.

Dermer remained in Virginia until spring and then turned

* Smith's Trav. & Works. 1-259.
† Mass. Hist. Col., 8-228.
‡ Purchase, 19-131.

northward once more. Eight months later his fate was made known to the colonists of New Plymouth by Samoset, who had lived in the East and learned to speak broken English "amongst the English men that came to fish at Monchiggon and knew by name the most of the Captaines, Commanders and Masters." He had met Dermer at Monhegan in the summer of 1620, whither that explorer and a companion had escaped after their conflict with the Nausites at Cape Cod. Dermer was then suffering with fourteen wounds from the effect of which he soon died.§

Smith assures us that the six or seven ships which visited New England that year went there "only to trade and fish; but nothing would bee done for a plantation, till about some hundred * * * went to New Plimouth." The arrival of the *Mayflower* at Patuxet upon November 11, 1620, had founded the first permanent settlement in New England.

February 27, 1620-1, claims were made in Parliament that "The fishinge at Monhigen exceedeth New foundland fishinge caryed into Spayne. Intercepted by the merchants of France: to the valewe of 100,000 l. per annum now brought home in tobacco."

Two months later, in the same forum, it was reported that, "The English, as yet, little frequent this" (Monhegan district) "in respect of this prohibition" (to fish without a license from the council); "but the French and Dutch * * * who come, and will fish there, notwithstanding the colony" of Plymouth.*

During 1621 Abraham Jennings and William Cross, known as Jennings and Company, sent the *Eleanor* from Orston to Virginia with a cargo of passengers and provisions. Such action disclosed the broad scope of the business of that company, which was engaged at that time in extreme northern and southern commerce with America.†

By September of that year English interest in the settlement of Maine had become so pronounced that a general plan of colonization was proposed by the Council of Plymouth. The reasons for this course were hopes of profit from sale of New England fishing licenses and fear of the public, which was insistent upon the rights of free fishery.

In the new scheme of settlement provision was to be made by

§ Mourt's Rel., 32.
* Brit. Proc., 1-28, 35.
† Min. of Va. Council. 58, 118; Hotten, 244.

every ship of sixty tons burden to transport "twoe Piggs, twoe Calves, twoe couple of Tame Rabbetts, two couple of Hens, and a cocke," which were to be delivered "at the Iland of Menethiggen" (Monhegan) "to the hands of such" as might be "assigned to receive them, for the use of the Colony."

Each shipmaster was to be instructed to leave every fifth member of his crew with adequate fishing tackle and provisions "untill the retorne of the fleete." These men were "to followe their fishing courses" during the winter and "to make triall of all the seasons of the yeare" as well as "make provision for the lading of some shipps as soon as the next fleete or shipping" should arrive.

The plan of the council was submitted to the "Merchant Venturers," a society composed of prominent citizens of the cities of Bristol and Exeter and of the towns of Barnstable, Dartmouth, Plymouth and Weymouth.

Inside of two months Bristol merchants filed their objections to the colonization plan, because Newfoundland fishing had failed in "late yeeres" and there were some adventurers in Bristol who were anxious to "make triall of that *new* fishing." It was not strange that Newfoundland returns were unsatisfactory, since at least three hundred fishing ships obtained cargoes at the island that year.

The names of those who signed the Bristol protest belonged to four Newfoundland patentees of 1610. These were Richard Holworthy, Humphrey Hook, John Langton and William Jones. The other subscribers were Humphrey Brown, Andrew Carleton, Richard Long, William Pitt and Thomas Wright. The last three, with Hook, and Robert, son of Thomas Aldworth, another original Newfoundland patentee, were associated subsequently in the settlement of Pemaquid.‡

Plymouth merchants, including Leonard Pomery and Nicholas Sherwill, who were later associated with David Thompson at Pascataqua, seconded the protest against taxing, or otherwise restricting, New England fishing vessels.

In November, 1621, the Virginia Company, in order to secure a part of the "rich trade in Furres" controlled by the Dutch and French, sent out the *Discovery* in command of Thomas Jones, who explored the coast from Jamestown to New Plymouth. He

‡ Am. Hist. Rev., 4-689, 693.

undertook to emulate Waymouth and Hunt by capturing several Indians, who escaped later at Cape Cod where the vessel was beached during a severe storm.

Thirty-five vessels fished on the coast during the year. Abraham Jennings and William Cross applied for council membership during the summer and were admitted as partners in the mainland upon payment of £110.§

October 28, 1622, owing to opposition to the inauguration of its colonization plan, the council modified the requirements for fishing privileges. Each ship was enjoined to "carry a man to New England" who was to be "Imployed by the fishermen there." The proportion to be left by the larger ships was to be one man in ten, or two in seventeen, for each thirty tons of capacity. Every master was directed to certify how many calves, goats, pigs, conies and fowl he would transport for the benefit of "ye publike."

At that time the only plantation begun by the English in Maine was that of Gorges at Damariscove. The public plantation was to be established upon two great islands in Sagadahoc River, now known as Georgetown and Arrowsic, and in the interior, between the Androscoggin and Kennebec rivers, was to be founded the seat of government for State County. William Pomfrett and George Dugdeale offered to become permanent colonists under the plan.*

During the fishing season there had been many fishing vessels stationed at Damariscove and Monhegan which did not recognize any council authority to exact license fees for local privileges and Francis West was appointed admiral with authority to compel their submission. January 28, 1622-3, a commission was issued to West to seize Monhegan, which most of the fishermen monopolized as their American port. That spring over thirty vessels, besides those employed by Jennings and Company, fished in the vicinity of the island.

Early in the year a plantation was begun at Monhegan by William Vengham and fishermen from Plymouth. The project was sponsored by Abraham Jennings, of Plymouth, and William Cross and Ambrose Jennings, of London, exporters and importers.†

Vengham was a master mariner of experience who, during

§ Am. Ant. Col., 1867-75.
* Am. Ant. Col., 1867-76.
† Bradford, 2-107.

the previous season, had been mentioned by Pory, at Damariscove, as an authority consulted by the Virginia Company in relation to fishing conditions to the south of Cape Cod; he may have been a superior officer in the *Eleanor*, of Orston, which was sent to Virginia by Jennings and Company in 1621.

During its early period of settlement Monhegan was merely a fishing plantation. Colonists were transported thither on some of the company's ships and remained on the island throughout the winter. William Pomfrett, the distiller, who had volunteered to become a resident for the council the year before settlement and was living at Monhegan, the year after, may have been an original planter in 1623.

About the last of June Admiral West arrived at New Plymouth from Monhegan in the *Plantation*. In the words of Governor Bradford, he had undertaken "to restraine interlopers, and shuch fishing ships as came to fish & trade without a licence from ye Counsell of New-England, for which they should pay a round sume of money. But he could doe no good of them, for they were to stronge for him, and he found ye fisher men to be stuberne fellows."‡

At that time, since he was unable to secure control of Monhegan, he had made his headquarters, during a brief sojourn, at Damariscove, where he discharged his crew and embarked for Massachusetts, as soon as he was satisfied that nothing could be accomplished.

Plymouth Colony was then on the verge of starvation and, influenced by reports of West that provisions were obtainable from the ships at the East, Myles Standish was dispatched to the Isles of Shoals, Damariscove and Monhegan for supplies. He returned in August with David Thompson, who had located his plantation at Pascataqua that spring.

Almost coincident with the admiral's arrival at New Plymouth was the departure of Robert, son of Ferdinando Gorges, with relatives and friends, from Plymouth for the New World.

September 10, Edward Winslow was dispatched for England to confer with the London partners and the council for the specific purpose of procuring patent rights at Cape Ann.

Within a week after Winslow's departure Robert Gorges reached the Massachusetts coast and after some survey selected

‡ Bradford, 2-100.

the premises abandoned by Weston's Colony as the site for his new plantation. He may have assumed that the fort and houses still standing at Wessaguscus were comprised within the bounds of his own grant, made the previous year on Massachusetts Bay. It was, however, a clear example of the compensating consequences of human avarice that, while the new proprietor was appropriating the unpatented location of Weston at Wessaguscus, agents of Plymouth Colony were seeking part of his definite allotment at Cape Ann.

After unlading his cargo Gorges sailed for the Eastward in the vessel in which he had arrived. He had expected to find Thomas Weston at Damariscove and, under orders from the Council of Plymouth, to confiscate the *Swan* for the failure of its owner to adjust overdue license fees and for misrepresentations made to his father and other members of the council in former transactions.

However, he encountered a severe storm on the coast and sought New Plymouth in order to procure an experienced pilot. After about two weeks' delay, during which he met Weston in that harbor, he left the vessel at New Plymouth, where it was being fitted for Virginia, and returned to Wessaguscus by land.

After some legal controversy with Bradford, Gorges sent Captain Hanson, one of his lieutenants, to take possession of the *Swan*, while it was still within the jurisdiction of Bradford's Colony. By this order not only the ship was "arrested" but Weston himself and "a great many men" were taken into custody. The bark was confiscated late in the fall, during a very cold period, with supplies for only two weeks.

Gorges selected a crew, disposed of the remainder and set his sails for the Eastward. Twenty days later he was found by Christopher Levett at Pascataqua, in company with David Thompson and Governor Bradford. After organizing the Council for New England he proceeded along the Maine coast as far as Monhegan, where he notified some of the fishermen, who had agreed to remain in Maine with Levett during the winter, to proceed to Little Harbor with the sailing craft required by the latter to make an exploratory trip to the Eastward.

Levett had sojourned at Pascataqua about a month when his boats arrived. He encountered severe snowstorms while examining the coast line as far as Cape Newagen, whence he returned to Casco and built his fortified house on the island in Portland Harbor.

Gorges, however, returned to Massachusetts before spring and restored the *Swan* to Weston with compensation for its detention. With reference to the settlement at Wessaguscus Bradford said, "This was in effect ye end of a 2. plantation in that place"; some of the colonists returned to England with Gorges, by way of Virginia, some settled in the South and a few remained for a time at Wessaguscus, where they were supplied subsequently by the Southern Colony.

In the parliamentary debate relating to free fishery, southern planters argued that their colony could not survive without the exercise of that privilege within the limits of the Northern Colony. There was no fishing south of Cape Cod, and when all other resources failed the early shipmasters relied upon the "catch" at Monhegan to ensure a profitable western voyage.

Consequently, lists of ships sent to the Southern Colony in 1623 and 1624 include many that, either on the outward or return passage, or both, fished upon the Maine coast. In this way some of the thirty vessels, which were reported to have been harbored at or near Monhegan during the former year, may be accounted for.§

While Levett was living at Casco, in the early part of 1624, Pemaquid Harbor was occupied by John Witheridge from Barnstable and Emanuel Altham from New Plymouth. Both were engaged in fishing and trading. During the same season other English fishermen were stationed at Sagadahoc, Cape Newagen and Damariscove.

At Monhegan a trading mart was maintained for the sale or exchange of commodities proffered by fishing masters. The deposition of Thomas Piddock, taken in an admiralty case, affords a glimpse of the nature and extent of the principal business at the island. The statement was made in 1628, when the witness was only twenty-seven years of age.

The testimony in these cases consists of questions and answers, but in the case of Piddock, who hailed from London, the statement has been reduced to the following abstract:

"In June and July, 1624, he and Edmund Dockett and William Pomfrett being then at Menhegen in New England as factors of

§ Rec. Va. Co., 2-496.

Abraham Jennings of Plymouth and Ambrose Jennings and William Crosse of London, merchants, did lade at Mendhegen, in the ship called the *Jacob* of (Nore)kham in Freezeland, whereof one Thomas Neeson was then master, from the ship *Prosperous*, Robert Bennett, master, 39,600 of dry fish containing 615 quintalls, from the *Golden Catt*, Mr. John Corben (master) 51,800 of the like fish weighing 893 quintalls, and from one William Vengam, *who was planted upon that island*, 82,300 of the like fish containing 1534 quintalls, which makes in all 173,700 weighing 3042 quintalls; one third of which fish did belong to the company of fishermen, for which one third the said Edmund Dockett gave the said Robert Bennett, John Corbyn and William Vangham bills of exchange on the said Abraham Jennings & Company; which fish when it was laden was all dry and well conditioned, and was consigned by the said Edmund Dockett to George Backlar then a merchant at Bordeaux."

More than half of the 150 tons of freight furnished for the lading of the *Jacob* was provided by Vengham who had been fishing on the island during the preceding winter. The name of Dockett, who later was interested in Virginia and made subsequent voyages with Vengham, was spelled "Doggett" in other connections.*

The disastrous sequel to this season's toil and hardships was disclosed by the same witness. He said that "after he came to England he met the steersman of the ship *Jacob* at Plymouth who told him that a Turkes man of war meeting with that ship about 30 leagues from the Polehead of Bordeaux, boarded and took that ship and the fish in her which they carried to the 'barr of Sally,' but the ship being of such draught that she could not go over that bar then the said Turkes took out of her what fish they pleased and gave the rest to the skipper for his freight."†

Salli is a seaport of Morrocco. At Bordeaux the cargo of the *Jacob* would have sold for more than $10,000.

In 1627, Jennings and Company who had acquired title to Monhegan, probably from the Earl of Arundel, sold the island and their entire stock in trade. The premises were bought by Abraham Shurt for Aldworth and Elbridge, all merchants of Bristol. Since funds were not available in this country to meet

* Putnam's Gen. Mag., 3-142.
† Putnam's Gen. Mag., Vol. 4, No. 1, 4.

the consideration, a bill of exchange was drawn upon Aldworth, to be paid in England.

The paltry price received for the island indicated the absence of valuable improvements. While some sort of shelter had existed there as early as the first visit of Rocraft in 1618, at the time of the sale to Shurt, according to Samuel Maverick, all of the building construction upon the coast of New England, except his own houses in Boston Harbor and a few dwellings at New Plymouth, would not have exceeded £200 in value. The fishing stages were built for convenience rather than comfort.

The price paid for the island was fifty pounds. The merchandise was also sold at the same time. The part of Plymouth Colony in the transaction was described at length as follows:

"Wanting trading goods, they understoode that a plantation which was at Monhigen, & belonged to some marchants of Plimoth was to breake up, and diverse usefull goods was ther to be sould; the Gover and Mr. Winslow tooke a boat and some hands and went thither. But Mr. David Thomson, who" (had) "lived at Pascataway, understanding their purpose, tooke oppertunitie to goe with them, which was some hinderance to them both; for they, perceiveing their joynte desires to buy, held their goods at higher rates; and not only so, but would not sell a parcell of their trading goods, excepte they sould all. So, lest they should further prejudice one an other, they agreed to buy all, & devid them equally between them. They bought allso a parcell of goats, which they distributed at home as they saw neede & occasion, and tooke corne for them of ye people, which gave them good content. Their moyety of ye goods came to above 400 li. starling. Ther was allso that spring a French ship cast away at Sacadahock, in wch were many Biscaie ruggs & other comodities, which were falen into these mens hands, & some other fisher men at Damerins-cove, which were allso bought in partnership, and made their parte arise to above 500 li. This they made shift to pay for, for ye most part, with ye beaver & comodities they had gott ye winter before, & what they had gathered up yt somer. Mr. Thomson having some thing overcharged him selfe, desired they would take some of his, but they refused except he would let them have his French goods only; and ye marchant (who was one of Bristol) would take their bill for to be paid ye next year. They were both willing, so they became ingaged for them & tooke them. By which means they became very well furnished for trade."‡

From this account, written in 1648, and from a deposition of Shurt, taken in 1662, it would appear that he was the Bristol merchant who arranged the terms of settlement between New Plymouth and Jennings and Company. That the deponent did not return to Bristol for several years may be inferred from his statement that his information relating to payment of the Aldworth draft was obtained from the drawee through correspondence. The will of Aldworth, made in 1634, implied a protracted absence for his "servant," and if Shurt's first residence in New England were continuous, as appeared to have been the case, the testator never saw him again. As it was, Elbridge as surviving partner settled the old company account and entered into a new engagement with him upon his return to Bristol the next year.§

Aldworth and Elbridge made no settlement at Monhegan until 1628, when the *White Angel* which belonged to the patentees was on the Maine coast and returned to her home port with four hogsheads of furs which had been consigned by Edward Winslow to the London partners, to be sold for the account of Plymouth Colony.

From the proceeds of the sale Elbridge, part owner with Aldworth in the *White Angel*, received, besides freight to Bristol, "125£. taken up at 50£. p. c." interest, computed for the year then elapsed. This loan must have represented the unpaid balance for the goods purchased at Monhegan in the spring of 1627. The colony's quick assets applicable to immediate payment, after it had assumed Thompson's full share of the French merchandise, disclosed a deficiency of some more than one hundred pounds.

The rate of interest paid was not usurious, even for that period, since it only reflected an extremely speculative condition of exchange at Monhegan. In 1625, Bradford complained that trading goods were bought at "deare rates, for they put 40. in ye hundred upon them, for profite and adventure, outward bound; and because of ye vnture of ye paiment homeward, they would have 30. in ye 100. more, which was in all 70. pr. cent."*

While Bradford assigned the year 1626 as the date of the sale at Monhegan, it must have occurred during the last month, ac-

‡ Bradford, 2-141.
§ Aspinwall, 30.
* Bradford, 2-137.

cording to the ancient style of reckoning. The island was sold in March, 1626-7, according to Sylvanus Davis.†

The master of the *White Angel* was Christopher Burkett, who afterwards made many voyages to the Eastern Country in the same vessel. Since the date of the first settlement on the premises was fixed in the patent of Pemaquid at 1628, or three years before its issuance to Aldworth and Elbridge, it is obvious that Burkett brought the first colonists to Monhegan, whence they were transferred later to the mainland.

In the summer of 1630 the *Swift,* which belonged to Thomas Wright, another Bristol merchant associated with the Aldworths, delivered passengers and provisions at Saco and Casco and withdrew to Damariscove and Monhegan islands. Reekes, as master of this vessel, had been instructed by the owner to relade on the coast with fish and train oil and to dispose of ship and cargo to the Portuguese at the West Indies.

The transaction had been prearranged in England but, as that country was then in a state of hostility with Spain and Portugal and the latter was a formidable rival of Great Britain on the sea, such act would have amounted to treason.

However, it happened that Reekes, in a moment of drunken fervor, disclosed his secret orders to a chance acquaintance and they were transmitted to Captain Thomas Witherly, who had arrived at Pascataqua in the *Warwick.* Acting by authority conferred upon him in English letters of marque, Witherly seized the ship at Monhegan and dispatched the crew to London as prisoners of war.

In the fall of 1631 Shurt had removed from Monhegan to the mainland, and the island had resumed its early status as a summer fishing station. According to the account of Winthrop, Pemaquid was on amicable terms with the savage Tarratines beyond Penobscot.

August 8, 1635, Monhegan had assumed so little importance that Richard Mather, who passed it on his way from England to Massachusetts, made only the following comment: "About eight of the clock we all had a clear and comfortable sight of America, and made land again at an island called Menhiggin, an island *without inhabitants,* about thirty-nine leagues northward or northeast short of Cape Ann."‡

† Sullivan, 392.
‡ Young's Mass. Chron., 470.

In January, 1642, eight men from Pascataqua, who had set their course for Pemaquid and were kept at sea for two weeks by adverse winds, "recovered" Monhegan where half of them died from exposure. The survivors "were discovered by a fisherman a good time after, and so brought off the island." There were then no inhabitants at that place.§

The next mention of fishermen at Monhegan was in 1647, when Valentine Hill, of Boston, and Robert Sedgwick, his wife's brother, employed John Devorex, of Marblehead, to manage their fishing operations and maintained boat crews at the island during the ensuing winter and spring. There were some summer fishermen at Monhegan who attorned to the Bristol owner, a fact which is shown by the account of Francis Knight, the agent, in which provisions received by "Monhigan men" were debited and fish delivered by Elias Hoskins were credited to the plantation.*

In the summer of 1648 four Ipswich shallops which had been fishing at Monhegan sought shelter at Damariscove on their return. One of the vessels lost its way in the storm and was capsized with its crew of four Englishmen and an Indian.

The next year Hill and Sedgwick agreed to lade a London ship with fish, and George Croskum, of Gloucester, testified that "he fished at Munhegan with Mr. Hill" and remained upon the island after Devorex had gone. Some swine were left there by the latter, who instructed the deponent and William Lullaby, another fisherman, to ship his property into the "Bay" by John Wilkinson, master of a vessel bound for New Britain. The witness claimed that Matthew Abdy and John Ridgeway had killed and "spent" one of the pigs "in their voyage."†

September 11, 1650, Thomas Elbridge as owner of Monhegan mortgaged it "wth all the houses" to Abraham Shurt and about two months later sold the same premises outright to Richard Russell, of Charlestown. At that time there may have been a few residents on the island, because Ridgeway, who was imprisoned in Massachusetts five years later for a civil debt, tendered his creditors notes signed by men who were supposed to "live at Monhegen."‡

Ten years later the County of Cornwall was organized by the

§ Winthrop, 2-60.
* Essex Rec., 1-216; Suffolk Deeds, 3-101.
† Essex Rec., 1-216, 325.
‡ Suffolk Deeds, 1-131; 2-144; 3-49.

New York government, but no islanders submitted. In 1672, there were fishermen living there and two years afterward a list of eighteen residents was compiled. The names were those of emigrants from Massachusetts or the Dutch Colony. In 1676, refugees from the mainland abandoned the island to the Indians and as late as 1795 Sullivan reported that the place was uninhabited.

PIONEERS

ALDWORTH, MATTHEW, witness, 1649.
BATEMAN, EDWARD, planter; removed to Woolwich, 1639; partner of John Brown; sold remnant of his land at Woolwich to James Cole, 1658.
BROWN, JOHN, mason; bought land from Robinhood at Woolwich with Bateman, 1639; New Harbor, 1654-1676; widow Margaret daughter of Francis Haywood, of Bristol, England; children Elizabeth, Emma, Francis, John, born 1635, and Margaret.
BUCKLAND, GEORGE, fisherman and planter, 1647; lived at Buckland's Neck on Corbin's Sound; wife Elizabeth; submitted to Massachusetts, 1665; children George, born 1630, and, perhaps, John of Wells.
CHAMPNEY, HENRY, planter at Pemaquid, 1639; died after 1665, in possession of Winnegance (East Boothbay); children James, Henry and William.
COCK, WILLIAM, planter, arrived from Bristol in the "White Angel" with Shurt, 1635; lived near New Harbor Hill; died before 1680; ancient homestead laid out to son Thomas, 1686; William, of Cox Head at Sagadahoc, may have been a son.
COLE, JOHN, fisherman at Pemaquid, at an early date; removed to Salem, 1676, and died there the next year; widow survived; only daughter lived at Salem.
DAVISON, NICHOLAS, born 1611; agent of Matthew Cradock at Charlestown, 1639; bought Damariscove, Monhegan and Pemaquid in instalments: from Paul White, April 27, 1653, Thomas Elbridge, April 14, 1657, and Richard Russell, July 21, 1657; Pemaquid, 1658; lived, died and was buried on the west side of Pemaquid Harbor, 1664; widow Joanna married Richard Kent; children Sarah (Lynde), born December 31, 1647, Daniel, born January 9, 1650-1.
DRAPER, NATHANIEL, merchant at Pemaquid, 1649; probably son of Nathaniel, the Indian trader of New Haven, who died in Virginia, 1647; Sheepscot, 1654; killed by Indians, 1689; widow Esther married Robert Scott; children Elizabeth (Stevens), Esther (Roberts), born 1655 and spared by the Indians in their attack upon Sheepscot, 1689, Lydia (Whittemore, Richardson) and Nathaniel.
ELBRIDGE, THOMAS, son of Gyles, the patentee, and Rebecca; a minor in 1646; took possession at Pemaquid, 1649; died in Spring Plantation, Liguanee, Parish of Saint Andrew, Barbadoes, 1682; children Aldworth, Elizabeth (Russell), born 1652, Gyles, John, Rebecca (Saunders), born 1659, Robert and Thomas.
HOSKINS, ELIAS, fisherman at Pemaquid, 1647; witness, 1653; son may have been John, of Pemaquid, who married Ruth Davis and was taxed at Jamestown, 1687.
KNIGHT, FRANCIS, brother of Robert, of Bristol, born 1610; overseer at Pemaquid, 1640-9; living there, 1669.
NORMAN, MATTHEW, planter, 1640; may have been the witness intended but transcribed as Newman in the Brown deed of 1625.

SHURT, ABRAHAM, born 1582; merchant of Bristol, England, who acted for Aldworth and Elbridge at Monhegan, 1627; Pemaquid, 1631-1646; Charlestown, 1653-1662.
TOOGOOD, RICHARD, trader, 1647; deceased 1651; his child may have been Edward of Berwick.

SAMOSET

There stands, far-off upon the hill,
    Upreared against the evening sky,
Tall and erect, unkempt and still—
    Like the lone wolf about to die—
        The wraith of Samoset.

Where he was born, or reared, or trained,
    Or what his creed, or if he thought
The forest empire where he reigned
    Should be supreme, it matters not;
        He was indeed a man.

His "Welcome Englishmen" survives
    As sentiment of after years,
And in its sway the nation thrives
    And world-wide malice disappears
        With universal peace.

His was no hope, no subtle plan,
    To conquer; his, no racial lore,
But just the call of man to man
    That seeks afar and evermore
        The sympathy of men.

The mist-wreaths wind along the lea
    And hide the form of Samoset;
The moon upon a silver sea,
    His crescent bark, sails onward yet—
        To westward and alone. *

---

* It was a belief of the American Indian, derived undoubtedly from the apparent movements of the celestial bodies, that at death the soul "goes up westward." N. Y. Doc. Hist., 3-29.)

MUSCONGUS RIVER

An Indian name for Muscongus River was Ananawapeske. The region about Round Pond was called Amobscot.

This part of the country was the patrimony of Samoset, an Indian sagamore who was always loyal to the English. His attitude towards strangers was one of intimate helpfulness. His favorite locality was Muscongus, also known as Hog and Samoset, Island. At Monhegan he met and strove to converse with the early fishermen in their own languages.

While at the island in 1619, and the following year, he had met Thomas Dermer, the employe of Gorges. The contact may have been as late as June 30, for on that date Dermer wrote to a friend in England. At that time the explorer had just returned in an open boat from Virginia where he had spent the winter. He had been in conflict with the hostile Indians of Cape Cod, whence he and one friendly native had escaped to Monhegan with many severe wounds. He did not remain long on the Maine coast since his critical condition soon compelled him to seek the South.

Samoset knew the circumstances and may have accompanied the explorer on his last voyage; at any rate, he reported the death of Gorges' agent to the first planters of New Plymouth March 16, 1620-1. Mourt then described him as "a Savage" who "was not of these parts, but of Morattiggon, and one of the Sagamores or Lords thereof." It was claimed by the visitor that in order to reach his country they would require "a dayes sayle with a great wind, and five dayes by land." He had already lived for eight months in their vicinity. In 1624, Samoset was an honored guest of Captain Levett at Casco, which was not his residence at that time.

The first occupation by the English was on the westerly side of Muscongus River. The first farm above New Harbor was purchased from Samoset by Richard Pearce January 9, 1641-2. The witnesses to this conveyance were John Brown and Richard Shute.*

Pearce married Elizabeth, eldest daughter of John Brown,

* N. E. Hist. Gen. Reg., 13-365.

and their children were recognized later as legal heirs of the Brown estate. The older children of Pearce claimed Muscongus Island as a special endowment from Samoset.

The Pearce homestead was situated at Round Pond, twelve miles above New Harbor, and at Passage Point, about two miles farther, was another concession from Samoset to Richard Fulford, who had married Elizabeth, daughter of Richard and Elizabeth Pearce. This deed was dated June 1, 1653, and witnessed by John Brown, Thomas Cole, John Hayman, Richard Pearce and Philip Swadden.†

Only one month later Samoset conferred title to one thousand acres at Saggohannago upon William England, William Parnell and Thomas Way. The latter had been a fisherman at Cape Neddock, but all were resident at Pemaquid at the date of the deed.‡

John Brown, who had witnessed two of the preceding conveyances, removed from Nequasseag (Woolwich) to New Harbor after 1654. At that date he was living at Woolwich, where he took the oath of allegiance to Plymouth Colony with other settlers on the Sagadahoc River. He appears to have been living at New Harbor in 1658, but he had not resided there long, because the deed in which he disposed of his last interest at Woolwich described him as "lately of Negausseg, and now of Pemaquid, planter."§

The Samoset deed, which purported to have conveyed to Brown a large tract of land above New Harbor at an early date, was discredited by the eldest son. While its acknowledgement by Shurt was dated July 24, 1626, the capacity of the magistrate was not indicated. Although he was a "servant" of Aldworth and Elbridge he had no civil authority in this country and there is no evidence of his presence at Pemaquid on that date. His first act was the purchase of Monhegan, which according to Sylvanus Davis took place in March, 1627.*

Another ancient conveyance of English origin was that of Thomas Elbridge, son of the Pemaquid patentee, who was described as "of Aldertown" (Pemaquid), to John Dollen, "of Mont Hegon," fisherman. It was in the form of a lease for ninety-nine years, dated August 1, 1669, and witnessed by Henry Champney and Francis Knight. The consideration was three gallons of

† York Deeds, 12-323.
‡ Me. Hist. Col., 5-188.
§ York Deeds, 35-55.
* York Deeds, 20 85

"strong water," and the description embraced a parcel of land "neare the River commonly called by the Name of Muscongus to the Valuation of Fower Hundred Acres * * * Seated at a place there commonly called by the Name of the Round Pond Limited within these Bounds following: vizt. on a Small River lying on the North or North East Side thereof & extending unto the Edge or Bounds of a Parcel of Land now in the Tennor and Possession of Thomas Cole of Pemaquid."†

The Samoset deeds were descriptive of tracts which terminated at Pemaquid River as their westerly boundary, beyond

THE SITE OF BROWN'S HOUSE AT NEW HARBOR

which were the lands at Damariscotta, subsequently occupied by the younger John Brown, Robert Scott and Thomas Kimball.

The homestead of John Brown was presumed by the early French colonists to mark the boundary between New England and Acadia, as established by the patent of Alexander in 1635, and was referred to as "La Maison de Jean bron qui fait la limite des terres de la Majesté d'avec celles de la nouvelle Angleterre."‡

A conveyance from one of his descendants described "the Homestead that was formerly John Browns of New Harbr Decd" as located "at the Head of sd Harbour where said Brown House & Garden formerly was." The entire tract contained but twelve

† York Deeds, 21-57.
‡ Me. Doc. Hist., 4-428.

acres and was situated at the extremity of the inlet on both sides of a creek known as "Western Brook."§

In 1671, when Massachusetts completed its Merrimac survey on a course due east from Upper Clapboard Island in Casco Bay, that province claimed the islands of New and Old Damariscove, Monhegan, Matinicus, Metinic and Saint George, with southerly sections of Harpswell, Phippsburg, Georgetown, Cape Newagen and Pemaquid. It was not stated whether the dwelling of Brown at New Harbor fell within that division or not, but the mere establishment of a boundary was a challenge to the title of New York as well as the pretentions of the French Government.*

PIONEERS

DENNING, NICHOLAS, planter at Pumpkin Cove, married Emma, daughter of John Brown, of New Harbor; children Agnes (Doliber), Emma (Elwell), Elizabeth (Paine), Mary (Stevens), George, Nicholas and William.

FULFORD, RICHARD, planter at Round Pond, where he bought land of Samoset, 1653; married Elizabeth, daughter of Richard Pearce, of Muscongus; children Elizabeth (Martin) and Francis of Marblehead.

PEARCE, RICHARD, carpenter, bought land from Samoset at Muscongus, 1642; married Elizabeth, daughter of John Brown, of New Harbor; children John, born at Pemaquid, 1644. Richard, born 1647, Elizabeth (Fulford), Francis, Joseph, Margaret (Ward), Mary (Hamlin), Sarah (Stockwell), William and George, born 1666.

§ York Deeds, 16-216.
* Mass. Col. Rec., 4-2, 696.

SAINT GEORGE'S RIVER

In 1605, George Waymouth, under patronage of the Earl of Arundel, sailed from Bristol in the *Archangel* with a crew of twenty-nine men and boys, most of whom had been recruited from the banks of the Thames.

He first sighted the eastern extremity of Nantucket, but pursued a northerly course for three days until "about sixe a clocke at night" on May 17, when land was discovered to the north-northeast which "appeared a meane high" island "some six miles in compasse."

This landfall was Monhegan and it afforded an unobstructed view of "the maine land from the West-South-West to the East-North-East" and for a great distance "up into the maine," where the Camden Hills, described as "very high mountaines" were visible above the low surrounding country. Here Waymouth erected a cross and named the place Saint George's Island.

From that point the vessel moved inland "in the rode directly with the mountaines, about three leagues," where among the group of islands at the mouth of Saint George's River was found a safe anchorage in "ten fathoms upon a clay oaze very tough." This haven was found to lie in 43 degrees and 20 minutes of northern latitude and was named Pentecost Harbor by the explorers, in grateful recognition of the day of their safe arrival.

The vessel was anchored near an island where the explorers found water, evidences of fire and cooked foods. There they assembled a pinnace which had been brought from England and with it made excursions to the vicinity of Thomaston, where a second cross was erected at the western trend of the river. Several voyages to New Harbor and Pemaquid, a distance estimated at four marine leagues, indicated that their rendezvous was Allen's Island. Waymouth embarked from Saint George's River June 16, and arrived at Dartmouth July 18, after a quick passage with no untoward events.*

The Indian name of Saint George's River was not mentioned by Rosier in his account of Waymouth's voyage, but, on an Eng-

* 3 Mass. Hist. Col., 8-129.

lish map of 1610, it was engraved "Tahanock" and the place where the second cross was erected, at the head of the inland bay above Thomaston, was marked by intersecting lines. In the census of Moashan it may have been misspelled but was rendered "Ramassoc." For positive identification of Waymouth's river, posterity is indebted to Briggs' Map of 1625, whereon the explorer's name was assigned to the first stream west of the Penobscot.†

The Earl of Arundel had intended to use the information secured by Waymouth in his discoveries to found a colony on the Northern Coast, but the exigencies of public political life would not permit him to proceed with the project. However, the relation of Rosier was published in London after his return and its favorable reception helped to stimulate a growing sentiment for immediate occupation by the Northern Company.

Yet the enterprise required more time than had been expected and a whole year intervened before adequate funds were subscribed and colonists provided. It is probable that members of the Sagadahoc Colony took with them a copy of Rosier's "Relation" or had discussed the subject with Waymouth or some of his seamen.

At any rate, after separation by adverse storms, their vessels met near the same point at Saint George's Island, where they believed they had identified "a Crosse Sett up the wch * * * was Sett up by George Wayman." Evidently, none of Waymouth's crew was present with the expedition to prove the fact.

From their island anchorage the colonists made a survey of the neighboring country and twice visited Pemaquid Harbor, whence Skidwaros, who was with them, and others had been deported by Waymouth, two years before. The account of the prospective colonists stated that they "rowed to the Weste in amongst many gallant Illands and found the ryver of pemaquyd to be but 4 leags weste from the Illand we Call St. Georges whear our ships remained still att anckor." After preliminary inspection and inquiry from the natives the colonists decided to proceed to the west.

The region about the mouth of Saint George's River was occupied by Salem colonists at an early date. Thomas Leverett, as trustee for the Massachusetts colony, was an owner in Muscongus

† Purchase, 14 424.

Patent. In 1630, which was the year when the grant was made, Roger Conant, Anthony Dike, Francis Johnson and Peter Palfrey formed a partnership at Salem for the purpose of "trading to the Eastward." Johnson was chosen manager and Dike master of their vessel.

SAINT GEORGE'S RIVER ABOVE PORT CLYDE

A plantation was begun on the west side of the river at Saquid Point, where Johnson was engaged in fishing, planting and trading with the Indians and English fishermen. An account of their property specified a "house with the debts due from the Indians" and "swine, boat, skiff, canoe, housall stuff and trading goods."‡

In 1632, according to the narrative of Roger Clap, the vessel of Anthony Dike and its master were captured by Dixie Bull and his confederates at the Eastward, after they had pillaged Pemaquid. The pirates insisted upon transportation to Virginia, but Dike declined to undertake the voyage on the ground that he was not familiar with the southern coast.§

April 15, 1633, Richard Foxwell, who had lived formerly at Dorchester, Massachusetts, returned to Pascataqua from Plymouth, England, in the fishing vessel of John Corbin, and July 16, following, acquired the plantation at Saint George's River.

‡ Essex Rec., 2-22.
§ Young's Mass. Chron., 362.

He complained subsequently that when he bought the premises at Saquid Point he had been guaranteed a confirmation of title from the Massachusetts government.

At the time of Waymouth's voyage to Saint George, Rosier had reported that among other commodities on the islands about Pentecost Harbor he found "spruce trees of excellent timber and height, able to mast ships of great burthen." Oak was mentioned as one of the products, but not pine, and it is still a fir country, where annual harvests of Christmas trees supply western market. Upon the hills on the mainland he observed "notable high timber trees, masts for ships of 400 tun."

The first allusion to the mast industry at the Eastward was made by Winthrop who mentioned a ship of Barnstable and the *Hercules* of Dover, which in the summer of 1634 "returned by St. George's to cut masts to carry to England."*

This statement disclosed that the English navy was being supplied with masts from Central Maine two years before shipbuilding was contemplated at Richmond Island or Saco. The timber may have been cut by the crews of the vessels or by some of the planters who were then occupying the trading house at Saquid Point.

The French seized the Plymouth trading post at Machabitticus about the first of August, 1635. The nearest English settlement was the house of Foxwell at Saquid Point, which was situated "about three score myles" westward.†

Saint George's Harbor was not molested by the enemy that year because it was occupied by English fishing vessels. Winthrop asserted that during the great storm of August 15, 1635, when the *Angel Gabriel* was destroyed at Pemaquid, John Witheridge, of Barnstable, and ships from Dartmouth were forced to cut their masts at Saint George's River. After the fishing vessels were gone Foxwell was at the mercy of the French and withdrew to Saco. The next year he visited Castine to confer with them in relation to future occupation of his premises at Saquid Point.‡

In 1701, Sylvanus Davis asserted that Foxwell had been a settler at Saquid Point as early as 1641. John Brown, of Pemaquid, also claimed "Lands at a place called Sawk Head" (Saquid)

* Winthrop, 1-134.
† Ford's Bradford, 2-108.
‡ 4 Mass. Hist. Col., 6-570.

"at the mouth of St Georges River about Three Leagues Eastward of New Harbr."§

According to Davis, the early settler on the eastern side of the river was Philip Swadden, who came thither from Pascataqua River about 1650 and resided at Quisquamego. Until 1654, however, the French were in control of the district beyond Pemaquid.*

It is significant that Swadden did not submit to Massachusetts jurisdiction at Sagadahoc in 1654, or elsewhere in the East. His residence at Quisquamego, or Sisquamego, was beyond the recognized bounds of Maine. The first and last trace of the pioneer east of Sagadahoc River was his signature on an Indian deed to Sylvanus Davis. The instrument conveyed land above the Oyster Beds at Damariscotta and Edward Bateman, of Woolwich, was present with him.

The earliest occupations at Saint George were fishing, cutting masts and trading with the natives, and posterity is indebted to John Jocelyn for his remarkable story of one of Foxwell's eastern business trips.

In 1656, after two years' disseizin, the French regained constructive possession of the river, but no fort was built there for a long time. However, in 1686, a commission recommended that some form of protection was necessary on account of the proximity of the place to the English. The decision was that "Un fort y seroit fort necessaire Estant le post le plus voisin des Anglois."

That Saint George had been abandoned by the English at an early date is plain. In 1727, Loron, a distinguished Penobscot Indian, stated that there was then but one "truck-house" or fort on the whole river. With relation to foreign occupation he said: "We do not remember of any settlements at St. George's, we remember a pretty while, and as long as we remember, the Place where the Garrison stands was filled with Great Long Grown Trees."†

§ York Deeds, 20-85.
* Essex Rec., 2-25.
† Me. Hist. Col., 3-390.

THE LOST PROVINCE

    Fabled city of the East
        Hidden in a wilderness,
    Where the golden hours obsess;
    Where the Indian princes feast
        And the princesses caress.
    Found but once in ancient times
        By romantic Spanish dons,
    Who exalted it in rhymes
        Over flowing demijohns.

    Norumbega, still obscure,
        Still enchanted in romance,
    Where all distances enhance,
    Where illusions all endure
        And all mysteries entrance;
    From thy void of olden days
        Men are carving greater things;
    From thy wilderness they raise
        Cities unsubdued by kings.

PENOBSCOT RIVER

This river was discovered by Portuguese and Spanish navigators early in the Sixteenth Century. The name Norumbega, given to the region by explorers and first mentioned by Ramunsio in 1537, was derived from that of an Indian village near Old Town, where was located the wigwam of the Bashaba, or king of Moashan.

Like other great rivers in Maine it was frequented by fur hunters many years before any settlement was established by Europeans, but in 1555 Durand de Villegagnon undertook to found a French colony in North America, which was then known as "Florida" by Spanish mariners. The location selected by him was at Norumbega, otherwise known as "Agoncy" by the natives and Pentagoet by the French. Its great water system was designated "Grand River" by map makers of the period and comprised Penobscot River and Bay.

Several years later Andre Thevet, companion of Villegagnon and official historiographer for the French king, who had traversed the Maine coast in 1556, wrote his impressions of Penobscot River and asserted that "upon its banks the French formerly erected a little fort about ten or twelve leagues from its mouth, which was surrounded by fresh-water, and the place was named the Fort of Norumbegue." This was the station of Villegagnon.*

Eleven years later Rene Laudonniere, who had served as an officer under Ribault in 1565, began a plantation at Saint Mary's River, in the present state of Florida.

November 8, 1603, Henry Fourth, of France, granted land on the Bay of Fundy to Sieur de Monts, who took possession of Dochet Island in Saint Croix River in 1604, but due to general dissatisfaction with that situation transferred his colony across the bay to Port Royal, now known as Annapolis, the next spring.

From Port Royal emanated other settlements, which reoccupied the island in the Saint Croix, in 1611, and soon after began a new plantation at Saint Sauveur on Mount Desert Island. The pioneers alluded to their province as "Nova Francia," a name

* Me. Doc. Hist., 1-416.

which had been assigned by Jacques Cartier upon discovery. However, French plans for expansion were interrupted by Virginians who were fishing on the coast during the summer after the southerly post at Mount Desert had been established. The English fishermen learned of the existence of the colony at Saint Sauveur from the Indians and, under leadership of Sir Samuel

DOCHET ISLAND, SAINT CROIX RIVER

Argal, proceeded to disrupt that and all neighboring settlements about the Bay of Fundy. The victorious fleet sailed for Virginia November 9, 1613. The captives were extradited, but refugees secured protection among the natives with whom they afterwards lived and intermarried.

Due to intimate relations with them, the disbanded colonists became expert dealers in furs and traded arms and ammunition with the Indians at exorbitant prices. In 1614, Captain Smith reported that the eastern natives stood in such great fear of the French that they importuned him to locate among them, suggesting as an inducement that he and a dozen assistants could regulate the whole northern trade.

September 10, 1621, Sir William Alexander became interested in the decadent fortunes of New France and obtained a grant of that territory which he renamed New Scotland, or Nova

Scotia. There occurred, however, an interim of several years before colonization of his Western Province could be undertaken. In the meantime, a memorial was presented to the English monarch by Count de Tillieres, the French ambassador, in 1624, in which demands were revived for the peaceable restitution of New France on the grounds of original discovery and colonization. The answer of the respondents, which was dictated by Gorges at the king's request, contained the gist of the contention and was expressed in the following paragraph: "It is argued that the pretensions of the French can only date from the discoveries made by Jacques de Cartier, and the foundation of a plantation at a place called Tadousac, by Champlain. Sir William Alexander's patent is also quoted and the right of Mons. Poutrincourt to the possession or settlement of any of those parts disputed." The colonies "planted by M. M. Villegagnon and René Loudonnière, from which they were expelled by the Spaniards," were declared to have been ineffectual to subvert English Claims.†

Gorges, who was recognized by the king and parliament as the highest authority on foreign relations, complimented himself upon the completeness of his answer and the resultant fact that for many years no further argument was advanced. Indeed, when the contention again arose it was only possible to settle it by a resort to arms.

According to Gorges, it was only at the urgent solicitation of his sovereign that he had been induced to part with his own rights in Northern Maine, then recognized as Canada County. Hence, it was with his acquiescence that the elder Alexander, in 1627, completed the organization of an English association, styled "The Merchant Adventurers of Canada," and began to recruit volunteers to found a colony in the New World. About one hundred of both sexes had been enlisted for the enterprise when King Charles issued the "pass," or commission, for the settlement of New Scotland. The royal edict was signed March 26, 1628.

At the call to embark some of the subscribers failed to respond for transportation privileges and were penalized subsequently, but the remainder amounting to about seventy were put in charge of William, son of the proprietor, and conveyed to Port Royal, where they constructed a fortification on the Granville shore.

In England the experiment of the Canada Adventurers and

† Sainsbury's Col. Pap., 1-61, 119.

the departure of the ship were attended with much publicity and followed with interest. Like Alexander himself the colonists, principally of Scotch extraction, expected to acquire wealth in the fur industry as well as agriculture.

For many years British fishing vessels had passed and repassed the Acadian shores without taking the time to investigate their resources; but at this particular juncture merchants of Bristol, who were operating in the vicinity of Monhegan, did not favor the establishment of a Scottish plantation in the East, because they had been accustomed to seine for herring and mackerel in Penobscot waters and to trade with the Etechemins about the Bay of Fundy.

Accordingly, it was not surprising that in April, of the year that the Scotch colony arrived at Port Royal, Edward Ashley should be sent from Bristol to Penobscot and furnished by merchants and relatives of that port with merchandise to be sold to the natives on a commission basis. One of these Bristol merchants was Thomas Wright.

The new trader adopted the French methods of living with the Indians and dealing in contraband articles. Such practices had been forbidden by royal edict, but Ashley excused his conduct on the ground that he had found eastern tribes already in possession of arms and ammunition, which they had obtained from French merchants.

Ashley's claim of French lawlessness was supported by a contemporary authority who, writing in 1628, deplored the fact that "Those Indeans to ye east parts, which had comerce with ye French, got peces of them, and they in ye end made a commone trade of it; and in time our English fisher-men, led with ye like covetoussnes, followed their example, for their owne gaine; but upon complainte against them, it pleased the kings majestie to prohibite ye same by a stricte proclamation, commanding that no sorte of armes, or munition, should by any of his subjects be traded with them."‡

Although Ashley was associated with Bristol trading interests at Monhegan far to the west, the proximity of the Scotch on the other side gave him some sense of security. At Port Royal, however, Alexander's colonists found the Indians adverse to trade, on account of the prejudice which had been created by their

‡ Bradford, 2-158.

predecessors, and advised the adventurers in England to that effect. The result was that, early in the year following the arrival of the new colony, Admiral David Kirke appeared off the Northern Coast with an armed fleet. By this means all alien opposition in the country was soon reduced and, due to losses of war and extradition, a surrender of Canadian territory to the English was effected July 19, 1629.

During the fall of this year Ashley returned to Bristol, either with, or in the wake of, the victorious squadron. In a deposition, dated February 11, 1631-2, he testified that "about 4 years past he first went to New England to inhabit, and stayed ther about sixteen monethes." This would fix the time of his departure at some time in August.§

Bradford reported that during the sojourn of this eastern trader he had "lived amonge ye Indeans as a savage, & wente naked amongst them, and used their maners (in wch time he got their language)." Ashley's own version of the experience was that he had been located "among the Indyans about three score myles from the Englishe," at a place called Machabitticus.

Ordinarily, two months were required for passage to England and Ashley remained there five months, in which interval he induced the Council of Plymouth, despite much opposition from Salem interests, to grant a concession at Muscongus, which extended as far west as the river of that name and included Machabitticus. The patent was issued March 13, 1629-30, but not in Ashley's name; it was ceded to John Beauchamp, of London, and Thomas Leverett, of Boston, England.

Beauchamp was associated with Richard Andrews, Timothy Hatherly and James Sherley, all of London. Leverett represented the Salem partners, including Matthew Cradock, John Humphrey, Isaac Johnson and John Winthrop.*

March 19, 1629-30, Sherley wrote to their associates at New Plymouth: "We have thought good to joyne with one Edward Ashley (a man I thinke yt some of you know); but it is only of yt place wherof he hath a patente in Mr. Beachamps name."†

The Salem contingent had insisted upon participation in the enterprise because they were convinced that Ashley would "strip them of all trade in those parts." Relatives of Ashley and mer-

§ Ford's Bradford. 2-179. note.
* Mass. Hist. Col.. 3-72.
† Bradford. 2-169.

chants of Bristol, including Thomas Wright, who had been interested in his former venture, were also anxious to refinance him in anticipation of large profits. However, only William Peirce, who had agreed to transport the company's employes and provisions, and New Plymouth, which was already engaged in eastern trade, were admitted to the commercial undertaking. Thomas Willett was chosen by the colony to represent its interests and the rest of the company, besides Ashley, consisted of a carpenter and four or five laborers. They took with them from Bristol a new boat and materials to construct another.

Peirce who was bound for Salem, but had promised to "bend his course," landed Ashley's party at Penobscot late in May.

After their arrival a substantial house was built near the margin of the river and supplied with merchandise for sale or exchange. This was the only building constructed by these traders at Machabitticus, and they relied solely upon small arms for defence.

Isaac Allerton was not merely a partner, but the chief advocate for the company's plan to establish Ashley and keep him stocked with goods for trading purposes. He came from Bristol with Peirce in the *Lyon* and after the colonists had been landed at Penobscot proceeded thence to New Plymouth. On his way westward Allerton engaged Captain John Wright, who then was quartered at Monhegan, to transport supplies in his shallop from New Plymouth to Ashley at Penobscot. This action was in accord with the request of Sherley, that the colony should furnish all the aid it could "either by men, commodities, or boats."

Wright was interested also in the arrival of the *Swift* at the Eastward. That vessel, which belonged to his brother Thomas Wright, of Bristol, had been dispatched by the owner, in company with Allerton and Vines, with passengers and provisions for Saco and Casco, where it was instructed to relade with fish and train oil.

Allerton, who had just traversed the eastern fishing grounds, accompanied Wright in his shallop as a passenger for Pemaquid, where there appeared to be the best prospect of securing a return cargo for the *Swift*. June 12, they were leaving Salem harbor just as Winthrop arrived and held a consultation on board the latter's ship. June 25, Allerton, Wright and Stephen Reekes, master of the *Swift,* witnessed the certificate of possession which was executed at Saco by Vines. Soon after, the *Swift* was taken at Monhegan as a prize of war.

Bradford reported that, as soon as Ashley had been landed at Penobscot, he wrote "& afterwards came" to New Plymouth, "to be supplyed with Wampampeake, corne against winter, and other things." His first supply was bound for Machabitticus about the middle of September, when Wright's shallop left passengers at Pullin Point on its way eastward.‡

With the resumption of trade at the Eastward Ashley was confronted with new competition. Sir William Alexander had not been inactive and April 30, 1630, had conferred upon Claude La Tour, a French Protestant, a large concession of territory extending eastward from the "Cloven Cape" about Cape Sable. Upon the premises thus acquired La Tour established a fort and settlement that year. The site is still distinguishable in the name of Port Latour in Barrington Bay.

The new French colonists sponsored by Alexander and the members of the first settlement about the Bay of Fundy, some of whom had lived among the natives and traveled inland with them, retained a monopoly of trade with the Indians. The further fact that French dealers were not prohibited from bartering weapons with the warlike tribes was in their favor.

Ashley, on account of previous experience, undertook to match such competition in kind. For this purpose he had imported rapier blades, guns, powder and lead. The result was soon apparent, for, to quote Bradford, "Ashley, being well supplyed, had quickly gathered a good parcell of beaver, and like a crafty pate he sent it all home, and would not pay for ye goods he had had of ye plantation hear, but lett them stand still on ye score, and tooke up still more." The complaint of the colony was that the London partners, on account of Ashley's larger volume of business with the natives and the advice of Allerton, "cast more how to supplie him then ye plantation."

The same historian added: "They were forct to buy him a barke allso, and to furnish her wth a mr. & men, to transporte his corne & provisions (of which he put of much); for ye Indeans of those parts have no corne growing, and at harvest, after corne is ready, ye weather grows foule, and ye seas dangerous, so as he could doe litle good with his shallope for yt purposs."§

‡ Mass. Col. Rec., 1-61.
§ Bradford, 2-174.

The scarcity of cereals in Northern Maine was explained by Pory at Damariscove in 1622. He reported that as for "Corne they set none in their parts toward the north, and that is the cause why Indian corne, pease and such like is the best trucke for their skinnes, and then in winter especiallie when hunger doth most pinch them, which is the season when the French do use to trade with them."

The bark provided for Ashley was the *White Angel*, purchased in 1631 from Alderman Aldworth, one of the Pemaquid proprietors, at Bristol, but early in May, before that vessel had arrived in New England, he was apprehended for selling dangerous weapons to the Indians.

Depositions of Plymouth employes at Castine, relating to his offence, were taken before Governor Walter Neal and Henry Keyes, master of the *Pide Cow* and deputy of the governor. The first hearing was conducted before Neal at Saco, July 19, 1631, and disclosed the names of Oliver Callow, John Deacon, James Downs, Thomas Richards, a servant who had died before the investigation, Henry Sampson and George Watson, as the earliest English residents of Machabitticus.

Isaac Allerton, who shortly before had arrived with a cargo of cattle at that port, was an interested observer, but was discharging his vessel in Boston Harbor three days later. Ambrose Gibbons, of Pascataqua, Vines and Lewis, of Saco, and Leonard Yeo, of Virginia, witnessed the proceedings.

A second hearing appears to have been conducted by Captain Keyes at Castine, in the presence of Vines, on July 30. There the deponents were William Phipps and Thomas Willett, the New Plymouth factor. Captions of proceedings described Ashley as a "late inhabitant of new England," and the deposition of "a servaunt" alleged that the respondent had been "forewarned and Advised by Captayne Neale and the governour of new Plymouth not to trade either armes or munition yett not withstanding since that time he traded with some Indians powder and shott."*

From the evidence adduced at the trial it was apparent that, "not long befoere Christmas when Edward Ashley went to New Plymouth," he had been admonished by the two governors to refrain from trading dangerous commodities with the natives.

* Mass. Hist. Proc., 45-493.

Only eleven days before the holiday Neal was in Boston in conference with the authorities.†

Some of the testimony was to the effect that "not long before Christmas" and "since Christmas," 1630, the trader had openly persisted in trucking contraband at the Eastward. With this express object in view he had imported prohibited articles since his first advent in the country.

After his arrest local authorities, of whom Neal was chief, undertook to confiscate a thousand pounds of beaver, from Ashley's accumulated stock, as a penalty for malfeasance, but finally acceded to the claims of Plymouth Colony and released the property.

According to the statement of the New Plymouth historian, the outcome of the investigation was that the respondent "was taken in a trape * * * for trading powder & shote with ye Indeans; and was ceased upon by some in authoritie, who allso would have confiscated above a thousand weight of beaver; but ye goods were freed, for ye Govr here made it appere, by a bond under Ashleys hand, wherin he was bound to them in 500 li. not to trade any munition with ye Indeans, or other wise to abuse him selfe; it was allso manifest against him that he had comited uncleannes with Indean women (things that they feared at his first imployment, which made them take this strict course with him in ye begining) ; so, to be shorte, they gott their goods freed, but he was sent home prisoner."‡

Ashley testified that he was deported in October following his arrest. Where he was confined during the interim was not indicated, nor is it known who was his bailiff but, probably, he was imprisoned on some fishing vessel off the coast. At the instance of the President and Council for New England, he was tried before a commissioner in England, where he was released under bonds, but never revisited America. He is reported to have died while returning from Russia, where he had been engaged in a similar employment by another trading company.

At the end of 1631 Allerton and Peirce sold their interests at Machabitticus to Plymouth Colony and the other partners withdrew from active participation in trade. The station, afterwards maintained wholly at the expense of agents of the colony and

† Winthrop, 1-38.
‡ Bradford, 2-179.

in charge of Thomas Willett, was regarded as the sole property of New Plymouth.

Soon after the subjugation of Canada by Kirke the English king was importuned to restore Port Royal to the One Hundred Associates, and on account of his marital and religious connections with France the foreign influences prevailed. In the case of Quebec there was some excuse for such compliance with international rules of comity, since the treaty of peace between England and France had been concluded April 24, and the conquest had not been completed until July 19, 1629, when the two nations had ceased to be belligerents.

Port Royal, however, presented different legal aspects, for it had been occupied by Scotch immigrants in time of war as a *vacuum domicilium*. July 4, 1631, after special consideration, the king agreed to transfer all sovereignty in that colony to French claimants, and six days later he ordered the Scotch settlers to evacuate the premises under the direction of Andros Forrester, the commander of the garrison at Granville. At the same time he requested Sir William Alexander to instruct Sir George Home "to demolish the Fort that was builded by your son there, and to remove all the people, goods, ordnance, ammunition, cattle and other things, belonging unto that colonie, leaving the bounds thereof altogether waste and unpeopled, as it was at the time your son landed first to plant there, by virtue of our commission."§

The royal orders were not executed that year, but the French assumed an attitude of supremacy in the territory forthwith. The premises at Machabitticus, however, were not molested until 1632, and trading continued to prosper there in the meantime. The location was ideal for that purpose. Cammock, writing to Trelawney from Richmond Island, drew a comparison in this respect between the western and eastern sections of Maine. His complaint was: "As for trade heer itt doth decay every yeare more and more * * * All the good that is to bee done in thes partes, for trade, is towards the Eastwarde * * * allmost to the Scotts plantation."

March 27, 1632, the One Hundred Associates made arrangements with Isaac de Razilly, as their attorney, "to go and receive restitution at the hands of the English and put the company of

§ Murdoch's Nova Scotia, 1-80.

New France in possession." As a retainer for this service Razilly was invested with a concession of land, centered on the

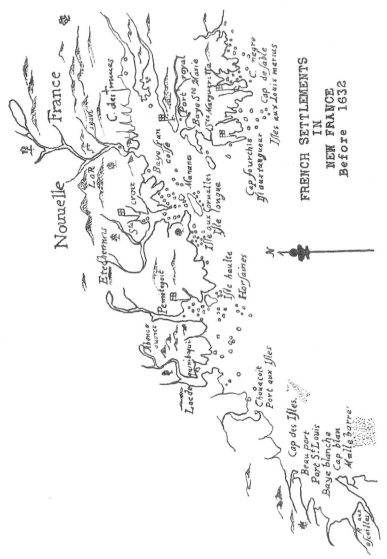

Saint Croix River, extending for twelve leagues along the coast and twenty leagues inland.

Two days later the terms of restoration were incorporated in the treaty of Saint-Germain-en-Laye. Razilly's commission "to make the Scotch and other subjects of Great Britain withdraw" was signed May 10, and he embarked soon after for Canada in a vessel which had been provided by the French Government. The Hundred Associates, who had been active agents in French development, still claimed the coast as far south as the forty-third degree of latitude by virtue of the original grant from Henry Fourth. Charles d'Aulnay, as lieutenant for Razilly, stated that when his superior first came to New France, to take possession of the country, he had orders "to clear the coast unto Pemaquid and Kenebeck of all persons whatever, and to cause them to withdraw, if there were any habitation seated on this side."*

It is evident that one of Razilly's vessels preceded him on the northern coast that spring and had been given special instructions to locate and displant the English settlements to the west of Cape Sable. The advance party fixed its headquarters at La Have and secured preliminary information about the English trading posts from countrymen in the vicinity, who were anxious to eliminate competition.

It did not seem wise to interfere with the tranquillity of Saint George or Pemaquid, because Massachusetts merchants, who visited the Indian resorts, and Bristol fishing masters, who frequented the region annually, would not permit retention for more than one season. On the other hand, an open act of war by known combatants might provoke direct retaliation from the British Government. Since it was nearest and contained a large assortment of merchandise which was readily convertible into needed funds, the New Plymouth post was made the objective.

June 14, 1632, it was reported at Boston that "The French came in a pinnace to Penobscot, and rifled a trucking house belonging to Plimouth, carrying thence three hundred weight of beaver and other goods. They took also one Dixy Bull and his shallop and goods."†

The account of the Plymouth historian was more explicit and described the method of operation. The Scotch accomplice was the sole survivor of Alexander's colony at Port Royal, which was about to be transferred to the French. The name of the "false

* 3 Mass. Hist. Col., 7-94.
† Winthrop, 1-79.

Scott" may have been William Hart, who advised Abraham Shurt of the French plans to seize Pemaquid three years later.

The story is as follows: "This year their house at Penobscott was robed by ye French, and all their goods of any worth they carried away, to ye value of 400 or 500 li. as ye cost first peny worth; in beaver 300 li. waight; and ye rest in trading goods, as coats, ruggs, blankett, biskett, &c. It was in this maner.

"The mr. of ye house, and parte of ye company with him, were come with their vessell to ye westward to fetch a supply of goods which was brought over for them. In ye mean time comes a smale French ship into ye harbore (and amongst ye company was a false Scott); they pretended they were nuly come from ye sea, and knew not wher they were, and that their vesell was very leake, and desired they might hale her a shore and stop their leaks. And many French complements they used, and congees they made; and in ye ende, seeing but 3. or 4. simple men, yt were servants, and by this Scoth-man understanding that ye maister & ye rest of ye company were gone from home, they fell of comending their gunes and muskets, that lay upon racks by ye wall side, and tooke them downe to looke on them, asking if they were charged. And when they were possesst of them, one presents a peece ready charged against ye servants, and another a pistoll; and bid them not sturr, but quietly deliver them their goods, and carries some of ye men aborde, & made ye other help to carry away ye goods."

"And when they had tooke what they pleased, they sett them at liberty, and wente their way, with this mocke, bidding them tell their mr. when he came, that some of ye Ile of Rey gentlemen had been ther."‡

In the meantime, Thomas Willett, master of the house at Penobscot, had been wrecked at Pascataqua with Shurt, of Pemaquid, and Captain John Wright. Their vessel was Wright's shallop and the master was transporting to Massachusetts English merchandise which had been unladen at Penobscot for the account of settlers living in "The Bay." Their disaster was reported at Boston June 14, 1632.

This casualty at Pascataqua was the first of its kind ever reported on the New England coast. A half-drunken sailor, addicted to smoking, insisted upon lighting his pipe before a land-

‡ Bradford. 2-189.

ing had been made. While doing so a spark fell into an open powder cask and a terrific explosion ensued, in which the smoker was killed outright and the other passengers barely escaped with their lives. The boat and its contents were never recovered. There was no further mention of Wright in Maine affairs. Although his boat was destroyed, he still followed the sea. His later residence was at Ipswich, but he appears to have been lost in a gale off the coast in 1654, when his administrator filed claims against residents of the Isles of Shoals.

Governor Neal, of Pascataqua, had served in the British army during that famous expedition to the Isle of Ré, and his proximity may have been known to the raiders. At any rate, as soon as he had been apprised of what had transpired at Penobscot, he provisioned his boat and sailed eastward. He was, no doubt, encouraged to take action by the eastern settlers and, probably, Shurt and Willett returned with him.

July 23, 1632, Neal's boat was still detained to the east of Richmond Island, where Captain Thomas Cammock, who had been injured in an accident, was awaiting him. The only hint at the nature of the governor's business in this instance is contained in the expression "urgent occasions." Nothing was accomplished by the voyage.

Dixie Bull, whose shallop was captured by the French at Penobscot, was a relative of Samuel Maverick, of Winnisimet. He was a merchant of London who had been named in the grant at Agamenticus that spring, in company with Maverick and Walter Norton, of Charlestown. Upon arrival in Massachusetts he had fixed his headquarters at Dorchester and, like Holman, Pyncheon and Way, proposed to engage in fur trading at the Eastward. Such a course was obnoxious to his neighbors who claimed a universal monopoly on the coast.

Bradford did not mention Bull by name, but did refer to him in the activities of Allerton. The latter had "set forth" that spring from Bristol in the *White Angel*, "with a most wicked and drunken crue," and upon his arrival in the country had sold commodities to anyone who would buy them. He not only accepted promises of payment from independent dealers, but he formed a company of traders and instructed them to dispose of his own goods at every point on the coast, or in the interior, where conditions favored.

From what ensued it is evident that Bull had hired his shallop from Maverick and obtained his goods from Allerton upon credit. When he and his crew of three or four were conveyed to La Have by Razilly's scouts, they found a few Scotchmen in possession at Port Royal. Lower Canada, however, was still British territory, for it was not until July 13 that Quebec was restored to Emeric de Caen, and not until August 22, that Bouthellier, the French secretary of state, forwarded to Razilly the English mandates, which had been issued the year before for the evacuation of the fort at Granville.

The attitudes of Razilly and La Tour were mutually hostile, each assuming an uncompromising position with relation to territorial boundaries and rights which were not even doubtful. With this critical situation it was but natural for the former to offer Bull the freedom of the seas if he would become his ally against the latter.

Bull acceded to the proposition and, joining with a few Scotch settlers at the fort and some Virginians in the vicinity, successfully raided La Tour's premises at Saint John.

The failure of the English plantations to avenge his losses at Penobscot and the favorable outcome of his exploit against the French preyed upon Bull's mind. He chose to regard his countrymen as inimical because they did not come to the rescue. He should have realized the fact that Penobscot was helpless, Saint George, impotent, and Pemaquid, committed to neutrality, because of an oral agreement with Razilly which guaranteed peaceful relations between them.

With sixteen associates he decided to proceed westward in open boats. When they had advanced to Saint George, they commandeered the vessel of Anthony Dike and obtained passage to Pemaquid, where they seized "500 li. of beaver" and provisions belonging to the Bristol patentees and their partners.

One of the assailants was killed by a musket shot from Pemaquid shore and four or five were detained against their wills. The refugees, suddenly overcome with a sense of the enormity of their offence against their countrymen and fear of summary punishment by western planters, impressed Dike's vessel and importuned him to proceed with them to Virginia, where some of them had lived. The southern colony was regarded by them as a safe refuge. It was described by a contemporary writer as a "nest of rogues, whores, dissolute and rooking persons."§

The winds, however, continued unfavorable for their plan, and, like superstitious seamen of the period, they became irritable by delay and fearful of the sounds of the tempests and the rattling of the cordage in their rigging at night. With such aid from the inauspicious elements Dike soon succeeded in convincing his captors that southern navigation was impossible on account of his unfamiliarity with that coast.

John Winter afterwards claimed that if conditions had favored, the pirates would have raided his plantation at Richmond Island and taken possession of one of his three employes, Andrew or Thomas Alger, or John Baddiver, who had offended them in some way. Roger Clap maintained that it had been Bull's intention to return to Massachusetts and discipline the magistrates at Dorchester, who had been severe in their treatment of the adherents of Gorges and Mason.

But fears of further invasion were groundless, for the fugitives from justice recanted during their retreat eastward and were content to purchase supplies from the fishermen and planters at market prices. They also made double restitution, in the form of another boat and its equivalent in beaver, for Maverick's vessel which had been taken from them that spring by the French at Penobscot.

About the time of Bull's arrival at Port Royal Razilly took possession at Granville. Fate had dealt harshly with Alexander's colony during its four years in Nova Scotia. Thirty had died in the first twelve months, some had deserted before the transfer and the residue "all fell victims to the savages or disease, one family only escaping."*

With prospects of foreign domination, the Merchant Adventurers were anxious to recoup a part of their losses in New France and readily assented to French offers for their holdings in Acadia. The transfer of the fort was described by Winthrop as a sale, and that was what the transaction really amounted to. It had been agreed in the peace treaty of the two nations that the French Government should provision and equip a ship for the outward and return voyages and that all personal property at

§ Me. Hist. Gen. Rec., 1-59.
* Murdoch's Nova Scotia, 1-78.

Port Royal should be paid for at English schedules of prices, "with thirty per cent of profit, in consideration of the risk of the sea and port charges."†

Aulnay asserted later that a bill of exchange was drawn upon a French merchant "for satisfaction of certain Indian corn, cattle and ordnance, which the said Scotts left with us."‡

The piracy at Pemaquid was not reported at Boston till November 21, 1632, when the governor obtained the information in a letter from Neal. At first consideration it was agreed to send twenty men to Pascataqua to join forces in an eastern drive, but subsequent inaction was excused on account of the inclemency of the weather. Neal and Hilton, however, were alive to the danger and dispatched all the forces they could muster. They made expeditious progress as far as Pemaquid Harbor, where they were wind-bound for about three weeks and temporarily abandoned their quest for the pirates.

While at the Eastward, they learned from a note, signed by Fortune le Garde, a French accomplice, that Bull and his men, who had reformed, had made amends in some cases and promised not to molest English plantations further, if left alone, but that they did not propose to be taken alive.

It was ascertained later that Bull had "gone to the French" and so "got into England," where, according to Clap, "God destroyed this wretched man," but not before he had had an opportunity to appear before the Council of Plymouth in an attempt to repeal the Massachusetts charter.§

Bull had not resided in New England a full year. The identity of some of his lawless confederates, who were described by Bradford in uncomplimentary terms, is apparent from subsequent allusions by contemporary writers. Most of them seem to have been connected with the eastern operations of Allerton, Maverick and Oldham.

Some of the outlaws remained in Nova Scotia under protection of the French, and "Bay magistrates," while in conferences with agents of Governor Aulnay over reparations, complained that that official had "entertained our servants which ran from us, and refuseth to return them, being demanded."

Others, however, went back to the colony of their own accord

† Me. Doc. Hist., 7-177.
‡ 3 Mass. Hist. Col., 7-94.
§ Young's Mass. Chron., 362; Winthrop, 1-96, 98, 104.

after public excitement had subsided somewhat at the close of the year. Even Winthrop admitted that "Three of the pirates' company ran from them and came home" to Boston—a statement which clearly indicated the port from which they had hailed.

Although former employes of Massachusetts planters, the refugees are known to have been in general disfavor in all of the eastern plantations, except at Saco, where Vines, and possibly Oldham, then had supervision. They seem to have had no alternative course but to enter the service of Allerton and Vines at the Eastward, where they were engaged in trade with the fishermen and Indians.

Allerton himself, after dismissal from the position of manager at New Plymouth, had been forced to seek new business alliances in Maine, where he was accused by his colony of combining with other "consorts" and procuring "a company of base fellows" to disrupt its Indian commerce at Kennebec and Penobscot, where, as if by irony of fate, Bull's vessel had been captured by the French.

In his account, relating to 1633, Bradford complained that Allerton had not only interfered with the colony's trade on the Kennebec, but had endeavored to establish a post farther east, beyond Castine, in order that he might intercept eastern commerce with the natives. Vines was one of the "consorts" and had some of the Massachusetts renegades in his vessel when he encountered La Tour about the Bay of Fundy, during that year. In consequence of the meeting, the former members of Bull's crew were arrested by the French commander, who charged that they had abused his men and damaged his property at Saint John the previous summer.

At the urgent intercession of Vines the culprits were released and set their course westward with the clear understanding that they would not trespass again upon French premises. Nevertheless, the English landed their unsold merchandise at Machias and fortified a wigwam near the shore as their trading post. Vines returned to Saco with their vessel and a few days later the French ship appeared in the offing.

La Tour's account of what transpired appears authentic. He stated that "coming to the house, and finding some of his own goods, (though of no great value,) which had a little before been taken out of his fort at St. Johns by the Scotch and some English of Virginia, (when they plundered all his goods to a great value and abused his men,) he seized the three men and the goods and sent them into France according to his commission, where the men were discharged, but the goods adjudged lawful prize."*

The greater part, if not all, of the property taken by the French at Machias belonged to Allerton. As Bradford explained the situation, although some of his associates would have been partners, he was obliged to trust them for their shares. This mishap proved so disastrous for Allerton and Vines that they decided to dissolve all business connections at that time and withdraw from eastern trade. Subsequently, Allerton was accused of an attempt to recoup this and other private losses from the public funds of New Plymouth.

Tranquillity reigned at Machabitticus until 1635. That year, said the narrator, "they sustained an other great loss from ye French. Monsier de Aulnay coming into ye harbore of Penobscote, and having before gott some of ye cheefe yt belonged to ye house abord his vessell, by sutlty coming upon them in their shalop, he gott them to pilote him in; and after getting ye rest into his power, he tooke possession of ye house in ye name of ye king of France; and partly by threatening, & other wise, made Mr. Willett (their agente ther) to approve of ye sale of ye goods their unto him, of which he sett ye price him selfe in effecte, and made an inventory therof, (yett leaving out sundry things,) but made no paymente for them; but tould them in convenient time he would doe it if they came for it. For ye house & fortification, &c. he would not alow, nor accounte any thing, saing that they which build on another mans ground doe forfite ye same. So thus turning them out of all, (with a great deale of complemente, and many fine words,) he let them have their shalop and some victualls to bring them home."†

The house at Machabitticus had been garrisoned a greater part of the time with only seven men. Mather, previously quoted, who with other passengers was bound for Massachusetts, asserted that after a delay of a few days at Richmond Island their ship, which was the *James* from Bristol, proceeded westward accompanied by the shallop of the refugees from Penobscot. He

* Winthrop, 2-111, 126.
† Bradford, 2-207.

described the party, which was returning to New Plymouth, as "Mr. Willett, of New Plymouth, and other three men with him, having been turned out of all their havings at Penobscot about a fortnight before." Willett was afterwards mayor of New York. All of his associates in the eastern trade resumed their residences in Massachusetts, where they were concerned later with the affairs of the colony.

Persons who would not otherwise be known as employes in the East may be identified through land grants from the colony soon after their terms of service had expired. Thomas Willett, overseer of Penobscot trading post, testified that he had often seen the indenture of William Phipps who, in 1636, was described in a twenty-five acre grant as "the late servt of the partners." That tract, as sold by him, comprised all of the land "due unto him by his service of apprenticeship" which had then expired. The partners were lessees of the trading privileges at Cushnoc and Castine. Another early employe in Maine was John Richards. He was not the person who, born in 1625, married the widow of Adam Winthrop, but an older colonist who, in 1638, was assigned land "due him by Indenture for his service" for the colony.‡

Thomas Richards, who died at Penobscot before 1631, may have been a relative of John. At any rate, the latter was living at Arrowsic in 1649, when he bought the island of Robinhood. In 1656, he was styled "Old Richards" by his companions at Kennebec, who regarded him as a sort of captain. In a controversy, which then took place over the confiscated property of Joshua Teed, Richards was asked if he had an authorization from New Plymouth to make the seizure. It was evident that he had none and expressed unusual concern when it was intimated that he might be held accountable.

New Plymouth proprietors were much perturbed at the loss of their post at Penobscot and were apprehensive of similar treatment at Kennebec River. Consequently, with the approval of the authorities "in ye Bay," they engaged Captain Richard Girling with the *Hope,* an armed vessel of three hundred tons then lying in Boston Harbor, to dislodge the trespassers and "deliver them ye house." The remuneration for the successful performance of this service was to have been "700 li. of beaver."

‡ Plymouth Col. Rec., 1-92, 175.

In due time Captain Myles Standish with twenty men piloted Girling's ship eastward and with their bark "brought him safe into ye harbor."

The narrator stated that "he was so rash & heady as he would take no advice, nor would suffer Captaine Standish to have time to summone them, (who had a commission & order so to doe,) neither would doe it him selfe; the which, it was like, if it had been done, & they come to affaire parley, seeing their force, they would have yeelded. Neither would he have patience to bring his ship wher she might doe execution, but begane to shoot at distance like a madd man, and did them no hurte at all; the which when those of ye plantation saw, they were much greeved, and went to him & tould him he would doe no good if he did not lay his ship beter to pass (for she might lye within pistoll shott of ye house)."

"At last, when he saw his owne folly, he was perswaded, and layed her well, and bestowed a few shott to good purpose. But now, when he was in a way to doe some good, his powder was goone; for though he had * * * peece of ordnance, it did now appeare he had but a barrell of powder, and a peece; so he could doe no good, but was faine to draw of againe; by which means ye enterprise was made frustrate, and ye French incouraged; for all ye while that he shot so unadvisedly, they lay close under a worke of earth, & let him consume him selfe. He advised with ye Captaine how he might be supplyed with powder, for he had not to carie him home; so he tould him he would goe to ye next plantation, and doe his indeour to procure him some, and so did; but understanding, by intelligence, that he intended to ceiase on ye barke, & surprise ye beaver, he sent him the powder, and brought ye barke & beaver home. But Girling never assaulted ye place more, (seeing him selfe disapoyented,) but went his way; and this was ye end of this bussines."§

That naval bombardment of the house at Machabitticus, now known as Castine, was the first of the kind recorded in the annals of the state, and if its object had been attained might have advanced the English development along the northern coast and changed the whole history of Maine. It is apparent that the post was not fortified with cannon, because the English vessel could "lye within pistoll shott" without dangerous exposure. There

§ Bradford, 2-208.

were but eighteen defenders and the only additional defences erected by them were earthworks.

It had transpired that during the summer before Penobscot was taken by the French, Sir Richard Saltonstall and his English partners, who were interested in the development of 1600 acres at the mouth of the Connecticut River, sent thither William Gibbins with twenty pioneers. For diplomatic reasons John, son of Governor Winthrop, had been selected by the patentees as chief executive for the new plantation.

After these colonists had been delayed for more than a week in Boston Harbor, where they had sought the services of an experienced pilot, they proceeded to their destination. Upon landing at Connecticut they were opposed by immigrants from New Dorchester, who had preceded them and taken unwarranted possession of their patrons' location and buildings.

As a consequence the discouraged settlers reëmbarked for England. Following the northern coast line near the Isle of Sable, they encountered a severe equinoctial storm which wrecked their pinnace and cast them ashore wholly destitute. From that island they made their escape to La Have on the mainland, where they had been entertained by the French, but turned towards Massachusetts as the only alternative. By coincidence they reached Penobscot during its bombardment and were detained until the conclusion of the siege.*

In spite of the fact that Pemaquid had furnished additional powder for Girling, Bradford did not hesitate to arraign that plantation in specific terms in his chronicles for that year. He claimed that Pemaquid supplied the French with provisions as well as kept them informed about the movements of the English. The writer, on account of personal interest, may have been prejudiced because the Bristol establishment could have been expected to profit by the elimination of competition at Castine.

According to the anonymous "Relation," written late in 1635, the patent of Penobscot was the largest in extent of all that had been granted by the Council of Plymouth in the Maine district, "comprehendinge (as is pretended) nere 40 leagues in length yett *it is planted but wth one house,* And is now possessed by the ffrench."†

* Winthrop. 1-161. 171.
† N. E. Hist. Gen. Reg. 40-7?

Although New Plymouth was anxious to resume trade at Castine and the eastern settlements were interviewed and invited to participate in the conquest, no subsequent attempt was made by that colony to recover its post.

Pemaquid, however, was vitally concerned in the issue, and correspondence of Shurt described the feeling of insecurity that was agitating his community. His letter to Winthrop, dated June 28, 1636, contained the following pertinent information on the subject: "Richard Foxwill, cominge from the French at Pennobscott, spake with a boate of ours (draylinge for mackrell) & tould them that Wm. Hart had him comended unto me, & that I should looke to my selfe, for that the French were gone to the Eastwards to fetch more helpe to take this plantation & others, & that they had left but five men at Pen: & withall that he had an English heart although he were with them: wishinge his freedom from them; & that he knowes a meanes to take Pennobscott with five men without losse of bloud."

"Here comes natives from thence & sayes that they will remove to some other parts, they are soe abused by them. Me seemes they should not leave such a small crew at home, neyther blason their intents. It is lamentable that a handfull should insult over a multitude. We must feare the worst, & strive our best to withstand them. They wrote unto me of desired freindship & amitye, with mutuall correspondence: & they pretended the same at their beinge here: A Franciscan ffryar insinuatinge unto me that Mr. Comander & Mr. Donye desired nothinge but fayre passages betwixt us, & that he was sent purposely to signifie so much unto me."

Eight years later another attempt to recover this house from Aulnay resulted in the death of Captain Thomas Wannerton, of Pascataqua; the expedition which was in the interest of La Tour was unsuccessful, but the English participants in the undertaking were encouraged to believe that they could recover the Eastern Country for themselves, and planned reprisal at an early date.

While New Plymouth evinced no further interest in the recovery of Machabitticus territory, Massachusetts mercenaries who had been implicated in the La Tour exploit advocated recapture and retention from Aulnay, to control the Indian trade about

Penobscot River. The former proprietors, however, did not ignore the prospect of collecting outstanding claims, and August 31, 1644, Edward Winslow, then governor, assigned to John Winthrop, the younger, Samuel Maverick and Captain Thomas Hawkins, the right to force Aulnay to pay for personal property, valued at 500 pounds sterling, which had been taken "violently and injuriously" about ten years before.

The conversion had taken place when Aulnay had seized Castine and retained the merchandise and equipment of "the Agents and servts. of Edward Winslow, William Bradford, Thomas Prence, and others their ptners at Matchebiguatus, in Penobscot."‡

The claim was presented to the French governor the following year, but no warlike demonstration was undertaken and Muscongus district, as well as Pemaquid plantation, remained undisturbed, until 1654. February 8, of that year, a commission was issued by Cromwell to Major Robert Sedgwick, of Boston, to subdue the Dutch and other English enemies in North America. To accomplish that purpose, a fleet of four vessels, comprising the *Augustine, Black Raven, Church* and *Hope*, was mobilized in the Thames and sailed from Portsmouth, England.§

After the Dutch settlements in New York had surrendered without bloodshed, the victorious squadron undertook to exhibit real prowess and proficiency by sweeping up the Northern Coast and overwhelming the French strongholds in Eastern Maine and Nova Scotia. While Acadia was reoccupied, without opposition, by New England troops, it was retained only until 1656, when the entire province was restored to interests representing both nationalities and defined as extending westward to "Pentacoet and the River of St. George to muscontus."*

The district was bounded westerly by New England and northerly by an imaginary line situated one hundred leagues inland. All specific measurements were augmented by the expression "et plus avant, jusqu'à la première habitation faite par les Flamans ou Francois, ou par les Anglois de Nouvelle Angleterre." Such liberal interpretation extended each dimension to "the first dwelling erected by Flemings, French or English in New England." With that idea in mind French inhabitants of Nova Scotia

‡ Savage's Winthrop, 2-220.
§ 4 Mass. Hist. Col., 2-230.
* Suffolk Deeds, 3-22; Hazard, 1-616.

regarded the house of John Brown at New Harbor as the eastern boundary mark of New England.

In 1688, Edward Randolph accompanied Governor Andros in an eastern tour of inspection. He described the old English fort at Penobscot, "formerly made up with stone and turfe," as "gone to ruin;" in fact, nothing was found on that site. In that vicinity, however, they visited a fortified dwelling which had been built by Aulnay after the Plymouth employes were evicted in 1635; the French establishment was then in possession of Sieur de Castin as sole proprietor in that district.†

Pioneers

ASHLEY, EDWARD, Indian trader at Castine, 1628-9; England, November, 1629, to March, 1630; Castine, May, 1630, to October, 1631, when he was extradited for selling contraband to the natives; never returned to Maine, but died while returning from Siberia, where he had been employed by a trading company.

CALLOW, OLIVER, sailor and employe of Plymouth Colony at Castine under Ashley and Willett, 1630-5; married Judith Clock February 29, 1655-6; died at Boston of old age, 1674; widow Judith; no issue.

DEACON, JOHN, servant of Edward Ashley at Castine, 1628-9; employe of Plymouth Colony at Castine under Ashley and Willett, 1630-5; died at New Plymouth in February, 1636.

DOWNS, JAMES, employe of Plymouth Colony at Castine under Ashley and Willett, 1630-1; with Hilton at Dover, 1631.

PHIPPS, WILLIAM, gunsmith and employe of Plymouth Colony at Castine under Ashley and Willett, 1630-5; covenant servant of the company, who disposed of his land, 1636; deceased before 1658.

RICHARDS, THOMAS, employe of Ashley at Castine, 1630; had deceased the next year.

SAMPSON, HENRY, arrived at New Plymouth in the "Mayflower," 1620; employe of Plymouth Colony at Castine under Ashley and Willett, 1630-5; returned to Duxbury; married Ann Plummer February 6, 1636-7; died 1685; children Elizabeth (Sproat), Caleb, Dorcas (Bonney), Hannah (Holmes), James, John, Mary (Summers) and Stephen.

WATSON, GEORGE, born 1602; employe of Plymouth Colony at Castine under Ashley and Willett, 1630-5; returned to New Plymouth and married Phebe Hicks that year; died 1689; children John, Mary (Leonard), Phebe (Shaw), Elizabeth (Williams), born January 18, 1647-8, Elkanah, born February 25, 1656-7, and Jonathan, born 1659.

WILLETT, THOMAS, son of Andrew and Jacobina (Goad), born at Barley, England, 1605; arrived from Amsterdam in the "Lyon," 1630; overseer for New Plymouth at Castine until 1635, when he was evicted by the French; returned to the colony and married Mary, daughter of John and Dorothy Brown, July 6, 1636; first mayor of New York, 1665; died

† Hutchinson Col.. 562.

at Barrington, Rhode Island, August 4, 1674; children, born in New Plymouth, Mary (Hooker), November 10, 1637, Martha (Saffin), August 6, 1639, John, August 21, 1641, Sarah (Elliott), May 4, 1643, Rebecca, December 2, 1644, Thomas, October 1, 1646, Esther (Flint), July 6, 1647, James, November 23, 1649, Hezekiah, November 17, 1651, David, November 1, 1654, Andrew, October 5, 1655, and Samuel, October 27, 1658.

WRIGHT, JOHN, brother of Thomas, of Bristol, England; mariner employed by Isaac Allerton to assist Ashley at Penobscot, 1630; made three trips to Plymouth with Ashley's shallop that year; wrecked at Pascataqua, 1632; removed to Newbury, but died at sea and left accounts at the Isles of Shoals, 1654; son John.

MACHIAS RIVER

In 1632, Isaac Allerton, who had been discharged as manager of the trading posts of New Plymouth at Kennebec and Penobscot, formed a partnership with Richard Vines, of Saco, and some others, to trade with eastern Indians.

In the summer of that year, while returning from a coasting expedition, both witnessed the delivery of seizin of Cape Elizabeth to John Winter. Other persons present at that time were John Oldham and Thomas Cammock.

The latter must have been convinced that the partnership venture would be a profitable one, for he remarked only a few days later: "All the good that is to bee done in thes partes, for trade, is towards the Eastwarde with a good shallopp * * * allmost to the Scotts plantation, wher I know ther is more store of beaver and better tradinge than is heer with us."*

The governor of New Plymouth complained of the aggressive conduct of Allerton as a rival in eastern trade. He claimed that the former manager of that colony's business had engaged unprincipled agents to do his trading along the coast; that he not only sent them up the Kennebec "to gleane away ye trade from ye house ther," but also had established a new post "beyoned Penobscote to cute of ye trade from thence also."†

However, it was not until 1633 that Vines undertook to establish the post to which Bradford alluded. In that year, while trading on the eastern coast of Maine near the site of the former Scotch plantation, which had been acquired by the French within a few months, Vines and La Tour, the Canadian governor, met and exchanged commodities to mutual advantage. At that time, by reason of the treaty of Saint-Germain-en-Laye, La Tour claimed exclusive right to trade as far west as Pemaquid, but he gave Vines special permission to dispose of his unsold merchandise in the ordinary course of trade on his way home, with the express condition that no station should be built or fortified within French territory.

* Me. Doc. Hist., 3-17, 19.
† Bradford, 2-188.

Nevertheless, the English upon arrival at Machias erected a small wigwam for shelter and stored their goods. Five men were left in charge by Vines, who reëmbarked with the rest of his crew for Saco. The Indian name for the river was Damache.

Two days later La Tour reappeared and took possession of the premises which, he afterwards asserted, had been fortified with two small cannon. After some resistance three of the English defenders were killed, or fatally injured, and the others with their confiscated property were conveyed to Port Latour.‡

According to the account of Bradford, previously quoted, "This was the end of yt projecte," and the loss was "most, if not all, Mr. Allerton's; for though some of them should have been his partners, yet he trusted them for their partes."

In January, 1635-6, Allerton returned in his vessel from the French settlement at Port Latour, where he had failed to ransom his two Englishmen, who had been taken by La Tour at Machias and sent to France as prisoners of war.

‡ Winthrop, 2-125.

APPENDIX A

OLD PLANTERS IN MASSACHUSETTS BAY COLONY IN JUNE, 1628

The Number:
    June 29, 1629, Higginson reported 200 colonists at
        Salem and 100 outside,   300
    March 28, 1631, Dudley listed 180 living and 80 dead
        colonists in the last two immigrations,   260

    Old planters,   40

The Same Result May Be Approximated in Another Way:
    June 29, 1629, Higginson made the census,   300
    September 6, 1628, White's estimate was 50 or 60,
        which with Higginson's 200 passengers made   260

    Old planters,   40

The Tentative List:

Braintree (Mount Wallaston):
1. Thomas Morton, arrived 1622, on his own account.
2. Thomas Walford, 1622 or 1624, for Captain John Mason.
3. Jeremiah Walford, came with his father.
4. John Peverly, 1622 or 1624, for Mason.
5. Thomas Moore, 1624, for Mason.
6. Walter Bagnall, 1624, for Morton.
7. Edward Gibbons, 1624, for Morton.

Weymouth (Wessaguscus):
9. John Bursley, 1623, with Robert Gorges.
10. William Jeffrey, 1623, with Gorges.
11. Edward Johnson, 1622, for Weston.

Hull (Natascot):
12. John Oldham, 1624, on his own account.
13. John Lyford, 1624, for Plymouth Colony.
14. Walter Knight, 1622, for the Dorchester Merchants.
15. John Gray, 1622, for Dorchester Merchants.
16. Thomas Gray, 1622, for Dorchester Merchants.

Boston (Shawmut):
17. William Blackstone, 1623, with Gorges.

Salem (Nahumkeag):
18. William Allen, 1624, for Dorchester Merchants.
19. John Balch, 1623, with Gorges.
20. Roger Conant, 1623, with Gorges.
21. Thomas Gardiner, 1624, for Dorchester Merchants.
22. Richard Norman, 1622, for Dorchester Merchants.
23. Richard Norman, the younger, with his father.
24. John Tilly, 1624, for Dorchester Merchants.
25. William Trask, 1623, with Gorges.
26. John Woodbury, 1624, for Dorchester Merchants.
27. Humphrey Woodbury, 1628, with his father.
28. Thomas Purchase, 1628, one of the Dorchester Merchants.
29. John Stratton, 1628, for Matthew Cradock.
30. Richard Bradshaw, 1628, for Dorchester Merchants.
31. Edward Ashley, 1628, on his own account.
32. George Lewis, 1628, with Purchase.
33. John Sanders, 1622, for Weston.
34. Peter Palfrey, 1622 or 1624, for Dorchester Merchants.

Mystic (Winnisimet):
35. Samuel Maverick, 1623, with Gorges.
36. Amias, 1623, widow of David Thompson.
37. John Blackleach.

Gloucester (Cape Ann):
38. John Watts, 1627, for Dorchester Merchants.

APPENDIX B

THE THIRTY NEW ENGLAND PATENTS

1621,
June   1, John Pierce (New Plymouth).

1622,
March   9, John Mason (Cape Ann).
April   20, John Pierce (surrendered).

July	24,	Duke of Richmond (Cape Elizabeth and Richmond Island).
		Sir George Calvert (Casco and Seguin Island).
		Earl of Arundel (Pemaquid and Monhegan Island).
August	10,	Gorges and Mason (Merrimac to Sagadahoc River).
October	16,	David Thompson (Pascataqua River).
December	30,	Robert Gorges (Massachusetts).

1623,

May 5, Christopher Levett (Casco).

1624,

January 1, Robert Cushman for Plymouth Colony (Cape Ann).

1628,

March 19, Massachusetts Bay Colony (East. Massachusetts). (Confirmed by Charles First March 4, 1628-9.)

1629,

November 17, Gorges, Mason and Associates (Laconia).

1630,

January 13, Plymouth Colony (Cushnoc).
February 12, John Oldham and Richard Vines (Biddeford).
Thomas Lewis and Richard Bonython (Saco).
March 12, Edward Hilton (Dover and Squamscott).
March 13, John Beauchamp and Thomas Leverett (Muscongus).
June 26, Lygonia Company (Sagadahoc).

1631,

November 1, Thomas Cammock (Scarborough).
Richard Bradshaw (Pejepscot).
November 3, Gorges, Mason and Associates (Pascataqua).
December 1, Ferdinando Gorges and Associates (Agamenticus).
John Gorges and Associates (Agamenticus).
John Stratton (Cape Porpoise).
Robert Trelawney and Moses Goodyear (Cape Elizabeth).
December 2, Walter Bagnall (Richmond Island).

1632,
February 29, Robert Aldworth and Gyles Elbridge (Pemaquid).
June 16, Thomas Purchase and George Way (Pejepscot).
1638,
March 23, Oliver Godfrey and Associates (Cape Neddock).

APPENDIX C

ANCIENT MAPS OF MAINE

Simancas, 1610.	Brown's Genesis U. S., 1-456.
Champlain, 1612.	Champlain (Prince Society), 3-228.
Smith, 1614 (Surcharged).	Am. Ant. Col., 1875-90.
Hendricksen, 1614.	N. Y. Doc., 1-12.
Jacobs, 1621.	N. Y. Doc., Frontispiece.
Brigges, 1625.	Purchase (Glasgow Edition), 14-424.
Nuova Anglia, 1631.	N. Y. Doc. Hist., Frontispiece.
Champlain, 1632.	Champlain (Prince Society), 1-304.
*Wood, 1635.	Young's Mass. Chron., 388.
*Godfrey, 1653.	Eng. Arch. (Jenness' N. H.), Frontispiece.
*Copy of the Godfrey Map.	Baxter Collection (State Library).
*The map of "I. S.," 1665.	Baxter Collection (State Library).

APPENDIX D

THE RECALL OF NEAL AND ASSOCIATES

There is no doubt that the Laconia Company recalled its Pascataqua employes because "returns" had been unsatisfactory. The list of those who returned with Neal in 1633 is a compilation based on later statements of the men themselves or other persons of equal veracity. Subsequently, all but three appear to have come back to America.

Those who remained in England were Adrian Tucker, Neal who, although an experienced military officer, failed to secure

* Western part only.

appointment as governor of New England, in 1637, and "Mr. Card," a householder who, from the nature of his personal belongings, appears to have been a clergyman. The residence of Card at Pascataqua was not indicated. He may have lived in Maine or New Hampshire. His location seems to have been farther from Dover Point than Newichawannock, where he stored his household furniture. His habitation may have stood at Thompson's Point, where the Indians had ancient planting ground. This position would have been about midway between the cabin of Cammock in Eliot and the fort at Newichawannock.

APPENDIX E

The Wannerton Deed

This Identure made the Twentieth day of November in ye Seventeenth year of the Reigne of our Soverign Lord King Charles by the Grace of God of England Scotland France and Ireland King Defender of the faith &c: Between Thomas Wannerton of Piscattaqua Gentleman of the one ptie & Alexa Shapleigh now resident in Piscattaqua aforesaid merchant of the other ptie That whereas it pleased ye president and Counsel of New England to grant a pattent of Lands and Territories upon the River of Piscattaqua aforesaid unto the right worshipfull Sr Fardenendo Gorges Knight Capt John Mason Esqr. and their Associates and the said Ferdenando Gorges Captain John Mason and their Associates for the well ordering and settling of Collonies and Plantations within ye Precincts of their said Pattent did constitute Capt Walter Neal Governour of their said Plantations by virtue whereof ye said Capt Walter Neal by his Deed under his hand and Seal bearing date the ninth day July Anno Domini 1633 had and made between ye said Walter Neal of thone ptie and ye aforesaid Wannerton of other ptie for ye Consideration in the said Deed expressed did assign and allot unto the said Thomas Wannerton a Certain pcel of Land scituate lying and being on the East Side of the aforesaid river of Piscattaqua being bounded on ye North side with a small Currant and adjoyning to the Corn Land planted in ye year 1633 aforesaid by Capt Thomas Cammock and on ye South Side bounded with asmall

freshit adjoyning to asmall head Land commonly called point
Joslen on ye west side bounded with the aforesaid River of Piscattaqua and to the Eastward the bounds Extend so farr as to the
one half of the way between ye sd River of Piscattaqua and the
River of Accementicus To have and to hold the afore said Land
to the Sd Thomas Wannerton his heirs and assignes forever
under the yearly rent of Ten shillings of Lawfull English money
with other Covents and Conditions in the said Deed Expressed,
as in & by the same more at large it doth and may appear, and
whereas the aforesaid Thomas Wannerton by his Deed Indented
under his hand and Seal bearing Date the first Day of March 1637
had and made between the Sd Thomas Wannerton of thone ptie
and John Treworthy their agent in these parts for and behalfe
of ye aforesaid Alexander Shapleigh of the other part for ye
Consideration of Thirty pounds Starlin and other Considerations
him the said Thomas Wannerton thereunto Especilly moving did
aliene Sell and Confirm all those lands in ye Deed before Specified
unto the Said John Treworthy agent for ye sd Alexander Shapleigh . . . Now these presents further witnesseth that the said
Thomas Wannerton . . . doth . . . confirm unto the said Alexander Shapleigh his heirs and heirs and Assigns that aforesaid
Tract of Land . . .

In witness whereof the parties above said to these present
Indenture their Signes and Seals Interchangably have Sett yeer on
ye Day and year first above written—
Thos — (Seale) Wannerton

Sealed Signed & Delivered in ye Presence of those whose
names are under written
<blockquote>
Saml Maverick
Francis Champernown
Clement Camision
Roger Garde
</blockquote>

A True copy Examd P Wm Pepperrell Clerk.

APPENDIX F

The Anonymous "Relation" of 1635

Some years ago an attempt was made to identify the authorship of this document, on account of its important bearing upon

Maine history. All of the evidence points unmistakably to Walter Neal, who had had charge of Laconia Plantation. During his three years of service at Pascataqua he had traversed the Maine coast half a dozen times in the exercise of police powers and visited Massachusetts twice. He was at Pemaquid less than two months before July 15, 1633, when he left the country for England. He boasted, in 1637, that no European had made such extensive discoveries of the "inland parts" as himself.

The declaration of the number of cattle in New England at the time of his comparatively late departure, his knowledge of grants from the council, the intentional omission of the location of that to Hilton with whom he had had a controversy over boundaries, and the admission that his colony was far removed from others and adhered to the Church of England, all comport with Neal's relations.

The term "my selfe and Colonie" was previously used in the third person in Pascataqua patent; there the expression was: "Capt Walt: Neale and ye Colony wth him."

Furthermore, there is other evidence that Cape Porpoise and Casco had been "forsaken" in 1633, although the latter had been occupied continuously after that date by Cleave and Tucker.

That the "Relation" was written near the close of 1635 is apparent from internal reference:

1. The Indian Plague, according to Captain Smith, began in 1617 and prevailed for three years. The "Relation" referred to the medial year of 1618, which was seventeen years before 1635. William Wood, writing in 1633, asserted that the epidemic subsided "about 14 yeares agoe."

2. The year 1635 marked the fifteenth anniversary of the arrival of the Pilgrims.

3. The nine-year period of progress under governors Endicott and Winthrop was reckoned from the founding of Salem in 1626.

4. The mischief done by the Indians "last year" related to the murder of Captain Stone and his companions in Connecticut late in 1633, but not reported until the next year.

5. The seizure of Castine by the French occurred about August 1, 1635, and was alluded to in the "Relation" as already accomplished.

APPENDIX G
INDIAN TITLES AT SAGADAHOC
(West Shore)

Phippsburg. John Parker, Sabenaw Peninsula and Chegoney, 1648.
Thomas Atkins, Atkins Bay, 1654.
Nicholas Reynolds, First High Head, December 3, 1661.
John, son of John Parker, of Sabenaw, Parker's Head and six miles upriver, June 14, 1659.
Thomas Webber, Winnegance Creek, May 29, 1660.
Alexander Thwayts, Winnegance Creek, May 28, 1660.

Bath. Robert Gouch, city site, May 29, 1660.
Thomas Watkins, Merry Meeting Bay, August 19, 1661.

(East Shore)

Georgetown. John Parker, of Sabenaw, Raskegon Island, February 27, 1650-1.
Westport. Thomas Ashley and Thomas Joy, of Boston, Raskegon to Cape Saugs, August 21, 1661.
Arrowsic. John Richards, the whole island, April 22, 1649.
Woolwich. Edward Bateman and John Brown, Nequasseag, November 1, 1639.
James Smith, Tuessic to Merry Meeting Bay, May 8, 1648.
Thomas Ashley, New Merry Meeting Point above "The Chops," 1654.

(Both Shores of the Kennebec)

Alexander Thwayts, Swan Island, before 1649.
Christopher Lawson, Swan Island, October 18, 1649.
New Plymouth, Cushnoc, January 13, 1629-30.

APPENDIX H
SULLIVAN'S HISTORICAL BLUNDER

James Sullivan in his "History of Maine," published in 1795, asserted that "There were in the year 1630, eighty four families, besides fishermen, about Pemaquid, and St. Georges and Sheepscot." That statement was based upon reminiscences of Sylvanus Davis, in 1701, when Davis did not claim such antiquity for the eastern settlements and cited only two cases of early residence —both at Saint George. One of these was to the effect that Richard Foxwell had lived at Saquid Point sixty years before. That planter acquired Salem plantation at Saint George in 1633, while a resident of Dorchester. The other case was that of Philip Swadden who was residing at Quisquamego as early as 1651, but had lived at Kittery and Dover prior to 1640.

In 1665, in their official report upon conditions in eastern Maine, New York commissioners found that the only plantations east of Kennebec River were Sagadahoc, Sheepscot and Pemaquid, of which the greater had "not over 20 houses." That report, signed by Samuel Maverick, is entitled to full credence for he had then traded in Maine with his own vessels for forty years.

Six weeks after the issuance of the report the eastern planters submitted to New York. The number of families then in the district was apportioned as follows: Sagadahoc, eight; Sheepscot, fourteen; Pemaquid and Winnegance, four; and Cape Newagen and Monhegan, none.

INDEX

(Consult pioneers for descendants not indexed)

Abbagadusset, 239, 251
Abdy, Matthew, 351
Abermot, 258
Abochigishic, 258
Abraham (ship), 19
Adams, Abraham, 254
  Jonathan, 254
  Philip, 138
  Thomas, 136
Alcock, Job, 136
  John, 134-6, 138, 142, 212
Alden, John, 276-278
Aldworth, Matthew, 352
  Robert, 25, 173, 289, 313-16, 318-9, 324, 326, 328-9, 342, 347-50, 355, 371, 395
  Thomas, 342
Alexander, Sir William, 26-7, 365-7, 370, 373, 375, 379
Alger, Andrew, 67, 192-3, 201, 204, 212, 379
  Arthur, 193, 197
  Elizabeth, 193
  John, 193
  Matthew, 193
  Thomas, 67, 201-2, 225, 228, 232, 302, 379
  Tristram, 204
Allen, Arnold, 210, 213, 236-8
  Hope, 237
  John, 73, 289, 302
  Leonard, 302
  Mary, 237
  Robert, 284, 287, 325-6
  William, 204, 393
Allerton, Isaac, 23, 30, 51, 59, 82, 154-5, 171-5, 177, 224, 243-4, 274-8, 314-5, 318, 369, 371-2, 377-8, 380-2, 390-1
Alley, Peter, 172
Alt, Henry, 45
Altham, Emanuel, 20, 311, 346
Ambrose (ship), 300, 312
Ameredeth, John, 118
Amniquin, 258-9, 289
Amoret, 14, 260, 308
Amory, John, 205
Andrews, Dorcas, 254
  Edmund, 208
  Jane, 182
  John, 115, 117-8
  Richard, 173, 275, 368

Samuel, 179, 181-2, 186
Andros, Sir Edmund, 324, 388
Angel Gabriel (ship), 318, 361
Angell, John, 13
Anger, Sampson, 55, 134, 136, 138
Angibaut, Pierre, 14
Annes (ship), 199
Anthony, John, 21
Apomhamen, 258
Aramasoga, 258
Arbella (ship), 223
Archangel (ship), 14, 332, 358
Archer, Gabriel, 13, 123
Argal, Sir Samuel, 15-6, 265, 294, 333-4, 365
Arrowsmith, Edmund, 290, 303, 323
Arundel, Earl Thomas, 11, 25-6, 241, 259, 297, 309-10, 332, 347, 358-9
Ashley, Edward, 23, 28, 59, 60, 172-3, 224-5, 244, 276-7, 313-4, 318, 367-72, 388, 393
  Sir Francis, 247
  Thomas, 399
Assacomoit, 14, 260, 308, 335
Asticon, 258-9
Atkins, Thomas, 271, 322, 399
Atwell, Benjamin, 229, 232
Augustine (ship), 387
Aulnay, Charles d', 320, 375, 380, 382, 386-8
Ault, John, 45
Austin, Samuel, 150
Avelling, Arthur, 22

Babb, Thomas, 177
Baccatusshe, 258
Bachelor (ship), 52, 114-5
Bachilor, Rev. Stephen, 111, 231
Backlar, George, 347
Bacon, Lord Francis, 338
Baddiver, John, 67, 201-2, 205, 379
Bagnall, Walter, 22-3, 25, 28, 42-3, 60-1, 64, 67, 199, 200, 202, 205, 313, 392, 394
Bailey, Eleanor, 191
  Hilkiah, 191, 197
  Jonas, 191, 205
Bailleul, Isaac, 16
Baker, Edmund, 225, 232
  John, 132, 134, 142, 210, 212
Balch, John, 393

[401]

Ball, John, 55, 146
  Richard, 186
Banks, Richard, 140, 142
Baple, John, 117
Barker, Edmund, 22, 299
Barlow, George, 191, 197
Barnard, Bartholomew, 130, 134, 136-7, 142, 212
Barrens, John, 17
Barrett, John, 142, 148
  Walter, 314, 321
Bartlett, Nicholas, 157, 214
Barton, Edward, 142, 162, 254
Bashaba, 258-9, 261, 308, 364
Bashrode, Richard, 242
Baston, Thomas, 118
Bateman, Edward, 280, 283-4, 290, 322, 325, 352, 362, 399
Batson, Stephen, 149, 160, 162, 186
Batten, John, 55, 135
Batteshill, Henry, 17
Beals, Arthur, 135
Beard, Thomas, 111
Beauchamp, John, 26, 34, 84, 173, 275, 292, 368, 394
Beeson, Thomas, 136
Beetle, Robert, 112
Belknap, Jeremiah, 36
Bellingham, Richard, 130
Bendall, Philip, 285-6
Bennett, John, 17
  Sir Henry, 285
  Melchard, 20, 310
  Robert, 347
Berry, Ambrose, 159, 173, 179, 186, 212
Best, Edward, 205
  Ellis, 15, 260
Biard, Pierre, 16, 263, 334
Bickford, John, 55
Biencourt, Jean de, 14-6, 333, 334
Billings, John, 114, 116, 192, 203, 205
Billington, John, 199
Binckes, Bryan, 268
  Daniel, 266
  Roger, 266
Blackleach, John, 393
Black Raven (ship), 387
Blackstone, Rev. William, 28, 42, 131, 171, 393
Black Will, 67, 202
Blaisdell, Ralph, 134, 140, 142
Blake, Thomas, 58, 68, 86
Blessing (ship), 17, 336
Boade, Henry, 148, 152, 173, 179, 186, 210, 212, 253
Boardman, Offen, 237
Bodwell, John, 302
  Body, Ferdinand, 54
Boggust, John, 226
Bolt, John, 135

Bolton, Stephen, 21
Bona Nova (ship), 19, 294, 309
Bond, Nicholas, 129
Bone, Thomas, 205
Bonython, John, 174, 183, 213
  Richard, 23, 25, 82, 84, 115, 133, 171, 173, 177-9, 182-4, 186-91, 394
Booker, Lancelot, 15
Booth, Robert, 152, 181, 186
Bouden, Ambrose, 22, 197, 204, 230
  John, 182, 197, 204
Bouthellier, 378
Bowant, 258
Bowles, Joseph, 181-2, 186
Bowser, Sir John, 33, 292
Boyce, Antiphas, 279
Boyden, James, 21
Bradbury, Thomas, 52, 108, 114-5, 130, 134, 142
Bradford, William, 23, 38-9, 41-2, 45, 61, 82, 170, 221, 273-8, 300, 313, 344-6, 348-9, 368, 370, 377, 380-2, 385, 387, 390-1
Bradshaw, Richard, 25, 170, 242, 245-6, 249, 267, 393-4
Bragdon, Arthur, 134, 136, 139, 142
Brattle, Thomas, 279
Brawnde, Edward, 17, 331, 336-7
Bray, Richard, 236, 238
Brereton, John, 13, 123
Bridges, John, 20, 310
Briggs, 395
Brimblecome, John, 17
Brindley, Lawrence, 137
Bristol Merchants, 28, 60-1, 65, 105
British Government, 375
British Parliament, 69, 296, 341
Brock, John, 226
Brookin, William, 44
Brooks, Thomas, alias Parker, 103, 117
Brown, Arthur, 211, 230, 232, 235, 239, 251, 290, 321
  Elizabeth, 326, 354
  Emma, 326
  Francis, 326
  John, 280, 283-4, 289-90, 322, 324-9, 352, 354-6, 361, 388, 399
  Humphrey, 342
  Margaret, 326
  William, 13, 124
Browning, Christopher, 18
Buckland, Elizabeth, 322
  George, 289, 322-3, 352
  John, 159
Bucknell, Roger, 205
Bull, Dixie, 64, 67, 76, 78, 126, 137, 142, 175, 202, 317-8, 360, 375, 377-9, 380-1
  John, 137

Seth, 137
Bunker, James, 112
Bunt, George, 205
Burdett, "Ed," 112
  Rev. George, 78, 115-6, 132, 134-6, 142
Burgess, John, 199, 205
  Richard, 138, 142
Burkett, Christopher, 67, 313, 318, 350
Burrage, Benjamin, 197, 204
  John, 197, 204
Bursley, John, 42, 112, 126, 137, 392
Bush, John, 157, 160, 163

Cabot, Sebastian, 13
Cadogan, Richard, 55, 57, 138
Caen, Emeric de, 378
Callow, Oliver, 371, 388
Calvert, Sir George, 11, 24, 243, 297, 394
Cam, Thomas, 14
Camision, Clement, 397
Cammock, Margaret, 196
  Thomas, 25, 58, 64-5, 67-8, 70, 90, 97, 105-6, 111-2, 115, 127, 175, 177, 192-6, 210, 373, 377, 390, 394, 396
Canada Company, 61
Cannage, Matthew, 205
Canney, Hannah, 101
  Samuel, 102
  Thomas, 97, 100-1
Card, 90, 396
Carleton, Andrew, 342
Carlisle, Earl James, 26
Carter, Richard, 234
Cartier, Jacques, 365-6
Casherokenit, 258
Castle, Gregory, 21
Chabinock, 153, 159
Chadbourne, Humphrey, 92, 96-9, 103, 117
  Lucy, 98
  Patience, 95
  Seth, 98
  William, 90, 92, 94-7, 103
Chambers, Thomas, 140, 142
Champdore, Pierre, 14
Champernoone, Arthur, 19, 114
  Francis, 69, 70, 107, 114-8, 133, 397
Champlain, Samuel de, 14, 36, 165, 259, 331-2, 366, 395
Champney, Henry, 290, 323, 352, 355
  Margaret, 326
  Maurice, 326
Chapman, Florence, 142
Chapple, Anthony, 205
  William, 205
Charity (ship), 19, 21, 51-2, 293, 299
Charles, 58, 104

Charles I, 25-6, 44-5, 104, 242-3, 248, 312, 366, 373
Charles (ship), 52, 294, 321
Cheater, John, 159
Childs, Henry, 101
  Robert, 181, 183
Chudley (ship), 19
Church (ship), 387
Clap, Roger, 40, 43, 252, 317, 360, 379-80
Clark, Anthony, 205
  Oliver, 114, 192, 203, 205
  Thomas, 139, 183, 255, 270, 278-9
Cleave, George, 60, 131, 146, 152-3, 162, 168-9, 173, 183, 186, 198, 200-4, 209-14, 218, 222, 227-32, 235, 237-8, 246, 251, 253, 270, 398
Cleves, Thomas, 283-4
Cobb, Peter, 205
Cock, or Cox, William, 319, 327, 352
Cocockohamas, 258
Cogan, Henry, 252
Coke, Sir John, 21, 76, 221
Colcord, Edward, 59, 60, 93
Cole, Amias, 42
  James, 177, 186, 325
  John, 352
  Thomas, 182, 187, 355-6
  William, 149, 187, 210, 213, 285-6
Collicott, Richard, 61
Collins, Nicholas, 17
  Robert, 142
Colmer, Abraham, 36, 39
Conant, Roger, 63, 224, 227, 360, 393
Concord (ship), 13
Conley, Abraham, 106, 112, 117
Consent (ship), 22-3, 220
Constable, William, 20
Cook, James, 18
  Mark, 18
  Peyton, 176-7, 187
Cooper, David, 337
  Michael, 16-7, 334
  William, 58, 68
Coppin, Thomas, 137
Corbett, Abraham, 70
Corbin, John, 19, 21, 49, 347, 360
Cornish, Jeffrey, 21, 300, 312
  Richard, 134, 142, 300, 312
Cotton, John, 61, 90
Council of New England, 38
Council of Plymouth, 24-6, 33, 35, 44-5, 49, 56, 61, 76, 82, 106, 125, 146, 154, 156, 165, 171-2, 174, 176, 193, 196, 198, 201, 210, 227, 239, 241-3, 243, 245, 247, 265-6, 296, 315, 339, 341, 345, 368, 380, 385
Cousins, John, 22, 28, 169-70, 173, 187, 220, 230, 235-6, 238-9, 243, 322

[403]

Cradock, Matthew, 51, 63, 152, 154, 157, 159, 176-7, 209, 368
Crafford, Stephen, 52, 53, 117-8
Crampton, Samuel, 76, 334
Crimp, William, 55
Crispe, John, 25, 266, 268
  Thomas, 22, 300
Crockett, Thomas, 58, 68, 86, 93, 115, 118
Cromwell, Oliver, 387
Crookdeak, John, 21
Croskum, George, 351
Cross, John, 149-50
  William, 18, 341, 343, 347
Cullane, Matthew, 55
Cummings, Richard, 53, 110, 181, 205
Curtis, Henry, 284, 287
  Thomas, 143
Cushman, Robert, 394
Cutt, Richard, 54
  Robert, 118
Cutting, John, 50, 54

Dame, Henry Clay, 100
  John, 100
Damerill, Humphrey, 291
Danforth, Thomas, 139
David (ship), 17, 336
Davis, Daniel, 112
  George, 283, 285, 287
  James, 15, 217, 260-1, 264
  John, 15, 134, 139, 143, 162, 260
  Nicholas, 137, 143
  Robert, 15, 217, 260, 263-4
  Sylvanus, 290, 350, 355, 361-2, 400
  Theophilus, 173, 179, 187
  William, 134, 143, 255
Davison, Nicholas, 289, 352
Deacon, John, 23, 371, 388
Dearborn, Godfrey, 149
Dearing, George, 191, 205
Dehanada, 241
Deliverance (ship), 13
Denning, Agnes, 326
  Eliza, 326
  Emma, 326
  George, 326
  Grace, 326
  Mary, 326
  Nicholas, 326, 357
Derby, William, 242, 252
Dermer, Thomas, 17, 18, 35, 38, 165-8, 315, 325, 331, 335, 337-41, 354
Dermit, William, 58, 68
Derumkin, 253
Desire (ship), 133
Devorex, John, 351
Dexter, Thomas, 237
Diaman, John, 15
Dicer, William, 182

Dike, Anthony, 360, 378-9
Discovery (ship), 19, 292, 294-6, 342
Dixon, William, 134, 138, 143
Dixy, William, 80
Dockett, Edmund, 21, 346-7
Dole, John, 286
  William, 271
Dollen, John, 355
Donnell, Henry, 134, 136-8, 143, 232
  Thomas, 136, 138
Dorchester Merchants, 77, 104, 242, 244, 247, 299, 392-3
Downing, Dennis, 112
  Emanuel, 75-7
Downs, James, 75, 371, 388
  John, 17
Drake, Thomas, 149-50, 232, 234
Draper, Esther, 287
  Nathaniel, 283-4, 287, 290, 322, 352
Druillettes, Gabriel, 280-1
Dudley, Thomas, 30, 75, 392
Dugdeale, George, 296, 343
Dunton, John, 59
Dustin, Thomas, 205
Dutch, Osmond, 143
Dye, John, 266, 268
Dyer, William, 285-7

Eagle (ship), 20, 310
Earthy, Abigail, 324
  Ann, 324
  Elizabeth, 324
  John, 324
  Mary, 324
Edan, Luke, 20
Edge, Robert, 143
Edgecomb, Nicholas, 191, 205, 249
  Sir Richard, 249, 254
  Wilmot, 191
Edmunds, Henry, 205
  Robert, 187
Edwards, James, 17, 336
  John, 17
  Oades, 55
  William, 21, 205
Elbridge, Gyles, 25, 52, 132, 137, 146, 289, 313-6, 318-9, 321, 324, 326, 328-9, 347, 349-50, 355, 395
  John, 289, 322
  Thomas, 289, 301, 316, 322-4, 351-2
Eleanor (ship), 18, 341, 344
Elizabeth (ship), 50
Elkins, Thomas, 187
Ellacott, Vines, 238
Ellingham, William, 139
Eliot, Robert, 15, 260
Emerson, Joseph, 143
Emery, Anthony, 112
Endicott, John, 79, 154, 222-7, 398
England, William, 355

Epenow, 335, 340
Epps, Daniel, 153, 159
   William, 166, 339
Evans, Griffith, 187
Everett, Andrew, 136, 138, 143
   William, 112, 116
Exchange (ship), 132
Eyre, Eleazar, 61, 70, 88
   Thomas, 61, 246

Falcon (ship), 284
Farre, James, 17
Feake, John, 70
   Robert, 63
Fell, Thomas, 20
Fellowship (ship), 196
Felt, George, 234, 238
Fernald, John, 187
Field, Darby, 180
   Richard, 205
Fishcock, Edward, 205
Fleet, Henry, 49, 59, 62-3, 127
Fletcher, John, 15
Fleury, Charles, 16
Fogg, Ralph, 155
Footman, Thomas, 134, 143
Ford, Thomas, 252
Forrester, Andros, 373
Foster, William, 22, 299, 322
Fowkes, Henry, 266
Foxwell, Richard, 179, 186-7, 191, 210, 360-1, 386, 400
Francis (ship), 50
Freathy, Alexander, 192, 203, 205
   William, 114, 130, 134, 192, 203, 205
Friend, Richard, 302
Friendship (ship), 173, 244
Frost, Catherine, 106
   George, 173, 179, 187, 213
   Nicholas, 105-6, 110, 112, 116, 301
Fryer, Nathaniel, 70
Fulford, Elizabeth, 326, 355
   Richard, 326, 355, 357
Furrall, Thomas, 68

Gale, Hugh, 139
Garde, Fortune le, 380
   Roger, 130, 134, 137, 139, 140-1, 143, 397
Gardiner, Sir Christopher, 44-5, 75-6, 78, 125, 187, 200, 244, 247, 317
   Henry, 57, 61, 63, 70, 88, 125
   Thomas, 393
   Governor William Tudor, 282
Garland (ship), 17
Garland, John, 205
   Peter, 22, 169-70, 220, 230, 232
Gaude, Mark, 206
Gayne, William, 17
Gedney, Bartholomew, 235

Gee, Ralph, 58, 68
Gent, Elizabeth, 286
   John, 271, 286, 322
   Sarah, 289
   Thomas, 271, 285-6, 289-90
George (ship), 294
Gibbins, William, 385
Gibbons, Ambrose, 10, 33-4, 44, 49, 58, 67-8, 70, 76, 82, 85-93, 97-8, 103, 105, 109, 114, 129, 371, 392
   Edward, 22-23, 169, 183, 212
   James, 181, 186-7
   William, 19, 169, 181, 183, 187, 218, 230, 252
Gibbs, John, 19, 49, 293-4, 313
Gibson, Rev. Richard, 53, 178-80, 206, 270
Gift (ship), 43, 226
Gift of God (ship), 15, 260, 269, 294
Gilbert, Bartholomew, 13
   Sir John, 263-4
   Raleigh, 13, 15, 216, 260, 263, 308
Giles, John, 22, 299
Gill, Arthur, 206
   Peter, 206
Girling, Richard, 383-5
Glover, Ralph, 126, 137
Goalsworth, John, 226
Goddard, John, 90, 92, 94, 103
Godfrey, Edward, 29, 48-9, 58, 65, 67, 69, 70, 111, 115, 118, 125-8, 130-40, 146, 156, 177, 194, 210-2, 218, 333, 395
   Oliver, 395
Golden Cat (ship), 347
Goodwin, Ichabod, 95
Goodyear, Moses, 25, 193, 201, 209-10, 227, 245-6, 394
Gorges, Lord Edward, 20, 26, 298
   Ferdinando, 24, 126, 132, 182
   Sir Ferdinando, 9, 11, 17, 24-5, 28-9, 33, 35, 38-40, 44-5, 50, 52, 57, 61, 65, 69, 71-3, 77-8, 88-94, 108-11, 114-6, 125-7, 129-33, 135-41, 147, 149, 159, 165-6, 168, 171-2, 176, 180-1, 192, 194-6, 200-1, 209, 211, 213, 216, 220, 225, 228-9, 231-2, 234, 243, 245-6, 249, 258-60, 264, 266-7, 273-5, 292, 294-7, 309, 321, 335-40, 343-4, 354, 366, 379, 394, 396
   John, 24, 126, 394
   Robert, 20-1, 28-9, 36, 38-9, 46, 125-6, 183, 220, 297-9, 344-6, 392-4
   Thomas, 29, 108, 130, 133-4, 136, 141, 143, 146-9, 152-3, 160, 169, 210-11, 218, 236-7
   William, 29, 115, 129-30, 133, 143, 177
Gorrell, Philip, 55
Gosnold, Bartholomew, 13, 123-4, 258-9

Gouch, John, 134, 143, 146, 149
  Rev. Robert, 281, 399
  William, 206
Gould, Alexander, 326-8
  Margaret, 326
Goyett, John, 15, 260
Grant, Ferdinando, 187
  James, 100
Graves, Thomas, 126, 137
Gray, John, 28, 392
  Thomas, 28, 392
Green, John, 112
  Richard, 297
Greenway, Clement, 177, 179, 187
Griffin, Owen, 14
Griffith, George, 59, 61, 63, 70, 88
Grove, Mary, 244
Gullet, Peter, 206
Gunnison, Hugh, 118
Guy, Edwin, 61
Guyer, Arthur, 22, 221

Haborne, George, 149-50
Hakluyt, Richard, 258-9, 295
Haley, Thomas, 187
Hall, Edward, 290
  John, 117-8
Ham, William, 114, 146, 192, 203, 206
Hamerhaw, 258
Hamilton, David, 100-1
  Marquis James, 26
Hammock, Thomas, 206
Hammond, Catherine, 96, 106
  Joseph, 106
  Pentecost, 206
  Richard, 279, 285
  William, 106, 157, 163, 212
Hancock, Henry, 206
Hanham, Thomas, 14, 15, 260
Hanson, Captain, 345
  Thomas, 100
Happy Entrance (ship), 22, 170
Hardwin, Grace, 266
Harker, John, 135, 144
Harlow, Edward, 15, 17, 260, 335
  Henry, 260
Harmon, Johnson, 136
Hart, William, 319, 376, 386
Harvey, Elizabeth, 254
  John, 21, 63
Hatch, Charles, 206
  Philip, 134, 206
Hatherly, Timothy, 173, 275, 368
Havercome, John, 15
Hawkins, Narias, 192, 203, 206
  Sir Richard, 17, 336
  Thomas, 387
Hay, Daniel, 14
  James, 26

Haynes, Samuel, 112, 117
  Thomas, 239-40
Hayman, John, 355
Hayward, Francis, 326
  Margaret, 326
Hazelton, Hannah, 236
Head, Nicholas, 17
Hearl, William, 206
Hebert, Louis, 14
Heifer, Andrew, 116, 196, 206
Helson, John, 162, 182, 187
Hempson, John, 206
Hendricksen, 36, 331, 395
Henry IV, of France, 364, 375
Hept, John, 17
Hercules (ship), 53, 361
Hewett, Henry, 20
  Nicholas, 206
Hickford, John, 197
Higginson, Francis, 392
Hill, John, 17
  Peter, 182, 202, 206
  Roger, 182
  Valentine, 54, 351
Hilton, Catherine, 51
  Edward, 28, 36, 42, 50, 59, 60, 74-5, 83-4, 87, 104, 171, 174, 318, 380, 394
  Margaret, 326
  William, 28, 36, 65, 68, 75, 83, 104-5, 111-2, 117, 135-6, 194, 326
Hingston, Philip, 196, 206
  William, 53
Hitchcock, Richard, 179, 181, 187
Hitchens, Arthur, 17, 336
Hobbs, Hannah, 101
  Henry, 101-2
Hobson, Nicholas, 17, 335
Hocking, John, 74, 105, 277
Hodge, John, 18
Hodges, Nicholas, 22, 299
Hoff, Ferdinano, 162
Hogg, Peter, 187
Hole, John, 206
Holland, John, 322
  William, 21
Holman, John, 301, 377
Holworthy, Richard, 342
Home, Sir George, 373
Hook, Humphrey, 127, 132, 137, 146, 333, 342
  Thomas, 137, 146
  William, 67, 127-8, 131-4, 137-40, 144, 146, 318
Hope (ship), 383, 387
Hopkins, John, 271, 322
Horden, Adam, 18
Horrell, Humphrey, 55
Hoskins, Elias, 322, 351-2
  John, 206
How, Anthony, 187

[406]

Howard, John, 21
Howbeck, John, 20
Howell, Morgan, 159-60, 187
  Richard, 136, 144
Howes, Edward, 76-8
Howland, John, 275, 277, 280-1
Hubbard, William, 31, 36, 40, 58, 185, 231, 253, 286
Huddleston, John, 19, 294
Hull, Rev. Joseph, 141, 144
Humphrey, Jeremiah, 206
  John, 44, 75, 368
Hunkins, Hercules, 55
Hunnewell, Richard, 302
Hunt, John, 15, 260, 263
  Thomas, 16, 334-5, 337, 340, 343
Hunter, Leonard, 144
Hurd, Arthur, 206
  John, 72, 108, 116, 118
  Thomas, 187
Hutchinson, Ann, 147, 160
  Edward, 147
Hutton, John, 17

Ingleby, John, 144
Irish, John, 277, 282
Ivy, Martin, 195

Jackson, John, 234
Jacob (ship), 347
Jacobs, 36, 331, 395
James I, 24, 26, 67, 333
James (ship), 50, 294, 300, 318, 382
James, William, 119, 135, 285
Jeffrey, Gregory, 163
  William, 42, 91, 125-6, 137, 139, 171, 392
Jenkins, Reginald, 206
  Reynold, 155-7
Jenks, Joseph, 140, 144, 212
Jenner, Thomas, 157, 180-1, 188, 266, 313
Jennings, Abraham, 18, 21, 201, 333, 341, 343, 347
  Ambrose, 18, 343, 347
Jewell, George, 194, 232
Jocelyn, Abraham, 196
  Henry, 29, 31, 58, 68, 71-2, 90-8, 100, 106, 109-10, 115, 119, 133, 169, 177, 194-7, 209, 228
  John, 31, 194-7, 362
Jonathan (ship), 36, 39
  Margaret, 196
  Sir Thomas, 92, 133, 194-7
Jolliff, John, 152, 177
Jones, Alexander, 44, 119
  Christopher, 269
  Thomas, 19, 112, 130-1, 134, 144, 195, 292, 295-6, 342
  William, 144, 342

Johnson, Edward, 19, 42, 45, 79, 114-5, 130, 134, 138, 144, 212, 392
  Francis, 360
  Isaac, 368
  Peter, 268
Jope, Mr., 277
  Sampson, 206
Jordan, Robert, 178, 214, 218, 231, 240, 251, 270
Joy, Richard, 206
  Thomas, 399
Judith (ship), 17, 336
Juppe, Thomas, 266

Katherine (ship), 20, 298
Kelly, John, 55
Keyes, Henry, 58-9, 371
Kidder, Stephen, 58, 68, 86
Kimball, Thomas, 290, 356
King, Thomas, 14, 206
  William, 132
Kipling, Brian, 266
Kirke, David, 368, 373
Kirman, John, 268
Knight, Daniel, 134
  Ezekiel, 149-50
  Francis, 301, 321-2, 351-2, 355
  Robert, 67, 127, 134, 136, 140, 144, 252, 318, 321-2
  Roger, 58, 68
  Walter, 392
Knolling, Christopher, 22, 299
Knowles, Rev. Hansard, 78, 106, 112

Labrisse, 58, 104
Laconia Company, 48-9, 56-9, 61, 63, 67, 70-3, 78, 81, 83-8, 91-2, 97, 100-2, 104-6, 126-7, 194
Lake, Thomas, 69, 70, 73, 183, 255, 270, 278-9
Lakesley, John, 206
Lalemont, Jerome, 280
Lander, John, 114, 116-7, 146, 192, 203, 207
Lane, Ann, 236
  Elizabeth, 236
  Henry, 236
  James, 236
  Job, 236
  John, 236
  Samuel, 236
Langstaff, Henry, 58, 60, 68, 71
Langdon, John, 73
Langton, John, 333, 342
Lapthorne, Stephen, 207
Larkham, Rev. Thomas, 78
Lash, William, 22, 221
La Tour, Claude de, 127, 370, 378, 381, 386, 390, 391
Laudonniere, Rene, 364, 366

Lausey, John, 19
Laverdure, John, 324
Lawson, Christopher, 119, 278, 399
  Henry, 226
Lawton, Henry, 324
Leader, Richard, 97
Lear, Tobias, 70
Lechford, Rev. Thomas, 62
Lee, John, 163, 181, 188, 286
  William, 302
Leighton, John, 188
Leverich, Rev. William, 78
Leverett, Thomas, 26, 84, 359, 368, 394
Levett, Christopher, 20, 25, 28, 38-40, 43, 46-8, 74, 77, 124, 140, 154, 165, 168-9, 172, 198-9, 201, 217-27, 231, 233, 273, 299, 310-1, 325, 331, 345-6, 354, 394
  Thomas, 84
Lewis, George, 240, 248, 393
  Thomas, 23, 25, 75, 82, 84, 115, 171, 173-4, 177-9, 182-4, 188, 371, 394
Libby, John, 196, 207
Lissen, Thomas, 207
Littlebury, John, 69, 70, 73
Littlefield, Anthony, 159, 162
  Edmund, 147-50
  Francis, 149
Little James (ship), 20, 273, 310-1
London Company, 80, 81, 224, 242, 244, 246
Long, Richard, 342
Long Robert (ship), 16, 335
Looman, John, 157
Lopez, John, 207
Loron, 362
Love, John, 177
Lucas, William, 207
Lucks, John, 19
Ludlow, George, 105
Lullaby, William, 351
Luckham, John, 119
Luxon, George, 49, 50, 196, 232
Lyford, John, 392
Lynn, Henry, 44, 119, 134, 137-8, 141, 212
Lyon (ship), 172, 223-5, 314, 369
Lyon's Whelp (ship), 49

Mackworth, Arthur, 160, 169-70, 182, 210-2, 225, 228, 231, 233, 235, 252
  Jane, 182
Maddiver, Michael, 207
Maiesquis, 258
Maine, John, 234, 238
Manawormet, 220, 253
Mannedo, 14, 260, 308
Manning, John, 110
Marbury, Catherine, 160
Marmaduke (ship), 294, 313

Marsh, Hugh, 112
Martin, Elizabeth, 326
  Francis, 207
  John, 21, 113
  Richard, 207, 234
  Samuel, 326
Mary and John (ship), 15, 224, 260, 269
Mary Rose (ship), 134
Mason, Ann, 31, 70, 73, 111
  .Captain John, 24, 26, 31, 33-5, 39, 40, 43-5, 50, 57, 61, 65, 69-73, 76-8, 88-97, 101, 111, 125, 129-30, 173, 200, 243, 248, 266, 297, 299, 321, 337-9, 379, 392-4, 396
  John, 285, 288-9
  Joseph, 70, 73
Massachusetts Bay Colony, 61, 77, 125, 141, 226, 314, 394
Masse, Enemond, 16
Mather, Richard, 50, 203, 350, 382
Matthew, John, 17, 335
Matthews, Francis, 72
  Nicholas, 207
Maurmet, 258
Maverick, Amias, 42
  Antiphas, 54-5
  Elias, 137
  Samuel, 21, 28, 30-1, 36, 38, 40-2, 60, 63, 124, 126, 130, 137-9, 144, 184, 218, 231, 248, 265, 268, 280, 285, 316-8, 324, 348, 377-8, 380, 387, 393, 397, 400
Mayflower (ship), 341
Mayhew, Thomas, 51, 152, 177
Mellin, William, 207
Mendum, Robert, 119
Mentaurmet, 253, 258-9, 283
Mercer, Thomas, 157, 162, 284
Merchant, Walter, 314
Merchant Adventurers of Canada, 366, 379
Merchant Adventurers of Plymouth, 226-7, 342
Meriton, Robert, 13
Merry, Walter, 181, 232
Messant, Ann, 132, 134-5
Miles, Joseph, 119
Miller, John, 119
  Shadrach, 60, 68
Mills, Edward, 207
  John, 22, 28, 169-70, 202, 220, 224-5, 230, 233
  Mary, 184
  Robert, 137, 188
  Thomas, 181, 184, 188
Mitchell, Paul, 207
Mitten, Elizabeth, 209
  Michael, 209, 213-4, 232-3

Moore, Richard, 157, 163
  Thomas, 44, 392
Montague, Griffin, 157, 160
Monts, Sieur de, 14, 364
Morgan, Robert, 179, 188, 251, 289
Morritt, Peter, 20, 311
Morton, Thomas, 19, 21-3, 28, 30, 34-5, 38, 40-2, 45-6, 48, 74, 76, 78, 91, 170, 199, 200, 209, 212, 220-2, 229, 232, 238, 274, 313, 317, 392
Moses, John, 233
Mosier, Hugh, 177, 188, 229
  John, 237
Motte, Nicholas, de la, 16
Moulton, Jeremiah, 139
Munjoy, George, 232-3

Nachen (ship), 17, 336
Nahanada, 14, 241, 308, 332
Nanney, Catherine, 139
  Robert, 137, 139, 188
Narracommique, 258
Nash, Robert, 235, 270, 301
  Joseph, 237
Nason, Richard, 103
Natahanada, 254
Neal, Charles, 58, 68, 86
  Francis, 254
  Walter, 23, 29, 31, 48, 58-60, 62, 64-5, 67-9, 71, 73, 83-4, 86, 90, 101, 105, 115, 119, 126-7, 156, 194, 202, 211, 228, 246, 267, 289, 315, 318, 371-2, 377, 380, 395-6, 398
Needham, Nicholas, 147
Neeson, Thomas, 347
Nevell, Edward, 22, 299, 312
Newcomb, Elias, 55
  Simon, 302
Newgrove, John, 106, 113, 117
Newlands, Anthony, 188, 213
Newman, George, 67, 127, 130, 132, 138, 144, 318, 322
  Matthew, 327, 352
  Robert, 22
Nicholas (ship), 195
Nichols, Anthony, 19
Nightingale (ship), 19
Norcross, Rev. Nathaniel, 141, 144
Norman, Matthew, 327, 352
  Richard, 393
  Robert, 239
Norton, Eleanor, 128
  Francis, 96
  George, 137
  Henry, 129, 137-8, 140, 144
  Jane, 128
  Richard, 137
  Robert, 137
  Walter, 125-132, 137, 139, 144, 377
Nute, James, 110

Nutter, Hatevil, 113
Nyle, Richard, 207

Octoworokin, 258
Octoworthe, 258
Okers, Rowland, 207
Oldham, John, 22-3, 25, 45, 58, 61, 81-4, 170-2, 176, 188, 223, 380-1, 390, 392, 394
One Hundred Associates, 373, 375
Opparrunwitt, 220
Ormsby, Richard, 138, 141, 144
Osborne, Nicholas, 302
Otis, Job, 237

Page, Elizabeth, 184
  Thomas, 179, 184, 188, 210, 213
Paine, Eliza, 326
Palfrey, Peter, 360, 393
Palmer, John, 193
  William, 119
Parker, Basil, 78, 96-7, 103
  George, 138, 145
  James, 117, 174
  John, 138, 173, 177-9, 181, 188, 255, 268-71, 399
  Mary, 269-71
  Robert, 302
  Thomas, 268-9
Parnell, William, 355
Passaconway, 84, 135, 220
Pattistall, Richard, 302
Paul, Daniel, 113
Pearce, Elizabeth, 326, 354-5
  Francis, 326
  George, 326
  John, 326, 393
  Margaret, 326
  Richard, 325-6, 329, 354-5, 357
  William, 326
Peddock, Leonard, 272, 296
Peirce, William, 172, 223-6, 243, 314, 369, 372
Pell, Thomas, 284
Pelletier, Abraham, 21
Pendleton, Bryan, 72
Penley, Sampson, 232
Penrose, John, 19
Penwell, Walter, 188
Pepperill, William, 397
Pestor, William, 137
Peters, Hugh, 157
  William, 313
Petfree, 58, 104
Peverly, John, 12, 23, 44, 199, 200, 207, 392
  Thomas, 44
Philip (ship), 289
Phillips, John, 214, 234, 238, 268-9
  Thomas, 55, 302

[409]

Walter, 286, 289-90, 303, 322
William, 183, 254
Phippen, Joseph, 214, 233
Phipps, James, 283, 285, 288, 325
  William, 371, 383, 388
Phips, Sir William, 283
Pickering, John, 44, 88, 93, 105, 113
Piddock, Thomas, 21, 331, 346
Pide Cow (ship), 58, 91-3, 129, 176, 371
Pierce, Daniel, 159
  John, 145, 290, 296-7
Pike, John, 113, 116
Pitt, Thomas, 314
  Sir William, 342
Plaisted, Ichabod, 102
Plantation (ship), 20, 298, 344
Platrier, Captain, 16
Pleasure (ship), 313
Plough Company, 174, 245, 267, 394
Plough (ship), 267
Plymouth Colony, 25, 28, 34, 40, 81-2, 84, 155, 172-4, 270, 273, 299, 310, 313-4, 316, 333, 344-5, 349, 372, 394
Plymouth Merchants, 28
Pomeroy, Thomas, 201, 245
Pomery, Leonard, 36, 39, 342
Pomfrett, William, 21, 296, 343-4, 346
Pontgrave, Robert, 14, 16
Popham Colony, 28
Popham, Edward, 15, 260
  Sir Francis, 16, 17, 264-5, 309-11, 335
  George, 15, 241, 260, 263-4, 294, 308
  John, 11, 260, 263-4
Pormort, Philemon, 149, 150
Pory, John, 19, 294-6, 309, 344, 371
Potts, Richard, 239, 255
Pouning, Henry, 119
Poutrincourt, 366
Powell, Michael, 145-6
Pratt, Phineas, 19, 34, 37-8, 46, 88, 292-3
Preble, Abraham, 140, 145
Prescott, Benjamin, 328
Prince, Thomas, 387
Pring, Martin, 13-4, 124, 258-60, 332
Prosperous (ship), 347
Providence (ship), 19, 22, 36, 39
Puddington, George, 116, 134, 140-1, 145, 212
Purchase, Samuel, 261, 265, 289, 337
  Thomas, 25, 28, 97, 115, 169-73, 177, 189, 201, 210, 217, 226, 239-45, 247-55, 268, 321, 393, 395

Quentin, Francis de, 16

Radiver, Abraham, 111
Rainsford, Robert, 137
Raleigh, Sir Walter, 38
Ramchock, 254

Ramusio, 364
Randall, James, 22
Randolph, Edward, 324, 388
Rastell, Humphrey, 21, 299, 300
Ratcliff, Philip, 76, 78, 317
Raymond, John, 49
Raynes, Francis, 145
Razilly, Isaac de, 373-5, 378-9
Rebecca (ship), 19, 51
Redding, John, 160
  Thomas, 158, 160, 236, 240
Reekes, Stephen, 74, 171-3, 243, 350, 369
Reeves, William, 114-5, 119
Return (ship), 20, 23, 171
Reynolds, John, 54, 58, 119
  Nicholas, 399
  William, 19, 20, 159, 212, 277, 282, 293
Ribault, Jean, 364
Richards, John, 160, 183, 271, 282-3, 399
  Thomas, 371, 383, 388
Richmond (ship), 204
Richmond, Earl Ludovic, 11, 24, 26, 198, 201, 297, 394
  John, 180, 183
Ridgeway, John, 351
Rigby, Sir Alexander, 69, 152, 162-3, 174, 211-4, 230, 235, 238, 268
  Sir Edward, 69
Rishworth, Edward, 136, 139, 148-50
Roach, John, 266
Robbins, Edward, 302
Roberts, Esther (Draper), 287
  John, 207
  Thomas, 17
Robinhood, 220, 235, 253, 269-70, 281, 283
Robinson, Edward, 183, 189
  Francis, 174, 181, 183, 189, 210, 212
  John, 266
Rocraft, Edward, 18, 165-8, 335, 337-40, 348
Rogers, Captain, 19, 293
  Christopher, 145
  George, 134, 207
  John, 134-5, 145
  Patrick, 302
  Robert, 134
  Thomas, 189
  William, 134
Romer, 281, 302
Rosier, James, 13-4, 307, 358-9, 361
Rouse, Nicholas, 225, 233
Row, Anthony, 196
  Nicholas, 22
Rowles, 83-4, 97-8, 108-9
Royal, Phebe, 234
  William, 213, 228, 234-8, 250, 252

Runacwitts, 82-4, 108-9, 220
Russell, Henry, 22, 221
　Joseph, 22, 221
　Richard, 314, 351

Sabenaw, 258-9, 308
Saco Companies, 81- 2
Sadamoyt, 220
Sagamore, James, 104, 315
　John, 104
Saint Peter (ship), 172-3
Saker, John, 22
Salem Colony, 173
Saltern, Robert, 13
Saltonstall, Sir Richard, 72, 157, 385
　Robert, 117
Samoset, 220, 324-9, 354-5
Sampson (ship), 18, 340-1
Sampson, Henry, 371, 388
　Thomas, 207
Samuel (ship), 195
Sanders, John, 20, 37, 40, 53, 88, 150, 153, 159, 297, 393
Sandy, Walter, 314, 321
Sankey, Robert, 179, 181, 189, 239, 251
Sargent, Stephen, 207
Sasuoa, 258-9
Saterley, Robert, 207
Saunders, Charles, 322
　Robert, 207
Savage, Thomas, 21
　Timothy, 15
Savery, Thomas, 277
Sayward, Henry, 136, 139, 145, 235
　Roger, 302
Scadlock, William, 163, 173, 179, 181-2, 189
Scammon, Alexander, 73
Scawas, 258
Scotch Colony, 373
Scott, Richard, 158, 160
　Robert, 285, 287, 289-90, 356
　Samuel, 287
　Thomas, 21
Scottow, Joshua, 197
Searl, John, 119
Sears, John, 232, 238
Seavey, William, 49, 52-3, 55, 88, 101, 117
Sedgwick, Major Robert, 54, 351, 387
Seeley, George, 53
　John, 53, 55
　Richard, 53, 182, 184
　Robert, 114
　William, 53
Seely, Jope and Company, 227
Sellick, David, 284
Sewall, Samuel, 101
Seymour, Rev. Richard, 15, 260

Shapleigh, Alexander, 51, 105-6, 114-5, 117, 119, 396-7
　Catherine, 51
　Nicholas, 51, 53, 69, 70, 73, 111, 117, 120
Sharp, Samuel, 75, 81
Shaw, Edward, 191, 197
Shears, Elizabeth, 113
　Jeremiah, 113
Shepherd, Thomas, 207
Sherbourn, Henry, 54, 70
Sherley, James, 171, 173, 175, 224, 274-5, 368-9
Sherwill, Nicholas, 36, 39, 342
Short, Tobias, 207
Shrewsbury Merchants, 72, 78-9, 105
Shurt, Abraham, 23, 28, 63-4, 67, 127, 194, 202, 227, 301, 313-6, 318-22, 324, 327-8, 347-51, 353-5, 376-7, 386
Shute, Richard, 290, 303, 354
　Robert, 239, 251-2, 290, 303
Sibatahood, 258
Simpson, Henry, 128-9, 134, 139-41, 145, 212
　Jane, 128-9, 139
Singleman, Henry, 158, 160
Skanke, 258
Skidwaros, 14, 241, 260, 308, 359
Skillings, Thomas, 254
Slanie, John, 337, 340
Slatier, Martin, 299
Small, Edward, 106, 113, 116
　Francis, 92, 100, 214
Smart, John, 45
Smith, George, 94
　James, 210, 237, 239-40, 251, 280, 399
　Joanna, 234
　John, 17, 21, 134, 145, 163, 176, 179, 182, 189, 212, 234, 268
　Captain John, 16, 30, 36, 46, 79, 124, 165-7, 217, 242, 258, 264, 291, 293, 299, 309, 312, 320, 331, 334-41, 365, 395, 398
　Richard, 67, 194
　Thomas, 189, 235
　Sir Thomas, 334
　William, 189, 191, 213
Somers, Sir George, 15, 264, 333
Southampton, Earl Henry, 259
Southcoat, Richard, 173
　Thomas, 173-4
South Phenix (ship), 299
Southworth, Thomas, 279
Sparrow (ship), 34, 292-4
Speedwell (ship), 13
Spencer, Humphrey, 92, 95-6
　John, 150
　Patinece, 95-6
　Roger, 178
　Thomas, 58, 68, 92-6, 98, 103, 117

[411]

William, 95
Squanto, 35
Squibbs, Thomas, 20, 298
Squidrayset, 199, 213, 220
Squire, John, 134, 145
　Nicholas, 134, 145
Stackpole, James, 102
Stalling, Edward, alias Rocraft
Standish, Myles, 20, 204, 320, 344, 384
Starbuck, Edward, 110, 113, 117
Stevens, Benjamin, 207
　David, 54
　Mary, 326
　Thomas, 235
　William, 20
Stileman, Elias, 94, 98
Stilson, James, 283, 326, 329
　John, 326
　Margaret, 326
　Mary, 326
Stone, Captain John, 68, 128, 132, 398
Stoneham, John, 14
Storer, Augustine, 84
Stover, Sylvester, 111, 145-6
Strachey, William, 263
Stratton, Ann, 154-5
　John, 25, 147, 152, 154-9, 191, 393-4
　Joseph, 20, 298
Straw, Jack, 38
Street, William, 13
Stuert, William, 324
Sturton, 17, 335
Sullivan, James, 352, 399
　John, 73
Swabber, 309
Swadden, Philip, 106, 113, 115-6, 120, 290, 355, 362, 400
Swain, 132
Swan (ship), 19, 20, 22, 37-8, 40, 293, 297-9, 300, 312, 345
Swift (ship), 74, 171-3, 200, 223, 225, 243, 301, 314-5, 350, 369-70
Symonds, John, 114, 192, 203, 207
　William, 152

Tahanedo, 14, 260, 308
Talbot, Moses, 277, 282
Tarratines, 79, 80, 84, 315, 350
Taylor, George, 228, 230, 233
　John, 22, 289-90, 303
　Stephen, 252
Teed, Joshua, 383
Thet, Gilbert du, 16
Thevet, Andre, 13, 364
Thing, Jonathan, 150
Thomas, Richard, 115, 120
　William, 237
Thompson, Amias, 41-2, 393
　David, 19, 23, 28, 35-42, 47-8, 58, 71,

88, 102, 217, 220, 273, 297, 313, 342, 344-5, 348-9, 392-4
　Robert, 137
　Rev. William, 106, 108, 113, 131-2
Thorndike, Elizabeth, 155
Thresher, Robert, 300
Thwayts, Alexander, 239-40, 399
Tillieres, Count de, 366
Tilly, John, 393
Tisquantum, 35, 168, 335, 337, 339-40
Tobey, Thomas, 17
Tocher, Brian, 17
Toogood, Richard, 322, 353
Townsend, Henry, 207
Trafton, Thomas, 136
Trask, William, 393
Treby, Edward, 207
Treedel, William, 17
Trelawney, Edward, 25, 176, 204, 208
　Robert, 65, 67, 114, 159-60, 168-9, 175, 178-9, 183, 193, 201-4, 209-11, 219, 227-9, 231, 245-6, 373, 394
Treworthy, James, 52, 106-7, 113, 116
　John, 52-4, 97-8, 105, 107-8, 114-5, 120, 248, 397
　Lucy, 98
　Nicholas, 111
　Samuel, 109
Trial (ship), 17, 336
Trick, Elias, 302
Trigs, Thomas, 53
Tristram, Ralph, 163, 181, 189
Trott, Mary, 160
　Simon, 158, 160
Tucker, Adrian, 58, 68, 395
　John, 13, 383-4
　Richard, 60, 72, 174, 198, 200-3, 209, 213, 228-9, 232, 237, 244, 246, 398
　Thomas, 54
　William, 18
Turbet, Peter, 53, 56
Turnel, William, 16
Turpin, Thomas, 53, 56, 110-1
Tussuck, 254
Twisden, John, 140, 145
Tyler, Wat, 38
Tyng, Edward, 279

Underhill, John, 78, 116, 124, 131, 229
Unity (ship), 21, 299
Unnongoit, 325

Val, Jean du, 14
Varney, Mary, 287
Vassal, William, 173
Vaughan, George, 23, 68, 84, 174
Vengham, William, 19, 21, 294, 343, 347
Verrazano, John, 13, 122
Villagagnon, Duran de, 13, 364

[412]

Vines, Joan, 182-3
  Richard, 18, 23, 25, 29, 46, 64, 71-2, 82, 84, 115, 117, 129-33, 137, 152, 154, 166, 168-83, 189, 196, 201, 210-3, 226, 238, 251-2, 270, 273-5, 314, 338, 369-71, 381-2, 390-1, 394
Vinion, John, 208
Virginia (ship), 178, 263-5
Vow, John, 20, 311

Wadley, John, 147, 149, 152-3, 159, 173, 179, 183, 189, 212
  Robert, 153
Wahangnonawit, 84
Wakefield, John, 150
Waldron, Richard, 73, 94, 101-2, 110, 231, 324
  William, 73
Walford, Jeremiah, 44, 392
  Thomas, 44, 392
Wall, James, 90, 92, 94-6, 103
Wallaston, John, 21, 299
Wallen, Thomas, 184
Walton, George, 72-3
  John, 72, 189
Wannerton, Edward, 59
  Thomas, 52, 59, 61, 68, 72, 88, 90, 105-6, 113, 117, 320, 386, 396-7
Ward, John, 134, 145
  Nathaniel, 134
Wardell, William, 149, 151
Warner, Catherine, 184
  Thomas, 184, 189
Warwick (ship), 46, 49, 57, 59, 60, 62-3, 81, 126, 172-3, 294, 301, 350
Warwick, Henry, 174, 177, 179, 181, 183, 189
  Earl Robert, 65, 67
Waters, Nathaniel, 23, 171
Watkins, Thomas, 399
Watson, George, 371, 388
Watts, Henry, 174, 179, 189, 191, 212, 230, 270
  John, 104, 393
Way, Eleazar, 252, 254
  George, 25, 173, 189, 239, 242, 244, 247, 249-50, 252, 395
  Henry, 60-1, 64, 245, 301, 377
  Sarah, 252
  Thomas, 56, 146, 355
Waymouth, George, 14, 258-60, 307, 315, 332, 343, 355, 359, 361
Weare, Peter, 96-7, 103, 116, 146, 212
Webber, Joseph, 271
  Mary, 271
  Thomas, 17, 271, 399
Weeks, Oliver, 197, 203, 228
Welcome (ship), 202
Wenape, 335
Wentworth, William, 84, 149, 151

West, Francis, 20, 38, 40, 297-8, 343-4
  John, 159, 182, 190, 210, 212
  William, 17, 336
Weston, Thomas, 19, 20, 22, 28, 34-5, 37-9, 45-6, 219, 273, 291-3, 297-300, 312, 345-6, 392
Wetherell, Sackford, 21
Wetheridge, Edward, 54
Wharton, Richard, 255
Wheelwright, Rev. John, 61, 79-85, 147-8, 151, 204, 223, 275
Whethem, Nathaniel, 266
Whilkey, Richard, 19
Whinett, Unipa, 296
White, John, 96, 106-8, 113, 117, 151, 173, 244, 249, 252, 283, 285-6, 288, 325
  Nicholas, 208, 219, 232, 240
  Paul, 120
  Richard, 135
  Tobias, 21
White Angel (ship), 59, 67, 75, 154-5, 173-5, 244, 277, 313, 318-9, 349-50, 371, 377
Whitehouse, Emanuel, 302
Widger, William, 135
Wiggin, James, 135
  Thomas, 50, 59, 71, 74-8, 83-4, 171, 174, 244
Wight, Thomas, 84
Wilcocks, John, 92, 96-7, 103
Wiles, John, 17
  Philip, 17
Wilkinson, John, 202, 208, 212, 351
Willett, Thomas, 63-4, 278, 316, 369, 371, 373, 376-7, 382-3, 388
William and John (ship), 20
Williams, Francis, 58, 68, 104, 108-10, 113, 117
  Helen, 109
  Richard, 176-7, 190, 264, 300, 309, 311-2
  Thomas, 115, 176, 179, 181-3, 190
Willine, Roger, 159, 208
Wills, Bennett, 23, 230, 233
  Thomas, 98
Winslow, Edward, 19, 20, 22-3, 30, 35, 40, 163, 204, 220, 273, 275, 277-8, 297, 299, 320, 340, 344, 348-9, 387
  Gilbert, 237
  John, 279
  Nathaniel, 237
Winter, John, 17, 23, 52-3, 67, 114, 131, 156, 160, 169, 172, 175, 181, 192-5, 198, 201-3, 208, 210, 211, 213, 219-20, 228-31, 245-6, 270, 317, 336, 361, 379, 390
Winthrop, Adam, 161, 383
  John, 43-4, 50-3, 57, 62-3, 75-8, 95, 104, 124, 138, 152, 161, 165, 174,

183, 202, 204, 212, 223-4, 226-7, 249-53, 319-21, 350, 368, 379, 381, 385-6, 398
Wise, Thomas, 190, 229
Witheridge, John, 19-21, 300, 310-3, 346, 361
Witherly, Thomas, 172-3, 301, 350
Withers, Thomas, 117, 120, 210
Wood, William, 61, 65, 67, 84, 200, 395, 398
Woodbury, Humphrey, 80, 393
  John, 393
Woodman, John, 199
Woolsley, Joel, 137
Wormwood, William, 54, 117, 120

Wriford, John, 302
Wright, John, 63-4, 74, 171-2, 182, 225-8, 314-5, 369-70, 376-7, 388
  Thomas, 74, 170-2, 222-7, 314, 342, 350, 367, 369
Wulfrana (ship), 105

Yardley, Sir George, 338
Yeo, Allen, 135
  Hugh, 314, 321
  Leonard, 371
Yorkshire Court, 149, 159, 176
Young, Matthew, 136
  Rowland, 134, 145
  Thomas, 248, 251-2